Market as a Weapon

Market as a Weapon

The Socio-Economic Machinery of Dominance in Russia

Anton Oleinik

Transaction Publishers
New Brunswick (U.S.A.) and London (U.K.)

Copyright © 2011 by Transaction Publishers, New Brunswick, New Jersey.

All rights reserved under International and Pan-American Copyright Conventions. No part of this book may be reproduced or transmitted in any form or by any means, electronic or mechanical, including photocopy, recording, or any information storage and retrieval system, without prior permission in writing from the publisher. All inquiries should be addressed to Transaction Publishers, Rutgers—The State University of New Jersey, 35 Berrue Circle, Piscataway, New Jersey 08854-8042. www.transactionpub.com

This book is printed on acid-free paper that meets the American National Standard for Permanence of Paper for Printed Library Materials.

Library of Congress Catalog Number: 2010024039
ISBN: 978-1-4128-1129-3
Printed in the United States of America

Library of Congress Cataloging-in-Publication Data

Oleinik, Anton.
  Market as a weapon : the socio-economic machinery of dominance in Russia / Anton Oleinik.
     p. cm.
  Includes bibliographical references and index.
  ISBN 978-1-4128-1129-3 (alk. paper)
    1. Power (Social sciences)--Russia (Federation) 2. Political culture--Russia (Federation) 3. Control (Psychology) 4. Barriers to entry (Industrial organization)--Russia (Federation) 5. Organizational effectiveness--Russia (Federation) 6. State, The. I. Title.

HN49.P6O44 2010
306.20947'09049--dc22

2010024039

Contents

Acknowledgments		vii
1.	Introduction: Market Power on the Make	1
2.	A Taxonomy of Power Relationships	43
3.	Russian Power: Constructing an Ideal Type	75
4.	Continuity and Change in the Prevailing Model of Power: On Path-Dependence in Russian History	101
5.	Market as a Weapon: Domination by Virtue of a Constellation of Interests	143
6.	Minimizing Missed Opportunities: A New Model of Choice?	177
7.	Doing Business in a Russian Region: Controlling Access to the Field	199
8.	Existing and Potential Constraints Limiting State Servants' Opportunism	237
9.	Conclusion: Impossible Change?	277
10.	Methodological Appendix: Mixing Quantitative and Qualitative Content Analysis	301
Appendix		327
References		357
Index		379

Acknowledgments

This book has had a long and difficult history. Its roots date back to my PhD dissertation on prison subculture (published as a book) because, as it appeared, prison subculture emerged as a reaction to a particular model of power relationships prevailing in that institution. I focused my studies on power relationships in 2005, when I started to work at the Department of Sociology at Memorial University in Newfoundland (maintaining my teaching and research commitments in Russia, at the Institute of Economics of Russian Academy of Sciences and the State University—the Higher School of Economics). Colleagues at these places have contributed to a revival in my interest in studying power, sometimes without knowing it. As an example of the opposite, I would especially like to thank Professor Svetlana Glinkina and Professor Svetlana Kirdina of the Institute of Economics, Professor Volker Meja and Dr. Judith Adler of Memorial University of Newfoundland for creating an unusually tolerant atmosphere and helping solve a number of organizational issues related to my research.

A first, very rough, draft of the arguments outlined in this book was presented at the conference "What is Soviet Now? Identities, Legacies, Memories" (University of Toronto, April 6-8, 2006) and the workshop of the AdmReformNet (www.arts.mun.ca/admreformnet/), the international network of experts on the issues of administrative reform in post-Soviet countries (Memorial University of Newfoundland, August 26-29, 2006). Separate parts of the book were also discussed at other academic meetings, namely the annual conferences of the Association for Evolutionary Economics (Chicago, IL; January 5-7, 2007 and Atlanta, GA; January 2-5, 2010), the workshop "Le Goulag en héritage" (Fondation Maison des Sciences de l'Homme and Université de Paris IV Sorbonne; March 19-20, 2007), the seminar "Sociology of Markets" (the State University—the Higher School of Economics, Moscow; May 20, 2008) and the IV Moscow Open International Book Fest (June 14,

2009). I extend thanks to all those who assisted at these meetings and commented on my interventions. Comments and suggestions made by Professor Valeri Ledyaev (the State University—the Higher School of Economics, Moscow) and Professor Rumen Gechev (University of National and World Economy, Sofia) on early drafts of Chapters 2, 3 and 8 were particularly helpful.

The necessary level of intellectual concentration would have been impossible without the emotional support and devotion on the part of those closest to me: my parents, Natalia and Alexandra. Even though they have not always approved the sacrifices that my work has involved, they nevertheless have always been understanding and supportive. The overall pessimistic message of the book vividly contrasts with the sense of optimism that is carefully cultivated by Alexandra.

Reviewers of Transaction and Professor Irving Louis Horowitz, Transaction's editorial director, made a number of cogent and helpful comments; most of them have been incorporated in the final version of the manuscript. As always, it was a great pleasure to work again with Sheryl Curtis, my language editor for many years. Her devotion to the job of translation and editing is among the rare things that one can always count on. Memorial University of Newfoundland contributed to covering some costs of manuscript preparation through its Publication Subvention program (November 2008 competition); this financial support is greatly appreciated.

Some chapters of the book were published previously as journal articles (however, their present versions in all cases differ markedly from the journal version: they have been significantly extended and revised). Their previously published sections are reproduced with the kind permission of the publishers of the *Journal of Economic Issues* (a version of Chapter 6 was published in Vol. 32, No. 2, pp. 547-556; © The Association for Evolutionary Economics), the *Journal of Communist Studies and Transition Politics* (a version of Chapter 8 was published in Vol. 24, No. 1, pp. 156-189; © Taylor & Francis), and *Quality & Quantity* (a version of the Methodological Appendix was published in Vol. 44). A number of ideas developed in this book were initially outlined in a series of Op-Ed articles published in two newspapers, *Vedomosti* and *Nezavisimaia Gazeta* over the period of three years, from Fall 2006 to Fall 2009 (more than 40 articles in all). The discussions that followed some of them helped to sharpen my arguments.

1

Introduction: Market Power on the Make

"Le droit de battre monnaie n'appartient qu'au prince"
*(Dictionnaire de l'Académie française,
sixth edition, 1835, p. 171)*

"Those in power mint money"
(An official from the Presidential Executive Office, 2008)

Individual decision-making is not an easy task, especially when the complexity of a puzzle that one confronts increases. However, challenges of individual decision-making appear less serious when compared with those related to the coordination of individual actions, or actions in concert. The task of finding a solution to a system of simultaneous equations necessitates a solid understanding of basic mathematics and some technical skills. To find a solution to a problem of interaction, one needs something more. On the one hand, the individual has to take into account the behavior of the counterpart, which is difficult to accomplish even with the help of solving simultaneous equations. "Action is 'social' insofar as its subjective meaning takes account of the behavior of others and is thereby oriented in its course" (Weber, 1968, p. 4). On the other hand, the individual needs to signal his or her own intentions, in order to facilitate the solution of a similar problem by other parties involved in the interaction (Livet & Thévenot, 1994, p. 157). The fewer points of common references in this process of mutual interpretation and adjustment, the more "rounds"—one thinks the others think one thinks the other think—appear necessary to find a solution. Sometimes speculations as to the possible plans of the other parties have all chances of continuing *ad infinitum* (Orléan, 1994).

The problematic character of interactions between two or more people has several solutions nevertheless. This plurality of solutions characterizes most everyday situations, however banal they appear. The "battle of the sexes," a generic name for interactions between two mutually dependent persons with non-coinciding interests and priorities, represents one such situation. One of the partners would like to spend an evening in a theater, the other—in a bar, yet both value the company of the other: their relationship has not gone awry yet. Attempts of both partners to reason in a purely rational manner produce uncertainty. Provided that there is no communication between them (as if they both lost their cell phones and needed to figure out where to go unilaterally), no one has a strategy that simultaneously secures good company and a preferred event.

A solution, one of several, implies references of both parties to the same norm or convention. For instance, the principle that the "lady is first" represents common knowledge, which produces their "spontaneous" and "natural" decision to go to the event preferred by the female partner. The other solution means relying on trust. Trust paves the way to behaving "as though the future were certain" (Luhmann, 1979, p. 10). In practical terms, the individual goes to the partner's preferred event expecting some gratification in a similar situation in the future.

The partners may as well seek power as a solution for transforming the interaction between equals into a power play. With the help of various strategic moves, such as threats, the commitment or the destruction of communication (Schelling, 1960, Ch. 5), the individual can deliberately restrict the range of options available to his or her counterpart. "If you go to the event of your choice, then instead of joining you I will go to my preferred place alone anyway, even if it is going to be a punishment for me too,"—threatens one of the partners before they separate and make their plans for the evening. By doing so, he or she acquires power over the other—as long as the threat is perceived as credible—because of deliberate changes in the choice situation (Dowding, 1996, p. 24). Action in concert then results from the submission of one participant to the other's will, which means the exercise of power by the second. This second participant appropriates the right to decide what to do (e.g., where to go) under particular circumstances at will.[1]

Power helps solve problems related to social action by merging two (or several) centers of decision-making into one. The actor vested in power decides exactly how coordination and adjustment can be achieved. In other words, power maintains order in interactions. Michael Mann (1986, p. 146) highlights this function of power by introducing the concept of "compulsory cooperation": power facilitates action in concert and increases "the surplus extracted from nature."

Max Weber (1968, pp. 32-34) differentiates two types of order: "law," if it derives from the use of power, and "convention," if order is embedded in norms and traditions shared by all members of a community. Order based on generalized trust, or trust in personally unknown people, can be added to this list.[2] Various types of order refer to different supports to action in concert, or coordination devices: power, convention and trust. When all of them are available, people involved in social action have a choice and, hence, greater flexibility and more degrees of freedom. If necessary, they substitute power for trust and *vice versa* (see Section I of Chapter 2). The fact that power, trust and convention have partly complementary, partly substitutable characters complicates their studies as they rarely exist in "pure forms."

I. Critical Case of Compulsory Cooperation

Russia represents a rare occasion in this regard: the "repertoire" of coordination devices contains one element there, power. As a Russian historian and philosopher of the nineteenth century argues, "the struggle appears unavoidable when achieving cooperation of individuals each of whom has a unique inner self. The natural state in this struggle is not freedom, but either power or obedience" (Tikhomirov, 2006, p. 14). One century later, Yuri Pivovarov (2006a, p. 253), another Russian historian and social scientist, also sees a key particularity of Russian culture in an all-encompassing, overwhelming role of power: "the Russian cultural community is power-centered, power represents the substance of our being." Power mediates most interactions, ranging from everyday decisions as to where to go out for a Friday night to the choice of national development strategies. "Practically all Russian revolutions and all successful attempts to modernize Russia have been carried out in the 'top-down' manner" (Gaman-Golutvina, 2006, p. 5). Even the most recent administrative reform (started at the end of the 1990s) that is potentially intended to reshape the scope and the substance of the coordination through power was initiated and implemented by people vested in power (see Section I of the Conclusion).[3]

The language of institutional theory[4] facilitates a further understanding of a power-centered community. Instead of using rather imprecise terms such as "culture," institutionalists introduce a series of concepts deriving from the notion of institutions as "the humanly devised constraints that shape human interactions" (North, 1990, p. 3). The key function of institutions lies in supporting interaction and making adjustments of individual plans possible. In this sense, power, convention and trust are all institutions. To take a step further, institutional theory differentiates between formal rules (e.g., laws), informal norms (e.g., customs and traditions) and enforcement mechanisms (e.g., law enforcement or ostracism in the case of informal norms). A particular combination of these three elements in Russia, Russian "institutional matrix," contains a great deal of enforcement mechanisms, all deriving from power, but very few formal rules and some informal norms. This translation of the idea of a power-centered society into the language of institutions has an advantage of emphasizing that a *means* to maintain order (power as an enforcement mechanism) replaces formal rules and informal norms that determine parameters of order by setting appropriate "*ends*." The substitution of a means for the ends calls for an in-depth discussion (see Section V of Chapter 2).

The above-formulated arguments allow answering the apparently simple question as to whether this book is about Russia and mainly for those who have interests in this country (specialists in Russian studies and international relations, businesspeople exploring this new market or working on it and so forth). The answer is neither affirmative nor negative. On the one hand, all those people are going to find a wealth of relevant information in the book. On the other hand, the book fits less the format of country studies than that of an inquiry into the nature of power. The weakness or nonexistence of the other coordination mechanisms creates favorable conditions for such an inquiry. Russia simply represents a critical case for studying power in its pure form. A critical case "is chosen on grounds that it will allow a better understanding of the circumstances under which the hypothesis will and will not hold" (Bryman, 2004, p. 51). The Russian case allows for a better understanding of social action when only one coordination device, namely power, appears available.

II. Market as a Mechanism for Strengthening Power: Marx, Weber and Beyond

Despite all the differences between the approaches developed by Karl Marx and Max Weber, they both view the market a mechanism for reproducing and strengthening power, which places them on the same side of the barrier with regard to neoclassical economists.

For Marx, the market helps capitalists to acquire power (in pre-capitalist societies industrialists and merchants occupied a subaltern position) and to exercise it by purely economic means. In contrast to pre-capitalist societies, where the application of physical force prevailed, capitalism hides power relationships beyond the façade of the employment relationship between two free—at first glance—individuals, the owner of money and the free laborer. "For the conversion of his money into capital ... the owner of money must meet in the market with the free labourer, free in the double sense, that as a free man he can dispose of his labour-power as his own commodity, and that on the other hand he has no other commodity for sale, in short of everything necessary for the realization of his labour-power" (Marx, 1936, pp. 187-188). Under these conditions, however, the "free" laborer has no other choice than to enter into an employment relationship accepting the capitalist's power over the process of production in general, whose essence is social action because of the division of labor and the need for coordination that it involves, and his labor in particular.

The transformation of labor into a commodity and the formation of the labor market represent a necessary condition for exercising power by "purely economic means." "Now the surplus could be extracted by 'purely economic means' through production and markets themselves, without the need for assistance from independent ideological, military, and political power organizations" (Mann, 1993, p. 24). This constitutes the first connection between power and the market, namely the market as a link in a more global chain of commoditization: that of labor, that of land, that of products of labor, etc. When viewed from Marx's perspective, the market itself is not a site where power structures interactions; it can rather be compared with a road leading to such a site. The capitalist has power over the laborer within the firm, whereas exchanges on the market, including the labor market, remain formally free.[5]

Max Weber shifts the focus of his attention to the market as a place not immune to power. Writing his *Economy and Society* half a century after Marx's *Capital*, he observes the reality of monopolistic capitalism. Under conditions of monopoly, the assumption of the equality of participants in a market transaction no longer holds. This gives rise to Weber's interest in power exercised right on the market place and in the process of market exchanges. However, he did not explore the links between monopoly and power in detail, indicating only a useful direction for further explorations (Weber, 1968, pp. 943-946). These links represent the second eventual connection between power and the market discussed in-depth in Chapters 5 and 6 of this book.

A third connection between the market and power not considered either by Marx or by Weber merits consideration. The state plays an increasingly active role on the market in all countries around the world; the global crisis that started in the second half of 2008 only reinforces this tendency (see also Sections V and VI of the Conclusion). It seems instructive, for both theoretical and practical reasons, to assess the impact of the state's involvement in market exchanges in terms of power. Does the market restrict the expansion of political power or, on the contrary, contribute to its continuous reproduction and strengthening? The third connection implies taking into consideration the state as a participant in market exchanges along with businesses ("capitalists" in Marxist terms) and the population ("laborers" and consumers). Except in rare cases of the expropriation or nationalization of private businesses, the state does not "hire" any of these actors, which makes Marxist models less relevant. No formal employment relationships emerge between the state and businesses. At the same time, the fact that the state has a unique status on the market suggests references to Weber's thoughts with regard to the power of monopoly. Nevertheless, he says nothing about an eventual interplay between political and economic monopolies. Amitai Etzioni (1988, p. 227), a socio-economist, assumes that "'pure' economic monopolies are logically possible, but seem rare and unstable; on the other hand, monopolies based on political and economic power are common and stable." But he does not go into further detail either.

How does the triplet state/business/population work on the market in terms of the power that it generates or suppresses? If the state does not "hire" businesses in the same manner as the capitalist hires the laborer, can it maintain order coordinating (regulating) market interactions by "purely economic means"? Instead of offering a fixed "salary," the state can create such conditions that, in order to make profits, the private business has to accept the state's priority in decision-making even in the matters usually under its exclusive control. This can be achieved if the state performs the role of a "gate-keeper" at the entrance to the market by allowing only those businesses that accept the state's monopoly in decision-making to "get in." Restricted competition increases the amount of profits appropriated by the "selected few." In contrast to the fixed pay in the employment relationship, this particular recompense is neither received directly from the "employer," i.e., the state, nor guaranteed *ex ante*. Instead, the state rewards obedient businesses by granting them the right to make profits and by increasing their economic power. In exchange, the "selected few" are expected to contribute by all available means to the further strengthening of the state's political power.

The configuration of relationships between the state and businesses outlined above does not arguably have a country-specific character. However, it takes manifest forms in the Russian case, especially during the period of rapid economic growth between 1999 and 2008 (Table 5.3 shows growth rates over this decade). Hence, there is a second reason for considering Russia as a critical case: the analysis of interactions between the state, businesses and the population on the market in this country helps shed more light on the previously under-explored connection between the market and power. More specifically, the choice of Russia allows studying conditions under which the market transforms into a mechanism for reproducing and strengthening political power.

The task of exploring a web of connections between economic and political monopoly justifies the choice of the period of economic boom for an in-depth study. Russia's rapid economic growth created powerful incentives for entering the national market. Both national and foreign businesses could get more by entering the Russian market than by working elsewhere, as opposed to what happened at the early stages of the market reforms (1991-1998) when businesses, including national firms, were trying to "get out" immediately after making first significant profits. A "gate-keeper," the actor able to exercise entry control on the market, transforms the strong interest of businesses in "getting in" into a resource for reproducing and strengthening its power. Hence the state becomes a "gate-keeper" and appropriates "purely economic means" for securing businesses' submission to its power.[6] Chapter 5 shows how entry control works in the Russian retail trade industry, Chapter 7—in one of Russia's regions.

Similar processes characterize international economic and, hence, political affairs. After several decades of looking for status as a world power by mostly military means, since the late 1990s Russia has increasingly relied on "purely economic means" in its international policies. The policies of mercantilist domination that it adapts derive from converting biases in the market structure into a resource for strengthening power at the expense of the other coordination devices. By adapting such policies, the state "attempts to dominate international markets, authoritatively controlling such resources as it can, moving toward diplomatic sanctions ..., even shows force, but short of war and territorial expansion" (Mann, 1993, p. 34). Hence, the only difference between the internal and foreign policies pursued by the state in Russia during the period analyzed consists in the type of the market under control: national in the former case, international in the latter.

The world market for hydrocarbons, crude oil and natural gas, has a less than perfect competitive structure. The supply on this market is tightly controlled by few key players, including the Organization of Petroleum-Exporting Countries (OPEC) and Russia. As of the second half of 2009, OPEC controls about one-third of the global supply, Russia—more that a tenth of it. Since the 1980s, Russia has been one of the two largest world producers of crude oil, the second being Saudi Arabia.[7] European countries increasingly depend on supplies of hydrocarbons from Russia. In 2006, Russian supplies covered about one-fifth of their total energy consumption—all sources of energy, including nuclear and alternative, combined. This means a one-and-a-half percentage point increase in just two years, using 2004 as a point of reference (Table 1.1).

Proved reserves of oil and natural gas further confirm Russia's status as a key player on this oligopolistic market. Even if Russia's share in proven world reserves of oil, 5 percent, does not seem impressive, that in proven world reserves of natural gas, 26.9 percent, makes it the single most important world supplier of hydrocarbons in the future (US Energy Information Administration, 2009). Despite the existence of a few other important players on this market, Russia has a strong capacity for exercising entry control because of its heavy reliance on (and its exclusive control of) pipelines as vehicles for delivering hydrocarbons to the final consumer. Once the final consumer gets "wired" to a pipeline, it becomes increasingly costly to switch to an alternative supplier whose availability is furthermore limited because of an oligopoly. The secure access to supplies of oil and natural gas appears conditioned upon the acceptance of Russia as a world power. Subsections II [d1], [d2] and [e1] of Chapter 8 provide more details on making power out of the market for hydrocarbons.

The period of economic boom and the rise of Russia as a world energy power coincide in time with the rule of Vladimir Putin, president of the Russian Federation between December 31, 1999 and May 7, 2008. However, the present volume is not a book about "Putin's rule" similar to a large body of literature covering Yeltsin's rule, Gorbachev's rule, and so forth, going down to Peter I's rule or Ivan IV's rule. The question of particular personalities seems less important than that of the configuration of power relationships in the context of which they act. President Putin may embody a close junction of power and the market, but the relevance of this connection goes far beyond the limits of a specific period of time (his term in office) or a specific country (Russia).

Table 1.1
Coefficients of Total Energy Dependence on Energy Supplies (Crude Oil, Natural Gas and Coal) from Russia, member-countries of the European Union, 2004 and 2006

	2004	2006
Austria	21.351	22.312
Belgium	16.75	18.295
Bulgaria	37.504	38.705
Czech Republic	24.653	26.124
Denmark	5.67	5.635
Estonia	13	15.55*
Finland	40.882	36.896
France	8.0252	10.614
Germany	21.525	23.024
Greece	23.678	23.634
Hungary	48.699	51.089
Ireland	0	0
Italy	22.336	17.145
Latvia	67.701	37.28*
Lithuania	47.168	64.191
Netherlands	11.3	13.971
Poland	27	30.361
Portugal	3.7905	0.0536
Romania	22.28	19.611
Slovakia	53.702	52.56
Slovenia	7.2882	6.4752*
Spain	9.235	10.968
Sweden	8.2876	11.269
United Kingdom	2.7	6.3432
EU-27	17.187	18.716

Sources: European Commission, 2008; European Commission, 2007. The coefficient of dependence equals the sum of products of the share of a particular source of energy in total energy consumption, the share of import in its consumption and the share of supplies from Russia in its total imports. * Data on crude oil are missing.

III. Agency versus Structure in Making Power

The question about the role of particular personalities should be clearly differentiated from that of agency versus structure. Does the junction of power and the market result from the conscious and deliberate choices of actors? Or, alternatively, does it naturally emerge at a certain stage in the evolution of the power-centered society? Once again, the confrontation of several theoretical approaches, ranging from most determinist to most "voluntarist," can be instructive.

Marx would certainly opt for the latter assumption. When discussing the process of the accumulation of capital, Marx refuses to see any freedom in actions of not only the laborer, but also the capitalist. Instead of enjoying power over the laborer, the capitalist appears in Marx's writings as a simple puppet whose behavior depends on impersonal forces embedded in structures of the capitalist mode of production. "The circulation of money as capital is ... an end in itself, for the expansion of value takes place only within this constantly renewed movement.... Thus the conscious representative of this movement, the possessor of money becomes a capitalist. His person, or rather his pocket, is the point from which the money starts and to which it returns. The expansion of value, which is the objective basis or main-spring of the circulation M-C-M, becomes his subjective aim ... he functions as a capitalist, that is, as capital personified and endowed with consciousness and a will" (Marx, 1936, pp. 169-170). Even when the capitalist thinks he or she does something at will, these actions in fact, produce desired outcomes only when they contribute to the continuous accumulation of capital. Applied to the case under consideration, similar reasoning would lead to the conclusion that the introduction of the market in a power-centered society would sooner or later end up by its transformation—as a result of free only at first sight actions of people vested in power—into a mechanism for strengthening power. The accumulation of power does not significantly differ in this regard from the accumulation of capital.

Neoclassical economic theory lies at the opposite extreme of the continuum between determinism and the assumption of free choice. Neoclassical economists normally do not pay attention to issues of power precisely because of difficulties related to the task of explaining power relationships in terms of rational choice. Attempts to model the behavior of the actor vested in power on the basis of neoclassical assumptions, free and rational choice being one of them, raise a number of theoretical problems. For instance, can the trade-off between seeking power and using alternative coordination devices, convention and trust, be exclusively explained in terms of comparative costs? Ronald Coase adapts this perspective, arguing that the expansion of the firm based on power at the expense of the market[8] has limits expressed in a particular type of costs, transaction costs.[9] "The firm will tend to expand until the costs of organizing an extra transaction within the firm become equal to the costs of carrying out the same transaction by means of an exchange on the open market" (Coase, 1988, p. 44).[10] Viewed from this perspective, power emerges as a result of the free and rational choices of parties in interactions.

The comparative dynamics of transaction costs associated with alternative coordination devices prevents the total substitution of power for trust and convention. It also produces a sort of "equilibrium of power" (Dementiev, 2004, pp. 78-79; Dementiev, 2006, pp. 86, 89-90). However, this reasoning misses an important point: power does not necessarily have built-in constraints. More precisely, power does have built-in constraints only when used as a means to achieve other ends (utility, according to neoclassical economists). However, in a power-centered society power has a tendency to transform into an end in itself (this dimension of power is considered in-depth in Section V of Chapter 2 and Chapter 3). In contrast to utility, there is no such thing as the law of diminishing marginal attractiveness of power.[11] Getting an additional prerogative does not necessarily reduce its value to the power holder. The "consumption" of power may rather be compared to drug addiction, as a person vested in it suggests: "power is like a drug.... I can easily recall many cases when people became heavy drinkers, suffered a severe psychological crisis as a result of their loss of power" (63A: female, in her forties, former vice-governor of a Russian region; see the Appendix for the list of respondents and their characteristics).[12]

The task of modeling the behavior of the actor, who has a subordinate position in a power relationship, involves even more challenges. What kind of rational considerations lead the actor to sacrifice his or her freedom by accepting the exclusive right of the power-holder to take decisions? Neoclassical economists see a rationale in exchanging freedom for a secure remuneration under conditions of risk and uncertainty[13] (Simon, 1951). They tend to overlook, nevertheless, the fact that power significantly alters the structure of choices available to the subordinate and, hence, it necessitates major revisions in the model of rational choice. Furthermore, the neoclassical theory of the employment contract fails to explain the submission of the formally "free" capitalist to the power holder under conditions of the junction of power and the market. Chapter 6 sheds more light on this issue by showing how the capitalist starts to minimize missed opportunities instead of maximizing them or achieving "satisficing" results.

The theory of structuration associated with the name of Anthony Giddens represents an attempt to find a middle ground between determinism, as in the case of Marxism, and agency, as in the case of neoclassical economics. Before constructing his own theory, Giddens (1984, p. 9) offers a good definition of the latter assumption: "agency concerns events of which an individual is the perpetrator, in the sense that the individual could, at any phase in a given sequence of conduct, have acted differently." The major contribution of the theory of structuration consists in showing how structure—the institutional environment—simultaneously enables and constrains agency (Chapter 8 examines a similar thesis in the context of state service in Russia). The question as to whether agency produces structure, i.e., whether the junction of power and the market results from conscious and deliberate choices, remains somewhat out of its principal focus. In this respect Giddens (Ibid, p. 171) sounds rather deterministic: "it is not the case that actors create social systems: they reproduce or transform them, remaking what is already made in the community of praxis."

A similar critique can be addressed to the theory developed by Pierre Bourdieu. He explains the continuous production and reproduction of the institutional environment in terms of actors' dispositions or habituses. The habitus is "a product of the past ... it revives past experiences in the present" (Bourdieu, 1980, p. 91). In other words, the habitus represents the essence—expressed in a highly concentrated form—of the previous evolution of a power-centered society. The agent acquires a habitus in the process of primary socialization in the family, then at school, when using concepts underlying a particular world-view and so forth. As a result, he or she unconsciously reproduces institutions that lay at the origin of the habitus by his or her actions.

The habitus leaves some room for agency, which undermines a completely deterministic stance. When Bourdieu (2005, p. 130) discusses the actions of the French bureaucrats responsible for regulating the market at the local level, he observes that they "can always choose, at least to the extent that their dispositions prompt them to do so, between obedience *perinde ac cadaver* and disobedience (or resistance and inertia), and this *room for manoeuvre* [provides] a possibility for bargaining over—of negotiating the price of—their obedience or consent."

Alena Ledeneva (2006, p. 16) further develops this fruitful insight by proposing the notion of informal practices as "more or less regular strategies of navigating between ... formal rules and informal norms ... [guided by] a practical sense of what needed to be done in a given situation." Informal practices combine structural constraints (parameters of a situation) and agency (manipulative ways of mixing formal rules and informal norms). This means that the interplay between habitus and agency represents a better predictor for the behavior of actors. Returning to the explanation for the junction of power and the market, however, it is safer to put the critical sociology of Bourdieu in the middle range, while leaning toward the deterministic end of the continuum: after all, habitus determines the scope of agency.

The "new economic history" of Douglass North, a subfield of the new institutional economics, lies closer to the assumption of agency while incorporating some elements of institutional determinism. North links institutional innovations to the activities of entrepreneurs who produce new combinations from structures inherited from the past. "The motivating factor of institutional change is the desire to maximize profits.... A change in the potential profits from arrangemental innovation induces after some delay (or lag) the innovation of a new arrangement capable of capturing those profits for the innovators" (Davis & North, 1970, p. 139; see also North, 1981, pp. 207-208). The interplay between structure and agency seems to be at work again, with a heavier emphasis on the latter.

The failure to acknowledge the particularities of power as an institutional arrangement limits the applicability of this approach to the present discussion. First, it assumes an instrumental character of power, i.e., power as a means to maximize profits or utility. Second, it refers to a perfectly competitive market (the market for institutional innovations) instead of presuming structural biases, a major precondition for the conjunction of power and the market.[14]

An alternative hypothesis with regard to the origins of the embeddedness of the market in power has a point of departure in the differentiation between two components of power, strategic and structural, that represents a contribution of analytical philosophy. The structural component refers to biases in market structure, whereas the strategic one—to conscious efforts of power holders to reproduce or even amplify them. In the presence of the structural component only there is no power, only luck. "Luck ... enables some to get what they want without trying" (Dowding, 1996, p. x). Power, on the other hand, requires conscious efforts focused on getting the most from the existing situation and at laying groundwork for getting even more in the future.[15]

In practical terms, this combination of structure and agency—their two-way interaction is discussed in-depth in Chapter 5—requires that, first, there are some biases in the existing market structure, however small and insignificant they initially are, second, that power holders realize related opportunities and, third, that the actions of power holders contribute to reproducing and amplifying the biases. At the start of market reforms, there was no shortage of structural biases inherited from the centrally-planned past: between the production of means of production (so-called Group "A") and the production of consumer goods (so-called Group "B"), between various industries (see Kornai, 1980 and Subsection IV.8 of Chapter 4), between the legal and extralegal sectors in the economy (Timofeev, 1993), and so forth. Not surprisingly, the topic of monopoly was widely discussed in Russian economic literature in the mid-1990s.[16] By the end of the 1990s, power holders realized opportunities for transforming these biases into a lever for strengthening their power. During the period between 1999 and 2008 they learned how to take the existing opportunities and create new ones, which provides the additional justification for the selection of this timeframe.

The alternative approach toward finding a middle ground between structure and agency in making power suggests that one should neither overestimate nor underestimate the contribution of power holders. Particular personalities may be of a lesser importance, yet the power-centered society would have not survived post-Soviet reforms and a series of deep political and economic crises without the conscious actions of the people vested in power in the 1990s and, especially, during the period from 1999 to 2008. Sometimes they were simply lucky; as the years after the fall of the Soviet Union pass by, they become more and more powerful. What positions do these people occupy in the institutional structure and who they are? According to Wright Mills (1957, pp. 3-4), the question can be reformulated as to who can be considered members of the power elite in Russia? "The power elite is composed of men whose positions enable them to transcend the ordinary environments of ordinary men and women; they are in positions to make decisions having major consequences."

IV. Russian Power Elite

Expectations with regard to the power elite formed by analogy with Western countries may appear misleading in the Russian case. Mills (Ibid,

p. 5) includes representatives of the "hierarchies of state and corporation and army" in the American power elite of the mid-twentieth century. He would be certainly surprised to learn that forty years later, in the Russia of the 1990s, members of organized crime joined this company and even played a leading role in it. Charles Tilly (1985), however, should have been far less surprised by this fact as he emphasizes an uncertain, elastic character of the line separating the state from organized crime, especially at the early stages of state making around the world.

Decisions made by members of organized crime had "major consequences" and no understanding of how the Russian institutional system worked during that period seems possible without paying attention to this aspect (Oleinik, 2003; Volkov, 2002). This does not mean that Russia temporarily lost its character of a power-centered society at that time, as the metaphors of the "roaring nineties" and the *bespredel* commonly heard in Russia (literally—"with no limits," "everything is permitted") may suggest. Just power was concentrated also in the hands of gang members, who shared it with representatives of some other groups.

The progressive departure of the members of organized crime from the power elite, which has been observed since the end of the 1990s—some of them managed to completely legalize their status, some got marginalized, yet others got killed—have not produced a picture completely familiar to Western eyes either. A number of studies show that no social group in Russia meets the requirements set for the elite, namely the capacity for formulating a program of development and taking the lead in this process. "The Russian elite lacks not only for programs of development, its representatives acknowledge their own inability to produce them. One can assume an impotent nature of the elite in today's Russia because of its incapacity to produce leaders and even mere ideas of leadership" (Gudkov, Dubin & Levada, 2007, p. 205; see also *Summa ideologij*, 2008, p. 117). Elites in this sense of progress and Enlightenment may well be absent in Russia during the period of 1999-2008, yet a power-centered society without a power elite could hardly exist even for a short while.

The process of modernization involves progressive separation of three elements of the institutional environment responsible for structuring power relationships, namely ruler, state and society (Kharkhordin, 2001). In a power-centered society, their separation is never complete because of the embeddedness of everyday interactions in power. If it takes place at all, instead of a non-hierarchically organized triplet it produces a pyramid with the ruler at the top, society on the bottom and the state in the middle. Chapter 4 offers an historical perspective on this process in the Russian case.

Numerous proofs that the differentiation between the three elements is actually taking place can be found both in the results of social surveys and everyday discourse. Namely, society appears clearly separated from, often opposed to, the two higher layers in the pyramid. Contacts between society and these two layers tend to be minimal even at the local level. A pilot survey carried out by the "Public Opinion" Foundation (*Fond Obshchestvennoe Mnenie, FOM*) on representative samples in four regions of Russia in late October 2003 (Lubarsky, 2005) shows that a majority of the population had neither contacted representatives of municipal bodies during past two years nor had close relatives and friends who had such contacts.[17]

Everyday discourse further confirms the existence of a wide gap at the lowest level of the pyramid. Two of the interlocutors spontaneously and independently from each other cited Alexander Rosenbaum, a popular Russian singer and bard, when discussing relationships between society and the rest of the pyramid:

> "From my point of view, there is nothing good in references to state interests. Rosenbaum has very apt verse: 'Nightingales make hearts thrill near Kursk, // In Moscow people kiss bosses' asses. // I love my motherland, // And hate the state.' You see, what a nice expression of my feelings" (5A).

> "I like the following verses, from Rosenbaum. 'I love my motherland and hate the state.' I love this phrase; this is a perfect expression of my feeling. In Russia, unfortunately, the state is completely disconnected from the society, completely. It seems to me that the state represented by the [central] government, the president, regional governments, is too far from the society. I mean not all of them, but most of them" (43A).

A natural place for the power elite is located at the top of the pyramid, which leads to considering it as an embodiment of not simply power, but supreme power (see Subsection I.3 of Chapter 4 for more on the meaning of the concept of supreme power). Various institutions have performed the role of supreme power throughout Russian history: the court of the czar, the chancellery of his imperial majesty emperor of Russia, the Central Committee of the Communist Party of the Soviet Union and the Presidential Executive Office (Figure 1.1).

The task of understanding relationships between the two highest layers of the pyramid, supreme power (ruler) and the state, represents a serious challenge. Does the state simply service supreme power without acquiring any power on its own? Or, on the contrary, shall state represen-

Figure 1.1
Pyramid of Power in a Power-Centered Society

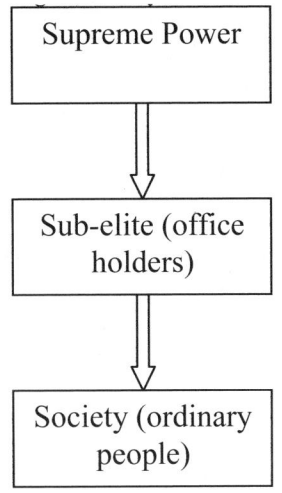

```
        ┌─────────────────┐
        │  Supreme Power  │
        └────────┬────────┘
                 ⇓
        ┌─────────────────┐
        │ Sub-elite (office│
        │     holders)    │
        └────────┬────────┘
                 ⇓
        ┌─────────────────┐
        │ Society (ordinary│
        │     people)     │
        └─────────────────┘
```

tatives be included in the power elite as their position enables them "to make decisions having major consequences"? Oxana Gaman-Golutvina (2006) and Richard Hellie (2005) describe state representatives in terms of "service class," which underlines their subordinate position vis-à-vis supreme power. On the other hand, public opinion in Russia perceives representatives of the state as grabbing and appropriating power. The results of a survey conducted on a representative sample by Levada-Centre in 1999 and 2008 show that most Russians see power concentrated in the hands of state representatives (Table 1.2).

The existence of several terms commonly used in Russian language to describe state representatives deserves mention: civil servants, public servants, bureaucrats, state servants, and office or rank holders (*chinovniki*, from *chin*—rank). The term "bureaucrat" has close connotations with the Weberian concept of rational bureaucracy and for that reason it has limited application in the Russian institutional context (Brym & Gimpelson, 2004). The concepts of civil and public service imply the other heroic assumption, that of state representatives acting in interests of society. Chapter 8 demonstrates the highly questionable character of this assumption, showing that state representatives act mainly in their individual or group interests. The concept of state service appears synonymous to that of service class. "The bureaucrats of Russia could not

Table 1.2
Distribution of Answers to the Question "In Your Opinion, What Is 'Power'? What Comes to Mind When You Hear This Word?"

	April 1999	June 2008
Violence, coercion	18	12
State, government	40	47
Office holders (chinovniki)	22	32
Bosses (nachal'stvo)	13	24
Opportunity to give orders	15	22
Constitution, laws	27	26
Management of public affairs	7	15
Privileges	21	17
Maintaining order	14	15
Delinquent behavior, opportunism	29	20
Social protection, help for the poor	10	10
Leading force	10	12
Individuals elected by the people and responsible to them	13	13
I do not know	4	3
N	2,000	1,600

Source: Obshchestvennoe mnenie, 2008, p. 29

be 'civil servants' but had to be 'state servants' above all else" (Ryavec, 2003, p. 53). Hence, it implicitly leads to the belief that state representatives do not acquire or appropriate any power, as they are simple translators, however imperfect, of a superior will.

The use of the term "office holder" does not rule out any of the hypotheses formulated above: state representatives as "lieutenants" of supreme power versus state representatives as members of the "power elite." Furthermore, it fits in well with the idea of the power-centered society in which the rank in the hierarchy of power, *chin*, transforms into the single most important predictor of behavior.[18] The concept of office holding catches the highly ambivalent position of state representatives in the Russian institutional structure: they translate the will of supreme power and simultaneously appropriate part of it. The tendency to appropriate some power with regard to society characterizes, according to Gaman-Golutvina (2006), the evolution of state representatives throughout Russian history. They never fully succeed but they never completely give up either.

In this sense, office holders occupy the position of sub-elites that are not completely deprived of power (Etzioni-Halevy, 1993, p. 96). Konstantin Pobedonostsev (1965, p. 270), a Russian high-ranking state servant in the nineteenth century, insightfully summarizes the ambivalences related to the position of his fellow *chinovnik*: "poor man, before he commands he has first to learn to obey." By passing the test of obedience on a continuous—almost daily—basis, office holders in Russia, *chinovniki*, usurp some power. Deprived of any autonomous, independent from supreme power, source of power, office holders reproduce the same model of power relationship that prevails at the highest layer of the pyramid in their everyday actions.

V. On Sources of Information

Any empirical research on the power elite necessitates solving at least two problems related to the collection of the primary data. First, this milieu has a closed character. A part of the explanation consists in the use of cooptation as a mechanism for recruiting new members of the power elite. "Men in the same circles choose one another" (Mills, 1957, p. 139).[19] Outsiders, including independent researchers, can hardly get even a temporary access to the power elite. The time when the rate of refusals to be interviewed did not exceed one-digit numbers—Lewis Dexter (2006, p. 35) recalls that in the early 1950s out of five hundred prominent southern politicians in the US only 3 percent turned down a request for interview from a personally unknown researcher—has gone not only in Russia, but probably in most other countries too. To get access to a closed milieu, one has to be introduced by an insider who then acts as a "sponsor" (Bryman, 2004, p. 297).

Most Russians do not have members of the power elite and sub-elite among their relatives, friends and acquaintances. The above-cited pilot survey carried out by *FOM* shows that more than two-thirds of respondents[20] do not have any personal connections with office holders (*chinovniki*). Furthermore, several government bodies, including the Presidential Executive Office, have formal regulations prohibiting interviews with "outsiders" without an explicit authorization: "By the way, we don't give interviews without permission of the department head" (21A).

Second, there are no reliable estimates for the overall "population" of the power elite, which makes the task of constructing a random sample virtually impossible to accomplish. In elite and specialized interviews "the population cannot be satisfactory randomized or stratified in advance" (Dexter, 2006, p. 43). Remaining options—convenience and theoretical samples—significantly limit the scope of possible generalizations.

For instance, what criteria can an outsider use to draw lines separating the power elite, the power sub-elite and the society? There is a kind of contradiction in definition: such criteria are set and applied by the insiders. One solution consists in relying on subjective evaluations and expert opinions as to how influential a particular individual is. A ranking of the most influential people in Russia (*Samye vliiatel'nye ljudi Rossii*, 2004) represents an example. It is also used as the sampling frame in a research project on the contemporary Russian elite (*Summa ideologij*, 2008, pp. 10-12).

The other solution implies using the office held by an individual as a criterion for including him or her into the power elite and sub-elite.[21] This approach conforms to a hierarchical logic proper to the power-centered society and allows constructing a sampling frame on the basis of the statistical data (without helping solve the problem of a high rate of refusals though). Olga Kryshtanovskaya (2005, pp. 17-22) assesses the overall population of the power elite (n=1,060) in a similar manner, as well as researchers from the Levada-Centre (Gudkov, Dubin & Levada, 2007, pp. 77-78). The official data, nevertheless, exists only in an aggregated form. The Federal State Statistics Service produces the total count of office holders in the state service equal to 846,307, or 0.6 percent of the total population, as of October 1, 2008 (Table 1.3). The list "A" (*categoriia "A"*) includes 35,123 of them, or 4.15 percent.[22] The decision as to how many of people from this list shall be included in the power elite (and how many from the remaining lists "B" and "C"—into the sub-elite) requires additional theoretical considerations.

Difficulties related to both getting access to the power elite and finding objective criteria for randomization and stratification prompt to apply elements of theoretical sampling in the presented study. Taking into consideration that representatives of supreme power remain completely out of reach of independent researchers—for instance, no known study incorporates interviews with individuals currently holding offices of the federal minister or higher—the present study focuses on the power sub-elite. This does not prevent from studying the prevailing model of power:

Table 1.3
Number of Employees Who Hold Offices in the State Service of the Russian Federation, by Branches of Power, 1999-2008

	Total	Legislative branch	Executive branch	Judicial branch	Other bodies
on January 1, 1999	485,566	7,995	397,236	78,281	2,054
on January 1, 2000	548,728	10,511	445,376	89,923	2,918
on January 1, 2001	576,050	10,368	456,665	105,655	3,362
on September 1, 2002	666,813	11,663	518,921	129,182	7,047
on January 1, 2005	684,202	11,989	558,931	105,672	7,610
on January 1, 2007	791,820	12,542	655,789	115,181	8,308
on October 1, 2008	846,307	12,716	699,160	124,750	9,681

Source: the Federal State Statistics Service, 2009. Retrieved from http://www.gks.ru/bgd/regl/B08_99/IssWWW.exe/Stg/tabl1.htm

representatives of the power sub-elite do not have an autonomous source of power and, hence, reproduce in their relationships with subordinates and ordinary people many features of supreme power.

Respondents were recruited from three categories: (i) associate ministers, department heads and associate heads—at this level key decisions with regard to the everyday operation of the government body are taken; (ii) bureau heads (*nachal'nik otdela*) and associate heads—the key servicing unit in the state administration and (iii) experts with a good knowledge of the milieu of office holders because of either their previous employment in the state service or current status as advisers. They represent both the federal and regional levels of the state administration. Further, all attempts were made to recruit as many respondents as possible from (i) the Presidential Executive Office—due to its closeness to supreme power and particular status "above" the other government bodies, (ii) ministries and agencies responsible for regulating economy and, more specifically, the market—because of the postulated importance of the junction of power and the market and (iii) the administration of a region in Siberia (Section II of Chapter 7 contains a detailed justification for the selection of this case). Informal divisions within the power sub-elite (see the next section) were also taken into account when selecting respondents.

Respondents who meet these criteria were contacted in two manners: through either official letters sent to the head of a particular government body on letterhead of an institute of the Russian Academy of Science or personal contacts using a snowballing technique. "If it's on letterhead, this means an official status of the document. I wouldn't even say the official status; it is simply dealt with through different channels" (52A). Surprisingly enough, both approaches brought some fruits, whatever unevenly they are distributed across the targeted government bodies. In most cases no informative interview appeared feasible without the help of a "sponsor." Researchers from the Levada-centre report similar problems with recruitment of respondents representing high layers in the pyramid of power (Gudkov, Dubin & Levada, 2007, pp. 80-81). The strategy of approaching respondents with the help of exclusively official means worked in only one case, that of a federal ministry (the Ministry for Economic Development), but allowed to organize a few informative interviews.[23] This ministry positions itself as taking the lead in administrative reform.

> "You're right now simply in a very special place, where everything is not representative of the whole.... If you make little efforts by searching for relevant information on the net, you'll quickly realize: this is not a typical place at all" (4A).

In total, 116 in-dept semi-structured interviews were conducted over the period from the start of 2005 till the end of 2008 (Table 1.4). Sixty-four of them (Set "A," see the Appendix for the list of respondents and the interview guide) were carried out in the framework of the project supported by the Social Sciences and Humanities Research Council of Canada (award Nos. 820-2005-0004 and 861-2005-0001). The research team includes Dr. Natalia Aparina (Kemerovo State University), Dr. Sergei Birjukov (Kemerovo State University), Dr. Karine Clément (Institute of Sociology of Russian Academy of Sciences), Prof. Oxana Gaman-Golutvina (Moscow State Institute of International Relations), Prof. Svetlana Glinkina (Institute of Economics of Russian Academy of Sciences), Evgenia Gvozdeva (Université Libre de Bruxelles), Dr. Galina Medvedeva (St. Petersburg Institute of Sociology of Russian Academy of Sciences) and the author who lead it. Full transcripts of 52 interviews (Set "B" and 9 last entries in Set "C," see the Appendix) were kindly made available for secondary analysis by Dr. Lev Gudkov and Natalia Zorkaya (Levada-Center) and Dr. Natalia Aparina (Kemerovo State University).

Transcripts of all 116 interviews (465,876 words in total, or 4,016 words per interview on average) were analyzed with the help of software

Table 1.4
Key Parameters of the Theoretical Sample Used in the Analysis throughout the Book Compared with the Other Samples

Study			This book Set "A"	This book Set "B"	Levada-centre♠	INOP†	GKS‡
N (n in the case of GKS)			64	43	568	326	846,307
Year			2006-2008	2005	2005	2007	2008
Gender of interlocutors, %	Male		73.4	83.7	n.a.	86	71.7
	Female		26.7	16.3	n.a.	14	28.3
Age of interlocutors, %	Under 41		39	0	n.a.	11*	55
	41-50		34.4	27.9	n.a.	27**	23.2
	51-60		18.8	44.2	n.a.	45***	19.6
	61 and older		7.8	27.9	n.a.	17	2.2
Group in the power sub-elite, %	Executive branch	Upper-middle	46.9	20.9	41	19.6	18.5
		Lower-middle	37.5	0	0	0	
	Legislative branch		0	27.9	8.6	10.4	1.5
	Judicial branch		0	0	8.4	9.8	14.7
	Expert		15.6	32.6	0	0	-
	Business		0	18.6	23.9	9.5	-
	Other		0	0	18.6	50.6	-

Legend: ♠ The study whose outcomes are discussed in (Gudkov, Dubin & Levada, 2007); † The study whose outcomes are discussed in (Summa ideologij, 2008); ‡ The total population of office holders in the state service, the data of the Federal State Statistics Service, retrieved from http://www.gks.ru/bgd/regl/B08_99/IssWWW.exe/Stg/tabl1.htm; * The age group of 18-34; ** The age group of 35-44; *** The age group of 45-59.

programs for content analysis QDA Miner version 2.0.8 and WordStat version 5.1.12 developed by Provalis Research (Montréal, Canada). The content analysis was performed using a number of codebooks (see the Appendix)—in function of a particular aspect of the junction between power and the market highlighted in various chapters of this book. Several iterations in qualitative coding and, hence, multiple re-readings of the same transcript (ten and more), appeared necessary to achieve a satisfactory level of validity and reliability. An original path model for triangulating the results of three types of content analysis: (i) the analysis of the co-occurrence of words; (ii) the use of dictionaries based on substitution with entries matching qualitative codes and (iii) qualitative coding allows to produce a quantitative assessment of reliability and validity in coding (see the Methodological Appendix).

The core idea lying at its origin consists in quantitatively measuring associations between transcripts of interviews ordered in function of co-occurrences of words ("themes"), particular combinations of words (categories of a custom-built dictionary) and qualitative codes. Strong associations indicate a high level of consistency in attributing qualitative codes (excerpts from them illustrate the analysis throughout the book). The achieved level of validity and reliability increases confidence in reported outcomes and their interpretation offered in this book. It also helps overcome usual criticisms addressed to purely qualitative, hermeneutic approaches (e.g., emphasis on their highly subjective character) without compromising their strengths (e.g., they make possible not only description and analysis[24] of social action, but also its interpretation consisting in the discovery of the subjective meaning attached to it).

VI. Anatomy of the Power Sub-Elite

Along with formal classifications and descriptions of offices, informal criteria play a significant, if not more important, role in determining the true position of an office in the pyramid of power. The vital role of informal institutions in structuring the power elite and sub-elite hardly surprises, considering the general prevalence of unwritten rules of the game in Russia over written ones (Ledeneva, 2006; Ledeneva, 1998). It should be kept in mind, nevertheless, that the spread of informal norms does not make them a key coordination device in a power-centered society. Informal norms play a secondary, complementary role with regard to power relationships.

For instance, the differentiation between three types of office holders in the economic sphere, the *khoziaistvennik*, the *apparatchik* and the *tekhnocrat,* emerged during the Soviet period. The first group includes "persons who perform resource allocation and held responsible for results" (Gregory, 1990, p. 54), the second—"persons who issue instructions and rules" and the third—"individuals who serve the former two groups in a technical rather than decision-making capacity." It is important to note, on the one hand, that these categories cannot be found in official job descriptions, and, on the other hand, that they describe a particular type of behavior and a membership in a particular informally constituted group rather than a particular office (i.e., the *khoziaistvennik* can hold an office with rule- and policy-making prerogatives[25]). What are key informal groups in the contemporary Russian power elite and sub-elite?

IV.1 Tops

If the formal boundaries separating the power elite (supreme power) from the power sub-elite appear somewhat blurred, office holders nevertheless do not have any difficulty when asked to identify the highest layers of the state service. Respondents' assessments suggest including people colloquially referred to as the "tops" (*topy*) into the upper-level of the power sub-elite. The "tops" commonly occupy positions as federal ministers and higher:

> "There are the minister and his associates. Most decisions are taken at this level, I think. Furthermore, if the associate touches upon some issues outside his competence, he will anyway ask the minister for advice" (37A).

> "They [federal ministers] act exclusively in a representative capacity. However, they believe that no one is above them, only the blue sky. They set such a big distance to anyone else and present themselves so unapproachable that no contact is possible for an outsider" (44A).

However, a better means for predicting membership in this group can be found in a particular type of behavior. Some respondents, who can safely be considered members of the power sub-elite, confess to not being able to understand and to correctly predict the actions of the "tops": they simply do not fit the behavioral model of other office holders.

> "The minister's motivation is a puzzle for me. It happened to me to hear how he explains his behavior a couple of times. It struck me as I'd never think in such a sophisticated and cunning manner" (13A).

Several patterns of "conspicuous consumption"[26] also distinguish the "tops" from the rest of the power sub-elite, although only few of them have a more or less formalized nature, such as the particular type of the company car. Federal ministers, directorate heads in the Presidential Executive Office and the presidential aides are entitled, as of October 2009, to an executive class BMW 750iL with additional options. The associate minister gets access to a less luxurious BMW 525i and so forth.

> "There are some differences in the type of the company cars [that office holders use]. Well, it is less the outcome of a particular corporate culture than the prescription stipulated by the law or something like that: who shall use which type of the car" (45A).

There exists no official regulation with regard to where the "tops" should live. Despite this, members of the power sub-elite are well aware of an informally set "sign of distinction": the "tops" tend to live in the most prestigious suburb west of Moscow, along the Rublvesky highway (colloquially called the *Rublevka*).

> "If I've got promoted to associate minister, I shall move to the Rublevka" (58A).

"They [the 'tops'] live separately even in a geographical sense. Along the Rublevka. It's not by coincidence that they cluster over there. They achieve a maximal isolation as a result" (42A).

VI.2 "Liberals" and "Siloviki"

The discourse about post-Soviet reforms often involves opposing two groups in the power elite and sub-elite, the "liberals"—advocates of the *laissez-faire*, neoclassical approaches toward economic reforms associated with their stronghold in the Ministry for Economic Development—and the *siloviki*, a nickname of representatives of power ministers: the Federal Security Service (FSB; former KGB), the Ministry of Interior, the Ministry of Defense, the Ministry of the Emergency Situations and some other government bodies with the privilege of the legitimate use of physical force. The RuNet, the Russian-language segment of the World Wide Web, for instance, contains a similar number of documents with each of the two terms.[27]

> "During the second half of 2004 a huge number of people were talking to the *siloviki* warning them: 'Guys, everything is going to end up by a disaster, and you'll have to disperse them [senior people protesting against a reform aimed at substituting monetary compensations for in-kind privileges; see more on this reform in Chandler, 2008 and Subsection II [h5] of Chapter 8] after all'. Two thirds of the *siloviki* replied: 'Great! After such a big mistake on their part it'd be easier for us to kick out these fucking liberals'" (50A).

Kryshtanovskaya (2005, p. 270) observes a progressive increase in the share of the *siloviki* in the post-Soviet power sub-elite compared with the late Soviet period: "The growing presence of the military among people vested in power has been observed all the time since the start of democratization. Their share has increased sevenfold between 1988 and 2002." Any assessment of the relative influence of the *siloviki* and the "liberals" based on the number of office holders, on the one hand, who wear the uniform (or who have worn it in the past) and, on the other hand, who graduated from the top programs with a strong neoclassical component (like the Higher School of Economics and the New School of Economics in Moscow—these two universities were often mentioned by the interlocutors in discussions about the "liberals") should be treated with caution, however. First, power does not necessarily directly correlate with the relative size of each group. One has to control at least two other variables: exact positions in the pyramid of power and the internal cohesion of the group. Public discourse may tend to overestimate the real involvement of the "visible hand" of the *siloviki* in making key decisions, however their total number is growing.[28]

> "I read a lot about [the expansion of the *siloviki*], but didn't observe any single time their involvement into decision-making. Well, it may be because my area of expertise [industrial organization] lies far away from their interests. It seems to me that either the power ministries are more passive than usually believed or they simply don't always understand very well what is going on" (45A).

Second, membership in each of the two groups tends to be conditioned less by formal links with a particular power ministry or university than by a distinctive "shared mental model" "that provide both an interpretation of the environment and a prescription as to how that environment should be structured" (Denzau & North, 1994, p. 4) and behavioral patterns. References to the ideal of service, *sluzhenie*, prevail in the discourse about the *siloviki*—in both their self-descriptions and characteristics provided by the other respondents. This ideal contrasts with that imputed to the "liberals," namely the spirit of entrepreneurship and a utilitarian, pragmatic orientation.

> "Quite diverse motivations could be found [in the state administration], everything depends on particular people. Some of them are profit-seekers, the others carve out careers, still the others think about the state's interests, my apologies if it sounds pathetically.... The state should appreciate such things as obligation, service, vocation" (38A).

> "According to some statistical data, 5 percent of the population feed themselves and create jobs for the others, they are called entrepreneurs. Some people with the spirit of entrepreneurship take state offices. The spirit of enterprise is not apparently the worst that could happen, but the state service is not the right place for doing business. When a businessman enters the state service because, as he believes, of higher profit rates, it's not a motivation we should look for" (40A).

Upon closer inspection, nevertheless, it appears that the emphasis on service proper to the *siloviki* and the pragmatism of the "liberals" may not necessarily contradict one another in the context of the junction between power and the market. Instead, they seem to possess comparative advantages in working on the same project of transforming the market into a mechanism for reproducing power. Neither of these groups has any interest in kicking the rivals out completely as a result of the partly complementary, partly substitutable character of their respective areas of expertise. The continuous reproduction of power, a major preoccupation for the *siloviki*, necessitates a good expertise in the economic matters that they do not possess. The maximization of profits, a major preoccupation of the "liberals," calls for using and increasing biases in the market structure and, hence, requires expertise in exercising the control that they lack.

> "They [the *siloviki*] are good lobbyists, lobbyists of the state's interests.... For instance, a large enterprise was privatized and the state kept a 5 percent stake in it. What to do with these 5 percent? The state doesn't need them.... The privatization was done improperly, the state initially had 17 percent that then transformed into 5 percent. There existed some serious concerns as to due procedure. Was it legal or illegal—I don't want to discuss. We, together with the law enforcement bodies, managed to prove that the state actually owns a 17 percent stake. It was a large insurance company. We made an arrangement and forced them buy the shares in question back at a more reasonable price. We twisted their arms leaving them no other choice but to buy these shares. We've got extra money for the budget; [the *siloviki*] got new epaulettes and got promoted" (13A).

The representatives of the Russian power elite who took highest offices in 1999-2008 gained, in fact, a unique experience that produces a strange—at first glance—mix of two "shared mental models," that of the "liberals" and that of the "siloviks." Many of those who wore the uniform in the late 1980s entered the business milieu in the early 1990s as a result of a deep financial crisis that lead to major lay offs in the power ministries. Some of them returned to the state service in the late 1990s with an "ambivalent consciousness that incorporates both the new market values and the old ideas of socialist equality and the great empire. Putin, like many other in the military, started leaning to the left and to the right simultaneously" (Kryshtanovskaya, 2005, p. 278).

VI.3 Teams as the Basic Unit of the Russian Power Elite and Sub-Elite

The composition of the Russian power sub-elite can hardly be described as focusing either on individuals or on large groups such as the "tops," the "liberals" or the *siloviki*. The core structural unit consists of a small group of people linked together less by official job descriptions and corresponding formal ties than by personalized relationships and loyalty.

> "A staff member is absolutely not considered separately, as an individual employee, but only as related to someone else. Consequently, everyone orients him or herself to a group and prioritizes group interests" (32A).

> "To make a career, one must hide any individual qualities and fit into the team well. He must understand and share the corporation's objectives, i.e., the [informal] structure he works for, he must limit his own ambitions" (2A).

> "Up to 90% of my work time I spent satisfying the interests of our group. Most people do the same. They simply work for the financial and industrial interests of their groups" (41A).

During the Soviet period, these key units in the state service took the form of clans (*klany*) and "cartridge clips" (a literal translation of *obojma*). The clan in the state service refers to an "informal inter-organizational community that exists in parallel with formal hierarchical groups" (Kryshtanovskaya, 2005, p. 83). The term *obojma* means a "group of people united around their leader" (Ibid, p. 62).

Today, the language for talking about informal groups in the state service has changed somewhat. The word "team" describes a small, hierarchically organized group of people united behind their leader. It usually contains from 2-3 (the administrative head plus 1-2 of his or her closest associates) to a dozen office holders who have some common social background: the military service in the same unit, studies at the same university or high school around the same period of time, previous life in the same neighborhood or town, common work at the government body and so forth. A play on words associated with this term—in Russian *komanda* means a team or an order given by a superior—may explain why it fits better in the context of power relationships. After all, small groups penetrate most layers of the pyramid of power, starting with the upper-middle level (the department head usually has his or her own team). The interlocutors mention issues related to the teams more often than most other topics, as the analysis of relative frequencies of qualitative codes from the codebook "Constitution [of the state service]" suggests (Figures 1.2 and 1.3; see also definitions of each code in the Appendix). The combined frequency of codes "Teams" and "Other teams" (312 in Set "A" and 34 in Set "B") has no match.

"By the way, the expression 'a member of the team' is relatively recent, during the Soviet time people did not identify themselves in such a manner" (52A).

"The team may disperse for some period of time when its members work for different government bodies and then they join each other again.... For example, a 'top' looses his position, like X., who worked since 1998 in the Ministry of Finances and the 'White house' [the federal government]. Let's have a look at the phone book: he created a team composed of quite a range of various people: his classmates from [the city of C.], young men from the [Higher School of Economics].... They worked together till 2001. Afterwards the situation had changed and most of them departed for the other government bodies. Now I look again and see that they reunited in the Ministry of Y. as soon as X. was appointed the minister. *How the team is usually composed? Does it have several layers?* It always includes the 'top' plus two, maximum three closest associates, those who follow him everywhere. Without them, mind I'm not talking about formal associates, the 'top' would not be able to survive" (30A).[29]

"There are people who unite in some natural groups and members of these groups do not necessarily occupy official positions. Some of them have enough influence to have a say when top officials make decisions. They, however, never sign any official documents" (1A).

Figure 1.2
Coding Frequency, the Codebook "Constitution [of the State Service]," Set "A"

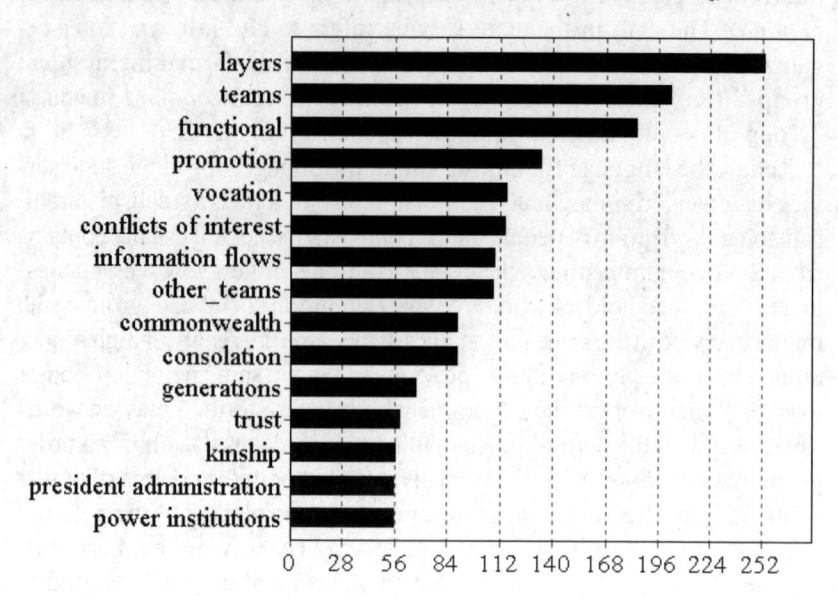

Figure 1.3
Coding Frequency, the Codebook "Constitution [of the State Service]," Set "B"

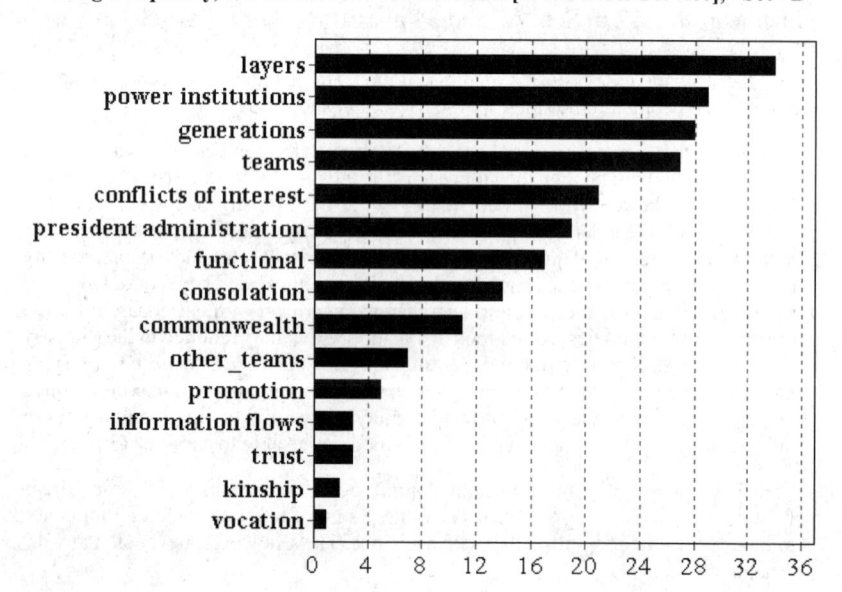

The bench (*skameika*) represents a special type of the team. It consists of a larger group of people loyal to the "top," including some support personnel: low-level specialists, company car drivers, secretaries, even cleaning ladies. These people often fulfill personal and sensitive requests made by the "tops" and their closest associates and, hence, have to be loyal and dependable. In any case, they have access to sensitive and personal information.

> "There is an expression: 'He departed together with his bench.' It means he left and took all his associates of various ranks. It may be a simple clerk or a secretary. Here is a common situation: the 'tops' leave and their secretaries follow them. They work at different levels, but form a team, broadly defined" (37A).

> "For a very long time, including now, the closest person to me has been—make a guess who?—my company car driver. He is my driver only according to his job description, in fact his functions are much closer to these of a 'special envoy.' I can entrust him any matter, however delicate and personal. Of course, he has no formal obligation to do all this, yet we have had good informal relationships and, it's going without saying, I pay him some extras out of my pocket" (63A).

Trust, if it exists in the state service at all, complements power as a coordination device only within the teams and "benches" as their particular form. Out of all possible sequences of the codes from the codebook "Constitution [of the state service]" when the second code is "trust," only codes "teams" and "other teams" form stable sequences whose probability far exceeds the conventional level of statistical significance.[30]

> "Trust is a key word for a team.... A loyal member of the team has no interest in establishing new illicit contacts on his own because they'd jeopardize his status within the team.... This means it's generally expected that the leader provides the members with some long-term benefits" (30A).

There are also several types of larger teams, whose size exceeds 3-10 persons; they were coded as "other teams." For instance, some ministries develop a kind of the *esprit de corps*, the sense of belonging to a meso-level community (the narrowly defined teams correspond to the micro-level, the state-service or a branch of power as a whole—to the macro-level).

> "In several areas there exists something like corporate solidarity. The Ministry of Foreign Affairs has it without any doubt. Not all people feel it, it's true, but it exists nevertheless" (8A).

People with the same educational background—graduates of the same university (but not in the same year), graduates in the same discipline such as physics or applied mathematics—may form the other type of the team in a broad sense of this word.

> "At my previous place of work, graduates in physics constituted an absolute majority at our department. More precisely, physicists who graduated from the Moscow Engineering Physics Institute. It happened somehow that the department of X. is staffed by them. Physics, then mathematics, at a lower level of this hierarchy" (6A).

> "You won't be able to talk with your fellows if you don't speak the same language. The same educational background allows you to understand each other" (36A).

In some cases, people belonging to a national minority also form a community by discriminating between "insiders" (office holders of the same nationality) and "outsiders" (office holders of the other nationalities). In the excerpt below, the interlocutor, who is a member of a national minority group, has doubts as to whether his nationality played a role in his rapid promotion. However, the widespread belief among the employees of this government body that it did counts far more. The case may, in fact, illustrate the so-called Thomas theorem at work: "if men define situations as real, they are real in their consequences" (Merton, 1995, p. 380).

> "In my case, I was told that the fact that I'm a Tatar played a very important role because our minister was a Tatar too. I think the Minister didn't pay attention to this. He didn't care about my nationality, even if he told me he was pleased to learn that I'm a Tatar. However, he closely controlled Tatars in the same way as he controlled the others. The people around believed that to be a Tatar, it's cool. According to them, it counts less if the candidate is good or not, the most important is too find an acceptable candidate. Instead of having an acting head for many years in a row, let's propose you as a candidate. And they did it" (13A).

Last, but not least, office holders tend to include fellows from other departments of the same government body or other government bodies with whom they once established a personal connection, however loose and occasional, in the broadly defined group of "their own people." Relationships within this group are maintained with the help of small gifts and mutually rendered services. At any rate, the strategy of "horizontal" contacts with a personally known office holder radically differs from that for dealing with complete "strangers."

> "As for practices of establishing contacts, in the milieu of office holders they don't seem to be very special. It's a kind of ritual. I don't know how radically it has changed since the Soviet time, yet it certainly continues to exist in quite manifest forms. Minor things that have a ritual nature determine the scope of established connections. For instance, on the eve of major holidays you see an astonishing numbers of gift boxes and packets circulating between offices" (1A).

What is said about the key role of small groups based on personalized relationships in structuring interactions within the power sub-elite seems to apply to supreme power as well. It can even be hypothesized that changes in the type of the body vested in supreme power represent the only significant variation in its constitution throughout history (see for further discussion Section IV of Chapter 4). Initially, supreme power was vested in the physical body of a particular individual: the czar.[31]

In the Soviet period (at least in post-Stalin Russia), supreme power was vested in the highest layer of the *nomenklatura*, the Central Committee of the Communist Party, especially its Political Bureau, the *Politburo*. A former high-ranking official of the Central Committee recalls:

> "These one hundred plus people, attendees of the plenary session of the Central Committee, constituted the key mechanism of decision-making. Even if the General Secretary's power tended to prevail" (33A).

This group vested in supreme power had a formal character: its boundaries were clearly set and "rules of the game"—spelled out in writing. All attempts to organize an informal small group similar to the "team" within the Central Committee and to make principal decisions within it would have immediately attracted the attention of the other secretaries of the Committee in the late 1970s and the 1980s. The clans and the "cartridge clips" existed, but were subject to policies of containment.

> "When [Gorbachev] arrived from the region of Stavropol and was charged with agricultural policies, he initially attempted to visit his colleagues at their homes.... He was told that people are not supposed to do this, it's under control to prevent the emergence of various companies having a hidden agenda.... Everyone for himself" (33A).

Since the fall of the Soviet Union, informal groups became the nest of supreme power: the "family" (a "team" embedded in the president's family), as under Yeltsin's rule, and the "teams." Both President Putin and President Medvedev, his formal successor, represent a particular team, in fact, formed on the basis of such common background as the previous place of residence (St. Petersburg and its suburbs) and/or studies at the same university (the faculty of law of the St. Petersburg State University) and/or common experience of work (the municipality of St. Petersburg) and/or experience of doing business together and/or extended family ties and so forth.[32]

> "The Minister represents a group of people close to the President. He is a personal friend of Putin, his business partner. Well, a business link goes not through the Minister

himself, but through his brother S., who had a common business with Putin when [Anatoly] Sobchak was Mayor [of St. Petersburg in 1991-1996]. It's a long-term family friendship. They are neighbors in the suburb, etc." (2A).

To summarize, the "small society"—a web of personalized and localized relationships based on a clear discrimination between *Us* and *Them*, Insiders and Outsiders (Oleinik, 2003, pp. 11-20)—represents the core building block in the social construction of the contemporary power elite and sub-elite. It means that mostly the teams, not individuals or formal groups, competing for access to the highest layers of the pyramid of power become key actors in mixing the market and power because success in climbing the pyramid of power since the start of post-Soviet reforms depends very much on the ableness, the ability to achieve desired results "with the presence of an opportunity" (Morriss, 1987, p. 80; see also Section I of Chapter 5) to transform the market into a weapon.

* * *

This book contains nine chapters, including an Introduction and a Conclusion. Chapter 2 outlines a general theoretical framework for analyzing power as a coordination device, as opposed to trust. The study of power relationships focuses on three axes: the technique for imposing will, the reason for seeking power (power as a terminal value, end in itself versus power as a means to achieve other ends) and the type of social action (familiar, normal, and justifiable). This taxonomy of power represents the first innovation—theoretical—related to the proposed approach.

The first axis structures the discussion in several other chapters, namely it helps explain (i) the violent nature of Russian power, i.e., the model of power relationships prevailing in the Russian institutional context (Chapters 3 and 4); (ii) how a previously under-explored technique for imposing will, domination by virtue of a constellation of interests in the market, works in theory (Chapters 5 and 6) and in practice (Chapters 5 and 7); and (iii) which elements in the existing institutional structure contribute to the continuous reproduction of Russian power (Chapter 8).

The second axis serves to explore the other important dimensions of Russian power, namely its self-justifiable character and the transformation of power into an end in itself (Chapter 3). In more practical terms, the second variable of the taxonomy of power sheds additional light on the origins of the discretionary behavior of office holders in Russia (Chapter 8). This book focuses on power in public interactions (in which the Generalized Other is involved) at the macro-level. They involve power relationships that potentially call for justification. The failure of Russian power to produce such justification can hardly be properly understood without taking into consideration the third variable of the taxonomy (Chapters 3 and 4). However, further studies are needed to make the third variable fully operational by exploring power relationships at the micro- (everyday interactions between socially close people) and meso- (interactions between people with a similar interest or plan) levels, as acknowledged in the Conclusion.

Chapter 3 offers an original conceptualization of Russian power which differs both from the concept of patrimonial power widely used in Western writings about Russia since Richard Pipes' pioneer application of this notion initially developed by Max Weber to the Russian case and the concept of *samoderzhavie* commonly found in Russian historiography. According to this conceptualization, Russian power lies close to power in its pure form and has five attributes: (i) a self-justifiable character, (ii) power as an end in itself, (iii) violent techniques for imposing will, (iv) an extreme asymmetry in the distribution of rights and obligations, and (v) the lack of feedback loops. Contrary to other conceptualizations of Russian power, namely those couched in terms of patrimonialism, the proposed approach shows its compatibility with a wide range of techniques for imposing will: from force to domination by virtue of a constellation of interests in the market and symbolic violence. If the proposed taxonomy of power (Chapter 2) facilitates the understanding of Russian power, Russian power in turn illustrates several elements of the taxonomy at work.

A closer look at Russian historiography is provided in Chapter 4. The goal of this chapter is not only to inquire into the historical evolution of Russian power, but also to highlight the complex interconnections between, on one hand, the discourse about power and, on the other hand, the underlying phenomenon, i.e., the prevalent model of power relationships. In other words, it shows how particular the categories and concepts that one uses to speak of power and to make sense of it may have an impact on its historical evolution. The analysis of secondary historical sources indicates the stability of the core characteristics of Russian power over time. Observed variability can be attributed to the context in which a particular historian assesses power (including his or her "doings," to use Quentin Skinner's term) and to changes in the repertoire of techniques for imposing will.

Chapter 5 explains the title of the book by offering an in-depth analysis of the eventual junction between power and the market. The concept of domination by virtue of a constellation of interests in the market was initially introduced by Max Weber, but it has not received enough attention on the part of social scientists since then, probably due to the fact that its development and successful application require a truly interdisciplinary approach combining political sociology, analytical philosophy, and economic sciences. This book intends to bridge the gaps that exist between disciplines: out of more than 430 references cited in it, 27 percent represent the contributions of economic sciences, 26 percent—sociology, 15 percent—political sciences, 13 percent—history, 5 percent—philosophy and 4 percent—management studies.[33] The explanation of how domination by virtue of a constellation of interests in the market works represents the second major innovation—theoretical and practical—developed in this book.

The technique of domination by virtue of a constellation of interests in the market is modeled in terms of a field of domination as a triad. One actor constituting the triad performs the function of drawing boundaries (institutional, spatial and financial) and controlling access. Domination by virtue of a constellation of interests in the market appeared in the repertoire of the techniques for imposing will associated with Russian power as early as in the Old Rus' (Chapter 4). Nevertheless, it became a key element of the repertoire only recently, with the progress of market reforms of the 1990s. The relevance of this technique for imposing will, however, goes well beyond contemporary Russia because of a recent intensification of the government's involvement into regulating the economy all around the world caused by the global crisis started in the second half of 2008 (the Conclusion).

Chapter 6 continues with the consideration of the issues raised in Chapter 5. Namely, it shows how power exercised through the market necessitates revisiting a core element of the neoclassical economic theory, the model of choice. Power makes it impossible to maximize profit/utility for one of the actors involved in coordination on its basis. The range of choices of this actor appears reshaped in such a manner that he or she minimizes missed opportunities, which does not fit in with the models of choice discussed in economic literature (maximizing behavior, satisficing behavior and coercion).

A case study demonstrating how the junction between power and the market works in practice contributing to strengthening positions of actors vested in power is presented in Chapter 7. Two types of rent are differentiated: resource rent and administrative rent. The latter is linked to restrictions on the access to the field of interactions. The theoretical framework proposed in the book is explicitly confronted with a "capture" theory of government regulation popular in economic literature. This chapter also deserves attention from a purely methodological point of view. The analysis proposed in it derives from triangulation of quantitative (econometric models and quantitative content analysis) and qualitative (qualitative coding) research methods.

Chapter 8 summarizes a wealth of empirical data collected from both primary and secondary sources. This data supports the assumption that, instead of limiting Russian office holders' discretion, the institutional environment in this country enables it. An assessment of the hardness of 21 potential constraints shows their rather loose character. The discretionary behavior of people vested in power represents an important precondition for—and a major outcome of—the continuous reproduction of Russian power. This conclusion suggests a possible strategy for administrative reform: it should be intended specifically to tighten the set of constraints that limit not only individual but also group discretionary behavior (taking into consideration the important role of the "teams" discussed in the Introduction).

The Conclusion indicates several directions for further research. More specifically, it contains formulations of two hypotheses: one about a "selective affinity" between the models of power relationships prevailing at the micro-, meso- and macro-levels in Russia (its verification calls for a more active use of the third variable of the taxonomy of power, the type of social action) and the other about the eventual drift toward negative convergence between models of power in Russia and in a number of Western countries (its falsification necessitates a comparative study with particular emphasis on how the power elites of various countries use domination by virtue of a constellation of interests in the market).

The Methodological Appendix contains a detailed and technical description of an original methodology for mixing three types of content analysis: (i) the analysis of the co-occurrence of words; (ii) the substitution model of quantitative content analysis and (iii) qualitative coding. It is used throughout the book, namely in the Introduction, Chapters 3, 6, 7 and 8 when referring to in-depth semi-structured interviews with Russian office-holders, a major source of primary data for the present analysis. This methodology can be considered the third innovation contained in the book, this time purely methodological. The methodology of triangulation serves to achieve a satisfactory—and quantitatively measurable—level of validity and reliability of outcomes and proposed interpretations.

38   Market as a Weapon

Supporting materials: descriptions of respondents, the interview guide, codebooks and dictionaries based on substitution are provided in the Appendix. They help the reader reconstruct the entire organization of the study and, eventually, make it replicable.

Notes

1. Game theory allows modeling the "battle of the sexes" in the following form:

		Male	
		To go to a theater	To go to a bar
Female	To go to a theater	3, 2 N_1	1, 1
	To go to a bar	0, 0	2, 3 N_2

   There exist two Nash equilibria, i.e., situations in which no player has interest in changing his or her strategy unilaterally, which makes the choice of a particular strategy a risky enterprise. Everything depends not only on the player's own preferences but also on the behavior of the other player. A commonly known norm, for instance, the "lady is first," allows eliminating risk and landing in cell (3, 2). Power, on the other hand, can be modeled as a deliberate restriction of the choices available to the counterpart by one of the players. For example, the male player informs the female player that if she goes to the theater, he will go to the bar penalizing both of them, but mainly—the female: compared to the alternative outcome, (3, 2), she is going to lose 2 units of "utility" whereas he—only one unit. In other words, the male attempts to restrict the female's choice to only two outcomes: 1 (she goes to the theater alone) and 2 (she joins the male in the bar). Under such conditions, a rationally minded female prefers joining the male to going to her preferred place alone.
2. Instead of considering order based on generalized trust as a particular case of conventional order, it is reasonable to put it into a separate category because trust does not necessarily have a traditional nature. Trust can have its origin in rational calculations or the belief in the efficiency of law enforcement as well (Oleinik, 2005b, pp. 58-60).
3. This also explains a major weakness in its design: if reforms are initiated and implemented by people vested in power only, one can hardly expect significant changes in the scale and scope of power holders' prerogatives (Oleinik, 2009b).
4. This generic name refers to a rather heterogeneous group of theories and analytical approaches that acknowledge the importance of institutions and put them at the center of analysis. This group includes the "old" institutionalism of Thorstein Veblen and John Commons, the New Institutional Economics of Ronald Coase, Oliver Williamson and Douglass North, the theory of conventions of Luc Boltanski and Laurent Thévenot, among several other theories.
5. A founding father of the New Institutional Economics, Ronald Coase (1988, pp. 35-36), in spite of his manifestly non-Marxist background, also equals power and the firm on the one hand, and opposes them to free exchanges on the market on the other hand: "outside the firm, price movements direct production, which is coordinated through a series of exchange transactions on the market. Within a firm, these market transactions are eliminated and in place of the complicated market

structure with exchange transactions is substituted the entrepreneur-co-ordinator, who directs production."
6. Interactions between the state and businesses during the global crisis started in the second half of 2008 do not rule out a similar logic either. Businesses can hardly survive the crisis without state subventions and loans. However, the access to the financial aid offered by the state appears highly selective: only the "selected few" can get the much needed money (the bankruptcy of Lehman Brothers as opposed to the US federal government's efforts to save some other investment banks; see Fink, 2008), which paves the way to entry control and the eventual reliance on "gate-keeping" as a lever of power.
7. As of August 2009, the total world production of oil averages 83.9 million barrels per day. The OPEC pumps 28.83 million barrels per day, whereas Russia—9.97 mb/d, which makes her the largest world producer followed by Saudi Arabia with 8.14 mb/d (OPEC, 2009, p. 32 and the data of the Russian Information Agency Novosty, retrieved from http://en.rian.ru/analysis/20090909/156074023.html).
8. Neoclassical economists acknowledge that market transactions necessitate some level of trust between their participants (Dasgupta & Serageldin, 2000) and, hence, involve some elements of convention.
9. Transaction costs are "comparative costs of planning, adapting, and monitoring task completion under alternative" coordination arrangements (Williamson, 1985, p. 2).
10. Vyacheslav Dementiev, a post-Soviet economist, generalizes this principle to all types of power relationships: "the imposition of will remains possible as long as costs associated with imposing will do not exceed those in the situation with no power involved" (2004, pp. 75-76; see also Dementiev 2006, p. 81).
11. The law of diminishing marginal utility states that "consumption of successive increments of a commodity yields not equal but diminishing increments of satisfaction or utility to the consumer" (Black, 2008, p. 578).
12. General parameters of the sample used in the present analysis and principles that guided the choice of interlocutors will be described below, in Section V of the Introduction devoted to sources of information.
13. Risk involves knowing all possible outcomes of an interaction and their quantitative probabilities, uncertainty allows the existence of unknown outcomes whose probability no one can carefully estimate (Harsanyi, 1977, Ch. 3). As a former US secretary of state for defense stated at a briefing in 2002, "there are known knowns; there are things we know we know [which refers to the situation of risk, A.O.]. We also know there are known unknowns; that is to say we know there are some things we do not know. But there are also unknown unknowns—the ones we don't know we don't know [which refers to the situation of uncertainty, A.O.]."
14. Institutional innovators consider "arrangemental alternatives in much the same fashion that a business firm considers the choice between alternative investment decisions" (Davis & North, 1970, p. 140).
15. In the battle of the sexes the male player would be simply lucky if the available choices did not fit in well with the female's preferences while matching his perfectly:

		Male	
		To go to a theater	To go to a bar
Female	To go to a theater	2, 1	1, 2
	To go to a bar	0, 0	2, 4 N

Under such conditions, the male can get what he wants—to go to a bar together with the female—"without trying," i.e., without acting strategically: there is only one Nash equilibrium. Thomas Wartenberg (1990, p. 157) finds a real-life example of this game structure: a non-discriminating husband who nevertheless lives in a society prone to male domination (see also Subsection III [Ie] of Chapter 2).

16. See, for instance, special issues of the leading Russian economic journal *Voprosy Ekonomiki* No. 11, 1995 and No. 4, 1998.
17. 60 percent in the Chuvash Republic, 57 percent in the region of Krasnoyarsk, 48 percent in the region of Samara and 47 percent in the region of Saratov, N=800 plus respondents in each of the regions. The author thanks Eugenia Gvozdeva for drawing his attention to this dataset.
18. "Matrixes of power" constructed by Simon Kordonsky (2006), that penetrate all layers of the institutional structure, show how such predictions may work in practice.
19. Mills refers in this passage to such members of the American power elite as top executives. However, a similar principle seems to prevail in the Russian power-elite as a whole. A carefully designed system of mutual references regulated the access to highest ladders of the pyramid during the Soviet time (Voslensky, 1984, p. 79). More recently, former president Vladimir Putin admitted that decisions as to who enters into office of the president are made within a narrow group of people vested in supreme power. When answering a question in September 2009 about presidential elections in 2012, he indicated: "Do you recall how we [President Dmitry Medvedev elected in 2008 and I] competed in 2008? So, we won't compete in 2012 either. We'll make an arrangement. We understand each other. We are of the same blood. We'll sit down and make an arrangement depending on the situation. Everything will be decided between us" (*Kommersant*, No 169 [4224] from September 12, 2009, p. 1).
20. 69 percent in the region of Saratov, 68 percent in the region of Samara, 66 percent in the region of Krasnoyarsk and 62 percent in the Chuvash Republic.
21. There also exists an option of approaching only individuals readily available for research. In other words, the availability for research then becomes the key criteria in sampling. It has been implemented in several studies focused on Soviet immigrants in the United States who, before their immigration, held offices at the middle layers of the Soviet pyramid of power (Gregory, 1990, pp. 168-176).
22. Comparable figures for 2001 are 25,450 and 4.4 percent (Gosudarstvenny komitet, 2002, pp. 1-16). The federal law "On basic principles of the state service in the Russian Federation" (version dated 7.11.2000) stipulates that individuals holding offices from list "A" (president, prime minister, heads of legislative bodies at the federal and regional levels, ministers, members of parliament, federal judges) do not receive prerogatives through delegation but are entitled to them, as per Article 1.1(1). In contrast to individuals holding offices from lists "B" (charged with servicing offices from list "A") and "C" (charged with servicing offices not included in list "A"), the law does not consider functions of individuals holding offices from list "A" as the "state service" (Article 2.1), which formally speaking suggests their membership in the power elite.
23. When tried in the region in Siberia, the "official" strategy initially produced a couple of non-informative interviews that ended up by frustrating both the interviewer and the interviewee, which led to the switch to the technique of snowballing. It worked only slightly better in the region of St. Petersburg having the status of a "second capital."
24. Technically speaking, analysis implies the discovery of causal relationships between variables, whereas description—the drawing of an exhaustive list of a variable's attributes.

25. The two most famous *khoziaistvenniks* of the 1990s (their group was also nicknamed "red directors"), Leonid Kuchma and Viktor Chernomyrdin, held top political offices (the first was the president of Ukraine in 1994-2004, the second—the prime minister of the Russian Federation in 1992-1998).
26. Thorstein Veblen (1934, p. 69) defines conspicuous consumption of goods as "honourable, primarily as a mark of prowess and a perquisite of human dignity."
27. Google.Ru produces 903,000 references to the "liberals" and 706,000 references to the "siloviki", as of October 1, 2009. It is worth noting that the "siloviki" is a more specific term, with very little usage outside the indicated context. An analysis of the one hundred most relevant outcomes of the search for the term "liberals" using Google.Ru shows that 72 of them contain references to the context of post-Soviet reforms, which allows a rough assessment of the total number of relevant documents of 650,000-700,000.
28. Studies of victimization highlight a similar disconnection between the number of delinquent acts and the intensity of concerns with the issues of crime (see, for example, Roché, 1993).
29. As this excerpt indicates, the only source of the "hard data" on the composition of the teams can be found in phone books of government bodies. More precisely, by comparing several phone books covering an extended period of time the researcher should be able to identify some patterns in simultaneous moves and transfers of office holders from one body to the other.
30. $p<0.0001$ in Set "A," see the table below:
Coding sequences, the codebook "Constitution [of the state service]", Set "A," start of second segment can overlap first segment, segments must be separated by no other code

Code A	Code B	Freq A	Freq B	Freq (B | A)	% of A	Freq (A | B)	% of B	% Events	Prob.
other_teams	trust	109	59	4	3.7	3	5.1	75.0	.0000
teams	trust	201	59	11	5.5	10	16.9	90.9	.0000
functional	trust	185	59	2	1.1	2	3.4	100	1.00
information flows	trust	110	59	3	2.7	3	5.1	100	1.00
conflicts of interest	trust	114	59	1	0.9	1	1.7	100	1.00
layers	trust	254	59	1	0.4	1	1.7	100	1.00
kinship	trust	57	59	1	1.8	1	1.7	100	1.00
promotion	trust	133	59	2	1.5	2	3.4	100	1.00
generations	trust	68	59	2	2.9	2	3.4	100	1.00
trust	trust	59	59	1	1.7	1	1.7	100	1.00
vocation	trust	116	59	1	0.9	1	1.7	100	1.00

Legend: Code A—the name of the first code in the sequence, Code B—the name of the second code in the sequence, Freq. A | B—the number of times that the first code is followed by this second code, % of A—the percentage of times that the first code is followed by this second code, Freq. B | A—the number of times that the second code follows this first code, Events—the total number of code sequences that have been identified.

31. The progressive emergence of the triplet ruler/state/society also involved the multiplication of the supreme ruler's bodies: along with his physical body he acquired a religious body, a moral one and a political one (Malinin, 1995). The political body of the Supreme ruler performing the function of a sovereign, a "lender of power of last resort," should not depend on his physical conditions, as expressed in the medieval proclamation "The King is dead. Long live the King."

32. The statement of President Putin that they are "of the same blood" with President Medvedev (see Endnote 19) can be better understood in this context.
33. Legal studies and linguistics account for 2 percent of the cited sources each, statistics—1.4 and the other fields—5 percent.

2

A Taxonomy of Power Relationships

Introduction

Despite a continuously growing body of literature, both scientific and popular scientific, power and its role in structuring everyday life is still under-explored. This outcome is partly attributable to an essentially contested character of the concept, which means that one cannot discriminate between alternative definitions of power "by appeal to theoretical criteria alone" (Wartenberg, 1990, p. 12; see also Cox, Furlong & Page, 1985, p. 29).[1]

This chapter is intended to cast some light on the existing gaps in our knowledge in this field and explore the strategies available for bridging them. The proposed approach provides a new outlook with respect to a variety of empirically observable forms of power relationships. It is argued that they can be studied within a single analytical framework. The new approach also highlights limits concerning the appropriateness of various forms of power and hence contributes to debates of the dialectics of power and resistance.

The fact that power relationships take various forms makes them a good differentiating variable with several attributes. As a result of a focus on power relationships, comparative studies can be conducted without using terms and concepts that are specific only to a particular case, country or area. The chapter also lays the groundwork for a discussion of "Russian power" (Chapters 3 and 4) and a particular element in the corresponding repertoire of techniques for imposing will: domination by virtue of a constellation of interests (Chapters 5 and 6).

Power is placed in the context of coordination and compared with an alternative coordination device—trust—in Section I. Section II discusses three types of social action: familiar, normal and justifiable. It will be shown, in particular, that a focus on the individual appears appropriate for analyzing some types of action. The study of the others, however, calls for shifting emphasis to the institutional environment in which actors use power for the purposes of coordination. In other words, one should be careful when outlining the areas of validity of both the methodological individualism and the holistic approach.

The exploration of relationships between the type of action and the technique for imposing will requires the production of a two-dimensional taxonomy of power relationships outlined in Section III. Section IV contains empirical illustrations for some cases in the taxonomy. The question as to whether it is worthwhile to include this in a third dimension, namely the purpose of using power (power as an end in itself vs. power as a means to achieve other ends), is discussed briefly in Section V. The correspondence between, on the one hand, the type of action and, on the other hand, the technique for imposing will might not hold if power transforms into a terminal value.

I. Power as a Coordination Device

Power is conventionally included in the field of political science, which explains the importance of this concept for studying the state, political institutions and processes. However, Max Weber's definition of power as the capacity of an actor to impose his or her will within a social relationship (1968, p. 53) broadens the scope of its application and makes it *a* key coordination device and, hence, one of the key categories of the social sciences as a whole. Power is ubiquitous everywhere there is a need for "co-ordination of the activities ... to achieve a common goal" (Wrong, 1980, p. 248).

The works of Hannah Arendt shed additional light on this aspect of power. She argues that "power corresponds to the human ability not just to act but to act in concert" (1969, p. 44; see also Stewart, 2001, pp. 6, 38). This means that power facilitates the task of coordinating human action and the achievement of goals that would otherwise remain outside the scope of the possible. The fact that these "enabling" effects of power may be mostly appropriated by one party involved in a power relationship (as shown in Chapter 6) does not undermine their existence.

The choice of coordination as a starting point in the study of power contrasts with methodological individualism and the holistic approach. The former methodology places the individual actor at the center of the analysis. Power relationships, which usually take the form of power dyads (the case of power triad is considered in Chapter 5), admittedly result from the conscious choices made by individuals; they are susceptible to rationalization. This reasoning makes economic models and game theory models applicable to inquiries into the nature of power.[2]

Advocates of methodological individualism also argue that the focus on the rational individual does not prevent them from going beyond power dyads and explaining power at the macro-level, namely power embedded in organizations and institutions. James Coleman's essay on the emergence of a corporate actor, a legal (juristic) person existing alongside the natural persons who established it, highlights this point. According to him, power relationships embedded in the corporate body gain a great degree of autonomy with regard to the power dyads that lie at their origin. The individual actor initially transfers control over a part of his or her actions to the corporate actor in the hope that it will allow him/her to better realize his or her interests. Yet "an increasing separation of power from its source in persons" (Coleman, 1974, p. 48) suggests that the corporate actor has its own "rationality" different from the individual rationalities of its constituents.

In a similar manner, Joshua Cohen demonstrates how, in the Lockean hypothetical situation of equal freedom and rationality, individuals might be interested in endorsing a state featuring the formal inequality of political rights, i.e., power of the members of a particular group over other citizens. His reasoning holds, however, only as long as one maintains a heroic assumption about the reduction of all civil interests (in fact, all individual interests) to pecuniary ones. If the level of material well-being is the individual's only concern, then under certain conditions he or she accepts a property owner's state (Cohen, 1986, pp. 314-320).

In this case, the task of embracing power relationships at the macro-level can be carried out with the help of rational choice analysis only at the price of attributing narrow pecuniary interests to the actor and "erasing" a moral dimension from his or her activities. Furthermore, claims that rational choices explain power both at the micro- and macro levels seem hard to falsify. The analysis of causal relationships (e.g., rational choice as an independent variable, power as a dependent variable) requires either the organization of experiments (in laboratory settings the validity of such experiments is limited, whereas natural experiments are rare) or a careful historical-comparative analysis. Yet, most advocates of rational choice analysis, including Coleman and Cohen, substitute thought experiments and artificial reconstructions on their basis for careful studies in history.

The holistic approach, which takes particularly elaborate forms in continental philosophy, emphasizes the role that institutions and the overall context of action play in producing power relationships and making them sustainable. The definition of power as a web of relationships embedded in existing institutions by Michel Foucault illustrates this change in analytical focus. "Power, it seems to me, should be understood as a plurality of relations of strength (*rapports de force*) that exist in a particular sphere and play a constitutive role in it.... Power relationships are not external to other types of relationships—economic processes, face-to-face interactions, sexual relations—but they are embedded in them" (Foucault, 1976, pp. 121-124).

If methodological individualism can be labeled, using Mark Granovetter's useful distinction (1985, p. 483), as an *under*-socialized conception of power, the holistic approach then refers to an *over*-socialized one. The latter view of human action leaves virtually no room for freedom let alone resistance to power. In the holistic perspective, power is perceived as omnipresent and overwhelming. Steven Lukes' reading of Foucault contains a number of insightful counter-arguments. Lukes reproaches Foucault for being excessively deterministic and "de-facing" power, i.e., refusing to link power and agency (Lukes, 2005, pp. 92-95; Lukes, 2002). "Within a system characterized by total structural determinism, there would be no place for power" (Lukes, 2005, p. 57) as there would be no place for free will. Similar criticisms can be addressed to another example of the holistic approach, the Marxist theory of power (see Section II of the Introduction).

A further problem with the holistic approach consists in overlooking other mechanisms of coordination. In fact, power transforms into a unique coordination device structuring interactions in all spheres of everyday activities, from sexual relations up to politics and international affairs. This lack of alternatives further narrows the scope of the actor's freedom. Also, the holistic approach does not escape the methodological complexity outlined above, although it assumes the opposite causal relationship between power embedded in structures (independent variable) and individual choices (dependent variable). Although Marx produced impressive historical studies, the results of most natural experiments, whose design was inspired by Marxist thought, including a socialist experiment in Russia, at best seem inconclusive and at worst they refute the very idea of freeing the actor by overthrowing power embedded in macro structures (the analysis proposed in Chapter 4 suggests that the October 1917 revolution led to the strengthening of power instead of dissolving it).

The dissatisfaction with both a rational choice analysis of power and a deterministic reading of it suggests that the analytical focus should be shifted from individual decision-making, on the one hand, and structures to interactions and coordination, on the other, as a unit of analysis. In this sense, the following analysis relies heavily on interpretative sociology (which was first outlined by Weber) and institutional economics with its "shift from commodities and individuals to transactions" (Commons, 1931, p. 652).[3] Putting interactions and coordination in the center of analysis also means taking a more cautious stance on causal relationships between power and individual choices. The question as to how power is produced and reproduced through interactions is given higher priority.

Interest in coordination implies focusing the analysis on an area that lies in-between individual decision-making and its context. The individual, to achieve his/her goals, must be able to predict the behavior of people around him/her and, furthermore, help these people predict his/her own behavior (on interpretation and mutual adjustment as a basis of coordination see Livet & Thévenot, 1994, pp. 154-157). Occasionally, we run into other people whose actions then become an obstacle in achieving our goals; other goals of ours are simply impossible to achieve without joining forces with the people around us and "acting in concert." The institutional context provides the interacting parties with the information and procedures that make coordinated action feasible. Institutions supporting coordination are defined in a broad manner: "an institution [is] collective action in control, liberation and expansion of individual action" (Commons, 1931, p. 648). In particular, coordination can be achieved within a hierarchy (through asymmetric control), when one individual makes most of the decisions whereas the others are supposed to implement them and not take any initiative on their own.

It would be misleading to argue that power is *the* key coordination device, which would exclude its substitution by other supports in interactions. Coordination can be achieved in a spontaneous manner, by an "invisible hand," as neoclassical economists like to repeat. The cases of tacit coordination through referring to "focal points" brought to light by Thomas Schelling illustrate this point. "Any key [to "deciphering" the behavior of the vis-à-vis] that is mutually recognized as the key becomes *the* key—may depend on imagination more than on logic, it may depend on analogy, precedent, accidental arrangement, symmetry, aesthetic or geometric configuration, casuistic reasoning, and who the parties are and what they know about each other" (1960, p. 57). However, the tacit coordination of mutual expectations requires the existence of a minimum common cultural background expressed in convention (analogies and precedents have a culture-specific character: after all, people in different countries did not necessarily read the same fairy tales and watch the same cartoons in childhood), which direct us to the institutional environment.

Trust—in its generalized form, i.e., trust in people who are not personally known to one, or people in general—should be considered as the other alternative support for coordination (Figure 2.1). Trust refers to "the expectation of one person about the actions of others that affects the first person's choice, when an action must be taken before the actions of others are known" (Ostrom, 1998, p. 12). In this sense, trust implies "a gamble, a risky investment" (Luhmann, 1979, p. 24). In other words, trust involves the acceptance of unilateral dependence made in a tacit form: the "invisible hand" once again seems to be at work. A high level of mutual trust among interacting parties allows them to rely on each other with respect to enforcing promises, rights and obligations. On the other hand, a low level of trust calls for the involvement of a third party, whose task consists in making them respect the rules of the game, and, hence, leads to the transfer of the right to control one's actions (North, 1990, pp. 34-35; Gambetta, 1993, p. 15; Oleinik, 2005b, pp. 62-63). This transfer lies at the heart of power relationships (Coleman, 1990, pp. 66-67).

Niklas Luhmann (1979) suggests thinking about trust and power in terms of their complementary and, simultaneously, mutually substitutable character. Both trust and power help individuals "reduce complexity" and uncertainty resulting from the freedom of people around them to act at will. Trust and power make mutual adjustments and coordination possible, but in different manners. Luhmann considers trust a higher level concept: power necessitates a particular form of trust, "system trust" (a

Figure 2.1
Three Mechanisms of Coordination

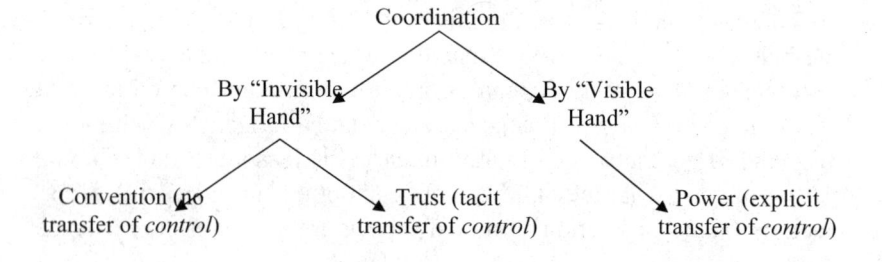

Coordination
By "Invisible Hand" / By "Visible Hand"

Convention (no transfer of *control*) — Trust (tacit transfer of *control*) — Power (explicit transfer of *control*)

Table 2.1
"Generally Speaking, Would You Say That Most People Can Be Trusted or That You Need to Be Very Careful in Dealing with People?"
(% of Respondents Who Chose "Can Be Trusted")

Year	Mean for the WVS sample	The United States WVS	GSS	The United Kingdom (WVS)	Russia (WVS)
1981-1984	36.5 (N=27,189; 25 countries)	39.2 (N=2,325)	36.5† (N=801)	42.5 (N=1,167)	35.9 (N=1,082)♦
1989-1993	34.6 (N=46,587; 38 countries)	48.1 (N=3,182)	38.4♣ (N=1,019)	42.1 (N=1,484)	37.5 (N=1,818)
1993-1999	25.2 (N=71,691; 57 countries)	35 (N=1,542)	33.6‡ (N=1,905)	30.4 (N=1.093)	23.9 (N=1,980)
1999-2004	28 (N=91,723; 70 countries)	35.5 (N=1,200)	37.2♠ (N=2,324)	28.5 (N=1,000)	24 (N=2,415)
2005-2006*	24.3 (N=65,497; 52 countries)	43.6 (N=1.249)	32.3◊ (N=3,923)	47.9 (N=969)	14.3 (N=1,918)

Sources: World Values Survey, 2009 and General Social Survey, Retrieved from http://www.norc.org/GSS+Website/ and processed by the author. †—The data on 1983; ♣—The data on 1990; ‡—The data on 1996; ♠—The data on 1998; ◊—The data on 2006; ♦—The survey was conducted on a non-representative sample, in one region; * The level of general trust was measured at the ordinal level, so the figures reported represent the sum of two answers: "Trust completely" and "Trust somewhat."

belief in the stability of the existing power relationship), whereas the opposite does not necessarily hold.[4]

According to the results of the World Values Survey (WVS), there is a general downward trend in the level of generalized trust throughout the world (Table 2.1). The situation in particular countries may vary (the dynamics of generalized trust in the US look especially volatile if one compares the results of the WVS with those of the General Social Survey, GSS), yet the mean value (unweighted) calculated for all countries included in the sample shows a steady decline. The low level of trust restricts the number of available choices and actors tend to rely on power relationships as a coordination device.

II. Analyzing Power Relationships through the Lens of Different Types of Action

The abstract and all-encompassing character of the concept of power calls for its operationalization, or, in terms of Marxist philosophy, for moving from the abstract to the concrete (Ilyenkov, 1982; see also Oleinik, 2009c). The first and still most cited attempt to develop a comprehensive taxonomy of particular forms (attributes) of power relationships dates back to the start of the twentieth century. Weber used different grounds on which power's claims to legitimacy can be based—legal, traditional, and charismatic—as the key criterion for developing the taxonomy. However, he did not provide explicit reasons for choosing this criterion by simply assuming that "every such system attempts to establish and to cultivate the belief in its legitimacy" (1968, p. 213). Why should the transfer of the right of control be necessarily assessed in terms of legitimation?

The other well-known attempt to make the concept of power more operational and useful for empirical studies was undertaken by Geert Hofstede. He focuses on the culturally acceptable degree of inequality in the distribution of the right to control one's actions, the power distance.[5] "The power distance between a boss B and a subordinate S in a hierarchy is the difference between the extent to which B can determine the behavior of S and the extent to which S can determine the behavior of B" (1980, p. 99). Unfortunately, the breakthrough in solving the problem of measurement is achieved as a result of skipping over all issues related to the legitimacy of power: the list of the predictors of power distance essentially includes physical indicators such as the geographical latitude of a country, its population size and wealth (GNP per capita). The strategy of a "big leap" from the abstract to the concrete has been adapted by a number of other scholars, most of whom decided to focus on structural issues, for instance:

- The degree of monopolization of the use of physical force (Tilly, 1985, p. 171; Tilly, 2004: 11; cf. the emphasis on the legitimate versus non-legitimate use in Weber, 1968, p. 54).
- Extensiveness: "The ratio of the number of persons who hold power to the number of the powerless" (Wrong, 1980, p. 15).
- Comprehensiveness: "The number of scopes in which the power holder(s) controls the activities of the power subject(s)" (Ibid; see also Lukes, 2005, p. 75; Cornell & Kalt, 1995, p. 405).
- Intensity (a variation on power distance): "The range of effective options open to the power holder *within* each and every scope of the power subject's conduct over which he wields power" (Wrong, 1980, p. 16).[6]
- The degree of "the division of powers and responsibilities across such tasks as… judicial affairs, … legislative affairs, … executive and bureaucratic function, and … international relations" (Cornell & Kalt, 1995, p. 405).
- Location: "the level of social organization … in which political power and responsibility are appropriately vested" (Ibid, p. 406).
- The degree of asymmetry: "the ratio of change in behavior of influencee to change in behavior of influencer" (Simon, 1953, p. 507).[7]

- The degree of activeness: active versus inactive forms of exercising power. In the former case, the imposition of the will produces an event, e.g., a change in the behavior of the subordinate, whereas in the latter case the exercise of power prevents some events, which are undesirable from the point of view of the power holder, from happening (Lukes, 2005, p. 77).
- Effectiveness with its two dimensions: "the first refers to an actor's ability to achieve the submission or compliance of another actor: this refers to the effectiveness of the very power relationship ... the second dimension refers to an actor's ability to achieve a desired result: this is effectiveness of management" (Ledyaev, 2009, p. 29).

Each of these structural criteria or their combinations helps produce taxonomies that the researcher can apply to a wide range of situations varying from tribes of Native Americans and terrorist groups to transnational corporations and states in the Western hemisphere. As often happens, improvements in reliability are achieved at the expense of validity:[8] the questions as to the conditions under which actors sacrifice a part of their freedom and autonomy and, broadly speaking, about a "social machinery" of power relationships remain unanswered. It calls for further developing Weber's inquiry into the process of the justification of power and attempting to move from the abstract to the concrete without sacrificing the interest in justification.

David Beetham's analysis provides us with a clue as to hidden obstacles along this path. He criticizes Weber for failing to systematically apply a clear-cut set of differentiating criteria while developing the three ideal types of legitimate power. According to Beetham, the legitimacy of power derives from (i) its conformity with established rules, (ii) justification of the rules by reference to beliefs shared by both the ruler and the ruled, and (iii) evidence of consent by the ruled to the particular power relation (1991, p. 16). Weber's legal authority, according to Beetham, fulfils condition (i), traditional—condition (ii), and charismatic—condition (iii). The three ideal types, he continues, result from the application of the three different criteria, which raises doubts as to whether the taxonomy is coherent and systematic.

Beetham also offers an explanation for the need to justify power. In the eyes of any moral agent "power relations involve negative features—of exclusion, restriction, compulsion, etc.—which stand in need of justification" (Ibid, p. 57). As a result, the concept of power and that of legitimation completely overlap: *failures* in legitimizing power call for violence and coercion (as a result, the last two forms are excluded from the list of power relationships; see also Arendt, 1969, p. 56). But a new problem then emerges: can legitimation be used as a *differentiating* criterion, if it is involved in *all* power relationships? In other words, Beetham seems to underestimate techniques for imposing will other than legitimation.

The idea of types of social action, familiar, normal and justifiable, proposed by Laurent Thévenot (Thévenot, 2007; Thévenot, 2000; Boltanski & Thévenot, 2000) seems appropriate for making further steps. It suggests that not all interactions require legitimation. For instance, localized (in time, geography and institutional space) interactions with those who are at "one's arm's reach" allow the actor to reduce the amount of attention and other cognitive resources spent on them. They range from intimate relationship to highly ritualized and routinized activities involving parties who know each other for a long period of time. Familiar action often relies on routines, which makes both justification and discursiveness unnecessary: coordination might occur "in silence." Routines act at the bodily level because they are "engraved" on the body. To use a common metaphor of power that opposes the body and the mind as the vehicles for imposing the will (Mitchell, 1990, pp. 545-546), familiar action clearly corresponds to the former.[9]

The register of normal action refers to those actors who have similar plans or projects. Physician-patient or instructor-student interactions, for instance, occur at this register. To coordinate their activities, they need to agree on common goals and interests. Thus, they speak the language of interests, opportunities, utility and functionality. Their task involves making coordination mutually useful and profitable, not in justifying it. The decision as to whether to transfer the right of control depends on rational calculations as a result. Either "one actor [transfers it to another] because the first actor believes that he will be better off by following the other's leadership" (the case of conjoint authority), or the first actor does it "without holding this belief, but in return for some extrinsic compensation" (the case of disjoint authority, see Coleman, 1990, p. 72). Rational choice analysis appears appropriate within the scope of normal action.[10]

Apparently, the existence of similar plans calls for coordination in other forms than power. Thus, Lukes equates power with domination: "*A* affects *B* in a manner *contrary to B's interests*" (2005, p. 109; emphasis added). On the other hand, the concept of transformative power, or power exercised, to use the same shortcuts, *in B's interests*, calls into question the assumption concerning the conflictual nature of all power relationships (Wartenberg, 1990, Ch. 9).[11] It may be argued that the commonality of interest does not exclude the use of power. On the contrary, power can help transform common interests *in potentio* into real common interests.

Finally, at the highest register, interactions have a depersonalized character; they are open to a potentially unlimited number of personally unknown participants. The public sphere is composed of such interactions, for example, between participants in debates over an issue of common interest (see also Section III of the Conclusion). Coordination of one's actions with the generalized Other requires their justification defined as a reference to commonly acceptable and understandable criteria for evaluation and moral judgments.[12] Here the mind becomes a key vehicle for imposing the will. It is worth noting that commonly acceptable and understandable criteria are external to the individual. They are embodied in the institutional environment and, at this register, one can hardly ignore the overall context of power relationships.

In the final account we avoid the dangers of both ignoring justification and making it *the* key element of power relationships. We also avoid confusing two concepts, power and authority. It seems reasonable to endorse a position in which authority refers to power relationships that are subject to moral justification and successfully pass this test.[13] "Legitimate power or authority ... provides [the subordinate] with moral grounds for cooperation and obedience" (Beetham, 1991, p. 26). On the other hand, *power*-holders do not need to justify their action to get subordinates do something: they rely on sanctions (positive and negative), strategies of manipulation, force (physical and psychic) or a monopolistic position in the market. Power is not subject to any external principle or institutional constraint and is limited only by a particular configuration of resources. Authority is subject to such constraints. Power exists in a quasi-physical realm of action-reaction force pairs and causal relationships. It should come as no surprise then that analogues borrowed from physics are commonly used in writings on power.[14]

III. A Two-Dimensional Taxonomy of Power

Power, as was argued in the Introduction and Section I, should be considered as a second-order concept with regard to coordination as a centerpiece of social action. Nevertheless, the above discussion suggests that we should probably search for a missing link between coordination and power. Can the concept of domination be considered a good candidate? Hardly, since there are two manners of exercising power: *contrary to* the subordinate's interests (domination) and *in* these interests (transformative power). Furthermore, the interpretation of domination in terms of institutions that make the imposition of the will sustainable and regular (Scott, 2001, p. 16), excludes its relevance at the registers of familiar and normal actions. The concept of influence, which James Scott places at the highest layer of his analytical scheme (2001, pp. 12-16), faces similar criticisms. First, its meaning often depends on a particular configuration of interests observed in relationships between *A* (Superoridnate) and *B* (Subordinate): Lukes (2005, p. 36), for instance, uses this term when there is no conflict of interests and attributes to it a purely "positive" meaning. Second, influence can have a concrete, not an abstract meaning: Warternberg (1990, pp. 104-105) sees in it a particular technique for imposing will and uses this term interchangeably with manipulation (manipulation as a particular case of influence).

Probably, the concept of control is abstract and neutral enough to make a link between coordination and power. Coleman (1990, pp. 66 ff.) defines power relationships in terms of a transfer of the right of control from one individual to the other. He focuses mostly on the cases of voluntary and rationally calculated transfers, which makes his analysis especially relevant at the register of normal action. Yet, if one takes into account the cases of involuntary or non-reflexive transfers and considers the fact that one of the solutions for coordination problems consists in fusing two centers of decision-making into a single one, i.e., in implementing control over one party's decision-making by the other party, then the concept of control might be a good candidate.

The process of the conceptualization and operationalization of power relationships can be illustrated in the following from (Figure 2.2). Dashed arrows represent connections whose exploration would lead us far beyond the scope of the present study. For instance, Foucault's insights into an association between a perfect command of the self and claims to control other people's actions (1984, p. 88) deserve a separate study. As was noted above, the control mechanisms over material objects have several elements in common with power over men in its pure form (see also Section I of Chapter 3). However, issues of property rights will be considered only tangentially.

Empirically verifiable definitions are provided in italics. As a result of the focus on asymmetric control in relationships with other people, most empirically verifiable definitions refer to political regimes: a standard definition of politics encompasses activities related to making and enforcing rules that help coordinate actions (Heywood, 2002, p. 4). Conditions under which particular political regimes function are square bracketed.

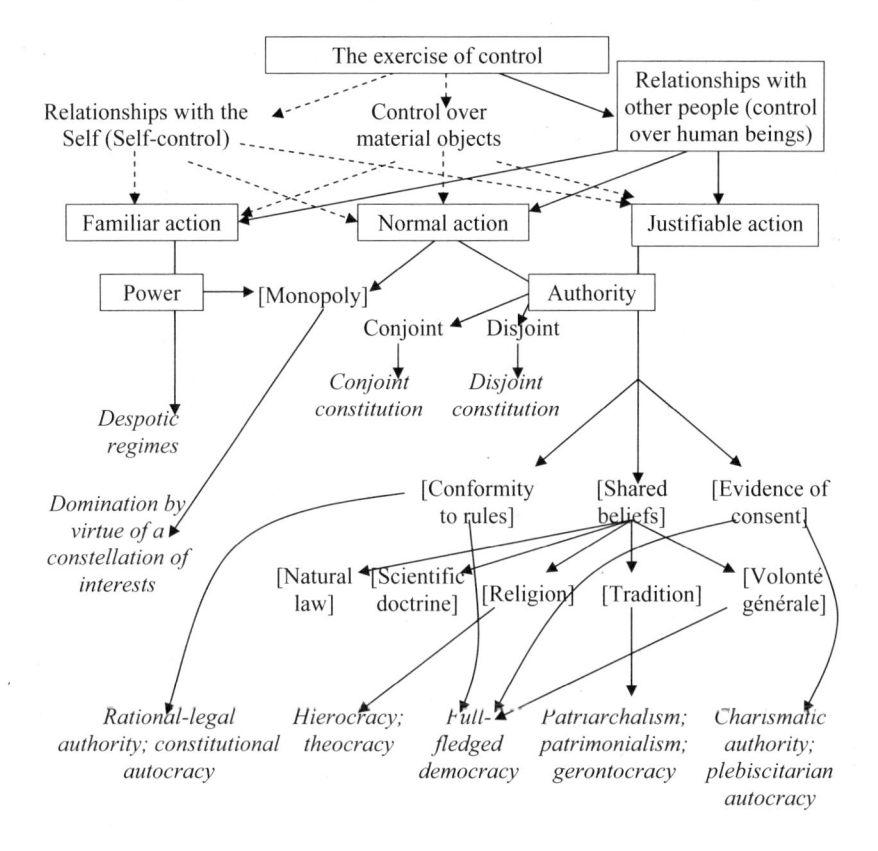

Figure 2.2
Conceptualization and Operationalization of Power Relationships

[Figure 2.2: A hierarchical diagram showing the conceptualization of power relationships. "The exercise of control" branches into "Relationships with the Self (Self-control)", "Control over material objects", and "Relationships with other people (control over human beings)". These connect to "Familiar action", "Normal action", and "Justifiable action". Familiar action leads to Power, normal action to [Monopoly], justifiable action to Authority. Power leads to *Despotic regimes* and *Domination by virtue of a constellation of interests*. Monopoly divides into Conjoint and Disjoint (Conjoint constitution, Disjoint constitution). Authority branches into [Conformity to rules], [Shared beliefs], and [Evidence of consent], which further branch into [Natural law], [Scientific doctrine], [Religion], [Tradition], and [Volonté générale]. These culminate in: *Rational-legal authority; constitutional autocracy*; *Hierocracy; theocracy*; *Full-fledged democracy*; *Patriarchalism; patrimonialism; gerontocracy*; *Charismatic authority; plebiscitarian autocracy*.]

For a more comprehensive discussion of rational-legal and charismatic authority, hierocracy, theocracy, patriarchalism and patrimonialism the reader can refer to Weber's writings (1968, pp. 217-219, 243-244, 1006-1011, 1059-1061). Richard Rose, William Mishler and Neil Munro (2006, Ch. 1) discuss the definitions of plebiscitarian and constitutional autocracies at length. Plebiscitarian autocracy or "realist" democracy implies relatively free and competitive elections and excludes the rule of law, i.e., the condition of conformity to established rules does not hold. On the contrary, full-fledged democracy inevitably includes all three elements of the justifiable transfer of the right of control: the rule of law, consent expressed through regularly held elections and a set of beliefs shared by both the superordinate and the subordinate and embodied in *volonté générale*, or the interests of a society as a whole (Beetham, 1991,

Ch. 6). One of the advantages of the proposed conceptualization lies in avoiding the danger of confusing and, hence, misusing the concepts that correspond to different stages of the movement from the abstract (coordination and control) to the concrete (empirically verifiable forms of power relationships).

This conceptualization lays the groundwork for developing a more formal taxonomy of power relationships. Since Carolus Linnaeus' nomenclature of plants and animals (1730) and Dmitri Mendeleev's periodic table of the chemical elements (1869) natural scientists have continuously been improving the standards for analytical description. In the social sciences—partly as a result of their non-paradigmatic nature (Kuhn, 1972, p. 86)—the progress made even with respect to key concepts seems far less impressive. The proposed attempt to develop a comprehensive taxonomy of power relationships refers to two differentiating criteria: (i) the type of action and (ii) the techniques for exercising control and imposing will (Table 2.2).

The previous taxonomies (Wrong, 1980, pp. 22-24; Beetham, 1991, pp. 16-21; Ledyaev, 1997, Ch. 12; Scott, 2001, p. 16) were one-dimensional. Lukes (2005, Ch. 1), who claims that his classification has a three-dimensional nature, uses a single criterion in fact: the level at which will is imposed. He differentiates between the actual decision-making, the process of agenda setting (the exclusion of some topics from the agenda) and the deepest level of individual preferences: power as an influence over what the individual wants. He does not indeed differentiate various techniques for imposing will as a function of the type of action and pays most attention to different configurations of normal action (including the deliberate change of the interests and wants of the subordinate). From a methodological point of view, Lukes' approach represents a critical extension of rational choice analysis. For this reason, it provides important insights essentially with regard to power at the register of normal action, leaving power relationships at the two other registers in shadow.

The criterion (i) lets us partially bridge gaps that exist between the major theoretical approaches in sociology, namely interactionism (focuses mostly on familiar action), positivism (emphasizes normal action) and critical theories (highlight the issues of justification). This brings to light a complementary character of two major methodological approaches in philosophy. The individualist and rationalist approach appears relevant for studying control embedded in normal action. Control at the register of justifiable action derives from the institutional environment, which

Table 2.2
3×3 Taxonomy of Power Relationships

			Type of action		
			I. Familiar	II. Normal	III. Justifiable
Imposition of will by	rationalizing it, namely by	violence, namely by	a. Applying force	(and/or)	Slavery	(and/or) Despotism
			b. Coercing (using threats)	Domestic abuse, parental abuse	Blackmail, racket	
			c. Manipulating	Guilt manipulation	Opportunism	Realpolitik
			d. Virtue of a constellation of interests	Specialization within a marriage	Monopoly	Monopolistic capitalism
			e. Structural bias of the system	Non-discriminating husband in a masculine society	Hybrids ("neoclassical" contracts)	Hegemony
			f. Making obedience paying (giving promises)	Marriage of convenience	Disjoint authority, "fordism"	Capitalism
	legitimizing it, namely by		g. Enforcing established rules	Legal marriage, religious wedding	Private bureaucracy, techno-structure	Rational-legal authority, constitutional autocracy
			h. Sharing beliefs	"Interpersonal interpenetration"	Conjoint authority	Traditional authority
			i. Getting consent	Common-law marriage	Wheel network	Charismatic authority, plebiscitarian autocracy

(Democratic enterprise; Full-fledged democracy)

calls for the holistic and interpretative approach. As far as the criterion (ii) is concerned, in keeping with particular research questions it can be defined either as various mechanisms for carrying out will, or as a set of constraints limiting power and facilitating resistance. For instance, physical or mental force underlies claims to power, if obedience is achieved through "the creation of physical obstacles restricting the freedom of another, the infliction of bodily pain or injury including the destruction of life itself and the frustration of basic biological needs" (Wrong, 1980, p. 24). On the other hand, one force can counterbalance the other force and so limit the scope of the latter. In other words, the proposed taxonomy can easily be adapted for the purposes of an inquiry into the constraints of power (Chapter 8).

The techniques for exercising control and imposing will are listed in keeping with the degree of violence associated with them: they range from violence in the most manifest forms to persuasion by utilitarian arguments and a three-fold process of justification. Violence, according to Arendt, "is close to strength" (1969, p. 46), the strength and perseverance necessary to keep going "one's own way" despite resistance. In terms of the master everyday metaphor, the progressive substitution of control over the mind (persuasion) for control over the body (coercion or, as Scott puts its, correction) results from the process of modernization (Mitchell, 1990, pp. 566 ff.). The emergence of capitalism with its impersonal and intangible forms of control makes the heavy and continuous reliance on the body as a vehicle for imposing the will less relevant.

The strategy of coercing (b) refers to the threat of applying negative sanctions, for instance, force. Coercion differs from force (a) because first it still leaves a choice to the subordinate (Wrong, 1980, p. 38; Wartenberg, 1990, p. 100) and, second, it makes the dominant worse off than he or she needs to be in the event the tactic fails. Namely, both of them lose in the case of an actual application of force (Schelling, 1960, p. 123).

Manipulation (c) means "any deliberate and successful effort to influence the response of another where the desired response has not been explicitly communicated to the other" (Wrong, 1980, p. 28). Manipulation requires control over information flows and the ability to turn them on and off at will. As the result of manipulation, the individual, who is subject to it, lives in a "virtual" world artificially designed according to the wishes of the powerful. "Control of the mass media is … key to control of the virtual world" (Wilson, 2005, p. 43) and the chief resource for manipulation at the macro level.

A combination of rational arguments and discretionary restrictions limiting the choice makes the next strategy for imposing will (d) feasible. Despite the appearance of free choice, the actor who is subordinated to the power of monopoly feels oppressed. "Because of the very absence of rules, domination which originates in the market or other interest constellations may be felt to be much more oppressive than an authority in which the duties of obedience are set out clearly and expressly" (Weber, 1968, p. 946). The actor subjected to monopolistic power has only two choices: either to accept conditions imposed by the monopolist or to abandon the task of the rational pursuit of his/her interests, which requires coordinating his/her activities with the monopolist.

The transfer of control by virtue of a constellation of interests (d) has a broader relevance than to the case of economic monopoly. In fact, it refers to a particular model of choice different both from the maximization of utility and coercion (Chapters 5 and 6, see also Oleinik, 2007a). The imposition of the will can result from mobilizing, as Lukes (2005, p. 25) puts it, a "bias of the system" as a whole. The powerless party then has no other option but to minimize missed opportunities instead of maximizing utility or minimizing pain.

"Changing the choice situation of people is ... an important way of altering their individual and collective power" (Dowding, 1996, p. 24). Thus, it is a good idea to introduce a new technology for imposing will in the taxonomy, power embedded in the structure (e) or structural power. Structural power should not be confused with luck. In the latter case, Keith Dowding suggests (1996, Ch. 4), the actor just gets what he/she wants without having to impose his/her will, whereas in the former case the actor makes efforts to activate or strengthen the bias of the system in his/her favor.

It is worth clearly differentiating the structural and strategic components of power. The latter refers to the institutions underlying the power, the former—to human agency.[15] The bias of the system takes at least two forms. First, the rules of the game, i.e., coordination procedures, provide one party with more options corresponding to his/her interests than the other party. In other words, the scope of the room for maneuvering might differ. "The possessors of superior resources restrict the autonomy of others by limiting the range of relevant considerations and, therefore, the courses of action that they feel are feasible and desirable" (Scott, 2001, p. 72). Second, the mere interests and desires of the actor subject to power embedded in the structure can be altered and "distorted" compared with what he/she would have in a "counterfactual" situation when not being subject to power. "*A* may exercise power over *B* by getting him to do what he does not want to do, but he also exercises power over him by influencing, shaping or determining his very wants" (Lukes, 2005, p. 27).

The strategy of making obedience "pay" (f) derives from the model of rational choice in a pure form: a promise of positive sanctions made by the superordinate increases the subordinate's gain if he/she transfers the right to control his/her actions. Finally, instead of combining moral, non-utilitarian techniques of persuasion (g, h and i) into a single case, I adapt Beetham's approach to provide a more nuanced picture.

The mere definition of the three types of action suggests that an association between them and the techniques for imposing will could exist. For instance, a "silent" and often non-reflexive coordination at the register of familiar action does not exclude a drift into power in its pure forms (shaded cells Ia, Ib and Ic). The orientation toward achieving a rationally chosen plan or realizing a project calls for using utilitarian arguments and speaking the language of particular interests (shaded cells IId, IIe and IIf). The coordination with the generalized Other requires reference to the most universal norms embodied in the law or traditions (g), a common set of values (h) and the procedures for expressing and aggregating particular interests (i), which points to the shaded cells IIIg, IIIh and IIIi. A detailed discussion of all the cells deserves a separate study; short comments on some of them are provided in the next Section.

IV. Empirical and Analytical Illustrations

[Id] The economic approach to marriage developed by Gary Becker illustrates the point. He argues that rational actors have an interest in deepening the gender division of labor and thus in making their marriage more sustainable (Becker, 1993, pp. 397-398). The more spouses are dependent on each other due to the complementary character of their skills (e.g., child-rearing versus making a living), the more stable their relationship is.

[Ie] Thomas Wartenberg (1990, pp. 157 ff.) considers the relevant case of a non-discriminating husband acting within the structure characterized by a bias favoring males, i.e., he lives in a masculine society.[16] Despite the fact that this particular husband does not personally discriminate against his wife, her action alternatives and available options derive from a gender bias embedded in the institutional environment. So, the wife appears dependent on her husband and has an unequal relationship with him despite his preference for non-discrimination. When coordinating his actions with those of his wife, the husband realizes his interests more fully than the wife and *de facto* he imposes his will on her.

[Ih] One of the "codes" of love outlined by Luhmann consists in labeling it as intimate relationships, or an "interpersonal interpenetration at an advanced level" (1990, p. 198). The actor who falls in love intends to explore and understand the personality of the loved one. The problem of finding a common denominator of two personalities has an open-ended character due to a complex and multi-level structure of each.

[IIb] Schelling's account of threats as a strategy of conflict illustrates a combination of violence and rational considerations that characterizes practices of blackmail and racketeering. On one hand, in order to achieve the desired outcomes, threats have to be carefully calculated. On the other hand, their effectiveness depends on the strength and resoluteness of the individual making them. "The use of thugs and sadists for the collection of extortion or the guarding of prisoners ... exemplifies a common means of making credible a response pattern that the original source of decision might have been thought to shrink from or to find profitless, once the threat had failed" (1960, pp. 142-143).

[IIc] According to a definition widely used in economic literature, opportunism implies that one is "seeking self-interest with guile" (Williamson, 1985, p. 30). In other words, opportunism allows one party to carry out a plan by deceiving the other parties involved in what initially looked like a common project.

[IIe] Institutional economists pay increasing attention to hybrids as a form of long-term cooperation among partners who maintain their formal autonomy. Long-term cooperation leads to the emergence of specific assets that cannot be redeployed outside it without a significant loss in their value (Williamson, 1991, p. 292). In the final account, the parties become so dependent on each other that they cannot escape power relationships, if the dependence has an asymmetric character (Ménard, 2005b, pp. 95-97). Specific assets produce a structural bias: their owner has important leverage with respect to negotiating his/her share in the profit from cooperation. In other words, he or she has more say in determining the exchange ratio in the situation of bilateral monopoly (see also Section II of Chapter 6 and Emerson, 1976, pp. 351-353).

[IIf] Economists usually speak of disjoint authority in terms of Principal-Agent relationships (Stiglitz, 1987, pp. 966-971). The "fordist" arrangement (named after Henry Ford) illustrates the idea of disjoint authority in its purest form. In exchange for good wages (the famous policy of $5 per working day), employees are expected to accept boring jobs at assembly lines and give up any attempts to challenge or merely limit the intensity and the comprehensiveness of their boss' power. Ford—like several other entrepreneurs at that time, including George Pullman—went so far as to claim his right to control the morale of his employees (Boyer & Orléan, 1990, pp. 23-29; Walzer, 1983, p. 295).

[IIg] Weber does not elaborate on private bureaucracy; he just opposes the public office to the private office or bureau created to run an enterprise (1968, p. 957). The concept of techno-structure sheds more light on this issue. John Galbraith uses techno-structure to refer to all employees, from the top managers to the white-collar workers possessing special knowledge and skills, involved in the process of decision-making in an organized way. In other words, techno-structure refers to all "organized knowledge" relevant to the operation of the firm (1967, Ch. 6).

[IIi] The wheel structure of networks implies delegating the right of control to the member who temporarily finds him/herself at the intersection of communication channels. In this case, power results from a consensual decision based on rational considerations (concerns in reducing information costs and optimizing information flows). Hence, "the appearance of hierarchy hardly constitutes a violation of a peer-group structure" (Williamson, 1975, p. 47).

[IIg+IIh+IIi] The list of arguments in favor of firms owned and democratically run by their workers usually includes references to established rules and shared beliefs, the necessity of evidence of consent by the subordinate. First, advocates of self-managed firms suggest transforming the structure of property without violating property rights (for instance, by allowing employees to buy out shares with the help of Employee Share Ownership Plans) and interpreting them as a "right to acquire the personal resources necessary to political liberty and a decent existence" (Dahl, 1985, p. 112). Second, the economic rationale of self-managed firms resides in the fact that they increase "the incentive for workers to report private information" which is valuable for managerial purposes (about the level of their efforts, for example; Bowles & Gintis, 1993, p. 77). In other words, self-managed firms help create a set of common interests and beliefs. In turn, the existence of common interests makes the evidence of consent with respect to all key decisions indispensable. Buying a team of people is not the same as buying a commodity (Putterman, 1988, pp. 245-246).

[IIIa] Michael Mann argues that coercion may appear justifiable if other attempts to organize and control people, materials and territories fail. He develops the concept of compulsory cooperation, namely the use of force and coercion in order to accomplish tasks necessitating a high level of coordination. Compulsory cooperation has no inherent immunity against the drift into despotism. "*Despotic power* refers to the range of actions that the ruler and his staff are empowered to attempt to implement without routine, institutionalized negotiation with civil society groups" (1986, pp. 169-170; emphasis in the original).

[IIIc] The history of *realpolitik*, or the political realm populated by corrupt people and corrupt rulers, starts with Niccolò Machiavelli's *The Prince*. "A prudent ruler ought not to keep faith when by so doing it would be against his interest, and when the reasons which made him bind himself no longer exist. If men were all good, this precept would not be a good one; but as they are bad, and would not observe their faith with you, so you are not bound to keep faith with them" (1940, p. 64). The principal task of political technologies, namely "black PR," consists in justifying power by distorting information flows when it cannot be justified on the basis of the non-distorted information. The toolbox of political technologists includes the construction of political parties, including those in "fake" opposition, the destruction of others, for instance, by staging internal conflicts and splits, the framing of general campaign dynamics, the creation of myths and so forth (for an overview, see Wilson, 2005; Ledeneva, 2006, Ch. 2).

[IIIe] The situation of hegemony, as was first described by Antonio Gramsci, derives from a bias of the system as a whole, not only from distortions in market structures (Scott, 2001, Ch. 4). Hegemony means that actors who are subject to power perceive the situation in such a way that they do not see any meaningful alternative and consent to their own subordination as the lesser of two (or more) evils. The point is that the actor vested in power can succeed in persuading the subordinate that his/her submission is the lesser evil even if meaningful alternatives exist. A bias at the level of cultural representations then produces a justification for the transfer of control. This bias results from the spread of particular ideologies "interwoven with moral and ethical judgments about the fairness of the world" (North, 1981, p. 49). Seen through the lens of a biased ideology, a number of alternatives lose their relevance, which contributes to the justification of the *status quo*.

[IIIf] The rationalization of obedience should not be confused with its justification by reference to rational considerations. The former corresponds to normal action (cell IIf), employment relationship serves as an illustration (salary makes the plans and interests of the boss and the employee compatible). The latter necessitates extending the scope of a particular plan or project to the sphere of money (Walzer, 1983, pp. 100-126; Turner, 2000) or the "market world" (*monde marchand*, Boltanski & Thévenot, 1991, pp. 241-252). There nevertheless exists a contradiction in utilitarian principles when used to justify obedience in the eyes of the generalized Other: "what goes on in the market should at least approximate an exchange between equals" (Walzer, 1983, p. 120). Because of this contradiction, one rarely hears rational arguments in favor of obedience to the rich outside the firm's boundaries made in public. On the contrary, such arguments must be "unveiled" by a critical analysis. Karl Marx defines capitalism as a system based on control exercised by the owners of capital over the process of production as a whole. The submission of the process of production to the purposes of the accumulation of capital lets its owner appropriate organizational functions. That "a capitalist should command on the field of production, is now as indispensable as that a general should command on the field of battle" (Marx, 1936, pp. 362-363).

V. Introducing a Third Dimension?

The association between the type of action and the technique for imposing will arguably exists as long as power has an instrumental value. This means that the actors pursue goals other than the grasp on power: power has no intrinsic value since it is one of the solutions to the problem of coordination. However, power might also have a terminal value, which places it on the same list as, for example, wealth or glory. This observation leads us to consider whether introducing a third variable in the taxonomy is worthwhile. The new variable relates power to end-means relationships, i.e., to reasons for seeking power. It has two attributes: power as a medium, a means for achieving some other goals, and power as an end in itself.[17]

The distinction between power as a means and power as a terminal value shares several common features with the other distinction, between power *over* and power *to*. As the latter opposition can be commonly found in philosophical discussions of power, it is worthwhile to offer a more detailed view of these two pairs of concepts. The concept of power *to* clearly indicates an instrumental character of the exercise of power aimed at achieving something. However, power *to* may or may not involve interactions with other actors, i.e., a social relationship. As Valeri Ledyaev rightly points out, power *to* "does not set apart two completely different cases: (1) *A* can do *x* (himself) and (2) *A* can achieve *x* by getting *B* to do *x*" (1997, p. 96; see also Wrong, 1980, Ch. 9; Wartenberg, 1990, p. 23; Stewart, 2001, p. 6). For this reason, power *to* appears useful in analyzing power as control over material objects and power as self-control (see Figure 2.2).

As for power *over*, it can also be present in all three types of relationships (with the actor him/herself, with material objects and with other people), yet it does not necessarily have an instrumental character. Thus, power *over* paves the way for inquiring into the specifics of power as a terminal value, as an end in itself. The case of management (getting subordinates to achieve some outcomes) suggests that the scopes of power *over* and power *to* partly overlap. On the contrary, the logic of the means-end relationship prevents the scopes of power as a means to achieve other ends and power as an end in itself from overlapping, which make the purpose for seeking power a good differentiating variable. Everything depends on the intentions of the power-holder and the order of his or her priorities (which, as it will be shown below, complicates the use of this variable in empirical research).

The example of a sergeant acting in various contexts helps sketch various configurations of power by putting the third differentiating variable to work (Figure 2.3), albeit in a highly schematic manner. In situation (a), the actor has power to operate a machine gun: he successfully hits a "bull's eye." This power does not involve any social action and, in fact, refers to nothing other than a training exercise. In situation (b), the sergeant applies his skills as to how to operate the machine gun in a battle, by targeting an enemy instead of the "bull's eye." The staff sergeant gives orders to subordinates, i.e., privates and corporals, in the situation (c). He gets the subordinate do what he wants. Both parties are clearly involved in social action. The staff sergeant gives apparently (and possibly substantially) meaningless orders to new recruits in situation (d).[18] He does so exclusively to show his strength and to secure their compliance. Finally, situation (e) refers to the sergeant commanding on a battlefield. He gets a private to do what he thinks is necessary to win the battle.

Power as an end in itself can be conceptualized as a zero-sum game: one party can win only at the expense of the other party.[19] On the contrary, power as a means to achieve other ends has several features of a non-zero-sum, or collaboration game. "'Winning' in a conflict does not have a strictly competitive meaning; it is not winning relative to one's adversary. It means gaining relative to one's own value system" (Schelling, 1960, p. 4). Scholars who focus exclusively on power *to*, accordingly overlook that power shall be modeled in two different ways. They argue, for instance, that power is never a zero-sum phenomenon (Morriss, 1987, p. 91).

Figure 2.3
Two Pairs of Concepts: Power Over vs. Power To and Power as a Means to Achieve Other Ends vs. Power as an End in Itself

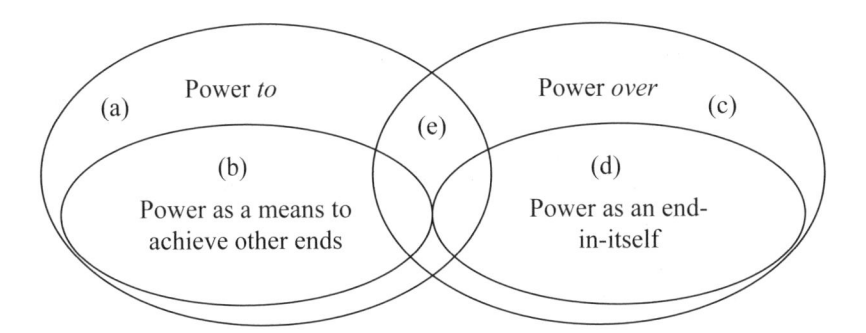

If power as an end in itself emerges at the register of justifiable action, then one can speak of a *failure* of justification. Justifiable action calls for the legitimization of power, i.e., for the persuasion of the generalized Other. Yet here the power-holder at best takes into consideration the subordinate's opinion in negative terms, as eventual obstacles in imposing will, or simply ignores it. In other words, power remains unjustified *despite* the expectance of the opposite, which highlights differences with a more simple case of power imposed by violent means (Rows a, b and c in Table 2.2).

The principal advantage of introducing a new dimension in the taxonomy consists in differentiating apparently similar cases of coercive authority and authoritarian regimes based on coercion: on a two-dimensional map both these cases should be placed in cell IIIb. This confusion leads Wrong to challenge the conventional opposition between power as control based on violence and authority as control based on either rational calculations or justification (1980, pp. 38 ff.). He argues, in particular, that the use of violence might be needed to achieve justifiable purposes (in fact, this is exactly what the modern state is expected to do according to a classical definition [Weber, 1968, p. 54], namely it applies violence for enforcing its order). However, the authoritarian state also uses violence to maintain its order. Josef Stalin's efforts, for instance, to broaden the area under his control in the early and mid-1930s looked for many external observers as if his major preoccupation consisted in reestablishing order (Solomon, 1996, pp. 153-154).

The task of differentiating coercive authority from despotism and authoritarianism requires knowledge of the reasons for seeking control. In the former case, control over other people has an instrumental value; it is mere a tool of coordination (power as a means to achieve other ends). In the latter case, control transforms into a terminal value, whereas coordination of common activities appears downgraded to the status of a means (power as an end in itself). This means that the major obstacle preventing the three-dimensional taxonomy from being fully operational consists in difficulties related to getting a clue about what is going on inside the "black box" of the mind of the actor who exercises control. What are his/her *true* intentions and interests? "A power relation cannot, therefore, be identified unless there is some reference to the intentions and interests of ... the principal" (Scott, 2001, p. 2).[20] In this sense, the proposed approach sides with deontology in its argument with rational choice analysis. "Deontology stresses that the moral status of an act should not be judged by its consequences, the way utilitarians do, but by the 'intention'" (Etzioni, 1988, p. 12). One should only add that the intention determines not only the moral status of power relationships, but also has an impact on their internal "mechanics" or constitution.

Several research strategies might help open the "black box" of the mind of the actor vested in power. First, the researcher can make a "heroic" assumption that the institutional environment determines the actor's intentions. Then a particular configuration of external constraints makes a difference: tight constraints limit the actor's opportunism and prevent him/her from abusing the right to control the other's actions. In a deterministic perspective, the tighter the constraints under which the actor vested in power acts, the better (see Chapter 8). Second, the researcher can describe and analyze the individual and group preferences of the powerful with the help of in-depth interviews. Special interviewing techniques, namely a "scenario" approach or "projective" methods,[21] have to be incorporated in the research design in order to "unveil" true intentions and interests. Third, the researcher's toolbox also includes a counter-factual analysis designed in a manner suggested by Lukes (2005, pp. 43 ff.). It focuses on the question as to what the scenarios of coordination are in a particular situation if the right of control has an instrumental value or a terminal value.

Conclusion

An attempt to explore the concept of power relationships was undertaken in this chapter. Despite the fact that power represents one of the core concepts in the social sciences, numerous gaps characterize most attempts to make this abstract category operational and apply it in empirical studies, especially in a comparative perspective. In contrast to the taxonomies of power relationships developed by Lukes, Wrong, Wartenberg, Dowding, Beetham, Ledyaev and Scott that have a one-dimensional character, the proposed classification refers to three variables: (i) the type of action: familiar, normal and justifiable; (ii) the technique for imposing will: by violence, by rationalizing it and by legitimizing it; and (iii) the purpose of looking for power: to achieve extrinsic ends (power as a means) or for its own sake (power as an end in itself). This potentially gives us a three-dimensional matrix (Figure 2.4).

It is worthwhile to outline a number of areas in which the new taxonomy has important implications. One such area involves debates of power and resistance. The dialectics of power and resistance has long attracted the attention of scholars in philosophy, sociology and political science. For some, resistance represents an important feedback loop in

Figure 2.4
A Three-Dimensional Taxonomy of Power Relationships

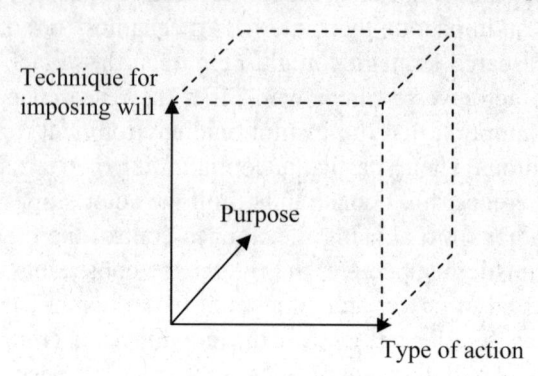

- Technique for imposing will
- Purpose
- Type of action

the reproduction of power. Resistance feeds power, as Foucault puts it: "Resistance is imminent to power relationships; it is embedded in them as an irreducible counterpart" (Foucault, 1976, p. 127). For the others, resistance challenges power and paves the way for changing it. "Theorized as non-conventional reiterations and unfaithful performances, resistance and critique—that is, oppositional forms of agency—involve a 'turning of power against itself'" (Swanson, 2007, p. 18). The contribution of the proposed approach to debates of power and resistance consists, on one hand, in differentiating inappropriate forms of power from unjust forms of power and, on the other, in justifying resistance to the former.

The right to resist unjust power is widely discussed both at the theoretical and practical levels. "A period of social conflict and political upheaval may be necessary, if costly, price to be paid for the transition to a more just or more progressive political order" (Beetham, 1991, p. 120). This debate omits, however, the idea that power does not always have to be justified. The opposition of just versus unjust power characterizes coordination at the highest register of action, justifiable action. Conflicts and tensions also derive from transferring a model of power appropriate to one register of actions to another register without adjusting and reshaping it. Power appropriate to familiar interactions may be "lifted" up to the register of justifiable action, which produces the drift into authoritarianism and despotism, or power backed by rational consideration structure relationships at the register of justifiable action instead of remaining at the register of normal action. The inappropriate character of a power relationship is as a good reason for challenging and resisting it as its failure to pass the test of legitimacy. In fact, in many cases, the latter can be attributed precisely to the inappropriateness of a power relationship for the context of interactions. The "new public management," i.e., attempts to reshape governmental institutions according to principles of economic rationality (Manning, 2003), potentially produces a gap between the emerging model of "rational" power and the general expectation that the power embodied in the state has to meet the requirements of legitimation.

Comparative studies represent a second large area for applying the multi-dimensional classification. It prevents us from using country- or culture-specific categories to label particular phenomena. The one-dimensional analogues are not sufficiently flexible and have fewer degrees of freedom for fine-tuning and catching details. New insights provided with the help of the proposed approach can be illustrated by studies of power relationships in Russia. A number of scholars label a particular model of power prevalent in this country "Russian power" highlighting its country-specific character (Makarenko, 1998; Pivovarov, 2006a). More specifically, they attribute the following characteristics to the prevailing model of power: the lack of any other justification apart from the mere fact of exercising it, the lack of constraints under which the power holder acts, a heavy reliance on violent techniques for imposing will, etc. However, the nature of the "Russian power" can be better understood in light of the new taxonomy (see Chapter 3). A model of power appropriate to familiar action is transferred without the necessary adjustment to the highest register of action: justifiable action. Under these conditions, both subjects and external observers generally expect the justification of power (from whence the insistence on the unjust, non justifiable character of "Russian power" in many writings about it) yet this is not offered by the individuals and groups vested in power. This is why "Russian power" lies closer to authoritarianism with an eventual drift into despotism than to coercive authority, even if the techniques for imposing will eventually include not only force, coercion and manipulation but also domination by virtue of a constellation of interests (Chapters 3, 4 and 5).

The new taxonomy also sheds new light on the related issue in comparative studies, namely the perception of political power in modern versus post-modern societies. There are plural definitions of what is modern and post-modern; one of them refers to the model of power. Ronald Inglehart argues that the erosion of institutional authority, namely the shift from the belief in rational-legal authority towards de-emphasizing authority, characterizes the transition from modernity to

Figure 2.5
"If It Were to Happen, Whether You Think Greater Respect for Authority Would Be a Good Thing, a Bad Thing, or Don't You Mind?"
(% Answering "Good thing")

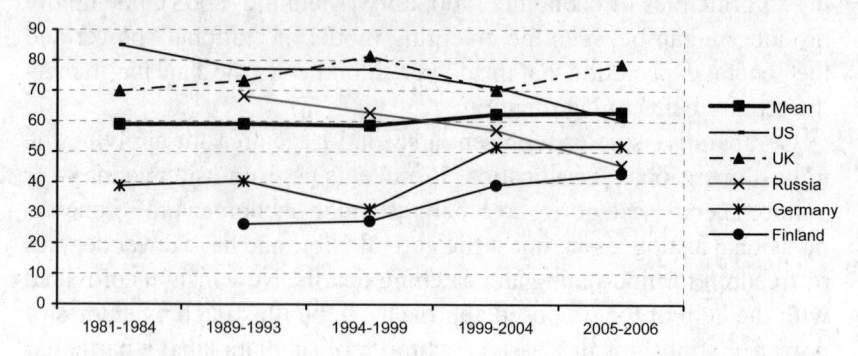

Sources: World Values Survey, 2009 and the author's calculations. In 1981, the data is for West Germany. The mean was calculated for the sample of size N=24,589 in 22 countries in 1981-1984, N=58,629 in 39 countries in 1989-1993 (first wave of the World Value Survey), N=72,159 in 52 countries in 1994-1999 (second wave), N=93,909 in 70 countries in 1999-2004 (third wave) and N=71,288 in 53 countries in 2005-2006 (fourth wave).

post-modernity (Inglehart, 1997, Ch. 10). He uses the downward trend in the dynamics of institutional trust (trust in the government) in most developed societies to illustrate this idea. Nevertheless, a closer look at answers to the question whether the respondent believes that a greater respect for authority would be a good thing indicates that the sample mean is *increasing* slightly over time, including in some countries that are usually considered post-modern (Figure 2.5).

Beetham's (1991, p. 98) assumption that standards for legitimate power in the context of modernity have significantly increased on all the three dimensions of it (g, h and i, see Table 2.2) provides useful insights in this regard. The more demanding the standards for legitimate power are, the greater the risk of disappointments and "broken expectations" (Oleinik, 2006a). If one agrees that the growing distrust in the government results from a raising of standards for judging the degree of its legitimacy, then the proposed approach suggests investing more efforts in meeting these standards through reviving democracy instead of minimizing the scope of the government and making oneself less dependent on it, which represents a liberal solution to the problem.

Notes

1. The concept of power is used not only in scientific discourse, but in everyday language as well. In this respect, Alfred Schutz (1987, p. 79) urges social scientists to build their concepts with the help of mental categories suggested by commonsense. However, the lack of agreement among scholars is aggravated by a plurality of uses of the word "power" in everyday life.
2. The following lines, for instance, look familiar to most neoclassical economists: "the incentive structure facing an actor is the full set of costs and benefits of behaving in one way rather than another. Typically actors have power over others to the extent that they can manipulate others' incentive structure" (Dowding, 1996, p. 5).
3. Richard Emerson's critique and reinterpretation of social exchange theory as one of the streams within rational choice analysis (1976, pp. 345-347) can be also mentioned here.
4. Nikolai Korkunov, a nineteenth-century Russian legal philosopher, developed a somewhat different argument in this regard and stressed the substitutability of trust and power. He saw in power a "last resort" in terms of coordination. Individuals resort to power if they appear unable to solve the dilemmas inherent in war with everyone against everyone by cultivating trust. "Men who are in fact dependent on one another may not agree on the rules that govern their relationships, and where men cannot agree on the rules, the only possible basis for their legal relationship is an agreement as to who has authority to act and decide" (Yaney, 1966, p. 482).
5. It allows measuring the "power" variable at the ratio (scale) level.
6. In this respect, Herbert Simon (1953, p. 513) refers to the scope of the "zone of acceptance."
7. Simon assumes that power always implies mutual influence, yet the degree of its asymmetry may vary.
8. A very similar situation emerges in studies of networks. A large variety of country-specific forms of networks prevents us from finding a common language in their analysis. Recent developments in this field of knowledge have resulted from shifting focus on the structure of networks and setting aside a series of substantial issues: the localization of transactions and its effects, the opposition between insiders and outsiders, and so forth (Oleinik, 2004a, pp. 98-100).
9. The concept of habitus as a power relationship "gene" (see Section III of the Introduction) seems appropriate as long as the exercise of power does not go beyond the register of familiar action.
10. When applied beyond this scope, it looses its validity and is subject to criticism as an instance of economic imperialism. Coleman (1990, pp. 428-429) argues that power resulting from rational choice has to pass the test of reciprocal viability (balancing losses and gains for each participant in a power dyad) or global viability (balancing aggregate losses and gains within a corporate structure or an institution). Yet, if a power relationship transcends the scope of a narrowly defined plan or project, this complicates the task of passing the test of viability. The larger the scope of a power relationship, the more diverse interests it involves. When non-pecuniary interests come into play, this further complicates the picture. Thus, an encompassing power calls for more than purely utilitarian rationales.
11. Transformative power requires more than a commonality of interests of *A* and *B*. It is intended to enhance *B*'s capacity for autonomous action, i.e., it puts an end to itself at some point in the future as a result of *empowering B*. Empowering is "understood as the enhancement of autonomy and solidarity" (Stewart, 2001, p. 1).
12. The fruitful assumption of socioeconomics according to which "individuals' decisions and behaviors, far from following one unified principle, or seeking to

maximize pleasure and minimize pain, or marching to one over-arching utility, empirically reflect the conflict between two—at least two—irreducible utilities. The first is our desire for pleasure; the other, our moral obligations" (Etzioni, 2003, p. 111; see also Etzioni, 1988, p. 4), can be the object of a new interpretation in the light of what has been said. The model of rational choice refers to the register of normal action, whereas morally oriented behavior refers to the register of justifiable action. The conflict between these principles exists as long as the same action has elements of both normal and justifiable coordination.

13. It is worth admitting that there exist a number of other manners for differentiating between power and authority. Dennis Wrong, for instance, refers to authority as the right of control deriving from a particular position or status (1980, p. 35). He also points out several language-specific definitions of power and authority, namely in French and German compared with English (1980, pp. 9-10; see also Hegy, 1974). Russian terms for depicting power are discussed in (Ledyaev, 1997, p. 95; Oleinik, 2005b, p. 63). However, the discussion of culture-specific concepts corresponds to the other step in moving from the abstract to the concrete (see Chapter 3).

14. For example, Aristotle compared power with physical compulsion (see Wartenberg, 1990, p. 79). In this sense, power shares several elements in common with the control over material objects embodied in property rights. As John Commons puts it, "the old distinction between the *possession of physical property* and *liberty of contract* becomes the distinction between the behavior of those persons who are subject to command and obedience and the behavior of those persons who are subject only to persuasion or coercion" (1939, p. 282, emphasis in the original).

15. Peter Morriss expresses this idea in terms of non-epistemic as opposed to effective epistemic ability. "A has the non-epistemic ability to do X if there exists W (a string of A's basic actions) such that if A does W then X results" (1987, p. 54). The effective epistemic ability adds to this list two stronger indications of A's human agency: "A knows that if she does W then X results, and A would do W if she wanted to do X" (Ibid).

16. "A society is called masculine when emotional gender roles are clearly distinct: men are supposed to be assertive, tough, and focused on material success, whereas women are supposed to be more modest, tender, and concerned with quality of life" (Hosftede & Hofstede, 2005, p. 120).

17. Arendt's reading of power as action in concert leads her to believe that power simply should not be thought of as a mean to achieve other ends. "Power, far from being the means to an end, is actually the very condition enabling a group of people to think and act in terms of means-end category" (1969, p. 51). However, because the positive effects of power can be appropriated by just one party or unequally distributed among interacting parties, the opposition between power as an end in itself and power as a means to achieve other ends shall not be relegated to the backstage.

18. Practices of hazing illustrate this situation (Sieca-Kozlowski & Daucé, 2006).

19. **Table Power as an End in Itself as a Zero-Sum Game**

		Second party	
		Impose will	Do not impose will
First party	Impose will	0, 0 [N]	1, -1
	Do not impose will	-1, 1	0, 0

Most combat sports (or even sports in general) can be conceptualized in a similar manner. It is worth noting that there is a single Nash equilibrium in this game: both players attempt to impose their will on the adversary (the upper left cell). In the end, nobody wins as a result of this struggle for domination.

20. Wartenberg encounters a very similar problem when he introduces a central position for his analysis difference between domination as a "negative" use of power and transformative power as a "positive" use. "Transformative power does not constitute a distinctive type of power...; rather, transformative power is a specific use of those types of power, one constituted by *the desire to empower the agent over whom it is exercised*... It is a use of power that employs such types of power as influence, force and coercive power" (1990, p. 195, emphasis added).

21. One of them implies putting the interlocutor in an imaginable situation in which there is no single socially approvable way of justifying his or her eventual actions (Oleinik et al., 2005).

3

Russian Power: Constructing an Ideal Type

Introduction

Peter Morriss (1987, p. 2) believes that "ordinary men and women frequently know more than academics about the meaning of 'power.'" Language serves a depository for this "folk wisdom." A simple search using two keywords "power" and "authority" in the Google database consisting of 8 billion documents shows that the relative frequency of the latter is almost two times higher in English (5.4:1) than in Russian (9.8:1). For instance, if people vested in power and their organizations are colloquially called "authorities" in English, they are referred to as "powers" (*vlasti*) in Russian. Upon closer inspection it appears that even the meaning of power as one's capacity to impose will has particular connotations in the Russian case. "In Russian the term 'power' is usually used for the description of someone's ability to control (dominate, compel, influence) *others*, 'power' is imagined as something that is 'over' us, that limits our freedom, creates obstacles, etc." (Ledyaev, 1997, p. 95; emphasis in the original). An attempt to inquire into what power is in Russian, or "Russian power," follows.

In the social realm, concepts and definitions have not only an epistemological but also an ontological value: they shape actors' perceptions and behavior (Skinner, 2002a, pp. 44-45). The Thomas theorem further stipulates that the manner in which actors define situations determines their subsequent developments (Merton, 1995).[1] The concept of power is no exception to this rule. Furthermore, it is reasonable to assume that its impact on everyday interactions exceeds that of other concepts because the underlying phenomenon in this case tends to "overrule" individual wills subject to it. The concept of power also has another distinctive feature: the manner in which it shapes actors' perceptions and behavior derives—at least partly—from the purposeful activities of those vested in power. Pierre Bourdieu (1994, p. 1) describes this process in terms of symbolic violence as the production and imposition "(especially through the school system) [of] categories of thought that we spontaneously apply to all things of the social world."

Unintended consequences of the spread of a particular perception of power deserve close attention as well. A particular model of power prevailing in the Russian institutional context left its traces even in Russian grammar. A socio-linguistic study has shown that the spread of impersonal sentences can be attributed to a progressive loss of the autonomy of people subject to "Russian power." Its authors, namely, argue that "the creation of the centralized state and the related formation of the imperial ideology led to the unconscious substitution of a system of impersonal categories underlining the subject's lack of control over an event for the system of grammatical categories that allows to identify the subject and his responsibility for the flow of events" (Ermakov et al., 2004, p. 104). Indeed, instead of the phrase "I cannot get to sleep" with the clearly identifiable subject, Russians would say *mne ne spitsia*, literally—"it does not sleep to me" where the responsibility is relegated to forces beyond one's control. In the same vein, Russian is poor in active perfect forms: "someone will have a house built in two years" emphasizes the expected accomplishment of an individual or a group of people, whereas Russian simply does not have future perfect active forms: *dom budet postroen cherez dva goda* ("a house will be built in two years").

The task of theorizing Russian power involves serious challenges. Studies of country-specific phenomena can be carried out with the help of two alternative approaches: *emic* or *etic* (Hofstede & Bond, 1984, p. 421; Newman, 2006, p. 449). An *emic* approach requires the researcher to use concepts and categories developed by "native" people in everyday interactions. "Russian power," when seen in this perspective, represents a unique phenomenon that can hardly be found elsewhere. Only scholars socialized in the Russian institutional context and specialists in Russian studies have the knowledge and skills necessary for an *emic* inquiry. An *etic* approach, on the contrary, calls for using universal, cultural-neutral categories and principles. There is no distinctive "Russian" power from this point of view, only a special case of power as the universal capacity to impose will on other people suitable to be studied even by an "armchair scholar" who has had a chance neither to visit the country nor to learn its language.

Russian studies in general—since debates between *zapadniki* and *slavianofily*—and studies of Russian power in particular show especially deep divisions between the two approaches. Yuri Pivovarov, for instance, argues that "the nature of Russian power, its particularities cannot be grasped without reliance on Russian thought and *vice versa*" (Pivovarov, 2004, p. 55; see also Pivovarov, 2006a, p. 66; Akhiezer, 1997, p. 195). Here my task consists in searching for a middle ground and in avoiding the excesses associated with both the *emic* and the *etic* programs of research. This can be done by identifying the key structural elements of power and considering a country-specific model of power, e.g., Russian power, in terms of their various configurations and "constellations."[2]

The methodology of constructing ideal types first developed by Max Weber helps in navigating back and forth between a universalistic vision of power and its country-specific forms. The ideal type "is no 'hypothesis,' but it offers guidance to the construction of hypotheses. It is not a *description* of reality but it aims to give unambiguous means of expression to such a description" (Weber, 1949, p. 90; emphasis in the original). After discussing prevailing approaches to the analysis of Russian power in terms of patrimonialism in Section I, the ideal type of power in its pure form is outlined in Section II. The term "pure state" highlights a "raw" state of power: unbounded, unlimited and not "contaminated" by other factors than the strength of will. It derives from the taxonomy introduced in Chapter 2 and has five attributes that allow for empirical measurement and falsification.[3] It is argued that Russian power lies very close to this ideal type, in contrast to the configurations of power relationships observed in other institutional contexts, namely in the West. In this quality, Russian power can be considered as a starting point in the evolution of other forms of power relationships. However, only a logical reconstruction of power in its pure form is offered in this chapter: the task of historical reconstruction requires a separate study and I will return to it in Chapter 4.[4] Section III contains empirical illustrations of each attribute of Russian power drawn from a series of in-depth interviews with persons vested in power and experts.

I. Prevailing Conceptualizations of Russian Power

When speaking about Russian power, scholars tend to emphasize its violent character: actors vested in Russian power primarily rely on violent techniques for imposing will (lines a, b and c in Table 2.2). In his list of attributes of Russian power, Pivovarov includes violence that sometimes takes its extreme form, despotism (Pivovarov, 2004, p. 66;

Pivovarov, 2006a, 22). Viktor Makarenko takes a further step, arguing that any power implicitly or explicitly involves violence and terror. According to him, in the Russian case, violence just takes acutest and the most extreme forms. He calls for a new "theory of power in which *force and terror are considered the key attribute*" (Makarenko, 1998, p. 85; emphasis in the original).

The thesis that Russian power contains the quintessence of any power relationship in its purest form and, hence, represents a necessary point of departure in all discussions of power seems fruitful and will be explored in depth in the following. At the same time, the exclusive focus on violent techniques for imposing will prevents consideration of the other attributes and adapting a multi-dimensional view proposed in the previous Chapter. This approach does not serve to differentiate power from authority either and, hence, to explain why the latter is so rare in the Russian institutional context.

The other distinctive feature of Russian power lies in its "solipsistic" nature. Actors vested in it tend to ignore the rights and interests of others; in their worldview, anything existing outside their own mind appears irrelevant. Pivovarov (2004, p. 89) opposes in this regard a power-centered social structure to a social structure with multiple subjects (and, accordingly, sources of will). The power-centered structure produces the drift into self-sufficiency and autocracy.

Two Russian terms that one can hardly translate into English or other Western languages without loosing important meanings, *samovlastie* and *samoderzhavie*, provide tools for speaking and thinking about self-sufficient power (while simultaneously being its products). Both concepts are deeply rooted in Russian history and Russian social thought: they derive from $\alpha \upsilon \tau o \chi \rho \alpha \tau \omega \rho$, the title of the emperor of Byzantium (Klyuchevsky, 1957, p. 123). In Byzantium, and initially in Ancient Rus' the terms "had meant no more than being free from outside control," in contrast to the status of a vassal (Hedlund, 2005, p. 140). With the emergence of the centralized Muscovite state they acquired a new meaning, namely unlimited and self-sufficient power within the realm. When translated into English, they accordingly turn into either "sovereign power," or "monarchy," or "despotism," or "tyranny"—depending less on the translator's discretion than on inherent ambiguities and contradictions in the underlying concepts.

Nikolai Karamzin probably made a first comprehensive attempt to distinguish *samovlastie* from *samoderzhavie*, associating the former with unlimited and self-sufficient power and the latter with limited, "modest" power subject to the imperative of justification. He asks "Can one limit autocracy in Russia without, at the same time, emasculating the tsar's authority, salutary for the country?" (Pipes, 2005, p. 138). In this canonical translation of Karamzin's *Memoir* Richard Pipes interprets *samovlastie* as autocracy, tyranny and *samoderzhavie*—as the tsar's authority, monarchy. However, in this case, Karamzin refers rather to an ideal he wanted to promote (the *Memoir* was submitted to Alexander I, Emperor of Russia in 1801-1825) than to an empirically observed and historically stable model of power. Russian power as it is, not as it should be, allows for contradictory interpretations and translations.[5]

Attempts to differentiate between *samoderzhavie* and *samovlastie* bring a new dimension to discussions of Russian power. In both cases, power relationships rely on violent techniques for imposing will, yet *samoderzhavie* calls for justification by referring to some superior principles, whereas *samovlastie* means a self-sustainable power that needs no justification other than the will of the person vested in it. This places *samovlastie* in cell [IIIa] of Table 2.2. Cell [IIIh] then represents *samoderzhavie*. Unfortunately, a serious flaw limits the use of both terms for the purpose of the conceptualization of Russian power. They imply a unique subject of power relationships, which makes the interests of the other people involved in them irrelevant. Rationality—in a particular form—and techniques for imposing will by rationalizing it seem completely alien to Russian power conceptualized in terms of *samovlastie* and *samoderzhavie*. It excludes the latest forms of Russian power embedded in the structures of the post-Soviet market from the analysis.

The concept of patrimonialism is intended to address the problems outlined above; it offers a comprehensive view of Russian power without falling into the traps of the *emic* and the *etic* approaches. Both Russian and Western scholars acknowledge the advantages of thinking of Russian power in terms of patrimonialism.[6] In fact, patrimonial power represents a rare case of the emerging "agreement reality" in the multi-paradigmatic social sciences—a description of the social realm on which most observers tend to agree (Babbie & Benaquisto, 2002, pp. 9-13, 40). The list of scholars endorsing patrimonialism as a way to think of Russian power includes people with diverse theoretical and ideological backgrounds: Richard Pipes (1974; 1999, Ch. 4), Michael Voslensky (1984, p. 71), Mikhail Afanasiev (2000, pp. 13-14), Karl Ryavec (2003, pp. 177-178), Yuri Pivovarov (2004, p. 65), Stefan Hedlund (2005, p. 125) and several others. They oppose Russian power as a particular form of patrimonial power to bureaucratic administration associated—following Max Weber—with the development of modern forms of organization because of its "stable, strict, intensive, and calculable" character (Weber, 1968, p. 224). This produces an analytical continuum with two extreme points: patrimonialism and Weberian bureaucracy. At different points in time, the exact position of Russian power may vary, yet it always lies closer to the patrimonial end (Yaney, 1973; Solomon, 2004; Brym & Gimpelson, 2004; Kryshtanovskaya, 2005, p. 82).

The "checklist" of the attributes of Weberian bureaucracy makes the task of its empirical falsification relatively easy: competitive recruitment of personnel, promotion based on merit, domination of internal over external recruitment, a high proportion of personnel with professional skills and higher education, transparent and predictable career paths in a clearly defined hierarchy of positions, mandatory retirement upon reaching a particular age or after a certain length of tenure and a comparatively good salary and a good return on investment in skills and tenure (Brym & Gimpelson, 2004).

Unfortunately, there is no comparably unambiguous and empirically falsifiable "checklist" for patrimonial power. When outlining the ideal type of this power, Weber highlights traditional regulation and justification, namely "the belief that [patrimonial] ruler's powers are legitimate insofar as they are traditional" (1968, p. 1020) and the close association of power over human beings with power over material objects, property: "the office had become a property object" (Ibid, p. 1033). The conceptualization of Russian power as patrimonial may be popular because of this unfinished and open-ended character of the underlying concept: some scholars focus on power-property relegating the imperative for traditional justification to the backstage, whereas others tend to overemphasize traditional features while forgetting that "politically oriented capitalism ... is very much compatible with patrimonialism" (Ibid, p. 1091).

The empirical falsification of both attributes in the Russian case reveals several problems and challenges. On the one hand, even if the normative view of *samoderzhavie*—as it should be—calls for traditional justification, tradition does not always limit the ruler's discretion, especially taking into consideration most recent developments of Russian power.[7] Traditional justification implies that both people vested in power and those subject to it refer to traditions, i.e., "age-old" traditions constitute the shared beliefs of the rulers and the ruled. Traditions in Russia have a discrete rather than continuous nature: they depend very much on a particular period of time. Gudkov, Dubin, and Levada (2007, p. 5) note in this regard that "the Russian historical time is composed of relatively short—compared with other societies—periods, each of them involves resetting institutional traditions and memory from scratch. Each period finds its justification in the total rejection of the previous one.... A quasi-historical mythology substitutes for the missing historical tradition as an instrument for justification and maintenance of the existing order."[8]

Within each of these historical periods, people vested in power and those subject to it do not necessarily endorse the same set of traditions either. When discussing models of development appropriate for today's Russia, 18 percent of the former group—members of the Russian elite (N=515, July-August 2005)—indicate Russian Orthodox traditions and "age-old" institutions of *"sobornost'*," which contrasts with far less intense support, 4 percent (N=1,600, June 2004), shown for this model by ordinary Russians (Gudkov, Dubin & Levada, 2007, pp. 87, 105).

Patrimonialism also implies deep embeddedness of power in the institution of family and its derivatives: the extended family, clans, etc. It "has its genesis in the piety of the children of the house toward the patriarch's authority" (Weber, 1968, p. 1050). The strength of this institution also varies across historical periods, reaching its lowest level in the early 2000s (Table 3.1). A world-wide survey conducted on random representative samples around the same period of time (World Values Survey, 2009) shows that the number of respondents who agree with the statement that "marriage is an out-dated institution" in Russia (21.7 percent; N=2,340, 1999) is quite comparable with that in some Western countries like Canada (22.3 percent; N=1,879, 2000) or Western Germany (18.6 percent; N=982, 1999) and largely exceeds that in the US (10.1 percent; N=1,183, 1999).

On the other hand, exclusive emphasis on power-property, i.e., practices of granting and enforcing property rights in exchange for services rendered to the ruler, overshadows other techniques of domination through the market proper to political capitalism. "Political capitalism ('politically oriented capitalism') includes the cases where profit is made through the state, via contacts with the state or under the direct physical protection of the state" (Swedberg, 2003, p. 60). In practical terms, this means that Russian power "at work" is identified only if property rights are at stake, such as in recent cases of de-privatization (e.g., the Yukos affair, see Subsection II [f1] of Chapter 8), whereas other forms of it remain overlooked. The necessary association of patrimonialism with power-property, especially land property, leaves some scholars puzzled as to why land property ceases to be the basis of the most recent forms of Russian power—does this signal its downfall (Pivovarov, 2004, pp. 228-235)?

Table 3.1
Crude Marriage and Divorce Rates in Russia, per 1,000 of Population, 1940-2007, Selected Years

	1940	1950	1960	1970	1980	1990	1992	1995	1996	2001	2002	2003	2004	2005	2006	2007
Marriage rate [1]	6.3	11.6	12.1	10.1	10.6	8.9	7.1	7.3	5.9	6.9	7.1	7.6	6.8	7.5	7.8	8.9
Divorce rate [2]	1.1	0.4	1.3	3	4.2	3.8	4.3	4.5	3.8	5.3	5.9	5.5	4.4	4.2	4.5	4.8
[1] to [2]	5.7	29	9.3	3.4	2.5	2.3	1.7	1.6	1.6	1.3	1.2	1.4	1.5	1.8	1.7	1.9

Sources: Tsentral'noe Statisticheskoe Upravlenie SSSR, 1978, p. 26; Federal State Statistics Service, 2006, p. 117 and http://www.gks.ru/free_doc/2008/demo/osn/05-06.htm. The data for 1940, 1950 and 1960 refers to the Soviet Union as a whole. For the purpose of comparison, crude marriage rate in Canada in 2001 was 4.7, crude divorce rate—2.3, which gives their ratio equal to 2 (Statistics Canada, 2008, pp. 74-75).

The conceptualization of Russian power as patrimonialism also excludes purely violent techniques for imposing will from consideration. Patrimonialism is a particular form of traditional authority, or a power relationship that actually meets the requirement of justification (see Figure 2.2). From this point of view, patrimonialism shares several features with *samoderzhavie* (and adds the power-property dimension to it) without having connections with *samovlastie*. Makarenko (1998, p. 84) rightly points out that "Weber's theory tells us nothing ... about elementary components of power such as physical violence, mass terror, internal spying or total control." All these considerations call for continuing efforts to conceptualize Russian power.

II. Theoretical Model: Russian Power as Power in Its Pure Form?

A better conceptualization of Russian power must meet several criteria. First, like patrimonialism and unlike *samoderzhavie* or *samovlastie*, it has to overcome the opposition between the *emic* and the *etic* approaches. It is argued that the ideal type of Russian power has an elective affinity with power in its pure form, namely it represents the starting point in the evolution of any other form of power. At more advanced stages of its evolution, both logical and historical, power can transform into authority, can be "framed," limited or constrained in some way. Yet, initially, power takes a "raw" form and observations of Russian power serve to outline its basic parameters.

Second, it must have several dimensions specified with the help of particular attributes. The issues of justification refer to one of these dimensions, techniques for imposing will to the other. The alternative conceptualization of Russian power shall be flexible enough to encompass techniques based on violence in pure forms (e.g., force and coercion) as well as those embedded in market structures: recent developments reveal the compatibility of Russian power with political capitalism. A third dimension, purposes for seeking power (two reference points, power as an end in itself and power as a means to achieve other ends, serve to map it, see Section V of Chapter 2) can be added to the first, along with some others.

Third, a more appropriate conceptualization has to be empirically falsifiable: a "checklist" of attributes of Russian power shall enable one to make a learned judgment about its presence or absence in a particular institutional context during a particular historical period. Attempts to conceptualize power in an empirically falsifiable manner are in keeping with measurements of the power distance by Geert Hofstede (1980, p.

99; see also Section I of Chapter 2) and the extensiveness and intensity of power by Ovsey Shkaratan et al. (2009, p. 552).

II.1 Self-Justifiable Power

A self-sufficient character of Russian power means that it finds its justification in itself, in the mere fact of being exercised. Russian power does not derive from external sources. Instead, it has only internal sources. "No other thing is required to introduce [this] power" (Pivovarov, 2004, p. 205; see also Pivovarov & Fursov, 1998).

It should be noted that, in contrast to situations in which justification is not required, e.g., interactions with personally known people in the private sphere (at the register of familiar action, see Section II of Chapter 2) or within a group of people pursuing a common rationally chosen plan (at the register of normal action), justification is expected by people involved in interactions. The ideal of *samoderzhavie* calls for the justification of power: "by its nature, power is founded on truth, and inasmuch as truth has as its source the All-High God and His commandments written indelibly in the consciences of all, we find a justification in their deep meaning of the words, 'there is no power but of God'" (Pobedonostsev, 1965, p. 253). Yet, even in this case, there is no built-in "enforcement mechanism." According to a commentator, the continuous use of the term *samoderzhavie* after the issue of the October 1905 Manifesto, that paved the way for the establishment of the Parliament, confirms the ruler's desire to highlight a self-sufficient nature of his power regardless "external" justifications. "By keeping the word of *samoderzhavie* the system of power (*vlast'*) showed its self-sufficient, as opposed to derived from something external, character" (Gribovsky, 1912, p. 25). In spite of the need for justification,[9] power in its pure form fails to pass the test: the power holder either justifies his or her rule by the fact of being vested in it, as in the case of *samovlastie*, or refers to a "faked" justification.

References to religious and ideological arguments should not deceive anyone: they are raised at the initiative of the power holders' and only if they do not constrain their autonomy and discretion (see also Subsections II [h1] and [h4] of Chapter 8). For instance, in Soviet times people vested in power referred to the ideals of communism as long as ordinary Soviets had taken them at face value—and progressively switched to more pragmatic and cynical "justifications." Soviets vested in power "no longer believe [as of the late 1970s] in the possibility of persuading their subjects, but want them to abandon all hope of liberation from the ideological conformism imposed on them from above" (Voslensky, 1984, p. 296; see also Shlapentokh, 1989).

II.2 Power as an End in Itself

The focus on continuous self-reproduction and expansion represents an additional feature of self-sufficient power. In the eyes of the ruler, the stability and continuity of power is given higher priority than anything else: the stability and sustainability of socio-economic development, population growth, and so forth. Instead of being a means to achieve these and other ends, people vested in Russian power perceive it as an end in itself, a terminal value (Pivovarov, 2006a, p. 92). Thus, their aim is to extend the comprehensiveness of power, or the number of spheres under the control of the power holder (see Section I of Chapter 2) and the intensity of control within each of these spheres. "A universal interest of power resides in expanding the scope of regulated activities" (Makarenko, 1998, p. 99; see also Voslensky, 1984, p. 170).

Surveys confirm the perception of Russian power as an end in itself by both people vested in it and those subject to it. For instance, a survey carried out on a sample composed of state representatives at the municipal and regional levels (N=300, 2005), shows that "in all groups of interviewed state representatives prevails the point of view that Russian bureaucracy has primary interest in maintaining its wealth and influence. In a group of state representatives, who consider the state service a separate class, about a half of respondents see state representatives' interests in expending the scope of their influence" (Byzov, 2006, p. 26; see also Tikhonova, 2006, p. 6). Ordinary Russians concur with this perception. When asked about the chief purpose of state representatives' activities, they see it in satisfaction of their own interests (55 percent, N=1,600, October 2007) rather than state interests (20 percent) or the interests of the population (12 percent; see Analitichesky tsentr Yuriia Levady, 2007, p. 24).

II.3 Violent Techniques for Imposing Will

Self-justifiable power whose primary purpose consists in reproducing and strengthening itself relies on violent techniques for imposing will as these attributes rule out persuasion and other techniques based on justification and substantially restrict the use of techniques based on rationalization. The purer power, the stronger its association with violence. In this sense, violence characterizes "not only technologies of power, but its substance" (Pivovarov, 2006a, p. 22; see also Pivovarov, 2004, p. 66).

People vested in power in its pure form prefer negative sanctions to positive ones both discursively and in practice. When advising the Russian Prince, Karamzin values the benefits of counting on fear: "fear is the most efficacious and common of all human motives" (Pipes, 2005, p. 195). In Soviet times, members of the ruling elite had a similar order of preferences: they "prefer the stick of propaganda and organization to the carrot of higher wages" (Voslensky, 1984, p. 154). Since then, the situation has not changed in this regard: a content analysis of 442 newspaper articles covering decisions and activities of regional leaders in two regions of Russia and Kazakhstan in the late 1990s—the early 2000s shows that negative sanctions are mentioned two times more frequently than positive ones (Ermakov et al., 2004, p. 223).

Power in its pure form prompts a broad definition of violence as one's strength crushing the other's strength and, therefore, violent techniques for imposing will. In addition to a physical form, violence can take on several other forms: structural, verbal, etc. Symbolic violence implies crushing one's beliefs and values "by universally imposing and inculcating … a dominant culture" (Bourdieu, 1994, p. 6; see also Section II of Chapter 5). Structural violence means crushing one's interests and rationally chosen plans by deliberately restricting the choice of available strategies and altering the pay-off structure. As a result, the real interests of actors subject to power are substituted for those that correspond to the power holders' preferences (Lukes, 2005, pp. 27-28; Dowding, 1996, pp. 5-8; see also Section II of Chapter 2). This plurality of violent techniques for imposing will explains the flexibility of Russian power and its adaptability to various institutional contexts ranging from the national economy as a princely manor to the post-Soviet market passing through the command economy. Viewed in this light, power-property refers to a particular violent technique combining physical (property rights involve physical control over material objects [Redmond & Shears, 1993, pp. 271-272]) and structural (since it produces distortions in economic interests see also Section II of Chapter 6) violence.

II.4 Extreme Asymmetry in the Distribution of Rights and Obligations

All power relationships imply asymmetry between the power holder and the subordinate: the first commands and rules, whereas the second obeys. Nevertheless, the self-justifiable character of power in its pure form and its reliance on violence produces extreme disproportions in the distribution of rights and obligations between people vested in it and those subject to it. What is allowed to the former appears forbidden to the latter. In fact, the language of rights and obligations does not seem appropriate in the context of power in its pure form: rights are concentrated at one pole of a power relationship, obligations at the other. For people vested in power, the possession of rights does not presuppose obligations; obligations of people subject to power do not entitle them to any rights. Instead of freedoms, the latter group of people has duties and obligations that, according to Pivovarov (2006a, p. 21), explain the yoke-type nature (*tiaglovy kharakter*) of the Russian social system.

The extreme asymmetry in the distribution of rights and obligations leads many authors to depict Russian power in terms of ultra-concentrated and monopolized decision-making: only one (few) subject(s) has the right to make decisions and initiatives. For instance, Olga Kryshtanovskaya formulates the following "iron law": "there can exist only one source of power and this source is located at the highest level" of the social organization (Kryshtanovskaya, 2005, p. 107; see also Pivovarov, 2004, p. 148; Holmes, 1994, p. 83; Voslensky, 1984, p. 104).

Shifting emphasis from the monopoly of power to the question of the degree of its asymmetry has several advantages. For instance, the monopoly of decision making reduces to zero elements of rationality in the actions of those who are subject to power in its pure form and precludes using a number of violent techniques for imposing will embedded in market structures. This complete monopoly can exist and rely on physical violence (the case of totalitarianism), although it is better to define power in its pure form as an infinite regression toward it.[10]

II.5 No Feedback Loops

Asymmetry in the distribution of rights and obligations coupled with the self-justifiable character of power in its pure form make feedback loops in relationships between the rulers and the ruled unnecessary. Feedback connections are a must if power derives its justification from external sources, especially from public support, as in the case of authority by plebiscite. On the contrary, people subject to power in its pure form have no say in the process; their opinion does not matter, let alone influence decision-making.

People vested in power can allow the expression of individual opinions, yet any attempts of the ruled to join efforts to increase the chances of getting their voices heard are considered a challenge. Russian power tolerates individual complaints as the only form that feedback loops can take (Kirdina, 2001, p. 129); as a matter of fact, they help the rulers discipline their "lieutenants." As for collective petitions, they are strictly forbidden (Voslensky, 1984, p. 173).

The lack of feedback loops produces a particular social structure that can be compared with an hourglass: "the narrow mid-point of the hour glass insulates individuals from the state; there is rich social life at the top and at the bottom" (Rose, Mishler & Haerpfer, 1997, p. 9). The hourglass structure implies that links between those at the top, the rulers, and those at the bottom, the ruled, are weak or non-existent. A survey carried out in 2005 on two samples, that of state representatives and that of ordinary Russians, confirms the disconnection between the two groups: "both ordinary Russians and state officials acknowledge the fact that in today's Russia the latter form a separate social group" (Byzov, 2006, p. 27).

The unilateral dependence of the ruled on the rulers (because of the self-sufficiency and the asymmetry of power), combined with the lack of feedback loops, produce the drift into bribery and corruption as artificial substitutes for missing links. By offering a bribe, the person subject to power in its pure form achieves two results: gets his or her voice heard and reduces the degree of the asymmetry in the power relationship. The ruled literally "buys out" a right that he or she is otherwise not entitled to. "A bribe is offered by someone who occupies a subaltern position and tries in this manner to reduce the asymmetry in his relationships with the person having more prerogatives" (Yakovlev, 1988, p. 150; see also Yaney, 1973, p. 26).

The proposed conceptualization of Russian power in terms of the five attributes does not undermine the value of previous attempts. Instead, it derives from them making them parts of a larger, multi-dimensional view. For instance, the violence associated with Russian power appears analytically connected with its other attributes, such as self-justification and missing feedback loops. In the same vein, power-property, an element of patrimonialism, represents a particular violent technique for imposing will. Figure 3.1 shows logical connections between the five attributes. The solid line illustrates just one set of them: the self-justifiable character of power excludes its status of a means to achieve other ends; the solipsism of power also causes asymmetries and makes any

Figure 3.1
Five Attributes of Russian Power

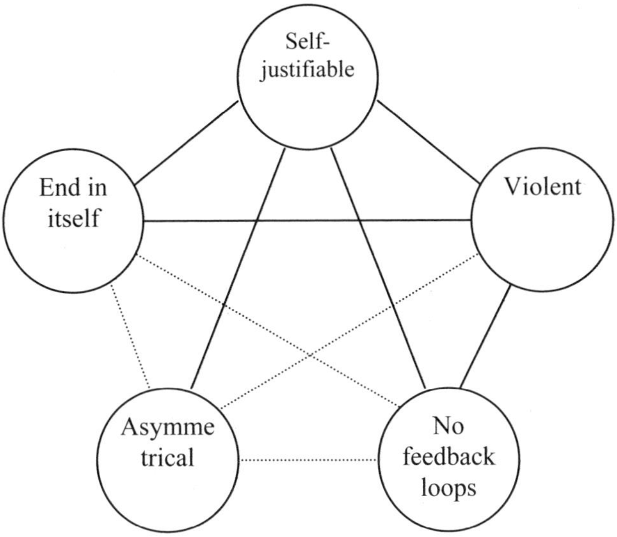

feedback loops unnecessary; finally, the task of imposing the alien will on someone without rights and means to have a say naturally calls for violent techniques.

Some characteristics can become more intense, whereas the others will be less intensive at a particular point in time.[11] The reliance on physical violence (and on power-property), for instance, can hardly be considered a constant.

If Russian power embodies power in its pure form, then one can expect to observe it not only in Russia. Total institutions in general and prison in particular represent an institutional setting particularly favorable to the continuous reproduction of power in its pure form (Oleinik, 2008d). Advocates of critical sociology go further and argue that the elements of power in its pure form, for example, symbolic violence, exist in any society, and only their particular configuration and intensity vary.

III. Empirical Illustration: Russian Power Seen by People Vested in It

The proposed analytical description of power in its pure form provides a "checklist" of attributes and, therefore, paves the way for its empirical falsification. One strategy derives from the assumption that power in its pure form is not constrained or limited by anything, be it the law (because of its self-justifiability) or the will of the ruled (because of the lack of feedback loops). Then, by gauging the strength of constraints, the observer can judge how closely a particular power relationship lies to the ideal of type of power in its pure form. Chapter 8 discusses outcomes of this test in present-day Russia.

The other strategy for testing the concept empirically consists in locating elements of public discourse that can be interpreted in terms of the five attributes. This involves content analysis of public speeches, publications in the printed media or transcripts of expert and specialized interviews (the parameters of the two series of interviews, "A" and "B," on which the present discussion is based, are specified in Section V of the Introduction and the Appendix).

Qualitative content analysis was performed using a codebook with codes corresponding to the five attributes of power in its pure form. For the purposes of detailing, the code "Violent techniques for imposing will" is subdivided into six sub-codes: "Force," "Coercion," "Manipulation," "Domination by virtue of a constellation of interests," "Structural bias" and "Symbolic violence". Table 3.2 provides coding frequencies (see the Appendix for full descriptions of the codes). In order to facilitate comparisons, the codebook comprises codes referring to two non-violent techniques, "Positive incentives" and "Legitimation" (because they do not fit the ideal type of power in its pure form, the descriptive statistics in their regard are placed in cells with a shaded background). In keeping with current standards of good practice (Gray & Densten, 1998, p. 422), two independent examples for each interpretation of codes (latent variables) are provided below.

III.1 Self-Justifiable Power

Probably the quintessence of self-justifiable power resides in the principle that someone vested in power is always right. Three interlocutors mentioned it spontaneously and independently from one another five times.

> "The main rule of the bureaucratic game says: when I'm a boss you're a dummy" (23B).

Orders and directions are simply given instead of being justified by referring to some superior principles or common sense.

Table 3.2
Coding Frequencies, Codebook "Power in Its Pure Form"

Code	Set "A" Freq	%	Set "B" Freq	%	Set "A" Cases	%	Set "B" Cases	%	Set "A" Words	%	Set "B" Words	%
Self-justifiable	60	4.7	18	2.5	32	50.0	14	32.6	2096	0.5	550	0.3
End in itself	49	3.9	66	9.2	33	51.6	32	74.4	1636	0.4	1983	1.1
Asymmetrical	232	18.3	89	12.4	62	96.9	37	86.0	8167	1.9	3373	1.8
No feedback	89	7.0	74	10.3	43	67.2	29	67.4	4214	1.0	2622	1.4
Violence 1: Force	62	4.9	47	6.6	31	48.4	28	65.1	2654	0.6	1476	0.8
Violence 2: Coercion	123	9.7	47	6.6	49	76.6	29	67.4	4674	1.1	1566	0.8
Violence 3: Manipulation	60	4.7	50	7.0	28	43.8	25	58.1	2870	0.7	1625	0.9
Violence 4: Domination by virtue of a constellation of interests*	238	18.8	118	16.5	57	89.1	36	83.7	14504	3.4	5517	2.9
Violence 5: Structural	108	8.5	94	13.1	44	68.8	35	81.4	5257	1.2	5453	2.9
Violence 6: Symbolic	69	5.5	57	8.0	32	50.0	25	58.1	2736	0.6	2204	1.2
[Non-violent techniques 1: Positive incentives]	143	11.3	32	4.5	53	82.8	23	53.5	5303	1.2	828	0.4
[Non-violent techniques 2: Legitimation]	32	2.5	23	3.2	22	34.4	17	39.5	1483	0.3	808	0.4

Legend: * Restricting the range of the subordinate's choices by controlling entry to a territory, the market, the legal field, etc. Monopolies resulting from various barriers to entry (cf. natural monopolies). The use of administrative resources for the purposes of restricting entry (see more in Chapter 6).

"You realize that an order is meaningless and useless, but it must be taken. This situation almost kills you, but you also know that nothing can be done without discipline. One has to have a very good health and intelligence to fight with this" (7A).

III.2 Power as an End in Itself

The decisions and activities of people vested in Russian power are intended, first of all, to keep and strengthen their grasp on power. Other political, economic or social goals have a secondary status.

"The chief purpose of the state service's (*apparata*) existence consists in its continuous reproduction and growth" (58A).

"Only one thing consolidates them [people vested in power], namely the fear of loosing power. They don't have anything else in common, yet this external fear transforms into an irresistible consolidating force, I think" (22B).

III.3 Extreme Asymmetry in the Distribution of Rights and Obligations

To use an apt metaphor first proposed by Michael Voslensky (1984), those vested in Russian power are always in the driver's seat: they get the privilege to decide where to drive, at what speed and how carelessly or carefully. Both ordinary Russians and business people feel like passengers in this car who travel at their own risk.

> "The sides of the bargaining process are absolutely unequal. The state official is the center of gravity; everyone else seeks how to approach him" (30A).

> "An ordinary person is powerless today.... I've just received documents from the tax administration—about my house, apartment, piece of land. Why such calculations? I receive first one version, then the second, with changes. Afterward they start to impose fines" (33A).

The last excerpt deserves particular emphasis as it shows the dramatic reversal in the perception of the situation as one moves from the driver's seat to the back seat (before retiring, the interviewee was a senior member of the Soviet and Russian *nomenklatura*).

III.4 No Feedback Loops

Many interviewees seem to agree with the "hour-glass" metaphor probably without knowing it. The lack of feedback loops characterizes relationships not only between people vested in power and those subject to it, but also within the state service. Information flows connecting its various layers tend to have a unidirectional, top-down, orientation.

> "[People vested in power] do not need accurate information! They are all idealists who are not interested in knowing what is going on in reality. They consider such information as an impediment" (6B).

> "If a brain over there, at the top, says 'don't do it,' there is not much discussion. Period. The task of the office holder is simple; it's not about discussing an order but about carrying it out. It doesn't matter if the order makes sense—no one will speak up" (53A).

III.5 Violent Techniques for Imposing Will

The discussion of violent techniques for imposing will starts with physical violence and ends with structural and symbolic violence. Chapters 2 and 6 provide their comprehensive theoretical overview.

III.5.1 Force. Force in the most manifest form, violence, is a costly technique for imposing will because it needs to be applied continually.

Only power-holders with unlimited resources can afford to rely on physical force, which restricts the scope of using it (there is an association between the amount of oil revenues at the disposal of the Russian state and its willingness to send people to prison, see Oleinik, 2008d, pp. 202-204).

> "Submission to force and loyalty is everything that counts" (23B).

> "If he has crossed someone's path, he may be accused of many things and sent to jail" (12A).

III.5.2 Coercion. The use of coercion requires fewer resources: force transforms into a last resort. This can explain the fact that the interviewees more often refer to coercion than to force (two times more often in the case of Set "A," see Table 3.2).

> "Everyone realizes that if he interferes with political interests—of the president, of his master, or someone else—he is going to be sent to jail or killed" (50A).

> "If you show him that his rear will be beaten with a stick, he'll become unbelievably accommodating and kind. What counts most, all these mediocre politicians just need to realize, with all their brain force and intellect, that the threat is not virtual but real" (38B).

III.5.3 Manipulation. Manipulation involves a deliberate distortion of the information available to the subordinate.

> "The information, that is made available to the mass media even by a seemingly open and transparent government body, is never complete. It is carefully selected" (19A).

> "Expert opinion is commonly used to manipulate decisions. For instance, X. [a top government official] I'm not sure if he continues to finance Council Y. as he did in the past. Because of his involvement, Z. stepped down. X. financed the Council only to show documents endorsing his position and signed by respectable people to Putin. They don't ask experts about what is going on in reality; they look for justifications of the position already taken" (42A).

III.5.4 Domination by Virtue of a Constellation of Interests. This technique consists in deliberately restricting the range of options available to rational—in their intentions—actors. Domination by virtue of a constellation of interests derives from imperfections and distortions of market structures and, hence, appears perfectly compatible with conditions on the post-Soviet "emerging" market. To be classified under this heading, a market distortion mentioned by the interviewee has to result from intentional activities of people vested in power. The corresponding code has the highest frequency in both sets of transcripts.

"The price of an entry ticket to these markets is high and the entire generation of young people appeared unable to make it" (6B).

"Business people keep asking us for help because, say, the firm controlled by a governor's daughter does not let them enter the [regional] market" (19A).

III.5.5 Structural Violence. In spite of "elective affinity" with domination by virtue of a constellation of interests, structural violence has its own particularities. Namely, it refers to broadly defined rules of the game as a factor limiting the subordinate's range of choices (cf. the limiting role of market structures in the previous case).

"In this structure, the choice is very simple. Either you want to be in and accept the existing rules, you don't criticize your superior, or you step down and start criticizing. Like in England, there is Her Majesty's Opposition; there is no opposition to Her Majesty" (23B).

"The current system of power is … self-reproducing. A normal person landing in such a place cannot behave otherwise. It's like in business. Everyone competes with anyone else and if you start living according to the other laws, you'll go bankrupt soon" (42A).

III.5.6 Symbolic Violence. Finally, symbolic violence implies an "ideological work" so widespread in Soviet times (Shlapentokh, 1989). More recently, it took the forms ranging from the search for a "national idea" to neuro-linguistic programming (see, for instance, Vasiliev, 2003).

"Now it's a troubled (*smutnoe*) time. One who manages to first formulate a new ideology of power [sic], will get a grasp on power after this phase transition" (6B).

"A paradox consists in the fact that methods of unconscious associations—the Orange plague [a reference to the 2004 Orange revolution in Ukraine], Pichugin the killer [a Yukos official sentenced to life for alleged killings], Nikitin the traitor [an ecological activist sentenced for alleged spying]—do work, rational arguments don't" (30B).

III.6 Non-Violent Techniques for Imposing Will

These techniques do not fit the model of power in its pure form. Respondents quite predictably mention them less often. For instance, the ratio of all codes covering violent techniques to all codes corresponding to non-violent techniques in set "A" is 4:1 (660 to 175), in set "B"—7:1 (413 to 55). 106 out of 107 interviewees referred to violent techniques at least in one form.

III.6.1 Positive Incentives. Positive incentives basically mean inducement: "the source of a subject's submission is a reward which he can get from a power-holder for compliance with his command" (Ledyaev, 1997, p. 186).

> "People vested in power (*vlast'*) will maneuver; they won't try to get everything they want with one stroke. They will be more careful and feed up the population—a bit" (43B).

> "The state has enough resources to stimulate a desired course of action on the part of some social groups: it can afford increasing pensions and wages, even at the price of inflation" (17B).

III.6.2 Legitimation. In practical terms, legitimation of power necessitates persuasion, or the appeal to reasonable arguments. "*A* presents arguments, appeals or exhortations to *B*, and *B*, after independently evaluating their content in light of his own values and goals, accepts *A*'s communication as the basis of his own behavior" (Wrong, 1980, p. 32).

> "The individual spends a lot of time at his job. When he understands the purpose of his work, he'll work effectively and life will make sense to him. A wise superior has to explain this to the subordinate—we work together to achieve a particular goal. Only then one can expect good results" (31A).

> "[Putin] played [in 1999] the role of a young successor to the tsar, the one from fairy tales. It's deeply embedded in the national culture and rings a bell for many people. It refers to deepest archetypes" (1B).

III.7 Relationships between Codes

The strength of association between various attributes of power in its pure form can be gauged by analyzing the co-occurrence of the codes. In both sets of transcripts, the code "Violent techniques" emerges as the "centroid", i.e., the code showing a highest degree of similarity with the other codes (see Sections III and IV of the Methodological appendix). It co-occurs in transcripts with the other codes more frequently than the others.

The codes "End in itself" and "Asymmetrical" lie closer to code "Violent techniques" than codes "No feedback" and "Self-justifiable" (Table 3.3). Figure 3.2 illustrates the relative position of the five attributes in a three-dimensional space in function of coding co-occurrences in set "A": the closer they lie, the stronger the association between them (set "B" has a similar constellation of the codes with code "Violent techniques" in its center).

Table 3.3
Jaccard's Coefficients of Similarity with Code "Violent Techniques"

Code	Set "A"	Set "B"
Asymmetrical	.953	.86
No feedback	.683	.744
End in itself	.5	.674
Self-justifiable	.484	.326

Figure 3.2
Co-Occurrence of Codes, 3-D Map, Set "A"

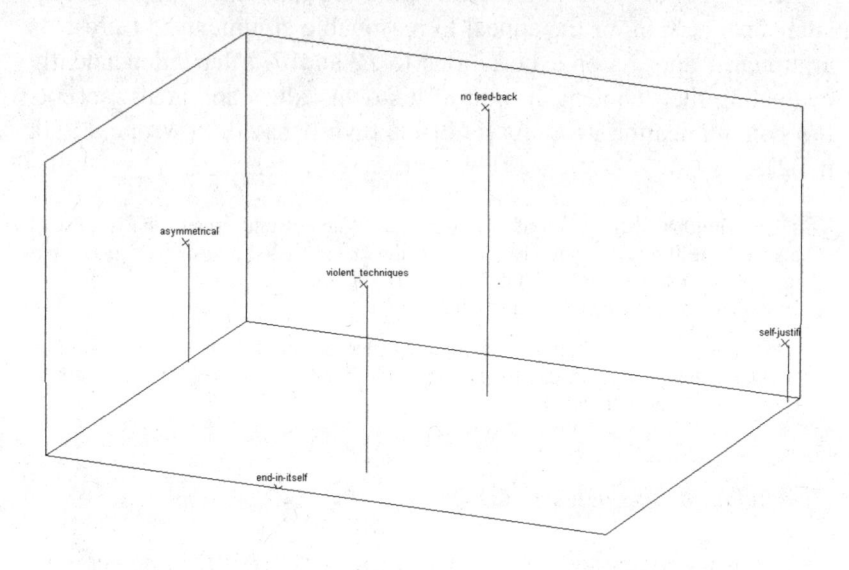

This pattern suggests that violence is indeed the alpha and omega of power in its pure form. The heavy reliance on violent techniques highlights a non-instrumental character of power in its pure form and its extreme asymmetry. A high priority attached to reproducing and strengthening power alienates the people subject to it. Only violence can ensure their obedience to orders. An extremely asymmetrical relationship between the powerful, the one who has rights but no obligations, and the powerless, the one with obligations but without any rights, also means the drift into violence. As the powerful party does not recognize any obligations, nothing prevents him or her from using violence. As the powerless party has no rights, he or she feels alienated and "uncooperative"—thus deserves a "stick," not a "carrot," in the opinion of the powerful.

Conclusion

The proposed conceptualization of Russian power in terms of power in its pure form occupies a middle ground between the *emic* and the *etic* approaches. A number of reasons explain the choice of a middle point when inquiring into the nature of Russian power. First, it helps bridge a gap between two strong intellectual traditions represented by *zapadniki* and *slavianofily*. Second, it serves to make sense of a wide range of discourses about power: interview guides neither from set "A" (see the Appendix) nor from set "B" were purposefully oriented to discussing power in its pure form.

Third, this analytical position enables the researcher to be simultaneously "in" and "out" of the field that he or she studies. A general ontological rule stipulates that "social researchers need to be simultaneously detached from and involved in the social-political world around them" (Newman, 2006, p. vii; see also Touraine, 1999, p. 160). This acquires a new meaning when studying power. David Beetham (1991, p. 110) argues that "it is only from a standpoint outside given power relations that it is possible to understand the processes whereby their legitimacy is maintained and reproduced, and what forces are at work eroding it, where such erosion is taking place." Yet being a complete outsider reduces the incentives to understand and, if necessary, criticize a prevailing model of power. Hence, the researcher has to be prepared to navigate back and forth between "in" and "out."

The analytical model of power in its pure form can be further developed in several directions. For instance, in the above discussion, its extreme asymmetry was assumed to be one-dimensional: this means an unequal distribution of rights and obligations within a sphere of activity, e.g., politics. A measure of comprehensiveness (see Section I of Chapter 2), if introduced in the analysis, would make it possible to see whether various spheres of activities have their own unique sources of power or not (see also Section III of the Conclusion). In other words, the extreme asymmetry of power in its pure form involves not only its intensity (e.g., all political rights are appropriated by people vested in power) but also comprehensiveness (e.g., people vested in political power appropriate not only political, but also economic and social rights). A quantitative measure of comprehensiveness consists in the number of spheres of activities in which rights are monopolized and appropriated by the same group of people vested in power.[12]

Further, it is worthwhile to differentiate between power relationships that structure interactions at the macro (most public) and the micro (within the organization, the family) levels. Does the model of Russian power reproduce itself not only at the macro level, as cited interviews with state officials and experts suggest, but also in everyday interactions in the family, at school, at the university and in the firm? If so, this could provide an additional explanation for the stability of Russian power over time that will be the subject of the next chapter.

Notes

1. Institutional economists express a very similar idea by emphasizing the role of "self-fulfilling prophecies": the anticipated state of something "is simultaneously an outcome of the process of anticipation" (Orléan, 1988, p. 237).
2. A similar approach to studying networks is discussed in (Oleinik, 2004a; Oleinik, 2004b).
3. This shall not be interpreted as a methodologically unsound attempt to directly falsify the ideal type. The ideal type here refers to the concept of power in its pure form; it guides the elaboration of empirically falsifiable hypotheses corresponding to the five attributes.
4. In terms of Marxist philosophy, the next chapter will address the question as to whether the proposed logical development of the concept of power has parallels in the actual historical process, as some Soviet Marxists argued (Ilyenkov, 1982) or not, as others insisted (Tronev, 1972).
5. A controversy dated 2006 around the term "sovereign democracy" coined by Vladislav Surkov, first deputy chief of staff of the Russian Presidential Executive Office (a fine example of how power holders produce categories intended to shape subordinates' perception of power) is worth mentioning. According to his definition, sovereign democracy, like *samoderzhavie* in Ancient Rus, implies freedom from outside control: "people vested in power (*vlasti*), governing bodies and their policies are elected, formed and directed exclusively by the Russian nation" (Surkov, 2006). Nevertheless, in full accordance with the inherent tensions of self-sufficient power, the term "sovereign democracy" does not rule out its autocratic interpretation. For instance, in his comments on this Leonid Poliakov (2007, pp. 62-63) interprets sovereignty as the right to overrule decisions deriving from any other sources of power located both inside and outside national borders. Viewed from this angle, sovereignty means first of all self-sufficient power concentrated in a single source. Not surprisingly, members of the Russian elite interviewed by *VTsIOM*—a state-owned public opinion center—appear deeply divided and ambiguous in their perception of sovereign democracy: only 40 percent of them acknowledge its usefulness, whereas 54 percent adopt a skeptical stance (the number of skeptics tends to be higher in capital cities, among members of the scientific, legal elite and leaders of mass organizations; see *Summa ideologij*, 2008, pp. 47-51).
6. The groundwork for this approach was laid down by Weber (1968, pp. 1059-1068—in a section on tsarist patrimonialism in *Economy and Society*) and Pipes in his *Russia under the Old Regime*. "Russia belongs par excellence to [the] category of states which in political and sociological literature it has become customary to refer to as 'patrimonial'" (Pipes, 1974, p. xxii).
7. Cf. "The power of the patrimonial official is, in essence, limited only by tradition; its violation is dangerous even for the most powerful official" (Weber, 1968, p. 1094).

8. For instance, in 2007 (and 2006) only 23 percent of Russians still considered the November 7 memorial day, the anniversary of the October 1917 revolution, a true holiday—despite all the importance attached to it in Soviet times (Analitichesky tsentr Yuriia Levady, 2007, p. 264; see also Table 4.8). According to a completely different account, Russia—along with the other post-Soviet countries—lies far from the ideal type of traditional authority and justification (Inglehart, 1995, pp. 444-449).
9. As early as in the fifteenth century, during the time of Muscovite tsars' expeditions to Novgorod and Pskov, it was believed that such exercises of power necessitated justification. Novgorod chronicles covering these events emphasized only facts, whereas Muscovite chroniclers went further and tried to justify the war waged by one Slavic state against the other. "It was important to explain and justify a 'crusade' against the city of Novgorod.... Because of this in the Moscow chronicle ... the prince of Moscow and his 'loyal' local supporters in Novgorod oppose the Moscow-Orthodox faith to the Lithuanian-Catholic one" (Ermakov et al., 2004, p. 242).
10. Attention to the degree of asymmetry also facilitates the task of developing quantitative—ratio-level—measures of Russian power, as opposed to presence/absence—nominal-level—measures.
11. If one measures the five attributes at the nominal level, e.g., present/absent, then this analytical model arguably describes Russian power throughout history, including most recent developments. However, if one measures them at the ordinal or ratio level, e.g., the degree of the asymmetry of power relationships, then some variations can be expected.
12. In this sense, power in its pure form characterizes "simple" societies as opposed to "complex" or "modern" ones. In a "complex" society each functional subsystem—the market, politics, science, etc.—has its own hierarchy, distributive criteria and corresponding asymmetrical distribution of rights and obligations (Walzer, 1983; Boltanski & Thévenot, 1991). The person who has few rights in one sphere can still achieve a superior position in the other. In "simple" societies, rights are unequally distributed in favor of the same group of people everywhere.

4

Continuity and Change in the Prevailing Model of Power: On Path-Dependence in Russian History

Introduction: Power as a Key for Understanding Russian History

Michael Mann (1986, p. 1) claims to add a new, previously under-explored, dimension to historical analysis by highlighting the role of power relationships in human history. "I have arrived at a distinctive, general way of looking at human societies that is at odds with models of society dominant within sociology and historical writing…. Societies are constituted of multiple overlapping and intersecting socio-spatial networks of power." The emphasis on power and its structures, however, has long characterized writings about Russian history. The present chapter aims to outline various aspects of this discrepancy between Western and Russian historiography, its sources as well as some of its outcomes.

The interest in the issues of power and its impact on historical process can be considered a *differentia specifica* of Russian historiography since its origins. Various ideological and theoretical approaches within it all acknowledge the importance of the issues of power. The focus on the state and other structures of political power "can be considered a common denominator of Russian socio-historical and political thought, regardless its particular stream: conservative, liberal, Leninist or social-democrat; traditionalist (*slavianofil'stvo*) or modernist (*zapadnichestvo*)" (Makarenko, 1998, p. 153; see also Krivosheev, 2008, pp. 10-11; Afanasiev, 2000, p. 29). Nikolai Karamzin, a prominent Russian historian and writer of the late eighteenth—the early nineteenth centuries was probably the first to equate the history of Russia and the history of power in Russia in a manifest and unambiguous manner (Pivovarov, 2004, p. 76).

The exclusive emphasis on power derives from its transformation into a quasi-unique driving force in Russian history. "Power should be written with a capital letter—Power. It is a leading force of the historical process" (Pivovarov, 2006a, p. 144). In practical terms, this means that changes in Russian history proceed in a "top-down" manner, necessitating the use of power as a lever. Attempts to modernize the country are no exception. They rely on power as a key resource even when reforms are intended to deprive power of its unique status and promote a more active involvement of actors other than those vested in political power (Gaman-Golutvina, 2006, p. 315; Holmes, 1994, p. 31).[1]

The exclusive reliance on power means that it replaces other coordination devices, namely trust (see Chapter 2). As a result, horizontal interactions tend to be mediated by a third party, an actor vested in political power. There exists a drift into excessive regulation of social, economic and political relationships: power starts structuring all of them. "The mediator, while trying to strengthen the organization of power, simultaneously undermines sources of the initiative of the masses" (Akhiezer, 1997, p. 168; see also Morozov, 1991, Issue 2, p. 108).

Notwithstanding numerous writings on power in Russian history, few efforts have been made so far to systematize them. This leaves important questions open, namely how the discourse about Russian power has been structured and whether there have been changes in the underlying phenomenon—the prevailing model of power relationships—over time. These research questions serve as guidelines in the following.

The discourse refers to "the way a particular set of linguistic categories relating to an object and the ways of depicting it frame the way people comprehend that object" (Bryman, 2004, p. 370). This chapter discusses various categories that help historians to make sense of the model of power prevailing in the Russian institutional context. Just like any other humans, historians are involved in social action while conducting their research: they react and adjust (for instance, endorse or criticize) to what others say and do. Hence, the categories and their uses by various authors shall not be taken separately; the correct interpretation of their meaning implies putting them in the context of interactions. In this regard, Quentin Skinner (2002a, p. 118) urges that "our main attention should fall not on individual authors but on the more general discourse of their times." Public discussions between Russian historians in the course of which they confront alternative approaches and conceptualizations were not rare in the past, with the public dispute between Mikhail Pogodin and Nikolai Kostomarov in March 1860 being a prime example (Publichny disput..., 1860). More recently, disputes take on less manifest forms and tend to be mediated through the text (sometimes the opponent is not even named, only implied[2]), which complicates the task of "deciphering" the discourse.

In a sense, the categories and concepts of power not only describe, but also constitute it. "The thought style sets the preconditions of any cognition, and it determines what can be counted as a reasonable question and true or false answer" (Douglas, 1986, p. 13). The discourse contains a number of templates for action indicating a thinkable course of actions, "the range of things that speakers are capable of doing in (and by) the use of words and sentences" (Skinner, 2002a, p. 3). This assumption implies that, by studying the historical discourse of power, one gains insights into the constitution of power, its stability or changes over time.

To summarize, the task of this chapter is two-fold. First, it analyzes the discourse of Russian historiography from the nineteenth century onward with respect to the prevailing model of political power. A major limit of the proposed study is its reliance on secondary sources—writings of Russian historians about power. For the purposes of discourse analysis, they appear more relevant than primary sources, namely archival documents.

The discourse of Russian historians is compared with that of Western scholars, who play the role of a "control group." Western historians writing about Russian power are less dependent on the concepts elaborated and imposed by actors vested in it. David Beetham (1991, p. 62) makes a relevant observation: "Both the evidence and the interests of the subordinate are so structured that the justifications advanced for the rules of power prove plausible to them within the given social context. Their plausibility can only be challenged from a position or standpoint outside that context." The concepts constitute the phenomenon under investigation, power, and *vice versa*, the prevailing model of power influences its perception by individuals directly involved in the power relationships through shaping their discourse (see Section I of Chapter 3).[3] The "control group" serves to assess the former aspect more carefully.

The second task of the chapter consists in assessing the continuity and changes in Russian power seen through the lens of Russian historiography. Do the historians describe the model of political power prevailing in the Grand Duchy of Moscow, the Russian Empire and the Soviet Union in a similar manner? If so, the continuity of their discourse suggests that the same "range of things"—uses of power—remain conceivable and possible in Russia.

The chapter is organized in four sections. The first section discusses key concepts in the historical discourse about Russian power. The notion of path-dependence is introduced in Section II. It helps theorize assumed continuity in the prevailing model of power. Variability in power, on the other hand, calls for the notion of the repertoire of techniques for imposing will. Section III considers a popular explanation for continuity in Russian power. It refers to a harsh and hostile environment, both natural and geopolitical. Finally, Section IV explores what historians say about Russian power during particular periods of time. Some consistent patterns in their assessments and disputes are considered in depth.

I. Lexicon of Russian Power

Skinner (2002a, Ch. 9) argues that a few key categories and concepts, which he refers to as the "cultural lexicon," describe the scope of the possible for all individuals, who are able to correctly understand and interpret them—for members of the same culture.[4] A lexicon structuring possible uses of power in the Russian institutional context would contain at least the following entries: supreme power, state, *samovlastie* and *samoderzhavie*.

I.1 Supreme Power

The independence of any higher instance makes power "supreme." There are some parallels between the concept of supreme power (*verkhovnaia vlast'*) and that of sovereignty conventionally used in the Western political and historical discourse. A sovereign state "is independent of any higher authority in the legal control of its own domain; [...] there is no superior legal authority to which it can appeal to confirm its own legitimacy, and to enforce its own rules" (Beetham, 1991, p. 122). However, the two concepts do not completely overlap. The failure to carefully differentiate them produces numerous confusions, both theoretical and practical.

Russian historians and political thinkers of the nineteenth century indicate three forms that supreme power can take in function of its subject: monarchy, aristocracy and democracy (Ivanovsky, 1895, p. 18; Tikhomirov, 2006, p. 29). In nineteenth century Russia, supreme power was vested in the monarchy, which, they continue, does not make it a case in its own right. However, putting people in the place of a monarch without changing other aspects of supreme power does not produce a democratic system. At best, a national-populist regime[5] with no internal checks and balances, no genuine representation of various social groups emerges.

Supreme power in all its three forms does not involve any division of powers. Various branches and bodies of power are ordered by rank instead, with supreme power at the top. The division of power exists only at the lower layers of the hierarchy, individuals and/or bodies vested in supreme power retain it in all domains. In other words, the Western concept of sovereignty describes a situation with at least three "superior authorities" (legislative, executive, and judiciary), none of which takes precedence of the others. The three branches of power appear subordinate to supreme power in the Russian context (see also Figure 8.3).

The division of powers at the lower layers of the hierarchy results from the overextension of power—it encompasses all activities in all domains (see also Section II of Chapter 2) rather than from conscious policies of checks and balances. The greater the extensiveness, the lower the effectiveness of power provided that supreme power does not rely on "lieutenants." "The influence of any power is restricted by certain limits" (Tikhomirov, 2006, p. 47).[6]

I.2 State

The existence of supreme power has a significant impact on the meaning attached to the concept of state. The emergence of the modern state in the West involved the differentiation of three bodies: that of ruler, that of state and that of society. State in a narrow, modern sense of this term refers to a system of administration (the executive branch of power) and the "means of coercive control that serve to preserve order within political communities" (Skinner, 2002b, p. 377). Society represents what French political philosophers call *volonté générale*, or priority given by people to their common rather than private interests (Boltanski & Thévenot, 1991, pp. 140-143). The English term "commonwealth" further develops this idea (Skinner, 2002b, pp. 385-386).

In a pre-modern situation, the three elements form a single, undifferentiated whole. Thorstein Veblen (1939, 161) highlights this aspect when characterizing the German state in the late nineteenth century. It "is neither the territorial area, nor the population, nor the body of citizens or subjects, nor the aggregate wealth or traffic, nor the public administration, nor the government, nor the crown, nor the sovereign; yet in some sense it is all these matters, or rather all these organs of the state. In some potent sense, the State is a personal entity, with rights and duties superior and anterior to those of the subjects, whether these latter be separately or collectively, in detail or in the aggregate or average."

Supreme power makes the process of differentiation hierarchical. The separate identities of the ruler, the state and the society were recognized in Russian historical and political discourse by the start of the eighteenth century (Kharkhordin, 2001, p. 225; Pipes, 1974, pp. 68-69). However, instead of three "sovereigns" the differentiation produced a hierarchy with the body vested in supreme power at the top, the state subordinated to it and the society ruled by the state (Figure 1.1).[7] The subordination of the state to the supreme power accounts for some of the difficulties with translating the main Russian term for the state, *gosudarstvo*, into English. Richard Pipes (1974, p. 78) suggests that "although we translate *gosudarstvo* as 'state' a more accurate equivalent would be 'domain,'" the realm under control of the master of a household.

The subordination of society to state gives rise to a police state heavily involved in regulating and "guiding" the everyday interactions of ordinary people. The police state does not necessarily have purely negative connotations[8]—it can have a civilizing mission. "Until almost the eve of 1789 Europeans viewed the development of civilized conditions as the result of action by the state rather than of the spontaneous operation of society. An *état policé* and an *état civilizé* meant roughly the same thing" (Malia, 1999, p. 28). The 1789 French revolution showed that societies in the West were ready for more autonomous action. The Russian discourse, on the other hand, derives from the belief that the society needs the state's guidance in its quest for welfare. The Russian police state implies "coercive activities carried out exclusively by governmental forces and aimed to increase welfare of the state and the population" (Ivanovsky, 1895, p. 57).[9]

I.3 Supreme Power: Attempts to Differentiate Despotism from Monarchy

When describing supreme power, Russian historians and political scientists focused on several features. First, supreme power excludes references to superior principles or authorities. It does not need any external justification. "Such power does not derive from anything, it does not depend on anything but on itself, and it has no other prerequisites to its existence but itself" (Tikhomirov, 2006, p. 89).

Second, the individual or the group of people vested in supreme power has full discretion when applying it. Nothing prevents them from transforming power into a resource for enhancing their privileges even more, instead of using it as a means to achieve other ends that have a broader appeal. The ruler can act "in a discretionary manner, according to his whims and interests only, without being concerned with welfare and interests of people" (Ivanovsky, 1895, p. 65).

Third, the lack of constraints also means the widespread use of violent techniques for imposing will. All other conditions being equal, the subject of supreme power prefers the shortest and simplest way to get what he wants from the subordinates. Hence, violence shall be added to the list of key features characterizing supreme power (Pivovarov, 2006a, p. 7).

Fourth, supreme power allows those who have it to enjoy rights without assuming any obligations vis-à-vis the subordinates (Khlopin, 1997, pp. 67-68; Morozov, 1991, Issue 2, p. 113). They make all the key decisions and take all the initiatives. "No one but the [supreme] ruler renders justice or grants privileges, powers of anyone else derive from [supreme power]" (Karamzin, 1991, p. 24). Supreme power does not tolerate independent and alternative sources of power, the principle of one-man management (*edinonachalie*) reigns at all layers of the hierarchy, down to the enterprise, the university or the workshop (Gregory, 1990, p. 57).

Fifth, links between supreme power and the ruled do not necessarily include feedback loops because all initiatives originate at the top of the hierarchy. Existing feedback loops perform a very particular function: instead of facilitating the information flow about the situation of ordinary people and their needs, they help the bearer of supreme power control his "lieutenants," the state apparatus. This is why, for instance, in the fifteenth century the ruler, Ivan IV the Terrible, encouraged ordinary people to submit their complaints and individual petitions about the eventual opportunism and misconduct of his representatives from the emerging state apparatus. In 1550, he even established a particular department, *chelobitny prikaz*, with a corresponding mandate (Livshin & Orlov, 2002, p. 100; Tikhomirov, 2006, pp. 245-249).

The characteristics of supreme power outlined above make a perfect match for the ideal type of Russian power discussed in Section II of Chapter 3. This leads to the assumption that supreme power represents the quintessence of Russian power, its practical realization. The concept of Russian power entered Russian historical discourse relatively recently. The evolution of supreme power since its emergence in the twelfth century has been conceptualized by Russian historians mainly in terms of *samoderzhavie* and *samovlastie* (see Section I of Chapter 3). As for the Western historical discourse about supreme power, it has been increasingly dominated by the concept of patrimonial power. All the three concepts incorporate the five features of supreme power yet they imply different emphases. Tensions between the alternative concepts and the corresponding debates between their advocates appear highly relevant as to the question about the continuity and changes in the prevailing model of power relationships.

Both *samoderzhavie* and *samovlastie* mean a highly centralized, autonomous and self-sufficient system of power. In the case of *samoderzhavie*, however, there exists a superior principle that guides actions of the subject vested in it. Religious beliefs—Orthodox Christian[10]—limit the ruler's discretion. Under *samoderzhavie*, "the monarch's will is clearly and unambiguously subordinated to God" (Tikhomirov, 2006, p. 87). The ruler simply translates the will of God, being his representative, or "lieutenant" on Russian soil.[11]

The reference to the ruler as a monarch in the above-cited statement deserves comment. For Karamzin and several other Russian historians, including Lev Tikhomirov, *samoderzhavie* equals a "true monarchy" (Pipes, 2005, p. 61). A "false monarchy," on the other hand, denies any restrictions on the ruler's will, which paves the way toward despotism. "A despotic monarchy, or *samovlastie*, differs from a true monarchy because under *samovlastie* the monarch's will does not have any objective guidance" (Tikhomirov, 2006, p. 87).

Returning to the five characteristics of supreme power, the key difference between *samoderzhavie* and *samovlastie* concerns the first of them, the presence or absence of a superior principle. The superior principle takes the form of religious faith, which places *samoderzhavie* into cell IIIh of Table 2.2, or law, as in the case of constitutional monarchy (cell IIIg). In the latter case, there are several parallels between *samoderzhavie* and Western monarchies that justify the eventual translation of this Russian term into English as "monarchy." "The distinguishing feature of monarchies is the rule of law, and the cooperation between the crown and the 'intermediate and dependent orders,' of which the most important is the nobility. In despotism (or tyranny) the whim of the monarch takes the place of law, and the rights of the estates are violated by the government which wishes to administer the whole country directly" (Pipes, 2005, pp. 60-61).

Samoderzhavie and *samovlastie* share, nevertheless, the four other features. This prevents them from being viewed as "limited power," even in the case of *samoderzhavie*, and causes numerous controversies in the discourse about supreme power. A legal scholar insists that "in the old Russian law *samoderzhavie* ... was closely associated with the word 'unlimited'" (Gribovsky, 1912, p. 24). A number of other scholars are of the same opinion (Pivovarov, 2006a, p. 7). Other scholars strongly object to this characterization, emphasizing that *samoderzhavie* involves a set of constraints limiting the discretion of those who are vested in it. "*Samoderzhavie* cannot be 'unconstrained' as unlimited power excludes the emergence of *samoderzhavie*" (Bol'shakov & Ermachkov, 1999, p. 77).

The Western discourse about supreme power acknowledges the importance of the opposition between despotism and monarchy. However, there is a clear tendency towards preferring the former concept to the latter. It takes manifest forms with the rise in popularity of the concept of patrimonial power as a particular form of despotism. Since the early 1990s, with the spread of Western theories in the post-Soviet social sciences, a growing number of Russian scholars have incorporated the concept of patrimonialism in their analyses (Pivovarov, 2004, p. 65; Fisun, 2003). Under patrimonial regimes, "the lines separating ownership from sovereignty either do not exist, or are so vague as to be meaningless, and ... the absence of this distinction marks a cardinal point of difference between western and non-western types of government" (Pipes, 1974, p. xxi). Seen from this perspective, well specified and enforced property rights constitute a new constraint of the ruler's discretion, along with religious faith and law (in fact, the law of property is a particular domain of the law). Alternatively, the ruler grants property rights to his subordinates (for instance, in order to reward their service), and also takes them back at will. "In the age of absolutism in Russia, unlike most of Western Europe, property presented no barrier to royal power" (Pipes, 2000, p. 180).

Does the tension between monarchy and despotism immediately undermine the initial assumption of the continuity in the prevailing model of power? No indeed: the same historical periods are often described using all three terms (one group of scholars opts for *samoderzhavie*, the second—for *samovslatie*, the third—for patrimonial power). Then what factors could account for a preference for one of them? It is time to develop some tentative hypotheses that will be considered more in-depth in Section IV.

The first possible reason for preferring one concept over the other lies in the different intentions of the scholar. The intentions of historians vary, which has an impact on their language: the use of a concept signifies the acceptance of a particular path of action, as Skinner argues. The author either adapts a critical or a sympathetic stance towards arguably unchanging supreme power. The sympathetic stance involves attempts to prove its legitimacy by showing its conformity to some superior principles, and the concept of monarchy enables the historian to do so. The mere nature of supreme power stimulates the search for justification: "people generally possess strong motives for seeking to legitimize any conduct liable to appear questionable" (Skinner, 2002a, p. 155). The critical stance, on the other hand, represents a reaction to these attempts, also natural because of the questionable and controversial nature of the underlying phenomenon. In other words, supreme power inescapably produces debates and controversies in the discourse about it.

The second possible reason implies some variability in supreme power that coexists with the stability of its core features over time. The possible combination of continuity and changes calls for introducing additional theoretical considerations in the next section.

II. Path Dependence and the Repertoire of Techniques for Imposing Will

The idea that the past has a significant impact on human interactions in the present is hardly new for historians.[12] An approach to theorize links between the past and the present initially developed by Douglass North seems particularly relevant because it highlights the inherent continuity in the institutional evolution of a country throughout history. The concept of path dependence occupies a central place in this approach. The range of options and alternatives available at any point in time is progressively narrowing because of the choices and events that have preceded it. "The consequence of small events and chance circumstances can determine solutions that, once they prevail, lead one to a particular path" (North, 1990, p. 94; see also Hedlund, 2005; Aslanov, 2009, pp. 82-82).

Several Russian historians and social scientists with an interest in history, even those who do not refer to North in an explicit manner, consider Russian history as path dependent. Svetlana Kirdina, for example, analyzes an "institutional matrix" that structures political, economic and social interactions in Russia throughout its history. The matrix represents a "stable, historically given set of core institutions" (Kirdina, 2001, p. 59) whose origins go back to the emergence of Russian states (Ibid, p. 7). The matrix includes a component responsible for the continuity in the political sphere (a hierarchical system of governance). The political, economic and ideological components are deemed equally important in this theory. In terms of the approach proposed here, however, the model of power would represent a core element of the institutional matrix and have an impact on all its other components.[13]

Aleksandr Akhiezer develops the other influential conceptualization of Russian history. In his view, the history of this country can be understood as a sequence of two long-term cycles, the first going from the Kievan Rus' to the October 1917 revolution and the second—from the October 1917 revolution to the fall of the Soviet Union in 1991. Both cycles have a similar structure. They "include three stages: the starting point, for instance, a communitarian ideal, the opposite pole, for instance, an authoritarian ideal and again the starting point, but this time enriched by the passage through direct and opposite inversions" (Akhiezer, 1997, p. 348). In contrast to a dialectical relationship between thesis, antithesis and synthesis in the traditions of German philosophy, the cyclical movement back and forth between the two poles produces little change in the Russian case. The system of governance and, hence, the institutional system as a whole, appear "locked in" this particular—cyclical—path. "It is not excluded, continues Akhiezer (1997, p. 733), that the third global cycle [started in 1991] would not open a way out, toward a liberal civilization, either."

Yuri Pivovarov and Oxana Gaman-Golutvina focus more specifically on path dependence in the evolution of Russian political institutions. Pivovarov emphasizes the continuity in principles according to which function organizations that embody supreme power: the court of the czar in the sixteenth—eighteenth centuries, the chancellery of his imperial majesty emperor of Russia in the nineteenth century, the Central Committee of the Communist Party of the Soviet Union in the twentieth century and the Presidential Executive Office most recently (Pivovarov, 2006b, p. 21). This continuity leads him to insist that "what we observe today does not mean a return to Soviet times. This is a more general return to the situation that has always existed" (Pivovarov, 2006a, p. 144). Gaman-Golutvina also agrees with the thesis that the political systems in the Grand Duchy of Moscow, the Russian Empire and the Soviet Union form a continuum. Such features as the central role of politics, the predominance of duties over rights for everyone but the ruler and the social hierarchy deriving from duties characterize all of them (Gaman-Golutvina, 2006, p. 227).

The idea of path dependence in Russian history finds some support in writings by Western scholars too. Like Gaman-Golutvina, Richard Hellie

(2005) sees continuity in the prevalence of state service throughout all Russian history. He discusses three periods in it—three "service-class revolutions"—that correspond to various techniques employed by supreme power in order to secure obedience of its "lieutenants." According to him, power has transformed into a unique key for solving all problems in Russia and has replaced the other solutions, which makes this country path-dependent.

Karl Ryavec's main ambition also consists in showing the continuity in the operation of the Russian state, this middle layer of the triplet ruler/state/ruled. Yet he focuses on a shorter period of time: from the late Russian empire up to the present. "Lasting patterns of thought and operation in Russian administration ... exist in one country over a period of more than a century and under three or more very different regimes" (Ryavec, 2003, p. 1).

Stefan Hedlund (2005, p. 25) considers the other form of path dependence, namely "a protracted absence of the rule of law." The failure to constrain the ruler by legal bounds—a distinctive feature of supreme power—has been observed from the old Muscovite order through the Soviet system. It is worth noting that some scholars include the most recent, post-Soviet, period, in the overall continuum, whereas others do not. The exploration of the question as to whether the most recent developments are "path-dependent" or not will guide the discussion in the following chapters.

A theory explaining path dependence in terms of ideology and mental models appears most relevant in the present context.[14] According to it, institutions do not change easily because they are embedded in an ideology as a particular world-view—and a corresponding set of concepts and categories. "The situation of today shapes the institutions of tomorrow through a selective, coercive process, by acting upon men's habitual view of things, and so altering or fortifying a point of view or a mental attitude banded down from the past" (Veblen, 1934, pp. 190-191; see also Zinvoviev, 1994, p. 257). Returning to the concepts and categories describing the prevailing model of power in Russia, their links with the past limit what current users of them "are capable of doing in (and by) the use of [these] words and sentences" and, hence, contribute to the continuous reproduction of the underlying model.

Ideology has its own dynamics that prevents significant changes. Namely, it produces a tendency toward interpreting any new experience in terms that derive from the past experience. Categories and concepts do not change at the same pace as the events and external conditions that they help interpret and make sense of (Denzau & North, 1994). As a result, "the subjective models of actors modified by very imperfect feedback and by ideology will shape the path" (North, 1990, p. 95; see also Zinoviev, 1994, pp. 41-42).

The theory of path dependence sheds some light on the continuity in supreme power: one of the mechanisms for reproducing an initial pattern of interactions consists in the continuous existence of a mental framework that it initially gave rise to. This theoretical framework, nevertheless, does not allow for introducing variability in the model of supreme power, which is necessary to explain oscillations that have been observed between *samovlastie* and *samoderzhavie* in the discourse about it. Consequently, the task of studying eventual variability around the general trend (path) requires further theoretical considerations.

Are all the five characteristics of supreme power equally stable over time? To put it differently, eventual variability in which characteristics would not undermine the status and functions of supreme power in the Russian institutional system? Although supreme power does not have built-in constraints, as has been shown previously, its exercise reaches some objective limits. For instance, its all-encompassing scope calls for the emergence of the state as an independent yet subordinate body. The set of the techniques for imposing will available at a given point in time also limit the ruler's discretion. "Objectives of individuals and groups vested in power are limited by the means at their disposal" (Makarenko, 1998, p. 63). These techniques vary in function of the stage of institutional evolution and depend on the availability of particular institutions and organizations, such as prison, the mass media or the market. When a new technique becomes available, it extends the scope of the possible for the ruler. Pivovarov (2006a, p. 171; 2006b, p. 55) reduces "revolutions" in the Russian context to major additions to the repertoire of techniques for imposing will. As long as techniques for imposing will remain violent (see Subsection II.3 of Chapter 3), however, their variability does not affect the overall character of supreme power.

The concept of repertoire serves to theorize changes in the violent techniques for imposing will. It was initially, in the late 1970s, developed by Charles Tilly and applied to studies of collective action. "The word 'repertoire' identifies a limited set of routines that are learned, shared, and acted out though a relatively deliberate process of choice... Repertoires are learned cultural creations ... at any particular point in history.... [People] learn only a rather small number of alternative ways to act collectively" (Tilly, 1995, p. 26). Since trust and power represent alternative coordination devices, different manners for organizing social action, the same observation applies to power relationships. Then the repertoire of techniques for imposing will refers to a limited set of alternative ways for securing obedience as a necessary precondition for using power to coordinate actions.

The concept of repertoire has two interpretations, purely instrumental and discursive. "Like their instrumental counterparts, which create templates for action, discursive repertoires provide contenders with a vocabulary of motives that can be used to legitimate their actions" (Traugott, 1995, p. 7). In the same vein, the discursive repertoire of techniques for imposing will provides the ruler with a vocabulary for making them acceptable to office holders (state servants) and the ruled (ordinary people). This means that the concept of repertoire also fits the methodological approach applied here, namely the inquiry into power relationships through an analysis of the discourse about it.

To summarize, continuity in the prevailing model of power relationships makes Russian history path dependent because power represents the centerpiece of the institutional environment in this country. This continuity can coexist with some variability, mainly in the repertoire of techniques for imposing will, as long as changes do not affect the essentially violent nature of these techniques (i.e., they remain in the range of the top five rows, [a] through [e], of Table 2.2).

III. Is Supreme Power a Result of Adverse Natural Conditions?

The theory of path dependence suggests that any event—however small and random it happens to be—could start a long-lasting path in the evolution of an institutional system. What events could lie at the origin of the specific model of power relationships embodied in supreme power? A popular explanation in Russian historiography emphasizes the adverse character of the environment, both natural and geopolitical, in which the Russian state has emerged and developed. On the one hand, the climate and soil in this part of Eurasia do not favor agriculture, which depends on the weather. A shortage of natural resources—oil and gas started to be appreciated relatively recently (cf. Subsection III [d1] of Chapter 8)—was a usual situation in early periods in Russian history. On the other hand, the warfare that was common everywhere in Europe (Tilly, 1985) became an especially recurrent pattern of interactions with the neighboring countries in the case of Russia.

To survive in such harsh and hostile conditions, human beings need to achieve a maximum concentration of their efforts. One cannot count on a spontaneous mobilization, as the argument goes; there is an acute need for the use of power on a continuous basis. "The model of development based on mobilization derives from the shortage of key resources.... The lack of freedom inside the country was a price to be paid for the independence of the external enemy" (Gaman-Golutvina, 2006, pp. 35, 37; see also Aslanov, 2009, p. 138; Tikhomirov, 2006, p. 13; Kirdina, 2001, p. 77).

Western scholars tend to acknowledge the importance of this factor. For instance, after comparing the fertility of soil in northern Russia and northern Europe, Pipes concludes that power and hierarchy are a necessary prerequisite for the accumulation of wealth above the subsistence level in the former, but not in the latter case. "Under the adverse economic conditions prevailing in Russia, groups aspiring to rise above the subsistence level had but one option open to them, and that was to collaborate with the state—in other words, to give up political ambition" (Pipes, 1974, p. 249). Hellie (2005, p. 88), in his turn, sees a rationale in the hypothesis linking recurrent wars with the neighbors to the rise of what he calls a "service class" (composed of "lieutenants" of supreme power).

This reasoning produces the following hypothesis (H_1): parameters of the external environment explain peculiarities of power in Russia.[15] Supreme power then finds its justification not in law or religious faith, but in the adverse external environment. If this hypothesis is confirmed, then supreme power enhances the ability to "act in concert" under these conditions.

Despite its popularity in Russian historiography, hypothesis H_1 has never been statistically tested using the data collected by historians. Although an empirical test involves a methodology that is different from discourse analysis, the quantitative test would significantly improve our understanding of the mechanism of path dependence by opposing external factors to factors under control of actors forming the triplet ruler/state/ruled. Were H_1 rejected, this would serve as an additional argument for focusing our attention on the discourse about power.

Hypothesis H_1 involves a causal relationship, under which three conditions must be met (Babbie & Benaquisto, 2002, p. 65): (i) the cause precedes the effect; (ii) the two variables are empirically associated and (iii) the observed association cannot be explained in terms of some third variable. The failure to meet at least one of these criteria would lead us to reject H_1. The empirical test refers more specifically to condition (ii) and has several components. At the first stage, it was run using the data from a comprehensive chronology of the most important events throughout Russian history (Rossiia, 2002). Special attention was paid to wars, especially defensive, initiated by countries other than Russia, because they serve as a proxy for the adverse external environment. The sequence of wars was compared with that of political regimes, using the classification of various decades into two groups: despotic and non-despotic, developed by Akhiezer (1997, p. 799).

It appears that for, the 113 decades from the 880s to the last decade of the twentieth century included in the sample there is no statistically significant difference in the frequency of wars during the "despotic" decades as compared to the "non-despotic" ones (with elements of communitarianism, or *sobornost'*, in Akhiezer's own words). On average, defensive wars lasted 1.34 years during the "despotic" decades and 1.14 years during the "non-despotic" ones. The *t*-test for equality of means shows that the difference is not statistically significant (Table 4.1).[16] It is worth noting that aggressive wars started by Russia were more frequent during the "despotic" decades, yet the difference only approaches the level of statistical significance. These outcomes fail to support hypothesis H_1.

At the second stage, the other sources of information about supreme power—and the other proxy for it—are used, which helps increase the reliability of the results. The test was based on the assumption that the "despotic" years (the unit of observation being year, not decade because of a shorter period of time) tended to be associated with more violent techniques for imposing will (for example, force), as measured by the number of people held behind prison bars divided by the total population (prison population ratio, PPR). The data on PPR covers the twentieth century only or, in other words, the second long-term cycle of Russian

Table 4.1
Group Statistics for the Average Duration of Wars under Despotic and Non-Despotic Political Regimes in Russian History

	Political regime	N	Mean duration	Standard Deviation	Standard Error Mean
Defensive war	Despotic	47	1.34	1.449	0.211
	Non-despotic	66	1.14	1.691	0.208
Aggressive war started by Russia	Despotic	46	1.89	2.387	0.352
	Non-despotic	66	1.27	1.802	0.222

Source: Rossiia, 2002 and the author's calculations

Continuity and Change in the Prevailing Model of Power   117

history according to Akhiezer. Two reasons account for this limitation. First, in Russia, as in most Western countries (Foucault, 1975), force as a technique for imposing will started to be embedded in the institution of prison relatively recently, since the nineteenth century. Prison was preceded by capital and corporal punishments and tortures. Second, the data on PPR in Russia covering the nineteenth century appear extremely scarce and non-systematic (it does not cover the entire Russian empire). The earliest known data dates back to 1820 and does not cover the two capital cities, for instance (Gernet, 1941, p. 229).

The t-test provides some support for the assumption that the "despotic" years had higher average PPRs, the pattern appears particularly manifest for the 1930s and 1940s (Figure 4.1). The mean PPR for the "despotic" years is 749.63 (prisoners per 100,000 of the total population), whereas the mean PPR for the "non-despotic" years is 474.62.[17]

Figure 4.1
Dynamics of Prison Population Ratio in the Twentieth Century, the Soviet Union

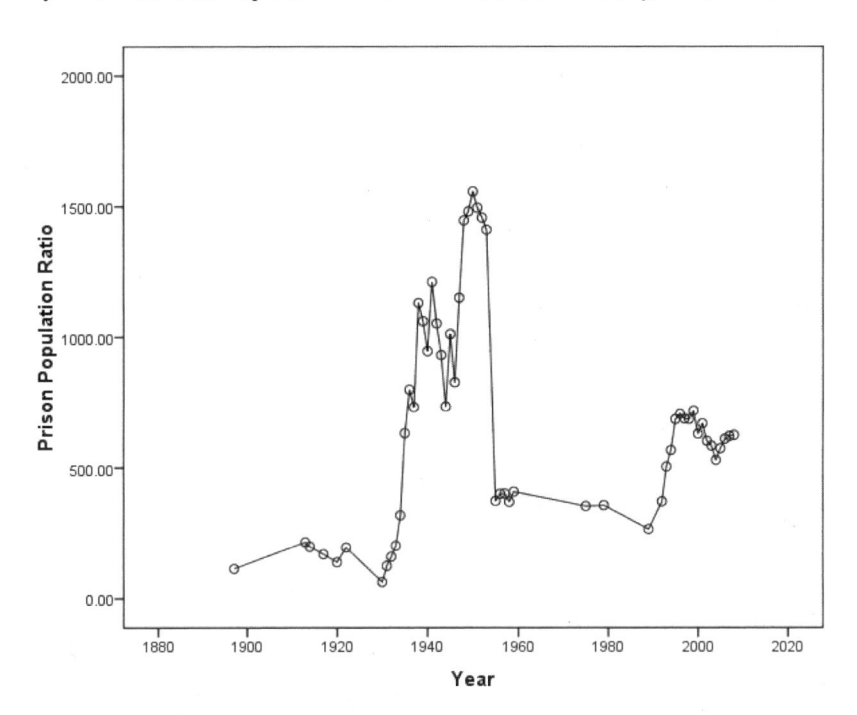

Sources: Gosudarstvenny komitet Rossijskoj Federatsii po statistike, 2003; Obshchestvo "Memorial," 1998

However, the *t*-test also shows that PPR does not differ significantly in function of the involvement of Russia in a defensive war. The mean PPR for years when Russia (the Soviet Union) was in a defensive war equals 666.87, which is very close to the mean PPR for years with no such involvement (627.02). In other words, the violent techniques for imposing will may indeed be associated with the "despotic" political regime, yet the test fails to confirm their eventual association with the adversary external conditions.

The reported outcomes of the series of statistical tests suggest that particularities of supreme power may be connected to some human-made factors inside the country instead of being derived from the adversary geopolitical conditions. During a time of defensive wars, supreme power does not get closer to its ideal type. On the contrary, the intensity of its characteristics may weaken, which draws the prevalent model of power away from its pure form.[18] It also provides some indirect support for the central thesis of this chapter, namely the idea that path dependence in the evolution of supreme power is closely connected with the continuity in the discourse about it, whereas variations in this discourse could be attributed either to the stance of a particular author or to changes in the repertoire of techniques for imposing will.

IV. Discourse about Supreme Power: Continuity and Change

Historians barely refer to a unique and prevalent model of power relationships during the earliest period in Russian history going from the ninth to the eleventh century. On the one hand, states only started to emerge on the vast and scarcely populated territory between the Dniepr and Volga rivers. On the other hand, the ruler, *knyaz'*, and the population initially had very limited opportunities for interaction. The *knyaz'* found a major source of income in long-distance trade, but not in agriculture or crafts. "The Kievan State ... did not emerge out of the society over which it ruled" (Pipes, 1974, p. 34; see also Hedlund, 2005, p. 38). Hence, the need for coordinated action inside what later became the heartland of the Russian empire, by relying on power or by using the other coordination devices, was weak if not nonexistent.

At the same time, power structured relations between emerging states, their neighbors and trade partners, which may have had an impact on the composition of the repertoire of techniques for imposing will. Karl Polanyi (1957, pp. 59-63) shows close connections between long-distance trade and warfare, one of the most violent techniques for imposing will. Several wars initiated by the rulers of the Old Rus', namely military campaigns against Byzantium in 907 and 941, were undertaken to get or secure privileged access to the markets of the late Roman empire (Aslanov, 2009, p. 212). This means that such wars can be interpreted not only in terms of the application of brute force, but also as early attempts to dominate by virtue of a constellation in the market. After all, the rulers of the Old Rus' wanted to acquire exclusive commercial privileges for their countrymen and to protect them against competition from the other merchants. The same logic later guided the transformation of the market into a weapon (see Chapters 5, 6 and 7).

IV.1 Andrei Bogoljubsky

The twelfth century represents a starting point in the evolution of supreme power according to Russian historiography. Andrei Bogoljubsky, the *knyaz'* of the Rostov-Suzdal principality between 1157 and 1174, was the first ruler who had embodied supreme power, at least some of its core elements. Kostomarov (2007, p. 57) views him as a path-breaker, precisely in the sense attached to the word "path" here: "In the second half of the twelfth century an embryo of the trend that would later prevail in the Russian world ... emerged on the Rostov-Suzdal soil."[19] In contrast to his predecessors, who were involved in an endless succession wars caused by the system of appanage, he undertook the first comprehensive attempt to concentrate all powers in his hands and to achieve a status independent from his "constituency" whose voice was expressed by the *veche* (a gathering of representatives of all major groups and families living in capital and "senior" cities), from his extended family members and from traditions as eventual constraints of the ruler's discretion. For instance, he transferred the capital of the principality from the "senior" cities with the well-established *veches*, Rostov and Suzdal, to a "junior" city without strong traditions of public representation, Vladimir (Klyuchevsky, 1956, p. 323; Kostomarov, 2007, p. 61). Whatever imperfect democratic institution the *veche* was,[20] it limited the *knyaz'*s power.

The discourse about Andrei also produces first—judging by the chronological order of events—debates as to the applicability of the two concepts, *samovlastie* and *samoderzhavie*. A number of scholars consider Andrei's legacy in a negative light, especially taking into consideration the fact that the succession of wars resumed immediately after his death, which leads them to label his rule as an example of *samovlastie* (Tikhomirov, 2006, p. 211). The others follow Karamzin (2003, p. 125) appreciating Andrei's policies, which focused on concentrating power, and describing them in terms of *samoderzhavie* (Krivosheev, 2008, p. 25; Bol'shakov & Ermachkov, 1999, p. 18). It is worth noting that some historians from the former group prefer *samoderzhavie* simply as a reaction to the negative image of supreme power as seen through the lens of *samovlastie*. Vasily Klyuchevsky (1956, p. 324), in turn, remains undecided and leaves the question as to the choice between the two terms open: "Was [Andrei] guided by thoughtful principles of responsible *samoderzhavie* or by instincts of petty tyranny?" To summarize, the disagreement and debates appear to be caused less by the substantial characteristics of supreme power than by the value judgments implicit in each of the two concepts.

As far as techniques for imposing will are concerned, Andrei's rule further indicates that such violent techniques as physical force and domination by virtue of a constellation of interests in the market may complement one another. After staging a failed war in 1170 against the Republic of Novgorod the Great, a North-Western state that initially embodied an alternative, with elements of democracy and oligarchy, model of political power (Kostomarov, 2008), he finally succeeded in using the market as a lever to get the citizens of Novgorod the Great accept his will. The shortage of food and basic products experienced in the city of Novgorod the Great during the years that followed the war—its citizens were mostly involved in trade with Western Europe and dependent on the supply of the basic necessities from the neighboring states, mainly from the Rostov-Suzdal principality—gave Andrei a second chance (Karamzin, 2003, p. 124). The goods in shortage were finally offered, but "under certain conditions": citizens of Novgorod the Great had to realize that it was in their best interests to invite a *knyaz'* nominated by Andrei.

IV.2 The Mongol Yoke

The Mongol yoke covering, in the Russian case, the period from the thirteenth to fifteenth centuries represents the other important milestone in the evolution of supreme power. Developments in the model of power relationships during the yoke consist in the strengthening of the core features of supreme power that emerged previously, not in radical changes of the path. The loss of sovereignty—Russian princes transformed into "lieutenants," plenipotentiaries of the Mongol Khans—neither constrained the *knyaz*'s power with regard to his subjects nor brought him any closer to them. In fact, the opposite happened. The *knyaz'* retained full discretion as long as he managed to collect the amount of tribute requested by the Khans. By performing the role of a "tax farmer" successfully, the *knyaz'* was able to prevent the Mongols' interference in his other affairs. "Russian princes practically 'bought out' the right to collect the tribute: they secured the 'output' wanted by the *Ord* [the Mongol state in Eurasia] and appropriated a part of the collected amount as a payment for their own 'service'" (Aslanov, 2009, p. 250).

The tax farmer needs neither to justify his activities by referring to a superior principle, nor to obtain any feedback—except the tribute[21]—from the population. The tax farmer does not assume any obligations vis-à-vis the population either. When performing his role as the tax farmer, the *knyaz'* has to possess a comparative advantage in applying force only. Not surprisingly, Russian historians see the deepening gulf between the prince and the population during the Mongol yoke (Makarenko, 1998, p. 159) and consider the prince's power under these conditions as a pure example of *samovlastie* (Tikhomirov, 2006, p. 201). Pipes (2000, p. 167) offers a similar account: "the Mongol manner of administering Russia through the agency of princes-collaborators led to the liquidation of democratic institutions and laid the foundations of her future autocracy."

The model of power embodied in the metropolis, the *Ord*, significantly differed from those in the dominions.[22] Relationships between the Khans and their own population had far fewer elements of supreme power, even taking into consideration the army-like structure of the state and principles of the statehood. "Heads of military divisions simultaneously acted as heads of civil administration" (Nyam-Osor, 2003, p. 135). The law played a significantly more constraining role in the Mongol case. The Great *Yasa*, a collection of laws and principles deriving from Mongolian customs and traditions, was a publicly approved and regularly updated[23] document whose norms were compulsory for everyone, starting with a rank-and-file person up to the Great Khan. In other words, the Great Khan's power had elements of legal authority because of these mandatory references to the *Yasa* and *toru*, norms of the underlying customary law (Nyam-Osor, 2003, p. 93; Trepavlov, 1993, p. 38).

IV.3 Ivan III the Great

The rule of Ivan III the Great (1462-1505) marked not only the *de facto* end of the yoke, but also the moment when the basic features of supreme power acquired a stable and sustainable character. The fact that supreme power took its final shape leads Pivovarov (2006a, p. 98) to view this period as the start of a "Great revolution" of supreme power. Its essence consists less in the gathering of Russian lands—Ivan III managed to create a unitary state in the place of a number of smaller and fragmented principalities—than in the gathering of powers, to borrow an expression from Aleksandr Presnyakov (1998, Ch. X). The Great revolution resulted in the concentration of all powers in hands of the ruler, which deprived the other actors of any initiative and capacity to carry out their own will. The mechanism of public representation, the *veche*, ceased to exist, whereas a substitute for it, the *sobor*, had completely different functions. The *sobor* "does not have the spirit of a free public assembly proper to the *veche*, it is a consultative body established from time to time, sporadically, on supreme power's initiative. Opinions expressed at the *sobor* and its decisions do not have a bounding character for the representative of supreme power" (Ivanovsky, 1895, p. 48).

Office holders, "lieutenants" of supreme power, found the freedoms that they enjoyed previously severely undercut as a result of two policies implemented by Ivan III. First, the *kormlenie*, or the imposition of additional taxes in a natural form on the local population, represented a usual way to sustain representatives of the *knyaz'* in remote areas of his principality. Ivan III issued special charters (*ustavnaia gramota*) in which he set "limits on the right [of his representatives] to impose additional taxes as well their obligations to the local population" (Krivosheev, 2008, p. 94). In doing so, Ivan III used legal instruments to constrain the discretion of his representatives, but not his own power.

Second, Ivan the Great made property rights relative and dependent on his favors. In contrast to the previous periods, the unconditional property rights of the prince's "lieutenants," *votchina*, were converted into conditional ones, *pomestie*. One could obtain them only in exchange for services rendered to the prince. There was no legal guarantee for security of property rights or any legal enforcement mechanism, the will of the prince overruled the law (Klyuchevsky, 1957, p. 130; Akhiezer, 1997, p. 115). Secure property rights limited the prince's room for maneuvering and simultaneously increased the capacity for autonomous action of those who had them. Hence Pipe's (2000, p. 160) "contention that the critical factor in the failure of Russia to develop rights and liberties was the liquidation of landed property in the Grand Duchy of Moscow." Conditional property rights are a centerpiece of patrimonial regimes: the ruler considers the country to be his domain. Patrimonialsm, however, refers to one aspect of supreme power, which limits the usefulness of this concept.

The consolidation of supreme power produced some changes in the discourse about it. The title of *czar* (from *cesar*) replaced that of *knyaz'* (Bogoiavlensky, 2006, p. 383). Ivan III was the first to introduce the title of *czar* in internal affairs: even the title of Great *knyaz'* fails to highlight an outstanding status of its bearer, his self-sufficient and self-sustaining powers. In contrast to the other powers, those of the *czar* do not derive from any terrestrial source.

The fact that supreme power acquires a sustainable character also explains the intensification of the tensions between the Grand Duchy of Moscow and the Republic of Novgorod the Great. Moscow staged wars against Novgorod in the past too. Yet Ivan III made the task of taking control over this rich Northern territory one of his top priorities. The relative wealth and prosperity of the city of Novgorod the Great, resulting from its institutional organization centered on the economy (Gaman-Golutvina, 2006, p. 77), made it an attractive target for hostile takeovers. Nevertheless, very good reasons were needed to justify an attack by one Christian state against another.[24] A more plausible reason is the inherent tensions between the two opposing models of power that the two states embodied. Supreme power hardly tolerates a success story of a close neighbor governed according to principles that completely undermine its very idea. The city of Novgorod the Great "developed the idea of people's sovereignty to such extent that Moscow managed to overtake it [in 1477] and make its citizens to accept the rule of the Great *knyaz'* only by applying force" (Tikhomirov, 2006, p. 81).

The appointment of a successor represents an even clearer example of the complete discretion that Ivan III enjoyed. He had first appointed his grandson Dmitry and then changed his mind and selected his son from a second marriage, Vasily, to be his official successor. This situation, according to Kostomarov (2007) and Klyuchevsky (1957), is an expression of extreme *samovlastie* that had never been seen before in Russia. It also indicates a combination of family tyranny (cell [Ia-b] of Table 2.2) and tyranny in exercising political power (cell [IIIa-b]). Karamzin (2003, p. 338; see also Aslanov, 2009, p. 285) disagrees with such an assessment of Ivan the Great's legacy and views him as the first ruler who truly embodied *samoderzhavie*. Once again, it seems that the debate reflects value judgments and divergent "doings" more than disagreements about historical facts. For instance, Karamzin, when choosing Ivan III as a role model for *samoderzhets*, aspired to become an adviser and councilor to the Russian emperor (see Section I of Chapter 3), whereas Kostomarov had a long record of thinking and acting critically (starting with a year in prison in his youth and finishing with a ban on his teaching in the 1860s).

Last but not least, the observation with regard to the rule of Ivan III concerns the composition of the repertoire of techniques for imposing will. Karamzin (2003, p. 220) observes that "the strengthening of the Muscovite state is associated with a significant spread of violent means that it deploys." Namely, the active use of corporate punishment in public (*torgovaia kazn'*) and the birth of prison in Russia mark this period. The Old Rus' did not know either of these techniques.

IV.4 Ivan IV the Terrible

In spite of his greater renown due to numerous historical and literary works devoted to his controversial personality, Ivan IV the Terrible, who ruled between 1533 and 1584, mainly continued along the path taken under his less-known predecessors. His actions, from the most extravagant (such as the temporary transfer of the title of *czar* to a third person) to the most violent, became possible only in the context of supreme power.

Ivan IV's original contribution to strengthening supreme power has several facets. First, he further restricted the freedoms of his "lieutenants" and the capacity for carrying out their will, as opposed to enhancing their capacity for carrying out his own will. This was done by abolishing the voluntary character of the service rendered to the *czar* by Russian nobles, *boyarstvo*. On the one hand, they lost the right to change their master at will. Without abolishing this right, the *knyaz'* was dependent on his servicemen and had no other choice but to be engaged in endless consultations with them and justifications of his decisions (Bogoiavlensky, 2006, p. 321). Peasants did not escape a similar fate either: their right to move from one lord to another was initially made conditional on the lord's approval, then restricted to a few days in November and finally completely denied (Hedlund, 2005, p. 96).

On the other hand, Ivan IV expanded the scope of the system of conditional property (this implies granting property in exchange for services only) and systematically enforced it, for example, through the practices of the *oprichnina*. The name for a land grant received from the *czar*, *dacha* (literally—the "give away"), entered the Russian language during that period of time and has remained in active use since then (Kryshtanovskaya, 2005, p. 291).[25]

The second contribution of Ivan IV consists in his attempts to make sense of supreme power and its particularities. In contrast to his predecessors, whose "doings" do not always have a discursive dimension (or, at least, there are no primary sources proving the opposite), Ivan IV was actively involved in debates about supreme power in the course of which he attempted to justify its particular nature. His correspondence (six letters and a pamphlet in all) with *boyarin* Andrei Kurbsky, his former close ally, who fled to the Polish-Lithuanian commonwealth and became the first Russian political émigré, represent an insider's take on supreme power (Klyuchevsky, 1957, p. 168). He defended himself and the supreme power that he embodied against accusations of despotism (several historians characterize the rule of Ivan IV in exactly these terms; see Karamzin, 2003, p. 451; Malia, 1999, p. 31). Without denying such features of supreme power as self-sufficiency and an unlimited character, he insisted on its necessity and on the harm caused by alternative sources of power, notably the *boyarstvo*. Needless to say, Ivan IV used the term *samoderzhavie* when discussing supreme power, not *samovlastie* or despotism.

IV.5 Peter I the Great

The rule of Peter I the Great (1682-1725) probably attracted more attention from historians, especially if one counts Western contributions, than any other period of the "Old Regime."[26] As in all cases considered in this section, in this large body of literature only aspects related to the continuity of and eventual changes in supreme power are emphasized.

The predecessors (Vasily Shuisky and Mikhail Fedorovich) and immediate successors (Ekaterina I and Anna Ioannovna) of Peter I represent a small deviation from the general path: when being vested in supreme power, they accepted—in the form of *zapis'*, or a particular contract—some conditions limiting their own discretion and enhancing the powers of particular groups of the nobility (Ivanovsky, 1895, pp. 52, 58). All the deeds of Peter I, from his first to last day in power, were aimed at "purifying" supreme power from such alien conditions and bringing it even closer to its ideal type than ever. Probably for this reason, Pivovarov and Andrei Fursov (1998) view this period as a continuation of the "Great revolution" of supreme power that resulted in "the stealing, expropriation of the subjectivity ... in favor of one and only one element of the Russian social structure."

Like Ivan IV, Peter I viewed the *boyarstvo* as a source of alternative power that created undue interference with the ruler's will. As a result, he radically reduced the frequency of meetings of a council composed of representatives of the *boyarstvo* that he inherited from the past, *duma*, and transformed it into a new body, *Consilia*, with a clearer mandate for servicing the *czar* and executing his will (Bogoiavlensky, 2006, p. 332). As if conditional property rights and an improved system of service ranks to which it was tied was not sufficient to limit the nobility's autonomy, Peter I went further and directly intervened in the daily routines of his subjects. An assault on what in the West would be considered privacy—the imposition of new daily routines and customs by force—can be better understood in the context of suppressing all alternative sources of will, both at the macro and micro levels. "When shaving beards off and extracting teeth by his own hands, Peter I performed the role of a *czar*, not that of a barber. In doing so he shows his power to even most ambitious of his compatriots and forces them to accept his superiority even in purely private affairs" (Makarenko, 1998, p. 234).

A major breakthrough concerns relations between supreme power and the Church. As previously shown, tensions between the two concepts, *samovlastie* and *samoderzhavie*, derived from the eventual role of Orthodox Christianity in limiting supreme power. To accomplish this mission, Orthodox Christianity had to be embedded in a strong organizational structure independent of the ruler (see also Subsection III [h1] of Chapter 8). Peter I deprived the church of elements of the institutional autonomy it had before: he abolished the patriarchy (the head of the Orthodox Church, the patriarch, is elected by representatives of various parishes and, hence, has an independent source of legitimacy) and replaced it with an executive body headed by his appointee, the *Holy Synod* (Gaman-Golutvina, 2006, pp. 108-109). "The Petrine clergy were also state servitors who, among other things, were obliged to report to the state anything that sounded subversive heard in a confession or elsewhere" (Hellie, 2005, p. 100; see also Hedlund, 2005, p. 188; Pipes, 1974, p. 222).

The loss of the Church's autonomy undermines a key argument in favor of interpreting supreme power in terms of *samoderzhavie* as unlimited power guided by the will of God. "For supreme power ... the destruction of the Church created a deadly danger, that of the evolution into despotism" (Tikhomirov, 2006, p. 260). This term prevails in the discourse about the rule of Peter I (Bol'shakov & Ermachkov, 1999, p. 77; Karamzin, 1991, p. 35). An even more telling fact lies in the endorsement of the concept of *samovlastie* by Peter I himself. Peter I personally supervised the drafting of major laws and decrees. One of them, the Military Code (*Voenny Artikul*) defined the individual vested in supreme power in the following terms: "his Majesty is a *samovlastny* monarch, who does not report to anyone in the entire world and has power and force to govern his, as a Christian ruler, states and lands according to his own will" (Ivanovsky, 1895, p. 56). This suggests that according to Peter I, the idea of *samovlastie* better expresses his "doings."

However, there is no consensus in assessments by historians even in this case. Some scholars argue that Peter I did not have unlimited and self-justifying power because of repeated references to a lay version of the common good as opposed to its religious reading. After all, Peter I was the first to differentiate, at the discursive level, two components of the triplet ruler/state/ruled, the person of the *czar* and the body of the country (Kharkhordin, 2001, p. 219).

Martin Malia (1999, p. 29) traces parallels between "civilization proceeding from the top down, from the enlightened few to the ignorant many" in Europe until the events of 1789 and in Peter I's Russia. He stresses changes in the vocabulary that Europeans use to think and speak of Russia in terms of their own situation and "doings." When "doings" of Europeans and those of Russian rulers have "elective affinity," the discourse tends to be less critical (this means with lesser emphasis on despotism and *samovlastie*), and *vice versa*.

Changes in the repertoire of techniques for imposing will during the second half of the seventeenth century also have to be taken into consideration as an eventual factor for explaining the variability in the assessments. While the application of brute force (corporal and capital punishment) remained widespread, prison progressively gained ground. The major collection of laws, enacted in 1649 and in force until 1832, the Council Code of Laws (*Sobornoe ulozhenie*), contains 30 (according to another count—41) references to punishments involving prison sentences compared to 61 references to capital punishment (Uporov, 2004, p. 91; Gernet, 1941, p. 86).

The inclusion of the law on "word and deed" in the Code is worth noting. According to it, not only any "doing" against the person vested in supreme power constitutes a crime, but even an intention expressed in thoughts and words (Hedlund, 2005, p. 149; Ivanovsky, 1895, p. 92). In other words, not only historians, but also Russian legal practitioners and even the general public at that time acknowledged the existence of links between concepts and "doings" (Ingerform, 1996, p. 739).

The other violent technique, domination by virtue of a constellation of interests in the market, also underwent some changes. Peter I granted serious privileges on the market to a few selected businesspeople, including foreigners—*gosti* (literally—guests). In exchange, they were required to provide services and produce goods of particular interest for supreme power, ranging from minting money to manufacturing cloth (Pipes, 1974, pp. 197-198). Hence, a privileged, close to monopolistic, status on the market had to be "bought" and had a conditional character. "As long as they operated the enterprise satisfactory, the manufacture was their 'hereditary property'; should they fail, the state would claim it back and punish them to boot" (Ibid, p. 210).

IV.6 Catherine II the Great

Controversies related to enlightened despotism take even more manifest forms in the discourse about Catherine II's reign (1762–1796). A group of scholars recognize her "version of the Enlightenment compatible with autocracy" (Malia, 1999, p. 75; see also Karamzin, 1991, p. 41). Under her reign, the triplet ruler/state/ruled was finally being formed, with the emergence of the last missing element, namely society as a separate entity (Pipes, 1974, p. 127). Oleg Kharkhordin (2001, p. 225) argues that this emergence results from policies of Enlightenment and the development of radical Enlightenment thinking.

Along with ideas of Enlightenment, the same argument continues, supreme power under Catherine is constrained by the strengthening of the nobility as an alternative source of power. By the end of the eighteenth century the nobility manages to return a number of important privileges, including more secured property rights on their property. "The elite has transformed from a service class to a privileged strata able to dictate its conditions to the crown" (Gaman-Golutvina, 2006, p. 140).

On the other hand, the Enlightenment also raised bar against which supreme power was judged. *A Journey from St. Petersburg to Moscow* (1790) by Aleksandr Radishchev containing a radical critique of supreme power in terms of despotism could hardly appear under a different, less severe, set of conditions. Once again, disagreements as to the most appropriate concept for making sense of supreme power derive from the particular context in which an assessment or utterance is being made rather than from significant changes in the debated phenomenon.

To this short overview—its size depends chiefly on the contribution of a particular personality to the movement along the path of supreme power—a significant addition to the repertoire of techniques for imposing will is worth mentioning. Policies of Enlightenment produced a surge in the arts and literature, and contributed to the emergence of the mass media. Instead of tolerating a new source of power independent of supreme power—the other proof of its basically unchanged nature—people vested in it established the first institutions of press censorship with the mandate to "screen" the increasing information flow. "Secular censorship had begun late in the eighteenth century, when Russia's autocrats had first sensed the full dimension of the threat that the ideas of the West posed to their authority" (Lincoln, 1990, p. 121). As a result, manipulation was being added to the repertoire. At that time, however, its key element, brute force, remained unchanged (the ratio of corporal punishment to prison sentences in the Collection of Laws issued in 1832 and in the Code on criminal and disciplinary penalties of 1845 does not differ from that in the Council Code of Laws, see Uporov, 2004, pp. 123, 200; Gernet, 1941, p. 87).

IV.7 Alexander II

The case of the *czar*-reformer, Alexander II, who reigned from 1855 to 1881, deserves mention because of his policies concerning the reform of the system in the top-down manner. What follows also applies to the other *czar*-reformer, Alexander I (1801-1825), even if the "attempt to restrict supreme power from the side of [this] bearer of it" (Ivanvosky, 1895, p. 59) had a significantly lesser scope.

The name of Alexander II is associated with the so-called "Great Reforms" of 1860-1874 that included not only the abolishment of serfdom, but also municipal, military and judicial reforms. Their initial design contained numerous elements copied from the "best institutional practices" of Western Europe. Nevertheless, while intended to improve almost every aspect of the state, they did not touch upon the centerpiece, the model of supreme power. In this sense, they did not go beyond limits of any other program of "conservative modernization" as "the leader's efforts to simultaneously import Western models and preserve his own hold on traditional authority" (Badie, 2000, p. 97; see also Oleinik, 2006b). Malia's account (1999, p. 168; see also Lincoln, 1990, p. 60) highlights this essential requirement of the compatibility of changes with supreme power: reforms "aimed to implement that part of the French revolutionary agenda which was compatible with preserving the two pillars of the Old Regime: absolutism in politics and aristocratic supremacy in society."

In fact, instead of limiting supreme power, Russia's Great reforms served to strengthen it by providing the individual or group vested in it with additional justifications. "Paradoxically, reforms intended to introduce modern economic relations and European political institutions in Russia ended by reinforcing power and moral authority of the autocrat" (Raeff, 1984, p. 182). Russian legal scholar Nikolai Korkunov, whose academic career started in the late period of Alexander II's rule, shows exactly how reforms served to reinforce supreme power. Reforms enlighten people in the sense of the increased awareness of their dependence on the state as "the only coordination device in town." Their growing autonomy and the conflicts that it produces lead them to seek supreme power as a supreme judge and guarantor of order. "The absolutist state is basically an attribute of the individual consciousness, arising from its citizens' growing awareness that they can cope with the forces around them by the use of reason and that they depend on each other in order to do so" (Yaney, 1966, p. 481).

The need to work on a deeper level, that of the individual consciousness, explains the spread of techniques for manipulation, the element included in the repertoire under Catherine II's reign. "In [late] tsarist Russia active manipulation of politics had long been a part of everyday life" (Wilson, 2005, p. 2). Namely, a mandate for manipulation had the "third section" of the gendarme corps whose activities added an "intellectual" dimension to otherwise violent means employed by supreme power.

It is mainly Western scholars (or Western-oriented Russian scholars), who declare that this reform of supreme power in the top-down manner was a success, while such connection between reforms and supreme power appears less pronounced in Russian historiography. For instance, Pipes (1974, p. xxi) believes that the Great reforms put an end to the Old Regime and lay at the origin of a new "bureaucratic regime." George Yaney (1973, p. 383) has a similar opinion: "One might well ask whether any systematization really took place in the tsarist government in 1711-1905…. The answer is yes." Does this assessment have more to do with a critical stance toward the Soviet regime that stopped the new—supposedly—path than with real changes in the nature of supreme power during the relatively short period of time that preceded the 1917 revolution? Would the revolution have been possible at all in the latter case?

IV.8 Soviet rule

Instead of considering the leadership of Vladimir Lenin, Joseph Stalin, Nikita Khrushchev and Leonid Brezhnev separately,[27] the assumption is made that supreme power during the Soviet time was a single continuous phenomenon. Arguably, the October 1917 revolution did not change the core characteristics of supreme power, in contrast to some other aspects of political, economic and social organization. Pivovarov (2006a, p. 52) calls the political regime that emerged in 1917 a republic embedded in supreme power, or *samoderzhavnaia respublika*. Communitarian principles inherited from the pre-revolutionary agricultural community, *obshchina*, allowed elements of republicanism to survive at the micro-level,[28] with the "vertical of power" originating from supreme power keeping all these local elements together. Supreme power penetrated the other elements of the institutional structure consequently substituting a meaning compatible with its own logic for their original meaning. "Activities and corresponding institutions that refer to particular criteria and values appear to be embedded in structures and relationships with a qualitatively different nature, namely hierarchical" (Levada, 1993, p. 87).

Like the Great reforms, the reforms carried out in the "top-down" manner during the Soviet time such as, for instance, the "thaw" in the 1960s, did not touch upon supreme power. "The masses are promised every conceivable reform and amelioration, including free housing and free lunch. But one line of change is unmistakably blocked off: they can look forward to no political right or institution that would enable them to exercise control over the now uncontrolled and uncontrollable party bureaucracy" (Shachtman, 1962, p. 13).

If before the 1917 revolution supreme power was vested in an individual, with the exception of periods when he or she signed the *zapis'* and shared supreme power with the selected few, the Soviet rule implied a collective, group exercise of it, again with the exception of Stalin's rule. The communist party's *nomenklatura* represented the new body vested in supreme power. "The *nomenklatura* is a list of the highest positions; the candidates for these positions are examined by the various party committees, recommended and confirmed" (Voslensky, 1984, p. 2; see also Konovalov, 2006, p. 163). There were two types of such lists: a basic one (candidates for all positions from this list needed explicit approval) and that for the purposes of control and registration (no approval required). The *nomenkatura* existed at all layers of the Soviet hierarchy, starting with the district up to the Central Committee of the Communist Party of the Soviet Union, CPSU. For example, the *nomenklatura* of the CPSU's committee in the region of Novosibirsk included 739 positions (heads of the lower-level party's committees, heads of key industrial enterprises and academic institutions) in 1946, 454 in the early 1960s and 805 in 1964. The *nomenklatura* of the CPSU's committee in the city of Slavgorod,[29] region of Altai, consisted of 260 positions in 1952 (Konovalov, 2006, pp. 82, 104 & 123). Voslensky (1984, pp. 92-93) assesses the total number of members of the *nomenklatura* at 750,000 people in the late 1970s, 3 million if family members are counted. However, not all these people enjoyed all the prerogatives of supreme power, only those at the very top of the hierarchy (the *nomenklatura* of the Central Committee and its Political Bureau).

Voslensky attributes all five characteristics of supreme power to the *nomenklatura*. First, its members did not need to justify their decisions and "suggestions" in other terms than references to their status inside the *nomenklatura*. A professionally incompetent fellow should not have any fears as long as he remained "on good terms with his influential *nomenklatura* colleagues" (Voslensky, 1984, p. 81). Second, the *nomenklatura* prioritized the strengthening of its own power and positions over any other objectives. "The *nomenklatura* ruling class endeavors ... to assure the security and maximum extension of its power" (Ibid, p. 125). Third, it relied chiefly on violent techniques for imposing will: its members preferred "coercion to offering incentives" (Ibid, p. 154). Fourth, the *nomenklatura* produced extreme imbalances in the distribution of rights and obligations between its members and the ordinary people. There was a "monopoly of decision making exercised by the *nomenklatura* on all important (and many unimportant) questions throughout the country" (Ibid, p. 104; see also Holmes, 1994, p. 83). Fifth, feedback loops in relations between the *nomenklatura* and the ordinary people took only the form of individual letters as the most harmless form that, furthermore, allowed the *nomenklatura* to control its "lieutenants" from the government, the legislature and the judiciary. "Collective complaints are forbidden" (Ibid, p. 173; see also Livshin & Orlov, 2002, p. 14).

Perhaps the ideology, namely a version of Marxism-Leninism, helped justify supreme power during the Soviet time and, hence, constrained the discretion of the *nomenkatura* by necessitating references to this eventual superior principle? Hardly, because scarce evidence—interviews with members of the *nomenklatura* either in the Soviet Union or in its "satellite" states—do not support the hypothesis about their strong ideological beliefs and commitment. For instance, factions (clans and "cartridge clips", see Subsection VI.3 of the Introduction) existing within the *nomenklatura* did not derive from ideological or policy disagreement. "Policy does not determine faction, but faction does determine policy" (Uri & Lukes, 1990, p. 37). A member of the *nomenklatura* in socialist

Poland further witnessed that "the Soviet model is the only political model which secures power for the handful of people on top as long as they desire. The leaders ... are not always enthusiastic about Marxism-Leninism. They are enthusiastic about holding power" (Ibid, p. 184).

The discourse about the model of power after the fall of the Soviet Union, since the early 1990s onward, shares some similarities with that of the short pre-revolutionary period mentioned in the previous subsection, with one apparent exception. Western scholars (and Western-oriented Russian scholars) seem to be more critical than most of their Russian colleagues. Again, divergences may be due to the context, namely to the criteria used when assessing most recent developments, than to real changes in the underlying phenomenon. From one point of view, the historical path radically changed around this period of time (Gaman-Golutvina, 2006, p. 41). From the other, supreme power continued to exist despite large-scale reforms. Advocates of the latter opinion emphasize the compatibility of the post-Soviet presidency with supreme power that has existed in Russia since the twelfth century.[30] The rest of the book is devoted to the further demonstration of the continuity of supreme power up to the present.

The lack of radical changes in the nature of supreme power does not prevent them from being included in the repertoire of techniques for imposing will. It can be argued that Stalinism, for instance, differs from the other periods in the Soviet history mostly because of an almost exclusive reliance on force, even at the expense of the other violent techniques for imposing will. This reduces the repertoire during the 1920s and 1930s to force at its core and coercion and manipulation in the form of propaganda at its periphery.

At that time, the use of physical force prevailed at all stages of maintaining order, starting with investigation through sentencing. Torture, a centerpiece of the repertoire until the nineteenth century, gained importance again. The Central Committee of the CPSU explicitly authorized the use of torture in investigation. In a telegram dated January 1938, Stalin confirmed the usefulness of this means of interrogation: "this method must be applied from now on, as an exception, to clear and still dangerous enemies as correct and expedient one" (cited in Solomon, 1996, p. 258; see also Solzhenitsyn, 1973, pp. 109-110). As for sentencing, custodial sentences progressively replaced non-custodial ones. While custodial sentences accounted for 10 percent of all court sentences in 1930, their share increased three-fold in just the three following years (Solomon, 1996, p. 98). The scope of crimes involving custodial sentences was also extended significantly. To land in prison in the early 1940s, it was enough to fail to meet a plan target, to come to work late three times or more in a month, to appropriate a small amount of the state's or the collective farm's property etc. (Ibid, pp. 138, 299).

Along with prison—more precisely, labor camps—force as a technique for imposing will was embodied in a number of other Soviet institutions because of their reliance on forced labor and restrictions of physical freedom (for example, through the passport regime): the collective farm (*kolkhoz*), the state's farm (*sovkhoz*), the construction site, the enterprise or factory, the army, the office (*uchrezhdenie*). "The Soviet countryside lies close to the Gulag, if one considers the intensity of coercion, and even leaves it behind if one takes into account disastrous consequences and the number of victims related to the process of collectivization" (Sokolov, 2005, p. 30).

Coercion, a technique whose mechanism cannot function without force as a point of reference (see Section II of Chapter 6), became a central element of the repertoire after the end of Stalinism. On the one hand, the use of force involves high costs, which makes this option available to supreme power either temporarily, or at moments when resources abound (Oleinik, 2008d, pp. 202-204). On the other hand, the extreme violence of supreme power under Stalin's rule allowed for it to be referred to subsequently as a point of reference instead of actually applying force. The KGB-style argument "it would be better not to resist" (Voslensky, 1984, p. 371) represents the essence of coercion at work. The number of prisoners does not have to return to the heights of the 1930s-1940s again. Yegor Gaidar (2006, pp. 134-135) offers a similar explanation for a decrease in the number of sentenced political dissidents (3,448 in 1958-1966, 1,583 in 1967-1974): a significantly larger number of them (63,100 in 1971-1974) were called up to the KGB for a "discussion." All of the "invited" got a "message": it is in your best interests not to continue this way. An absolute majority considered the threat credible.

The reliance on threats can also explain an apparent paradox in the Soviet-type policies with regard to human resources: people who made rather serious mistakes at some point in their career got promoted more often than those with a flawless record. Mistakes made by the subordinate in the past transformed into an important lever for the superior. "A character with a less than perfect character or record may be preferable since he may be controlled more easily" (Uri & Lukes, 1990, p. 12).

Manipulation gained importance after reforms of the 1960s, because of the surge in the intellectual life that they produced (very much like policies of Enlightenment implemented by Catherine II). In the 1960s, the KGB Disinformation Service was greatly expanded and granted special status (Albats, 1994, p. 175). Along with coercion, manipulation became an important tool that the KGB used for neutralizing political dissidents. One of the strategies that it employed consisted in disseminating, among dissidents, fabricated information about the collaboration of some of them with the state security. "The KGB succeeded in its manipulations to such an extent that mutual suspicion made effective collective action very difficult" (Wilson, 2005, p. 16).

However, the use of manipulation was far from restricted to operations of the KGB. Other "lieutenants" of supreme power depended on it too. The communist party incorporated elements of manipulation in its "ideological work," taking into consideration the belief that "the mission of the party press is not so much to inform as to instruct" (Uri & Lukes, 1990, p. 133). The number of people involved in ideological work on a full- or part-time basis is impressive. "By a conservative estimate 12-14 million people, about 10 percent of all employees, conduct ideological work on a daily basis in the framework of their profession" (Shlapentokh, 1989, p. 106).

Finally, despite the marginal place officially occupied by the market in the centrally planned economy, the technique of domination by virtue of a constellation of interests did not completely disappear from the repertoire. The Soviet leadership quickly realized how to use the biases of an oligopoly on the international market for hydrocarbons to their advantage (the Soviet Union has been a major player on this market since the 1970s). Gaidar (2006, p. 191) reports several successful examples of manipulating the market price of oil through terrorist activities on the part of the Soviet proxies targeting the infrastructure (pipelines and terminals).

Other examples can be found in the late Soviet period and particularly during the early stages of the post-Soviet reforms. They resulted from the growing importance of the "shadow" market in a system characterized by permanent shortages and structural biases. Most economic actors, even with a completely legal status, had no other choice but to look for goods and services in short supply on the "shadow" market (Yakovlev, 1988). Those with privileged access to such goods and services found themselves on the "short side" of the non-clearing market (see Section II of Chapter 6), which enabled them to exploit the structural bias at the expense of the others. "Deficit becomes a tool for obtaining the other goods and services in short supply" (Akhiezer, 1997, p. 598) and produces a "chain reaction."

Luc Duhamel (2004) shows how the transformation of deficit into a means for acquiring or strengthening power works in practice taking the trade network in Moscow as an example. Due to imbalances between two sectors in the Soviet industry, one producing means of production and the second—consumer goods, the shortage of the latter was particularly acute. People involved in the retail trade, hence, developed a power position in the economic sphere. Furthermore, they managed to convert this power position into political influence as well (the Moscow trade network was closely connected with one of the most powerful factions in the Central Committee). Unusually violent prosecution of selected members of the trade network in the early 1980s only confirms that not only corruption and bribery, but power is at stake in this case.

Structural biases do not disappear during first stages of post-Soviet reforms; the opposite happens. To structural imbalances in the economy inherited from the past one has to add regulatory policies adapted by the supreme power[31] and its "lieutenants," the central and regional governments. To start a business in industries with the highest rates of profit one must obtain a large number of licenses and permissions and/or the status of an "authorized" (*upolnomochenny*) agent of a government body. This access control exercised by the representatives of the supreme power only intensified the imbalances instead of helping to eliminate structural biases. "The greatest privilege in Russia of the 1990s consists in getting permission to start a business that yields excess profits. It counts for a *carte blanche* for enrichment" (Kryshtanovskaya, 2005, p. 315). Domination by virtue of a constellation of interests in the market has progressively transformed into the central element of the repertoire, which explains particular attention paid to it in the rest of the book, especially Chapters 5, 6 and 7.

Previous developments as well as the availability of new institutions, such as the market, made the post-Soviet repertoire of techniques for imposing will more diversified than ever in Russian history. This diversity naturally found its expression in the discourse about power. An all-Russian interdisciplinary conference "Power and power relationships in contemporary world" organized in Yekaterinburg in 2006 provides a rare chance for analyzing the discourse of Russian social scientists representing not only capital cities but also the regions. All the contributions to the two-volume proceedings (n=265) were coded with the help

Table 4.2
Various Techniques for Imposing Will Mentioned in a Conference Proceedings

Imposition of will by	Techniques for imposing will	Historians Freq.	%	All social scientists, including historians Freq.	%
Violence	Force	1	5	14	5.3
	Coercion	1	5	4	1.5
	Manipulation	0	0	43	16.2
Rationalizing it	Virtue of a constellation of interests	0	0	11	4.2
	Structural bias of the system	2	10	24	9.1
	Making obedience pay	0	0	8	3
Legitimizing it	Enforcement of established rules	6	27.3	42	15.8
	Correspondence of rules to beliefs shared by both the ruler and the ruled	5	22.7	25	9.4
	Expression of consent by the ruled	1	5	21	7.9
	No technique	6	27.3	73	27.6
Total		22	100	265	100

Source: *Vlast'i vlastnye otnosheniia v sovremennom mire*, 2006

of content analysis. It appears that all five violent techniques for imposing will attracted social scientists' attention, with manipulation being an absolute champion (Table 4.2). Furthermore, contributors discuss violent techniques more frequently (36.3 percent of cases) than techniques for legitimizing power (33.1 percent), which supports the thesis about the essentially violent nature of the prevailing model of power relationships. Interestingly enough, historians make an exception: they focus mainly on techniques for legitimizing power.

Conclusion

The proposed analysis of Russian historiography of the nineteenth century onward indicates significant continuity in the discourse about power. Variations appear less significant than one would have expected: they consist mainly in a continuous back and forth movement between two concepts, *samovlastie* and *samoderzhavie*. Both of them refer to essentially the same underlying phenomenon of supreme power. Different emphases derive from the context in which a particular assessment is being made and eventual changes in the repertoire of techniques for imposing will, the only element of supreme power that arguably varies throughout Russian history. The context refers to the scholars' values and ideology, their "doings" (how do they position themselves with regard to people vested in supreme power?), the other assessments made around the same period of time (in debates in which the scholars are involved, what statements do they criticize or endorse?), and finally, their location (inside or outside the Russian institutional system).

Relationships between the discourse and the underlying phenomenon, supreme power in this case, have a dialectical nature. On the one hand, the discourse produces the phenomenon through the template for actions, "doings" in Skinner's terms, that it contains. On the other hand, power enables those who are vested in it to structure the discourse about it, as shown in the works of critical sociologists (see also Section I of Chapter 3).[32] Only the former link is carefully considered in this chapter. In order to get a more complete picture the proposed analysis has to be complemented by an in-depth study of the latter connection.

The link from discourse to power suggests some responsibility on the part of historians, who are among the other participants in making the discourse. By using, developing or accepting particular concepts and categories they willingly or unwillingly contribute to the construction and continuous reproduction of a particular model of power relationships. The continuity of supreme power is at least facilitated by the fact that "almost all contemporary Russian historians instead of criticizing the [prevailing] mental models aim to keep them untouched" (Makarenko, 1998, p. 154).

The other possible extension of the proposed study lies in comparing the discourse about supreme power with the primary historical data about it, namely archival documents shedding light on its five characteristics. This task would help to further confirm or reject the assumption that the discourse and the underlying phenomenon are closely interlinked in a web of direct and feedback loops. Its accomplishment necessitates further operationalization of the supreme power through complementing the list of its five features by empirically identifiable and measurable attributes, which paves the way toward content analysis of archival documents using the methodology outlined in the Methodological Appendix.

Notes

1. A similar observation could apply to all countries of "catch-up" modernization where non-state actors appear too weak to take the lead, in contrast to the "leader" countries that were modernized in a "bottom-up" manner (Oleinik, 2006b; Gerschenkron, 1992).
2. Pierre Bourdieu (1984, p. 39) observes a similar tendency in French academia towards hiding disagreements and making them less explicit and links it to increases in the level of "symbolic violence" in the second half of the twentieth century.

Continuity and Change in the Prevailing Model of Power   139

3. Consequently, the same model of power can be perceived differently by those who are "in" and those who are "out." Speaking about the political regime in Germany of the nineteenth century, Thorstein Veblen (1939, p. 231) indicates: "The current Imperial system of mitigated repression and bureaucratic guidance is apparently acceptable to the German people and apparently works to good effect among them, although it would presumably not be workable if imposed on a population with a different recent historical past." There are several parallels in the historical evolution of Russia and the German states in the eighteenth—twentieth centuries (Zweynert, 2009; Raeff, 1983).
4. Specialists in semiotics develop a similar idea. For instance, Yuri Lotman (1990, Ch. 7) considers culture as a construct composed of a number of key symbols. These symbols play the role similar to that of "plot-gene" because they contain the information about past, present and future interactions in a highly condensed form.
5. For an overview of this concept and its application to Latin America, see Touraine, 1988.
6. The same can be said with regard to elements of popular participation and self-administration at the local level that do not completely disappear even at the height of strengthening supreme power. For instance, supreme power needed *zemstva*, a form of local self-administration in the nineteenth century, "because of the inability [of the former] to substitute [the latter] by some form of its own organization" (Ivanovsky, 1895, p. 417).
7. The Soviet system represents an example of how supreme power and the state interact in practice. The communist party—its Central Committee—embodies supreme power and closely controls the official governmental structure, the workers' and peasants' "soviets." In such a situation, "the government has little power of its own…. The party accepts responsibility for success while the government has to assume responsibility for all failures" (Uri & Lukes, 1990, p. 50; see also Malia, 1999, p. 300).
8. Cf. "Under a police regime, political activity is outlawed and security organs are given practically unlimited powers to make sure the proscription is observed" (Pipes, 1974, p. 312).
9. This idea continues to dominate the Russian discourse up to now: a July 2008 survey (N=1,600) shows that public opinion strongly endorses it. Eighty-one percent (74 percent in July 2007, 72 percent in April 1997) of respondents agree that ordinary people could not live in Russia without care and guidance provided by the state (Obshchestvennoe mnenie, 2008, p. 27). Public opinion surveys also indicate that the words "state" and "state's servants" arouse mostly positive feelings because Russians link them to public interests as opposed to private ones (Petukhov, 2006, pp. 9-10; Byzov, 2006, p. 25).
10. Since the rule of Ivan III, the Grand Duchy of Moscow claims the role of the unique and legitimate successor to Byzantium as the capital and stronghold of Orthodox Christianity. The second wife of Ivan III, Sofia, was the daughter of Byzantine emperor Justinian the Great and a living symbol of this continuity (Karamzin, 2003, pp. 283-284).
11. It is questionable whether religious faith can constitute an efficient constraint as the state and the church have been always expected to act "in concert." The concept of "symphony," singing in unison, not only characterizes this type of mutually agreeable relationship, but it was explicitly used by Russian theologians in their discourse (Pivovarov, 2004, pp. 66 ff.).
12. For instance, Skinner (2002a, p. 20; emphasis in the original) strongly criticizes the belief that historians should "take the greatest care *not* to select [their] topics

on the grounds that they seem to [them] to have some current interest or (worse still) some contemporary relevance or importance."
13. Path dependence in the evolution of Russian economic institutions is acknowledged in a number of studies. For instance, Jacques Sapir (1990, p. 24) indicates the continuity in the organization of planning between the late Russian empire (the military-industrial committees) and the Soviet Union. Vladimir Yefimov (2003), in turn, demonstrates the path dependent character of the evolution of agricultural institutions in imperial, Soviet and post-Soviet Russia.
14. There is no single explanation for the phenomenon of path dependence. Some scholars stress the impact of numbers—theorized with the help of the notion of evolutionary-stable strategy borrowed from game theory (Smith, 1982): the more people refer to a particular institution, the fewer incentives there are for those who have not yet made their minds to prefer alternative institutions. A similar approach consists in tracing parallels between the evolution of institutions and the "lock-in" effects related to the choice between alternative technologies (Arthur, 1988). After the number of uses of a technology reaches a certain limit, new products tend to be compatible with it at the expense of less widespread alternatives.
15. In more technical terms, the external environment is an independent variable, whereas the prevailing model of power—a dependent variable. An alternative (null) hypothesis, H_0, implies that there is no causal connection between the external environment and supreme power.
16. The assumption of homogeneity of variance was assessed by the Levene test, $F=0.465$, $p=0.497$; this indicated no significant violation of the equal variance assumption; therefore, the pooled variances version of the t-test was used. The mean duration of defensive differed non significantly, $t(111)=0.67$, $p=0.504$, two-tailed. The test is run "as if" the sample were random. It should be noted that, strictly speaking, omissions and errors in the data do not have a random character. So, the presented outcomes shall be treated with caution, even if the same "as if" assumption is routinely made in many similar cases.
17. The assumption of homogeneity of variance was assessed by the Levene test, $F=3.593$, $p=0.063$; this indicated a slight violation of the equal variance assumption; therefore, the version with no assumption of equal variance of the t-test was used. The mean PPR during the "despotic" years differed significantly, $t(45.7)=2.77$, $p=0.008$, two-tailed. The caveat with regard to a non-random nature of the sample has to be repeated here.
18. Peter I understood well connections between the defensive war and the rhetoric of commonwealth: he accepted the superiority of the common good over the supreme ruler's whims on the eve of the Poltava battle (Kharkhordin, 2001, pp. 227-229). Anecdotic evidence suggests that Joseph Stalin also weakened his grip on power during first years of World War II, when the Soviet Army suffered major defeats (Aksenov, 1993).
19. Pipes (1974, p. 24) also traces the origin of the path to the twelfth century but describes it in terms of patrimonial monarchy: "The patrimonial monarchy best defines the type of regime which emerged between the twelfth and seventeenth centuries and which ... has survived until the present."
20. Akhiezer (1997, pp. 88-89) indicates with this regard that "the *veche* was a field of conflicting monologues, a gathering of authoritarian heads of ... the families, [it produced] not a majority view, but an only acceptable opinion."
21. "A single self-interested monarch ... would maximize tribute, set costs so as to accomplish that maximization of tribute, and be indifferent to the level of protection rent" (Tilly, 1985, p. 176).

Continuity and Change in the Prevailing Model of Power 141

22. By definition, the imperial form of statehood implies a sharp contrast between the political regime in the metropolis and that in the dominion (Gaidar, 2006, p. 8). However, the thesis defended here challenges the widespread view that the model of supreme power was "imported" from the Mongolian "mainland."
23. At meetings of the *kurultai*, a council of Mongol chiefs and local khans, in 1211, 1219 and 1225.
24. The official explanation formulated by Moscow and found in several historical sources (see Endnote 9, Chapter 3)—Novgorod attempted to betray the Orthodox faith and to adopt Catholicism when asking the king of Poland and grand prince of Lithuania for a protectorate—does not hold under closer inspection. The Charter signed by the king contains a clause explicitly prohibiting the expansion of Catholicism on Novgorod soil (Karamzin, 2003, p. 279).
25. In the Soviet time, this term referred to a small piece of land in the countryside with a cabin used as a second home by a city dweller and his or her family. They had no property right to the land, however, using it under a conditional lease from a state enterprise, the condition being the employment at this enterprise.
26. According to Pipes (1974, p. xxi), it extends from the ninth to the late nineteenth century.
27. A more detailed historical study, of course, would allow highlighting particularities in the institutional environment during these time periods.
28. The continuity of the *obshchina* represents the other facet of path dependence in Russian history (see Ledeneva, 2006, Ch. 4; Oleinik, 2005a).
29. With the population of around 30,000 people.
30. The first post-Soviet leader, Boris Yeltsin, perceived the institution of the presidency in a manner that "was much closer to that of traditional Russian autocracy than it was to Western-style democracy" (Hedlund, 2005, p. 274; see also Kryshtanovskaya, 2005, p. 235).
31. As reflected in Presidential decrees—President Yeltsin relied heavily relied on his decree power (Remington, 2006).
32. For instance, Pierre Bourdieu shows how the state and its representatives produce the discourse, including the key categories and concepts, about the housing market. "The laws of construction of discourse … reside in the laws of construction of the space of the production of the discourse" (2005, p. 107).

5

Market as a Weapon: Domination by Virtue of a Constellation of Interests

Introduction

From the liberal perspective, freedom represents a fundamental value and the minimal basis for reaching a consensus between parties even if all their other priorities diverge (Rose, 1995). Freedom contrasts with dependence and submission, subjection to external control. Freedom and power as the manifestation of one actor's control over the other actor's behavior refer to two mutually exclusive forms of social and economic organization: "liberty is the absence of social power over one" (Dowding, 1991, p. 55). In the same vein, the market is seen as a liberating force, in both a literal and figurative sense.[1]

Because of this uneasy match, economists tend to leave the issues of power outside of the scope of their analysis. The task of explaining the origins of power is then outsourced to political scientists, political sociologists and analytical philosophers. This chapter is intended to bring power back into socio-economic analysis by placing special emphasis on its embeddedness in interactions. More specifically, it addresses the question as to whether power and domination—understood as the exercise of power over B, Agent, by A, Principal, contrary to B's interests (Wartenberg, 1990, p. 117)—can derive from what initially looked like "free" interactions in the market. If such a link does indeed exist, then this prompts a further inquiry into the relative contribution of structural factors and human agency to the emergence of domination out of the market. Does A's domination result more from a particular market structure or from A's rational choices and strategies?

The proposed research question appears valid independently of whether *A* and *B* refer to individual subjects or organizations. However, for the purposes of the present analysis, the organization as an entity on its own rather than an aggregate of individual subjects is chosen as the unit of analysis. The organization might presumably have specific interests on its own that do not equal the sum of its members' interests (Huntington, 1968, pp. 24-27). This entity has a depersonalized character: it does not disappear if some of its members depart or die. The organization can take the form of a small or medium size enterprise, a corporation, a university or a state—in other words, any *juristic* person as opposed to the *physical* person (Coleman, 1974, pp. 17-25).[2]

Two accounts of domination in the market are confronted, the neoliberal one, deriving from the neoclassical approach in economic theory and the *laissez-faire* ideology, and the critical one, developed in writings of Michel Foucault, Pierre Bourdieu and their followers. The former account highlights interests and their key role in shaping human behavior and organizational strategies. "Stable preference, rational choice, and equilibrium structures of interaction constitute the hard core of the microeconomic paradigm" (Eggertsson, 1990, p. 5). Choices are then the function of interests. The latter account implies, on the contrary, a deterministic stance: the institutional environment, not interests, shapes choices. At the individual level, the habitus determines behavioral patterns (see also Section III of the Introduction). "The habitus re-activates the meaning embedded in institutions" (Bourdieu, 1980, p. 96). At the organizational level, the group habitus takes the form of routines (Nelson & Winter, 1982).

In spite of the apparent contradiction between the two accounts, they can be treated as mutually complementing rather than excluding each other. The program of economic sociology initially outlined by Max Weber allows for the consideration of the institutional environment as a parameter of the function of the maximization of interests. "Interests drive people's actions but the social element determines what expression and direction these actions will take" (Swedberg, 2003, p. 3; see also Lindenberg, 1990, pp. 79-81). The interplay between interests and the institutional environment lies in the center of the present study. Namely, it aims at linking changes in market structures to strategies pursued by organizations in quest of domination.

Taking interests into account seems especially important because the current configuration of the institutional environment puts particular emphasis on them. At the level of ideology, a key component of the institutional environment, the growing popularity of "economic imperialism," or the application of the model of welfare-maximization outside the narrowly defined subject area of economics, makes the rational pursuit of interests look natural even in contexts where they were previously relegated to secondary roles: law (thanks to the contribution of "law and economics;" Posner, 1977), the family, education, crime and deviance (Becker, 1993), trust (Coleman, 1990, pp. 99-104) etc. The neo-liberal model of globalization with its heavy reliance on the "invisible hand" of the market also increases the scope of choices determined by interests (Strange, 1996). More specifically, the fall of "real socialism" in the former Soviet Union paved the way to a series of reforms that produced in the early 1990s the situation of anomie characterized by the imperative of the accumulation of wealth regardless of legal or social constraints (Shlapentokh, 1995; see also Merton, 1938, p. 675).

The spread of interest-driven behavior calls for rational decision-making. It also facilitates the coordination of actions with the help of rationalization. The model of rational choice then transforms into a support for social action: the fact that all parties involved in it try to behave rationally helps them to correctly interpret each other's intentions and adjust their plans accordingly. Rational action within a homogenous group of subjects refers in this sense to a subset of reasonable, i.e., understandable to the generalized Other, action, to a particular configuration of social action (Weber, 1968, pp. 4-24; Schuetz, 1953, pp. 21-26). Power relationships do not constitute an exception. When practices of rationalization become prevalent, this makes techniques of the imposition of will by rationalizing it particularly relevant (rows d, e and f in Table 2.2; with special emphasis on rows d and e). Applied to studies of power in its pure form (see Chapter 3), this gives particular importance to domination by virtue of a constellation of interests in the market.

This chapter has a two-fold purpose. On one hand, it intends to "reach across the aisle" and to unveil implicit inter-relations between concepts employed by both neoclassical economists and critical theorists. A careful review of the two approaches enables one to clear the terrain and minimize possible confusions.[3] On the other hand, it aims to take a step further by exploring an often-neglected concept, domination by virtue of a constellation of interests with the help of the two approaches. This works through restricting access to a transaction or a field understood here as a stable set of transactions and interrelations delimited in physical and institutional space by clear and non-permeable borders.

The chapter includes three sections. The neoclassical account of domination in the market is confronted with the critical one in Section

I. After outlining these two extreme positions, several attempts to find a middle ground between them are considered. I argue that Weber's concept of domination by virtue of a constellation of interests sheds new light on this issue and allows for finding some common ground between the mutually exclusive—at first sight—approaches. In Section II, I elaborate on a particular technique of domination in the market, namely the closure of the space of interactions. This technique works through controlling the entry and "not letting (potentially interested parties) in." Section III is devoted to an overview of three exemplifying cases. All of them call for bringing the concepts of space and territoriality back into the analysis of power and domination. The case studies rely on both primary and secondary data sources. Some possible generalizations of the proposed analysis are discussed in the Conclusion.

I. Power and the Market: Existing Approaches towards Making Sense of Domination in the Market

I.1 Neoclassical Economics

Starting with Adam Smith (1818, p. 11), mainstream economists have kept emphasizing a mutually beneficial character of exchanges in the market. From this perspective, the market exchange represents a "Win-Win" strategy: by engaging into it, both parties expect to achieve the maximum satisfaction of their interests. Both the seller, Producer, and the buyer, Consumer, appropriate a part of the surplus generated by the division of labor combined with the "invisible hand" of the market. The former gets the consumer's surplus, the latter—the producer's surplus (Marshall, 1920, pp. 104-105, 375-376).[4]

Neoclassical economists use exchanges in the perfectly competitive market (characterized by significant number of participants, free entry/exit, and homogenous products) as a yardstick by which everything else is measured. They label all other contexts of interaction as "deviant," especially if they limit freedom and give rise to market power. The list of "deviant" cases includes monopoly, various forms of imperfect competition and the firm. Market power represents a rare occasion when neoclassical economists actually use the concept of power, but at the price of detaching it from the context of interactions between two or more agents. Market power refers to the producer's capacity to set prices above its marginal costs, which overshadows any effects on the customer's range of options. To paraphrase Herbert Gintis (2000, p. 45), neither the producer nor the customer cares what the other is doing.

When considering monopoly (or its double, monopsony: monopoly of a single buyer), neoclassical economists accuse the monopolist of abusing its market power and appropriating a part of the consumer's (producer's) surplus. The situation of bilateral monopoly may lead to intensive and costly bargaining over the distribution of a rent (surplus) emerging as a result of the transaction (Friedman, 1987). However, they do not assume any changes in the behavior of either A, the monopolist, or B, who is subject to A's power. Both continue to act in their best interests, B is just less successful than A in doing so. B tries to get the maximum satisfaction but under a tighter set of external constraints. Economists believe that, even in such cases, one should be very cautious with the concept of asymmetrical relations. "They remind us of pre-Humeian and pre-Newtonian notions of causality" (Simon, 1953, p. 503).

Imperfect competition as the departure from one or more of the above outlined conditions characterizing the free market deserves special mention. By restricting the number of participants in market exchanges, e.g., by erecting barriers to entry, one can create and appropriate monopolistic profits or rents. This paves the way to a particular type of business, namely protection. It consists in eliminating or neutralizing the competitors of Bs (Tilly, 1985, pp. 175-180; Djankov et al., 2002). As long as the price of protection paid to A by B is less than the rent created by protection, buying it makes sense for B. It should be noted that B in this case gains market power in regard to some other subject, B', and becomes A' in relationships to the latter. Nevertheless, neoclassical economists tend to overlook new aspects emerging as a result of such an extension of the initial relationship.

The classical game theory "revolution" of the 1970s and 1980s paves the way for placing stronger emphasis in economic analysis on interactive aspects of exchanges in the market. In terms of game theory, the market exchange has several features of "pure collaboration games": their participants win and lose simultaneously and have identical preferences regarding the outcomes (Schelling, 1960, p. 84). Nevertheless, this important innovation does not involve serious changes in the hard core of the neoclassical paradigm, namely the model of rational choice. A high level of rationality is imputed to players, which overshadows the structural factors that lie at the origin of power in the market. Classical game theory links domination to such strategies as threat, commitment, promise and the destruction of communication. All of them require sophisticated calculus (Schelling, 1960, Chapter 5). These strategies help A dominate B by changing B's incentive structure and restricting the number of alternative strategies available to the latter (Dowding, 1996). *A* structures *B*'s conditions of choice in such a manner that *B* rationally decides to accept *A*'s dominance.

The firm as an "island of conscious power" in the ocean of unconscious coordination by the "invisible hand" represented a serious challenge to the mainstream economics. Neoclassical economists first ignored the firm considering it a kind of "black box," then either compared it with a "nexus of contracts" between independent and free economic subjects (Alchian & Demsetz, 1972), or elaborated a functionalist explanation for its existence. The latter account does not contain any indication of a conflict between domination and freedom. A hostile merger and the consequent transformation of a previously independent firm into a subaltern unit of the other firm, for instance, is seen in terms of the minimization of transaction costs in the market. Because "there is a cost of using the price mechanism" (Coase, 1988, p. 38), rational considerations can induce the subject to give up its autonomy and freedom. What initially looked like a hostile merger brings about a "Win-Win" situation thanks to economies on transaction costs.

In spite of its growing popularity, transaction costs economics as an extension of the neoclassical approach fails to provide an adequate framework for understanding all aspects of the relationship between the market and power. First, it overshadows conflicts resulting from domination. Second, the lack of interest in the issues of domination prevents study of the entire range of organizational forms. The introduction of the hybrid, a more flexible organization form occupying the middle ground between the market and the hierarchy embodied in the firm (Ménard, 2005b, pp. 95-97), into analysis does not bridge all gaps. For instance, the analysis of vertical integration in terms of the choice between three discrete alternatives, the competitive market, the hierarchy and the hybrid (Williamson, 1991), appears incomplete without taking market power into consideration. A firm able to influence the actions of the others in the market has fewer incentives to move toward vertical integration (Shervani, Frazier & Challagalla, 2007).

To summarize, neoclassical economic theory appears to be poorly equipped for explaining the emergence of power through interactions in the market. On rare occasions when it attempts to do so, the question about the relative role of structural factors and human agency remains unanswered, as illustrated by the following definition of barriers to entry. They refer to "the set of structural, institutional and behavioral conditions that allow incumbent firms to earn economic profits for a significant length of time" (Cabral, 2008, p. 383). Do structural and behavioral conditions replace one another or does the former derive from the latter?

I.2 Critical Theory

The critical approach highlights an omnipresent character of power and domination: they arguably structure interactions in spheres as distant as intimacy on the one hand and the market on the other (Foucault, 1976, pp. 123-124). Moreover, domination inevitably generates conflicts, including in the market. The market thus has no immunity against power and domination. Instead of considering market exchanges in terms of "pure collaboration games" critical theorists assume that one party can win only at the expense of the other, as happens in "zero-sum games".[5] The struggle for power then depicts reality more correctly than the "Win-Win" situation.

The distinction between "power *over*" and "power *to*" helps ensure better understanding of the changes in the analytical focus (Dowding, 1996, pp. 4-8; Section V of Chapter 2).[6] Power *to* bring about outcomes does not necessarily involve a conflict of interests between A and B. In fact, both might be interested in jointly producing an outcome that neither of them is able to achieve separately. Alternatively, the concept of power *over* underlines the ability of A to get B to bring about outcomes in the particular context of their interactions. Peter Morriss (1987, pp. 80-82) speaks of this "contextualized ability" in terms of "ableness," or the "can" under a given set of structural constraints. Critical scholars emphasize power *over*, whereas advocates of rational-choice theory—power *to*.

Foucault's account leaves virtually no room for agency. Domination appears embedded in existing institutions: family, school, prison, public and scientific discourse. Its self-reproduction through the everyday functioning of the institutions does not require input from either A or B. Steven Lukes, for instance, criticizes Foucault for "de-facing" power (Lukes, 2005, pp. 92-95).

Neither neoclassical economists nor critical thinkers assume that the behavior of A and B differ in kind. For the latter, both of them try to get the maximum satisfaction of their interests; for the former, A and B are engaged in plays of power and seek domination (Ailon, 2006, p. 776). The outcome of these plays, i.e., who dominates and who obeys, depends on a particular configuration of relations between positions of A and B. This distinct power structure shapes what critical scholars call a "field" (see Swedberg, 2005, p. 99). Were the power structure different, e.g., B occupied a position of strength, the outcome would be opposite (B would dominate A).

The institutional environment determines choices of A and B at a deeper level too. It not only shapes the structure of strategies available to them, but also affects their preferences by means of the habitus. For critical thinkers, there is no such thing as a free choice because the subject's preferences derive from the habitus embedded in the institutional environment. When connecting the emergence of a field of power, as a field of struggle for power over the state, to specific interests of actors, namely the jurists and state representatives, Bourdieu (1994) does not consider interests an independent variable and does not refer to the model of rational choice.

The habitus can be compared with a gene in its quality to influence the subject's subsequent behavior (Bourdieu & Passeron, 1970, p. 48). The habitus represents a link between the past, the present and the future: it contributes to the continuous reproduction of behavioral patterns inherited from the past (Bourdieu, 1980, pp. 91-92). Nevertheless, it remains unclear where the habitus comes from. The theory of path-dependence links today's structures to minor events coincidentally occurred in the past (North, 1990, p. 94). The accentuation of the phenomenon of path-dependence serves to relieve the subject of any responsibility for outcomes of current interactions. Even pedagogical action as *conscious* efforts aimed at the imposition of a habitus tends to reproduce the pre-existing patterns of domination (Bourdieu & Passeron, 1970, pp. 37-42).

Nevertheless, the habitus leaves some room for agency, which undermines a completely deterministic stance (see also Section III of the Introduction). Actors try to make rational choices informed by their interests, but interests derive from habituses whose origins seem obscure. After all, habituses determine the scope of agency and not *vice versa*.

I.3 Attempts to Find a Middle Ground

The strategy of taking into consideration both institutional constraints and strategic behavior (agency) seems promising from several points of view, especially when accompanied by the analysis of the interplay between these two variables. First, it helps to find a middle ground between two extremes, the neoclassical approach and the critical theory. Second, the combination of structuralism and rational choice theory has important applications to organization studies. Namely, it sheds new light on particular constellations of interests in the market that can give rise to domination, as in the above-mentioned case of the business of protection.

Socio-economists claim that they overcome the opposition between the individualist approach of neoclassical economics and the structuralist one of sociology in general and critical theories in particular. However, a "core theorem" of socio-economics represents in fact an axiom, postulated, empirically illustrated but not demonstrated logically. It, namely, stipulates that individual's decisions and behavior depend on two factors, the desire for pleasure and the moral obligations (Etzioni, 2002, p. 111; see Endnote 12 to Chapter 2). Or, the interplay between the freedom of choice and obligations can hardly be explored without finding a genuine combination of neoclassical economics and critical theories.

Samuel Bowles and Herbert Gintis (2008) argue that power emerges in all the non-clearing markets. Actors on the "short" side of these markets have significantly more degrees of freedom than their counterparts on the "long" side. For instance, consumer sovereignty derives from the excess of supply in the market for consumer goods. "Probably nowhere in the daily lives of ordinary people do they feel more power, and gain more respect, than when acting as consumers" (Gintis, 2000, p. 140). Labor and credit markets do not clear either.

This account has several merits. First, it highlights the fact that even B makes some profit while transacting in the non-clearing market (see also Chapter 6). The consumer, A, pays a price in excess of the marginal cost, which allows the producer, B, to earn a profit. The idea that both A and B tend to be better off when entering into a power relationship will help provide an understanding of the characteristics of domination by virtue of a constellation of interests. Second, the task of modeling interactions in the non-clearing market requires the use of evolutionary game theory (Gintis, 2000, pp. 134-147). In contrast to classical game theory, evolutionary game theory does not use the model of rational choice as a starting point. The degree of the actor's freedom and rationality becomes a new variable in the specification of a model (Ibid, pp. 229-230).

However, Bowles and Gintis interpret power too narrowly, as power *to* do something. For instance, the consumer has power to switch suppliers, if dissatisfied with the quality of a product. They see little interest in emphasizing aspects related to power *over* someone, as in the case of getting B to make the improvements to the product which A would appreciate.

Anthony Giddens' theory of structuration represents another attempt to reach across the aisle. The major contribution of the theory of structuration consists in showing how structure—the institutional environment—simultaneously enables and constrains agency. The issues of power and domination remain somewhat out of its principal focus. Furthermore, the question as to whether agency produces structure, i.e., whether the junction of power and the market results from conscious and deliberate choices, remains unanswered in a clear and unambiguous manner.

Tony Lawson (1997, p. 169) does not elaborate more on this point when applying the theory of structuration to economic analysis either: "the reproduction/transformation of social structure is rarely an intended project, it is equally the case that the individual agents are not always aware, certainly not discursively or self-consciously so, of the structures upon which they are drawing."

Steven Lukes proposes a version of the critical approach consisting in "*combining* a 'faced' with a 'de-faced' account of power's mechanisms" (2002, p. 492; emphasis in the original). He argues that structural biases create favorable conditions for domination. However, the task of transforming domination *in potentia* into something real and tangible requires human agency. "To identify a given process as an 'exercise of power,' rather than as a case of structural determination, is to assume that it is *in the exerciser's or exercisers' power* to act differently" (Lukes, 2005, p. 57; emphasis in the original). At the same time, Lukes falls short of clearly acknowledging that the transformation of the bias of the system into a resource for power necessarily results from conscious and deliberate choices. "The bias of the system can be mobilized, recreated and reinforced in ways that are neither consciously chosen nor the intended result of particular individuals' choices" (Ibid, p. 25).

I.4 Domination by Virtue of a Constellation of Interests: Weber and Beyond

Weber opposes two types of domination, by virtue of a constellation of interests and by virtue of authority (1968, p. 943). The former originates in a monopolistic market and "may be felt to be much more oppressive than an authority in which the duties of obedience are set out clearly and expressly" (Ibid, p. 946). The behavior of A and B is driven here by interests, not by moral duties or affects. A aims at getting the maximum satisfaction of its interests and has the ableness, or the contextualized ability, to do so (Morriss, 1987, pp. 80-82). A's ableness has two components: structural (it occupies a position of strength in relationships with B) and strategic (it uses this position in the most efficient way and further strengthens it). If the strategic component is missing, then A should be considered lucky rather than powerful: the organization achieves its goals "without trying" (Dowding, 1991, p. 105; 1996, Ch. 3). The strategic component implies that A mobilizes the "bias of the system," to borrow Lukes' expression. Behaving strategically, A reproduces and reinforces the bias of the system, which makes its domination more sustainable in the future.

Domination by virtue of a constellation of interests refers to nonzero-sum games as a "mixture of conflict and mutual dependence" (Schelling, 1960, p. 87; see also Gintis, 2000, p. xxiv). B also derives something from the relationship yet its behavior can be hardly described in terms of maximizing. Domination means that B does something that it would not otherwise do (Lukes, 2005, pp. 43-44). Assumptions as to what exactly B would otherwise do depend on the theoretical approach (Ailon, 2006; Morriss, 1987, pp. 73-74). The discussed combination of structuralism and rational choice theory allows for safely assuming that B would otherwise try to get the maximum satisfaction too. However, B's alternatives are structured in such a manner that its first-best choices are simply unattainable. B then *minimizes missed opportunities*, which differs from maximizing behavior (the choice between the first-best and the second best), coercion (the choice between the worst, a negative sanction, and the second worst) and satisficing behavior (getting a positive reward fixed at the outset and acceptable for B). A changes B's incentive structure inducing B to accept A's domination as a condition for being better off by entering into the relationship (Oleinik, 2007a; see also Chapter 6). B gets a part of potential (counterfactual) profits that would be available if there were no bias in the relationship between A and B.

A's ableness to get B to minimize missed opportunities instead of maximizing gains requires the existence of a number of structural preconditions. A and B must be interdependent: their activities are characterized by reciprocal effects. The interdependence between firms, for instance, can refer to various types of task interdependence (Crook & Combs, 2007): pooled (suppliers and a departmental store), sequential (a technological chain) or reciprocal (a network R & D project). Furthermore, these reciprocal effects have to be asymmetrical, which means unequal sensitivity and vulnerability of the counterparts. The level of sensitivity depends on how quickly changes in one organization's behavior bring costly changes in the other's situation. Vulnerability, in turn, signifies "the relative availability and costliness of the alternatives that various actors face" (Keohane & Nye, 2001, p. 11). If A is a buyer, then its domination over supplier B rests on B's high sensitivity and vulnerability because one or several of the following conditions are met (Cox, 2004a, p. 352; the second and sixth conditions influence sensitivity, the remaining seven—vulnerability):

1. there are few buyers and many suppliers,
2. A has a high percentage share of B's total market,
3. B is highly dependent on A for revenue with few alternatives,
4. B's switching costs are high,
5. A's switching costs are low,
6. A's account is attractive to B,
7. B's offering is a standardized commodity,
8. A's search costs are low,
9. B has no information asymmetry advantages over A.

Several of these conditions, namely 1, 3-5 and 8, can be subject to A's manipulation by means of regulating the entry to the market. Entry control represents a possible strategic component of A's ableness (see also Grosse, 1996, p. 474) that helps create and/or reinforce the structural component. Entry control implies that B is better off when being "in" than when "out". B gains something by entering into the relationship, yet the price of entry consists in accepting A's domination, which implies, in fact, the minimization of missed opportunities.

I.5 Enclosure of the Field of Transactions as a Condition for Domination

There exist various definitions of what constitutes a field. For instance, in economic sociology "the field metaphor implies that firms watch one another, engage in strategic behavior vis-à-vis one another and look to one another for clues as to what constitutes successful behavior" (Fligstein & Dauter, 2007, p. 111). To express a similar idea, Neil Fligstein (1996) also uses the metaphor of market as politics highlighting struggles between organizations for control over competition and, more generally, rules of the game in the particular market. Bourdieu (1994, p. 4) defines a field through conflicts over the access to the different species of capital: physical force, economic, informational and symbolic. According to these definitions, the idea of the border, central for the present discussion, is at best relegated to the back-stage: in this chapter the field is understood to be a clearly delimited space of interactions.

It is worthwhile to differentiate between the control of access to a rare resource, e.g., the different species of capital, and the control of access to a transaction, to a field. In the former case, the control does not necessarily involve social action. Such control most often takes the form of property rights. In the latter case, the control aims to structure social action in a particular manner, to make it compatible with domination. Weber (1968, p. 43) calls social relationships with clear and impermeable borders "closed": not everyone, who wishes to join, is actually in a position to do so.

Power and domination may result from both types of control. For instance, patrimonial power (see Section I of Chapter 3) means nothing less than B's acceptance of A's domination in exchange for getting "conditional" property rights to a resource of B's interest. The history of traditional societies provides ample examples of "how chiefs come to power" by controlling access to rare resources (Earle, 1997).[7] A can also dominate B as a result of granting him or her "conditional" access to a transaction. B's interest in transacting with A may derive from the exchange of resources (the link [i] in Figure 5.1), but also from the need to coordinate activities, without which social action becomes simply impossible (the link [j]). Because of the link [j], A's control of access to resources, however rare and specific (see Subsection IV [IIe] of Chapter 2) they may be, is not absolutely necessary for his or her domination over B.

Entry control can either be exercised by A or result from the intervention of a third actor, C.[8] C performs the role of a "gatekeeper" regulating access to the field and making it conditional upon acceptance of particular "rules of the game" underpinning domination.[9] This possible transition from the dyadic relationship between A and B to a triad of A, B and C provides us with the other reason for an in-depth analysis of entry con-

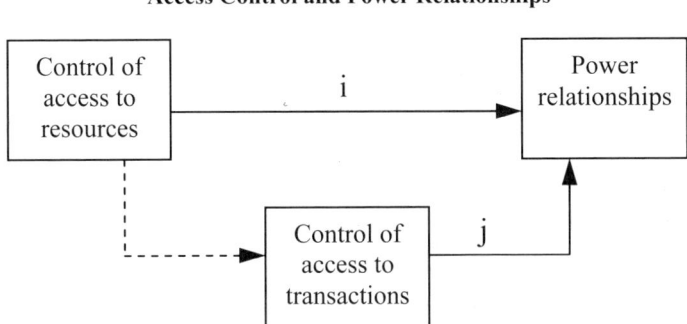

Figure 5.1
Access Control and Power Relationships

trol.[10] The triad, not the dyad seems to be an elementary configuration of the field of power (see also Welch & Wilkinson, 2005) because the idea of field prompts the completion of its image with boundaries and, eventually, gates with gatekeepers on duty.[11]

The intervention of C both gives A an upper hand in relationships with B and creates conditions for C's domination over A. The triad then gives rise to a chain of power relationships by superimposing one power relationship (C—A) over the other one (A—B, Figure 5.2). If the field is structured in this manner, C has an ableness to dominate over A and, indirectly, B. B might not be aware of its subaltern position because neither domination by A nor domination by C takes manifest and easy-to-grasp forms. Because the interests of B and A are "expediently aligned," A can control B "without the need for any explicit direction or any expression of [its] wishes" (Scott, 2001, p. 71). C's domination remains even less visible for B as the latter might have never directly dealt with C (if conditions 1-9 hold, C restricts access of organizations of the same type as A, i.e., buyers, letting B-type suppliers in without restrictions). In other words, C and, to a lesser degree, A remain "behind the curtain."

Along with obfuscating its dominance, C gains in more pragmatic terms as well. First, C can cash in on the advantages associated with entry control to the spot by getting A to buy an "entry ticket." C then uses a kind of "capitalization rate" when calculating the price of the "entry ticket." Second, by controlling entry, C avoids the need to enumerate and specify things, actions and relationships that C wants to happen or not to happen (Sack, 1986, p. 22), which may be time and resource consuming. Instead of telling A and B what to do, C just gets them behave in its interests by structuring relationships between them in a particular way.

Figure 5.2
Power Triad

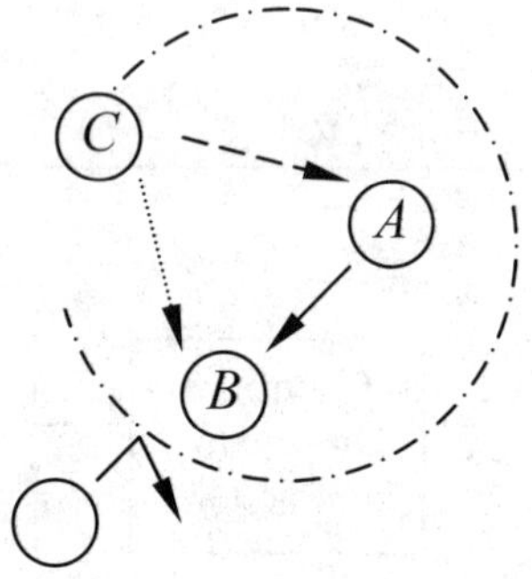

It is worth noting that the behavior of *A*, *B* and *C* is assumed to be driven by interests, only their functional roles differ (e.g., gatekeeper, buyer and supplier). Like Smith's pin-makers (1818, pp. 4-5), *A*, *B* and *C* all profit from the division of "labor." Hoverer, only *C* maximizes its satisfaction (gains both in absolute and relative—by appropriating the biggest share of monopolistic profits, a particular kind of rents, resulting from entry control—terms), whereas *A* and *B* minimize missed opportunities (gain only in absolute terms). *B* would gain less when not entering into the relationship with *A*, *A* would also get less without *C*'s assistance in limiting the number of *B*'s eventual counterparts, *C* would not make any profits without *A* and *B*—this is the constellation of *A*'s, *B*'s and *C*'s interests lying at the origin of the transformation of the market into a weapon. Similarly to the critical theory of law viewing in it a "form or dimension of social power" (Turk, 1976, p. 276), a critical institutional theory unveils structures of domination embedded in the market and studies their emergence.

What type of organizations has a comparative advantage in performing the functional role of *C*? Economists argue that a key function of states consists in regulating access to rare resources by establishing and enforcing property rights. Some of them, namely advocates of the New Institutional Economics, are particularly interested in studying the impact of secure property rights on economic subjects' incentive structure (North, 1981; Eggertsson, 1990, Part IV). The state's involvement into the business of gatekeeping makes sustainable structural distortions that constitute the field: unlike the firm, the state is protected against bankruptcy even if mismanaged.[12] Stability differentiates purely economic monopolies (i.e., established by *A* only) from politico-economic monopolies deriving a constellation of interests between *A* and *C* (Etzioni, 1988, p. 227).[13]

If there are several *A*s (i.e., the triad transforms into the field), the function of gatekeeping can be performed by *C* as a self-governing institution created by *A*s. The emergence of associative mechanisms for regulating access to common-pool resources (Ostrom, 1990) illustrates this alternative. *A*s then can appropriate and share the rents generated by entry control without losing advantages associated with the division of "labor" between *A*, *B* and *C*.

Gatekeeping makes sense only if there are clear-cut and impermeable boundaries delimiting the field. A differentiating feature of the organization as a particular coordination structure consists in "identifiable boundaries" (Ménard, 1993, p. 13; Hodgson, 2006, p. 8). Boundaries of the field have a larger scope and they contain a gate through which organizations (not individuals, as in the case of the organization) can get in upon acceptance of *C*'s domination. These boundaries can have an institutional (ethnic groups, clans, and other *Us* versus *Them* divisions, as well as restrictions imposed by the law and contracts), a spatial (an area or a territory), a financial (entrance fees, membership dues, and minimum capital requirements) or a symbolical (professional jurisdictions and credentials, tastes and lifestyle in connection with class divisions) nature. For instance, the embeddedness of states—at least in the case of Western nation-states—in the territory explains their inclination towards using spatial techniques of entry control. Only state logic can confer on a territory its clearest political identity (Badie, 2000).

The concept of territoriality developed in political geography seems highly relevant in this regard: "Territoriality establishes control over area as a means of controlling access to things and relationships" (Sack, 1986, p. 20). In other words, territoriality means domination by virtue of a constellation of interests embedded in a spatially delimited field.

Territoriality represents one of several possible configurations of the field of domination. Cross-tabulation of two variables, the type of boundaries and the type of flows subject to regulation, gives us a taxonomy of fields of domination suitable for empirical research. Institutional boundaries are subdivided in informal (social) and formal (written rules, regulations and laws). What can be moved across the boundaries of the field also counts: people, organizations, cultural patterns, goods and money (Table 5.1). The cells on the diagonal going from the upper left to the bottom right corner are shadowed in keeping with the assumption that institutional boundaries appear appropriate for regulating movements of people and organizations, symbolical—cultural

Table 5.1
Taxonomy of the Field's Boundaries and Flows Subject to Regulation

Boundary / Flow	Institutional A. Informal (social)	B. Formal	C. Symbolical	D. Spatial (territoriality)	E. Financial
1. People	1A	1B	1C	1D	1E
2. Organizations	2A	2B	2C	2D	2E
3. Cultural patterns	3A	3B	3C	3D	3E
4. Goods	4A	4B	4C	4D	4E
5. Money	5A	5B	5C	5D	5E

(Human agency applies to rows 1–3)

patterns; physical boundaries—movements of physical objects (goods) and, finally, financial boundaries—monetary flows.

Without pretending to fill all cells in this taxonomy, it would be instructive to see how it applies to a few empirically observed phenomena. For instance, access analysis of the internal configuration of space in houses, namely, the differentiation between more "public" and more "private" areas and the distance between them, illustrates the cell [1D] (Richardson, 2003; Bourdieu, 1979, pp. 79-90, 133-153). Spatially restricted access to some areas and the multiplication of rooms simultaneously reflect social distance and contribute to its reproduction.

Monetary flows embedded in social structures such as what the Arabs call *hawala* and the Chinese *fei ch'ien* serve as examples of the situation [5A]. In order to participate in a reliable system of money transfers and pay far less than when sending money through the regular banking system, one has to be a "good citizen" of a diaspora and accept the patterns of domination embedded in it (*Economist*, 2008; El-Qorchi, 2002). A similar configuration can be found in some corruption schemes. In fact, in order to be accepted as a bribe-giver, one often needs to have a dependable reputation built on the basis of previous interactions in a social network. "Not everyone is equally well positioned to access this market" protected by a net of social connections and mutual guarantees (Robbins, 2000, p. 436; see also Bourdieu, 2005, p. 140). Again, social boundaries help reproduce patterns of domination in the field where "contact-makers," who act as gatekeepers (called *blatmeisters* in the Soviet Union; see more on this institution in Ledeneva, 1998, pp. 104-123), and bribe-takers, not bribe-givers, have an upper hand.

II. Technique of Power: Not Letting in Versus Not Letting Out

Domination by virtue of a constellation of interests in the market rests on a particular technique for imposing will by restricting access and "not letting in." In spite of apparent similarities, the technique of "not letting in" ought to be clearly distinguished from that of "not letting out." The latter, in fact, has much in common with force and coercion (see Section III of Chapter 2). This works under the assumption that B's best interests consist in not entering into the relationship with A or in getting out of it. Applied to power relationships between individual actors, the technique of "not letting out" takes the most manifest forms in the case of prison. Restrictions of personal freedom progressively substituted for torture and corporal punishment as techniques of making the person disciplined and obedient. "The nineteenth century saw the spread of techniques of power proper to the disciplinary grid and their application to the space of exclusion (lepers, mad people, delinquents)" (Foucault, 1975, p. 200).[14]

The other example of the technique of "not letting out" at work can be found in the practices of racial segregation in the United States. The subjugation of African Americans by the dominant majority was first based on the institution of slavery, then on involuntary segregation giving way to "voluntary" segregation in ghettos and, more recently, to the incarceration of growing numbers of young black men in "judicial ghettos," i.e., prisons (Wacquant, 2001, pp. 98 ff.).

The work of police as a disciplinary institution also contains elements of the strategy of "not letting out." When pursuing a suspect, police officers must first seal off potential avenues of escape by creating a number of physical obstacles and barriers. A participant observation study shows that "police officers' subculturally constructed sense of themselves as successful rests quite basically on their capacities to control the flow of action across space" (Herbert, 1997, p. 87).

In management, employees might be kept living in particular locations such as company towns, which facilitate the control and surveillance of the workforce by the business owners and their lieutenants (Taylor & Spicer, 2007, pp. 330-332). For instance, both Henry Ford and George Pullman, designer and developer of the first sleeping car, were known for their attempts to subject the workforce to rigorous moral discipline by accommodating the workers in the specially built factory towns (Walzer, 1983, pp. 195-199).

The *territorial* "monopoly of the legitimate use of physical force in the enforcement of its order" (Weber, 1968, p. 54) gives states a comparative advantage in not letting people, organizations, goods or money out. This highlights an "elective affinity" between force and coercion, on the one hand, and *exit* control, on the other. States investing heavily in their ability to control the spatial movements of their subjects, e.g., the Soviet Union or China, prevent them from moving out of particular locations (using the system of mandatory registrations like *propiska* in the Soviet Union[15] or *hukou* in China, see Zhang, 2001, Ch. 1) and out of the country (issuing exit visas) without permission from the authorities. Applied to power relationships between organizations, exit control finds its expression, for example, in export duties as an element of mercantilist trade policies, the fight against capital flight (the Russian case is discussed in Oleinik et al., 2005, pp. 111-117) or restrictions on profit repatriation by MNEs.

The technique of "not letting in" works under the other set of assumptions. First, it implies that B is better off by "being in," i.e., by entering into the relationship with A, than by "being out." Second, it refers less to force and coercion, in spite of the fact that fences, walls or barbed wire might remain, than to the exclusion of some alternatives available to B and/or their substitution for the other alternatives (e.g., making a deal with A under the condition of accepting A's domination). A gets B to do something because of a constellation of their interests resulting from this "surgical intervention" on B's order of preferences.[16] Third, states also have a comparative advantage in exercising entry control, this time due to their *territorial* monopoly over the use of *symbolic* violence (Bourdieu, 2005, p. 92). Symbolic violence consists in shaping and reshaping at will the other's actor order of preferences, in "determining the good and the beautiful" (Ibid, p. 128). It also contributes to shaping symbolical boundaries (Lamont & Molnár, 2002).

The state has the ability (ability refers to the generic, unconditional "can"; see Morriss, 1987, pp. 80-83) to draw and enforce all types of boundaries: institutional, spatial, financial and symbolical. For instance, all these boundaries appear "at play" in the production of the housing market by the French state analyzed by Bourdieu. The state sets the criteria for admission to the field. For example, the demand for detached or semi-detached houses is far from being "naturally given" (Bourdieu, 2005, pp. 16-20, 121). Being a condition of the access to the field, the desire for owning a house reflects a particular social organization, a lineage, promoted by means of symbolic violence over the others, namely classes, socio-professional groups[17] or even neighborhoods. The state further lays down a set of general and specific regulations structuring interactions between subjects in the field: property law, commercial law, contract law, price freezes or controls, etc. (Ibid, p. 92). Urban zoning policies reflect spatial boundaries at work. Finally, the institution of mortgage helps "screen" potential entrants to the field by financial means (Ibid, p. 89) by enabling some of them to get in and keeping the others out. Gatekeeping provides the state (C) with an upper hand in its power struggles with the other subjects: construction firms, developers, real estate agents (As) and households (Bs).

Lynne Chester provides further examples of the markets with conditional access for either buyers or sellers or both. Namely, she shows that Australian electricity, water, employment services, housing, and carbon trading markets all involve setting criteria for the eligibility of buyers and sellers, as well as conditions for their access. "Ongoing market participation is not assured even if eligibility criteria are satisfied. Participants may be required to make regular payment (e.g., annual fees), be limited to a fixed term by contract, be subject to regular re-assessment of eligibility, or make payment for goods and services by supplier-determined time and method" (Chester, 2010, p. 15). The criteria and conditions are set by the government, which seems particularly surprising considering the prevalence of neo-liberal discourse in that country.

The comparison between entry visas with exit visas highlights the mechanics of "not letting in." Both intend to restrict the mobility of individual subjects yet in different ways. Entry control has several similar features with the admission to a club, especially in the case of immigration. "Individuals may be able to give good reasons why they should be selected, but no one on the outside has a right to be inside … it is a question of ideological affinities" (Walzer, 1983, pp. 41, 50). Exit control works at the level of physical constraints, entry control—at the level of preferences, even if the check-points as "a concrete, local, and powerful experience of the state, … the site where citizenship is strongly enforced" remain in play (Lamont & Molnár, 2002, p. 183). In order to be admitted, one has to "fine-tune" his or her preferences to those predominant in the field. Techniques for the subjugation of native populations and migrant populations differ accordingly. To control the former, ghettos or prisons might be needed, the procedure of "conditional admission" might well suffice to control the latter.[18] In the same vein, import duties and licenses, a tool for regulating flows of goods, work differently from export duties and licenses. The former distort the market play only to the extent necessary to produce a constellation of interests underpinning domination (e.g., protectionist policies) whereas the latter derive from anti-market mercantilist policies.[19]

There are a number of factors limiting the state's ableness to perform entry control. Their list includes, first, "the imperative to induce companies to invest" into the national economy (Farnsworth & Holden, 2006, p. 475). The model of welfare state makes C dependent on A's (businesses') willingness to invest, i.e., to enter into relationship with C. C's obligations in regard to ordinary citizens, Bs (social security, education, etc.), and the imperative of material welfare (pecuniary interests prevail over the other interests) necessitates A's ableness to generate a continuous flow of resources. In other words, structures in which domination by virtue of a constellation of interests are always enabling and constraining C's ableness to carry out its agenda. Interests *constellate* instead of being suppressed.

Second, in a given moment in time, numerous fields produced by state actors coexist at the national and the international levels. Boundaries drawn by regional authorities overlap with each other, as they overlap to some degree with those drawn by the central government. This creates loop-hopes in the fence and limits C's domination within a particular field (Bourdieu, 2005, pp. 136-137). A also has a choice of moving from one national field to the other. "The possibility of moving from one jurisdiction to another with lower regulatory demands puts downward pressure on regulations across all jurisdictions" (Sassen, 2000, p. 380; see also Farnsworth & Holden, 2006, p. 481). Globalization in this sense strengthens the structural component of A's power.

A countervailing factor that structurally strengthens C's domination consists in its control over resources with limited mobility (e.g., natural resources) for which A can hardly find substitutes. C's control of access to unique resources increases A's vulnerability and allows C to extract additional rents. For instance, the Russian government's control over the world's major oil and gas deposits enables it to extract significant resource rents in relationships with oil and gas companies, including MNEs (Gaddy & Ickes, 2005; see also Keohane & Nye, 2001, p. 13; Section II of the Introduction, and Section III of Chapter 6).

Third, some non-state organizations challenge the state's monopoly over drawing borders. Such classical activity of trade unions as the picketing of the site of a strike represents one of such challenges. Not surprisingly, states usually respond abruptly to trade unions' efforts to draw and enforce their own boundaries. The 1984-1985 coal dispute in the UK, in which the government aimed to prevent the National Union of Mineworkers' from picketing, serves an excellent illustration (Blomley, 1994, Ch. 5). The territorial embeddedness also characterizes activities of the Sicilian Mafia: each "family," *coscà*, tends to control a particular territory (Arlacchi, 1986, pp. 176-178). Conflicts abound because the state and the Mafia claim sovereignty over the same territories: "the government intervention is tolerated only as long as it does not interfere with the usual business of the Mafia" (Padovani, 1987, p. 15).

III. Three Exemplifying Cases

Three exemplifying cases represent various configurations of the field. They can be classified with the help of four variables: the type of organization occupying structural positions C, A, and B in the field and the type of boundaries drawn by C (Table 5.2). The buyer occupies subaltern position B in all cases but one, (3). Social boundaries prevail

Table 5.2
Taxonomy of Exemplifying Cases

Case	Organization in position			Type of boundary
	C	A	B	
1. Open-air market in Russia in the 1990s	Organized crime	Seller	Buyer	Spatial
2. Supermarket/mall	Retailer	Seller	Buyer	Spatial and financial
3. Supply-chain	Buyer	Buyer	Supplier	Institutional

in relationships between individuals. When they structure relationships between organizations, as in the case of interlocking directorates or industrial districts (for an overview, see Oleinik, 2004a, pp. 94-101), they combine with other boundaries, spatial or institutional. This explains why the three case studies do not include an example of social or symbolical boundaries at work.

III.1 Open-Air Markets in Russia in the 1990s

Prices of all goods and services, as well as their nomenclature were subject to state regulation in the command economy. The liberalization of trade and prices decreed by Boris Yeltsin, President of the Russian Federation, on December 3, 1991 (Decree No. 297), was one of first steps in the radical market reforms started shortly before the fall of the Soviet Union. Due to the lack of market infrastructure, buyers and sellers first flooded streets and places in the cities and towns. However, they quickly realized the need for finding a place where buyers can meet sellers and *vice versa*, i.e., the need for the market in its simplest, an immediate sense of a "place of sale" (Ménard, 2005b, p. 91). Markets for agricultural products existed during Soviet times, yet in a very restricted number and in a format that did not meet the new requirements.

The New Institutional Economics predicts that entrepreneurs maximizing their profits will create new institutional arrangements and organizations that help capitalize on new opportunities (Davis & North, 1970). Nevertheless, they fail to indicate that such innovations make commercial sense only if institutional or organizational innovations take the form of a club good having two characteristics: non-rivalrous and excludable (Sandler, 1992, Ch. 1). The latter calls for drawing boundaries, controlling access, and charging entrance fees. The creation of the market by a "visible hand" requires only the fencing of a piece of land in the downtown area or close to a nexus of transport connections, the organization of a check point and the building of a few hundreds of booths or small shops for lease (Figure 5.3). The gatekeeper (*C*) can not only capitalize on the new opportunity, but also extract monopolistic rents by limiting the access of sellers to the marketplace. A limited number of sellers (*A*s) enjoys an upper hand in relationships with buyers (*B*s), but in return *C* charges *A*s an "entrance fee" including a significant portion of the monopolistic profit. *A*s, *B*s and *C* are all better off by entering into the relationship (*B*s—because of the lack of alternatives and general shortages of consumer goods).

As in southern Italy, organized crime was the first to understand and seize the opportunity. In the early stages of its development, the Mafia was "protecting" local fruit and vegetable markets by limiting competition (e.g., the "Mafia of the Gardens," see Rusakov, 1969, pp. 96-102). Later, the Mafia extended the same technology for extracting rents to the other local and regional markets (Gambetta, 1993, p. 198; Arlacchi, 1986, pp. 106-108). Investments in open-air markets occupied a privileged place among the economic activities of the organized crime in Russia in the 1990s. First, they could be made more or less legally, which helped launder the money generated by purely criminal activities. Second, they were a safe and very profitable bet (a middle-size open-air market in Moscow generated a yearly rent of up to $1 million for those who controlled it; see the excerpt from an interview below). Third, this business has some "elective affinity" with the regular activities of organized crime: control of movements and flows, the principle of territoriality, extortion. There is, nevertheless, a notable difference: the victim

Figure 5.3
Layout of an Open-Air Market in Moscow (existing since the early 1990s)

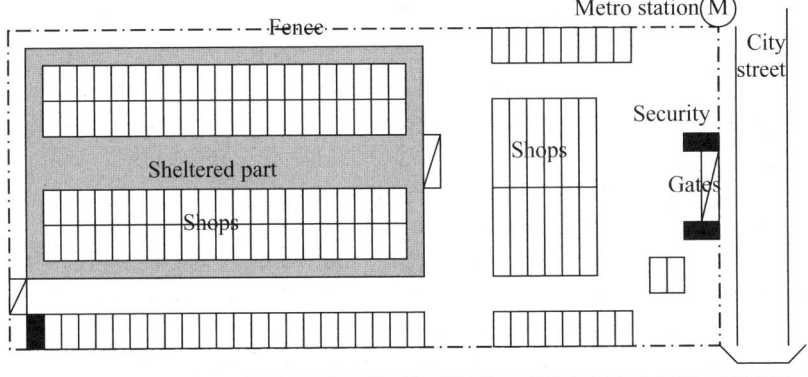

of extortion chooses between the worst and the second worst, the firm willing to sell on the open-air market minimizes missed opportunities by agreeing to pay a "tribute."

> "They [members of large criminal 'syndicates'] became legal owners [in the mid-1990s]. *If I follow you, they purchased the shares in the name of their members?* Yes. Of course, not all members [got the shares], only a narrow circle of those at the top. They become owners of such enterprises as a large market for agricultural products, a large department store ... an open-air market, these are especially popular now" (from the interview with a male criminal gang member conducted in summer 2001 in a maximum security prison, in the region of Sverdlovsk).

> "One can make megabucks on an empty spot without doing anything. I mean it would be enough to put up 600 shops and that's it.... I've just had my man taking care of everything, our man in fact.... *Did you control him?* I don't care whether he gets any extras. I care only about my share, in cash.... I get this cash and the rest is not my business: whether he pays the security guards out of it or just pockets it.... In the past, [the fee was] $1,500 [per shop, per year], the rest is not my business.... I don't really care—there are 600 booths, one and a half [thousand] from each gives 900 [thousand]. After that, everything is in his hands—he can rent them for two [thousand]—it's all his business. He must know all this stuff" (from the interview with a thief-in-law—*vor v zakone* is the highest informal rank in the traditional criminal milieu in the former Soviet Union[20]—conducted in fall 2000 in a high security prison, the region of Murmansk).

III.2 The Supermarket/Shopping Mall Field

In the case of Russia, open-air markets since the end of the 1990s started to progressively transform into supermarkets and shopping malls (sometimes the latter were even built in the spots previously occupied by the former) that also represent a field of domination by virtue of a constellation of interests. The share of open-air markets in the total turnover of retail trade decreased from 26.6 percent in 1995 to 21.1 percent in 2005 (8.3 percent in 1990; see Federal State Statistics Service, 2006b, p. 545). At the same time, the emergent field is not country-specific. A few large retailers dominate retail trade in most developed countries. For instance, the ten largest US retailers accounted in the early 2000s for 80 percent of the average manufacturer's business (Corsten & Kumar, 2005, p. 80).

The supermarket/shopping mall field comprises the same subjects as the open-air market: the gatekeeper (the retailer,[21] C), the seller (the manufacturer, A) and the buyer (the final customer, B). To this list, as shown below, a second gatekeeper, the state (C'), has to be added. Yet the configuration of their relationships differs significantly. The supermarket business flourishes in a mass consumption society in which the aggregate supply tends to exceed the aggregate supply (open-air markets emerged during the process of the transformation of the shortage economy with the aggregate demand exceeding the aggregate supply; see Kornai, 1980). The supermarket represents a "focal point," a place where manufacturers meet customers. The number of meeting places cannot be large; otherwise, instead of facilitating coordination, they render it more complicated, as illustrated by "pure coordination" games (Schelling, 1960, Ch. 3; Schotter, 1981, pp. 22-23). This creates a structural bias: the control of access to a limited number of meeting places paves the way to domination of C and C'. Property rights over site-specific assets, i.e., assets whose maximal yield is a result of their particular location (Ménard, 2005a, p. 55), facilitates the appropriation of the gatekeeper's role but is not an absolute must. For instance, a supermarket located at a crowded intersection or near a subway station loses its value if, for some reason, sellers and/or buyers stop considering it a "focal point."[22] Domination in retail trade derives less from property rights over particular assets than from the capacity to control access to the meeting place of producers and consumers.

The excess of supply means that the meeting place becomes overcrowded: the number of manufacturers willing to sell their products to final customers is larger than the actual capacities of the retailers. In the words of the owner of a large Russian retailer, "I recently asked my staff to calculate the size of a store that could accommodate all manufacturers that would like to sell their goods through our chain. It appeared that it must have a surface of 140 thousand square meters. We don't have such stores and, probably, the customers would not like them either" (Khasis, 2006). It is worth noting that the turnover of the Russian retail trade has grown faster than the GDP (one should keep in mind that the Russian economy as a whole had exceptionally high growth rates between 1999 and 2008, see Table 5.3).

These tendencies further strengthen the structural position of the retailer, C, who controls the access to the final customer, B. B also gains from the reconfiguration, yet to a lesser degree. In other words, A loses a part of its structural power, C and B gain at A's expense. Yet even A does not lose in absolute terms as a result of the benefits associated with increased and more stable sales. Because of the new structure of the field, C's room for maneuvering when extracting rents from B and, especially, A increases. The practice of charging As "entrance fees" does not disappear.[23]

Table 5.3
GDP (real volume) and Turnover in Retail Trade (physical volume), the Russian Federation, 2000-2007, % to previous year

	GDP	Turnover in retail trade
1995	95.9	93.8
2000	110	109
2001	105.1	111
2002	104.7	109.3
2003	107.3	108.8
2004	107.2	113.3
2005	106.4	112.8
2006	107.7	114
2007	108.1	116

Sources: Federal State Statistics Service, 2006, pp. 36, 542 and retrieved from http://www.gks.ru/bgd/regl/b08_11/IssWWW.exe/Stg/d02/21-04.htm and http://www.gks.ru/bgd/free/b01_19/IssWWW.exe/Stg/d000/i000230r.htm

> "The retailer dictates the rules of the game; there is no doubt about this. If the supplier wants to enter into any chain store, they must pay and, further, cast itself on its knees. Up to us to decide whether they will sell their products here or not" (from the interview with a senior manager of a large chain store conducted in spring 2006, Moscow[24]).

In the new structural conditions C can go further and demand from A a number of other concessions. The list of conditions under which the manufacturer is "let in" might include side payments for enlarging its nomenclature of goods offered in the retailer's stores, side payments for "renting" the shelves (especially located in "hot spots"), payment arrears (up to 45 days) for the goods sold, compensations for the goods stolen in the retailer's stores, side payments for promotion companies carried out by the retailer, severe fines for breaking contractual terms and others (Radaev, 2007, pp. 182-184).

> "Metro and Auchan make money by getting kick backs from the suppliers: bonuses, primes, etc. One pays to 'get in' a few thousand on the spot, then some thousands— each quarter. They have a very small margin, about 10%, the key source of profits being charges paid by the manufacturers."[25]

Western retailers use more sophisticated strategies for extracting rents in their home markets. For instance, they launch expensive Efficient Consumer Response (ECR) programs. These programs help C attract new customers by improving the level of service, but C has the ableness to place the burdens of ECR adoption on Bs while appropriating its benefits (Corsten & Kumar, 2005). As a result of *C*'s domination, *B*s occasionally sell their products for the cost price, which in some countries prompted the state to intervene and limit *C*'s domination at least partly. The law sets a minimum selling price covering the manufacturer's costs in France (Barrey, 2006, p. 147). This strengthens *B*'s ableness to resist *C*'s requests to give *C* the lowest, exclusive price.

"We insist that they [the manufacturers] give us the best price" [in the market].

The intervention of the state is not necessarily benevolent in nature, especially in Russia where the state embodies power in its pure form (see Chapters 3 and 4). In fact, the state may transform into a second gatekeeper, the one who controls access to retail trade as a particular industry (cf. the supermarket controls access to the "shelf" as a meeting place). The Russian case provides ample examples of the state playing the role of *C'*, the second gatekeeper. The state uses institutional boundaries, namely, the law, in order to control access to retail trade and to grant it under certain conditions.

The evolution of subsequent drafts of the Federal Law on Principles of State Regulation of Retail Trade enacted on the 1st of January 2010 is telling (Oleinik, 2008f). The January 2008 draft enabled the government and its regional bodies to cap prices. According to the March 2008 draft, the state lost this privilege but acquired another one—the right to limit the market share of a particular retailer in the local market. The maximally allowed market share was set so low[26] that this would open the door to discretionary behavior and corruption on the part of state servants. In the subsequent versions, the emphasis has completely changed. Instead of limiting them by means of anti-trust policies, the state supports large retailers that assume responsibility for the situation in the politically sensitive market of consumer goods in exchange. This creates favorable conditions for converting economic rents into political benefits, as happened on the eve of the March 2008 presidential elections in Russia: the major retailers were asked to cap prices on basic necessities in exchange for the promise of *carte blanche* in pricing and further expansion after the elections. The final version makes a U-turn and reintroduces the control by means of anti-trust policies. It appears that the benefits associated with controlling access to the market did not escape the attention of Russian office holders. They managed to gradually—toward the end of the 1990s—push organized crime out of this

**Figure 5.4
Field of Retail Trade in Russia**

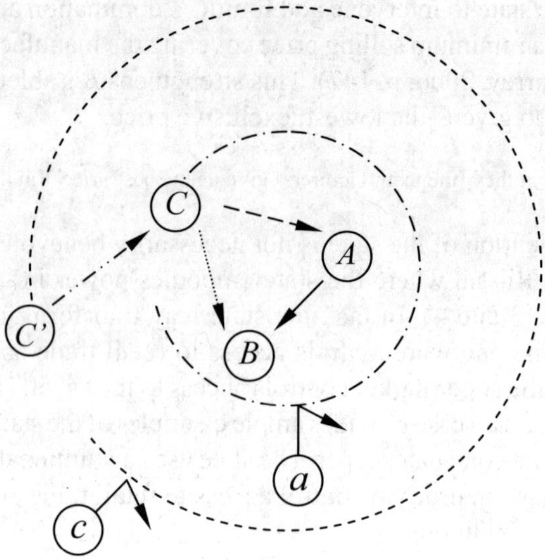

business and re-shape the field of retail trade (Figure 5.4, *a* and *c* are would-be producer and would-be retailer respectively).

The supermarket/shopping mall model can be generalized beyond retail trade. "It is evident that bureaucrats may exercise their power over business through ... selling various permits to enter the market and then to operate in it (licenses and certificates).... [This technique helps] establish *control* over the market field, which in turn ensures the constant flow of rents" (Albats, 2005, p. 17; emphasis in original). If the state or regional authorities manage to control access to the national and/or regional markets, then they might behave in a similar manner with respect to firms interested in entering this market and force them to buy "entry tickets." The structure of the field underpins the state as the gatekeeper's (*C*) dominance over multinational enterprises or enterprises with headquarters located in other regions (*A*s), on the one hand, and over customers of their products (*B*s), on the other. An in-depth case study of such a configuration of the field is discussed in the next chapter.

III.3 The Supply-Chain Field

Supply chains, a topic actively discussed in organization theory and managerial literature, can also be managed by using the technique of "not letting in." Supply chains differ from a dyadic relationship between the supplier and the buyer. They include, along with first-tier supplier, second-tier and, eventually, higher-tier suppliers. Supply chain management means "a sourcing technique that involves the buyer undertaking proactive supplier development work, not only at the first-tier of the supply chain but also at all stages in the supply chain from first-tier through to raw material supply" (Cox, 2004a, p. 350). This serves to classify the supply chain as a field with the buyer in its center.

Supply chain management spreads rapidly in many industries, namely retail trade and car manufacturing. The Japanese car manufacturers were among first to introduce a multi-layer structure of relationships with the auto parts makers. The most intensive, collaborative contacts are maintained with the first-tier suppliers and the intensity of mutual obligations decreases as the distance from the center, the car manufacturer, grows (Aoki, 1991, pp. 223-224). The operation of the Japanese transplants in North America stimulated the adoption of a similar model by American car manufacturers (Benton & Maloni, 2005). As a result, top car manufacturers do not buy parts in the open market but rather create their own "fields" with restricted access.

The structure of the US car manufacturing industry—five top producers account for 85 percent of the market share (Ibid, p. 7)—explains the buyer's ableness to configure the supply chain at will and to control access to it by deciding with whom to sign contracts (boundaries have an institutional nature here being embedded in the contractual law). In other words, the buyer in these conditions performs two roles: C (by shaping the field and controlling entry) and A (by being directly involved in relationships with the suppliers).

In this field, the supplier occupies a subaltern position, B. Nevertheless, B is neither forced nor coerced to enter into the contractual relationship with C/A. B still has a positive incentive to cooperate because it benefits from increased volume and greater input/output stability, which allows it to reduce its production and transaction costs (Crook & Combs, 2007, pp. 550-552). B clearly minimizes missed opportunities, B and A/C's interests are aligned in a constellation instead of being mutually exclusive. Taking into consideration the fact that the application of coercive power within supply chains affects A/C's situation negatively (Benton & Maloni, 2005, p. 14), A/C has very pragmatic reasons for learning the art of aligning its interests with those of B (Cox, 2004b; Cox et al., 2004).

This type of task interdependence further limits C/A's ableness to go "too far" in extracting rents. The supermarket model is based on pool-

Figure 5.5
Supply Chain as a Field of Domination

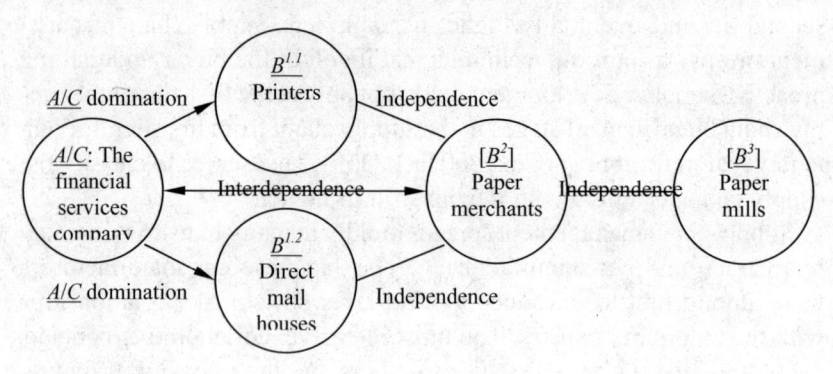

```
A/C domination ──→  B^{1.1}        Independence
                   Printers  ──→
A/C: The                            [B^2]                    [B^3]
financial    ←── Interdependence ──→ Paper  ──Independence── Paper
services                            merchants                mills
company
                    B^{1.2}
A/C domination ──→  Direct     Independence
                    mail
                    houses
```

Source: Adapted from (Cox et al., 2004, p. 361).

ing supplies, whereas the supply chain in manufacturing is based on the sequential transformation of supplies (Crook & Combs, 2007, p. 549). As C/A deals directly only with first-tier B^1, higher-tier Bs (B^2, B^3, etc.) have more room for maneuvering. In fact, in intermediate dyads, B^1—B^2, B^2—B^3 and other local configurations of domination or interdependence (when parties are equally vulnerable and sensitive) might emerge (see Figure 5.5 with the supply chain of a financial services company buying marketing print services as an example). They help some Bs compensate at least partly for opportunities missed in the relationship with C/A at the expense of the other Bs. Empirical studies also show that the strategic component of C/A's ableness to capitalize all opportunities embedded in the field might be weak due to subjective misperceptions on the part of C/A's management and/or to their failure to efficiently undertake necessary steps (Cox et al., 2004). Yet, this discussion calls for changing the unit of analysis and shifting the focus towards individuals and groups rather than organizations.

Conclusion

The proposed sketch of how domination by virtue of a constellation of interests works allows for moving toward reconciling the individualist (neoclassical economics) and structuralist (critical theory) approaches. Domination is neither an outcome of free and conscious choices, as the former suggests, nor a product of depersonalized and invisible forces embedded in institutions, as the latter implies. Lukes' emphasis on the bias of the system, the structural component of one's ableness to dominate, overshadows the need to get it mobilized.

The argument developed in this chapter lies in the middle ground between the individualist and the structuralist extremes. Domination in the market is continuously produced and reproduced by actors, both individual and organizational, in their day-to-day business. Initially small structural distortions and biases embedded in the institutional environment as a result of consciously chosen and implemented strategies transform into larger ones that can be used as a lever in relationships. The slightest departures from the conditions of perfect competition, this "nirvana" situation for neoclassical economists, can be reinforced and aggravated by conscious efforts of actors to turn the biases to their own advantage. Once presented with an opportunity for extracting monopolistic rents by limiting competition, rationally minded actors try to make this opportunity enduring by further distorting the structure of the field to their advantage. The strategic component of one's ableness to dominate helps strengthen its structural component and so forth. The access to the field limited by structural factors (e.g., the physical capacity to accommodate all potential traders) is further limited by humanly designed and made boundaries (e.g., by entry control carried out by the gatekeeper).

This reasoning can also shed new light on the evolution of the individual/group habituses, namely the question as to where it comes from (see also Section II of the Conclusion). The habituses are products of the lust for domination "engraved" in the institutional environment. Small events and decisions progressively transform the field of interactions. This strengthens the structural component of one actor's ableness to dominate and weakens that of the others. Further choices of the interacting parties, hence, are limited by their past interactions. So, the habitus of domination and maximization of satisfaction emerges and shapes the behavior of A and, especially, C. The opposite side of the coin consists in the development of the habitus of submission. It leads B to minimize missed opportunities (in the case of domination by virtue of a constellation of interests) instead of maximizing satisfaction.

The proposed analysis suggests interesting theoretical implications calling for further research. Following Smith, neoclassical economists argue that exchanges in the market are mutually profitable. They refer to the "Win-Win" situation as an analytical and practical (justifying antitrust policies) yardstick even when they speak about monopolistic and oligopolistic markets. If there were no distortions, they argue, interacting parties would be interested in maintaining the conditions of perfect competition as long as possible. This optimism seems unjustified in the light of the present study. When presented with an opportunity for extracting rents, interest-driven actors will not only take it, they will also try to make this opportunity permanent by aggravating the structural bias of the field.

Perfectly competitive markets are not sustainable in this sense. Most transactions in the real, not ideally designed, market are biased to some extent, which means that one party has an upper hand over the other with respect to splitting the profits generated by the interaction. "While there will be no situations in transactions in which both parties can fully achieve their 'ideal' value capture goals, there will be many in which both parties achieve some of their goals even though one party wins slightly, or even a great deal, more from the exchange than the other" (Cox, 2004b, pp. 415-416). This further implies that the model of the minimization of missed opportunities ought to be considered as a necessary complement of the model of maximizing behavior. They can be compared with two sides of the same coin.

Notes

1. The market, as the argument goes, has literally saved many lives by allowing the redemption of serfs and prisoners (Frey & Buhofer, 1986).
2. The issues of the organization's internal structure remain beyond the scope of the proposed analysis, namely the task of identifying a stakeholder who has the most influence on the process of setting organizational goals and their implementation. The inquiry into power and domination *within* organizations deserves to be the subject of a special study that could be carried out with the help, for instance, of the theory of coalitions (Andreff, 2003, pp. 240-242) or of the concept of the "field of the firm" meaning "the structure of the relation of force between different agents that belong to the firm" (Bourdieu, 2005, p. 69).
3. "Because many scholars use similar concepts but identify them by different terms, confusion results about the degree to which people are saying different things" (Fligstein & Dauter, 2007, p. 106).
4. The social exchange theory further generalizes the model of mutually beneficial exchanges well beyond the marketplace, to all social actions (see an overview in Emerson, 1976).
5. Western people with experience in doing business in post-Soviet countries witness a widespread belief among their local counterparts that only one party of a market transaction wins: "There is no win-win strategy. It is a win-lose mentality: one of us gains, the other loses" (interview with a French businessman operating a business in Russia cited in Muratbekova-Touron, 2002, p. 223); "We've got an impression that for them [Russian counterparts] the most important is not to conclude a deal, after all, it's all about gaining the upper hand. This seems to be the most important. So, for us, the relationship is biased a bit" (the interview with a top manager of a large French company operating in Russia cited in Oleinik et al., 2005, p. 41).
6. It should be noted that only power *over* clearly contradicts freedom, as stated in the Introduction to this chapter. Power *over* involves restrictions over *B*'s range of choices that are imposed by *A*. Power *to*, in fact, represents a key precondition for

freedom, as Peter Morriss argues. "A concern about people's inabilities (or lack of power [*to*]) is far more important than a concern about their unfreedoms" (2009, p. 65). However, shifting emphasis in this manner would lead us far from the context of interactions, namely, between *A* and *B*, and blur the distinctions between human and unhuman-made constraints.

7. Controlling access to material objects (the institution of property rights) historically evolves into controlling access to potential counterparts, to a relationship. John Commons (1939, p. 237) speaks in this regard of "an evolution of the notion of property from the ownership of visible things to the ownership of invisible encumbrances on behavior and opportunities."

8. The label *C* is used taking into consideration conventional notations in analytical philosophy. In fact, a more explicit, yet less compact and universal system of notations would include Principal (*A*), who controls entry, Agent (*B*), who profits from structural biases, and Client (*C*).

9. The third party to a transaction as a gatekeeper shall be clearly differentiated from the third party as a contract enforcer. Douglass North (1990, pp. 34-35), for instance, considers the latter case in depth when discussing three forms of exchange: personalized exchange, and impersonal exchange without third-party enforcement (kinship ties, merchant codes, etc.), impersonal exchange with third-party enforcement.

10. Brym, Lie and Rytina (2008, pp. 10-11) offers a sketch of the structural differences between the dyad and the triad.

11. Karl Marx's account of the enclosure of Commons (lands in communal property) in eighteenth-century England suggests multiple parallels between drawing new physical boundaries and restricting access to agricultural land, on the one hand, and the emergence of the field of capitalist domination, on the other (1936, Ch. XXVII). Yet, in this example, the access to a capitalist field is mediated by the control of access to a resource, which makes it less pure.

12. Cf. the idea of considering the state a "juristic person" potentially subject to bankruptcy (Churkin, 2006).

13. On uses of government regulations and "strategic" corporate social responsibility policies by multinational enterprises, MNEs, to raise rivals' costs and not let them in, see Rodriguez et al., 2006, pp. 738-740.

14. Here prison is understood in its "ideal-typical" functions: custody and punishment (Sykes, 1958, pp. 18-31). The task of rehabilitation paves the way to conditional release as a form of "not letting in" (the control of access to the society outside the prison walls). Nevertheless, the latter task is usually sacrificed to the previous two: "If society is not sure of the priority to be attached to the tasks assigned the prison, the overriding importance of custody is perfectly clear to the officials" (Ibid, p. 18).

15. The roots of this institution can be found in the police state that existed in Russia before the October 1917 revolution. "According to the Russian law, the passport serves as a document identifying its holder and confirming his right to live in a particular location" (Gribovsky, 1912, p. 206).

16. It is worth mentioning that the "hard core" of neoclassical economics includes the assumption of stable and exogenous preferences (Eggertsson, 1990, pp. 5-6), which makes it blind to domination by virtue of a constellation of interests.

17. These two have more "elective affinity" with living in such dwellings as apartment buildings and low-cost housing, *HLM* in French; see more on links between the class habitus and the life in *HLM* in Bourdieu, 1979, pp. 79-92.

18. Illegal immigrants—illegal aliens as they are called in the US—escape this screening and, hence, remain outside the scope of the host state's control.

19. The policies encouraging to "Buy American" (or Russian, or any other national product) popular at the time of economic crisis started in 2008 create particularly

20. The institution of "thieves in law" is discussed in more detail in Oleinik, 2003, pp. 73-78.
21. In the Russian case, organized crime often managed to convert its control over open-air markets into a significant stake in the chain store business. For instance, the owner of a large regional chain store Sberegaika (the region of Orel) reportedly has a background in organized crime, see *Kommersant* No. 14 (3831) from January 31, 2008, p. 5.
22. This happened with Arbat Prestizh, once the largest Russian cosmetics retailer (comprising 95 stores with the turnover of $471.5 million in 2007), after criminal charges were laid against its owners in January 2008. Producers started to change their preferences in favor of smaller retailers. Consumers, who had found fewer and fewer brand names on the shelves, followed their lead. The last store working under the trademark Arbat Prestizh was closed in early 2009 (*Kommersant*, No. 23 [4078] from February 10, 2009, p. 8).
23. The price of the "entry ticket" varies in function of the commodity group: minimal in the case of goods for children, maximal in the case of strong alcohol (Khasis, 2006).
24. The interviews cited in this section were conducted in the framework of a research project carried out at the State University—the Higher School of Economics (Moscow) (Ovchinnikova, 2006).
25. Large international retailers started to open outlets in Russia relatively recently: Metro—in 2001, Auchan—in 2002. In spite of the fact that the share of top 10 retailers in the total turnover of retail trade was about 4 percent in 2004 (calculated by the author on the basis of the data from Federal State Statistics Service, 2006b, p. 545 and Radaev, 2005, p. 12), it is rapidly increasing and, according to interviews, rules of the game are set now principally by these largest retailers.
26. Twenty-five percent, cf. the 60 percent market share of a retailer does not prompt any severe restrictions in the UK and Germany (Boeri et al., 2006, p. 67).

6

Minimizing Missed Opportunities: A New Model of Choice?

Introduction

A set of key axioms of "hard core" neoclassical economic theory (Eggertsson, 1990, pp. 3-32) suggest that there is a solid link between the model of rational choice and the existence of a unique, stable, and Pareto-efficient market equilibrium. The market "clears" and reaches equilibrium as a result of individual choices by economic agents who intend to maximize their utility. Sub-optimality at both the micro (if economic agents fail to maximize the utility) and macro (the existence of multiple equilibria and market failures[1]) levels has always puzzled economists.

This chapter focuses on differentiating two potential sources of sub-optimal outcomes at the micro level; the first refers to the nature of individual choice and the second—to interactions between agents and coordination of their actions. Special attention will be paid to the latter, namely to sub-optimal outcomes resulting from a particular configuration of power relationships, taking into consideration that "power is an intended or desired casual effect" (Scott, 2001, p. 5). In what follows, power will be understood mostly in the narrow sense, as domination (see also Chapter 2).

Power relationships produce an asymmetrical situation: the Principal[2] tries to realize his or her agenda whereas the Agent chooses between sub-optimal outcomes. While doing this, the Principal employs several strategies. One of these, domination by virtue of a constellation of interests in the market, is the subject of the present analysis (see also Chapter 5). The Principal structures the Agent's incentives in such a way that the attempts of the latter to behave rationally lead him or her to produce effects desired by the former.

Monopolistic power illustrates this form of domination. Neoclassical economists show how monopoly leads to sub-optimal outcomes at the macro level. Nevertheless, they appear less interested in modifications in the model of individual choice (the assumption of rational choice still holds) induced by monopoly and in the interactive side of relationships between the Principal (monopolist) and the Agent.

Section I is devoted to differentiating sources of sub-optimal outcomes embedded in individual decision-making from those that reside in interactions and coordination of actions. Power is considered as one of the coordination mechanisms. A special case of power relationships, domination by virtue of a constellation of interests, is discussed in Section II. This involves minimizing the Agent's missed opportunities. In this context, interactions between the Principal and the Agent produce a model of individual choice that has been under-explored in the existing literature. Empirical examples considered in Section III illustrate the idea of domination by virtue of a constellation of interests. They refer to recent tendencies in emerging markets in post-Soviet countries, namely Russia. These tendencies took especially manifest forms in 1999-2008.

I. Sources of Sub-Optimal Outcomes: Individual Decision Making Versus Interactions

Particularities of approaches developed, on the one hand, by neoclassical economists and, on the other hand, by sociologists, game theorists and advocates of the old institutional theory facilitate the task of analytically differentiating sources of sub-optimality. The former group focuses attention on individual decision-making, whereas the latter examines interactions.

Neoclassical economists indicate that limited cognitive capacities and high transaction costs prevent the economic agent from finding and implementing a solution that guarantees maximum satisfaction. The model of bounded rationality shows "how we use limited information and limited computational capacity to deal with enormous problems" (Simon, 1978, p. 13). Uncertainty, or unawareness of all possible "states of nature," further complicates the task of finding an optimal solution (Langlois, 1986, p. 228). Socio-economists add a new dimension to the model of bounded rationality. They argue that moral values and convictions should be added to the list of constraints under which a choice is actually made. That which appears to be the most technically expedient might contradict one's moral convictions. The conflict between values and rational considerations calls for ordering preferences. If values transform into meta- or second-order preferences, then they can "overrule" first-order preferences referring to the model of rational choice and lead to sub-optimal—in terms of technical expedience—outcomes (Jonge, 2005).

Models of rational choice remain focused on individual decision-making. In spite of the existence of various institutionalist interpretations of bounded rationality, they just add new parameters, or constraints under which an individual attempts to maximize his or her utility (Figure 6.1). If transaction costs are taken into consideration, which becomes common in standard economic analysis, economists interpret them as "taxes" on exchanges (see, for instance, Ménard, 2005a, pp. 48-50).

The search for an alternative source of sub-optimal outcomes involves focusing on transactions, not commodities or individuals, as the unit of analysis. This approach characterizes interpretative sociology with its focus on social action, game theory and the "old" institutional economics. In this perspective, sub-optimality can be attributed to coordination failures. This causal link takes especially manifest forms in so-called "pure coordination" games: in order to achieve desired outcomes, everyone needs to adjust their behavior to that of their counterparts. For example, each of two motorists on a narrow road depends on the counterpart's choice (turn left or right) to achieve the ultimate goal of avoiding collision (see Schelling, 1960, Ch. 3; Schotter, 1981, pp. 22-23).

It is worth noting that, even if individuals manage to find common references and coordinate their behavior, there is no guarantee against falling into sub-optimality. Common references (convention) are embedded in institutions that "are products of the past process, are adapted

Figure 6.1
Sources of Sub-Optimality in Individual Decision-Making

Maximization of utility under constraint of
- Scarcity of resources
- Scarcity of information
- Scarcity of cognitive capacity
- Moral preferences
- [...]

to past circumstances, and are therefore never in full accord with the requirements of the present" (Veblen, 1934, p. 191; see also Sugden, 1989).

Power relationships emerge as one of the tools that help to solve coordination problems: instead of trying to predict the counterpart's choice, the individual transfers the right to control his or her actions to the former who then becomes the Principal. The Principal decides how the Agent is to behave and what actions the latter has to undertake when confronted with unforeseen contingencies (Coleman, 1990, pp. 66-67; Kreps, 1990a, pp. 92-93). Two or more centers of decision-making merge into one. In other words, the Principal *causes* the Agent's actions. The Principal's decisions do not necessarily refer to the past; thus in conditions of uncertainty, coordination through power relationships has greater potential than spontaneous coordination embedded in institutions.

Employing power as a solution to coordination problems has its price, however (Figure 6.2). The Agent is expected to maximize not his or her own utility, but that of the Principal. The Principal acts under a new constraint too: the Agent's utility transforms into a parameter of the utility function of the former. The Principal-Agent literature helps emphasize the opposition between the Principal's model of choice and that of the Agent. Joseph Stiglitz (1987, p. 969) reduces the Principal-Agent model to the following system of simple equations (EU refers to expected utility; $\bar{U}$—to the minimal compensation that the Agent would be willing to accept in exchange for transferring the right to control his or her actions):

$$\begin{cases} \max EU_{Principal} \\ EU_{Agent} \geq \bar{U} \end{cases} \quad [1]$$

Figure 6.2
Sources of Sub-Optimality in Interactions

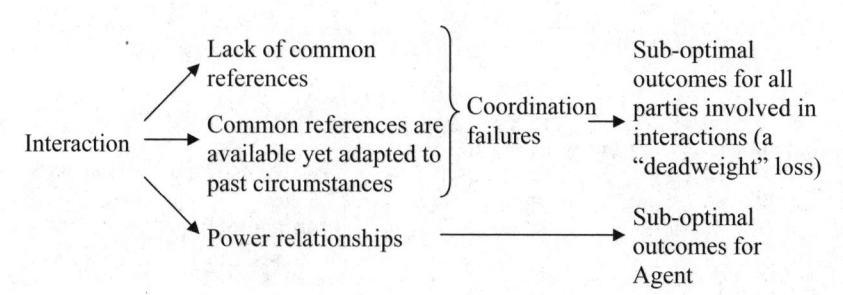

Interaction →
- Lack of common references
- Common references are available yet adapted to past circumstances
 } Coordination failures → Sub-optimal outcomes for all parties involved in interactions (a "deadweight" loss)
- Power relationships → Sub-optimal outcomes for Agent

The Agent does not always voluntarily transfer the right to control: the Principal can also appropriate it. In function of the grounds on which the transfer is made, power relationships might or might not require justification and legitimation. This means that not all power relationships have a moral dimension (see Section II of Chapter 2). Power backed by force or coercion (the threat of force), for instance, does not suppose any justification.

The case of coercion deserves special attention. The Principal gives the Agent a choice, but a very special one: neither alternative (the use of force by the Principal or the lack thereof if the Agent complies with the Principal's requests) corresponds to the Agent's preferences. The Principal puts the Agent in conditions in which the latter's choice minimizes eventual losses; in terms of Equation [1], $\bar{U}<0$.

Monopolistic power, especially in the case of natural monopoly,[3] does not suppose justification either, in spite of the restrictions imposed on the set of choices available to the Agent. A particular industrial organization produces a "bias" in the market structure (see Chapter 5).

Justification can appear faked, as in the case of manipulation. The information supplied by the Principal to the Agent prevents the latter from realistically evaluating his or her actions, their objectives and outcomes. The Principal leads the Agent to believe in the legitimate character of the transfer of the right of control "by limiting or determining selectively the subject's information supply, e.g., by withholding pertinent information not easily available to the subject from other sources, or by structuring the agenda of meetings" (Ledyaev, 1997, p. 191).

Finally, there are cases of truly justified power relationships. The list of arguments appropriate for justification purposes includes rational considerations (compliance pays off) as well as references to values and norms shared by both the Principal and the Agent that allow speaking in terms of legitimate power (Beetham, 1991). An employment contract (Simon, 1951) creates positive incentives for transferring the right to control: in the case of compliance, the Agent's expected utility has a positive value, $\bar{U}>0$.

Domination by virtue of a constellation of interests represents a form of power that potentially calls for justification. Justification becomes a must if the Agent is subject to other than natural monopolies. Unlike the situation of natural monopoly, here a bias of the system derives from the conscious actions of the Principal who, for example, erects barriers to entry. Monopolistic structures result from the Principal's attempts to shape the Agent's incentives in such a manner that the latter can avoid the "worst"—which nevertheless has a positive value compared to coercion—only by contributing to the achievement of the results desired by the former. This type of power relationship can be observed not only in the market, but also in other spheres. For instance, a constellation of interests seems common in politics and in international affairs. Political elites in a number of states align their interests with those of political elites in more powerful states as long as their inferior status provides them with some benefits that do not necessarily take a pecuniary form (see Scott, 2001, pp. 83-84).

The Agent's expected utility has a positive value here. Yet, instead of maximizing it or getting a "satisficing" reward, he or she aims at minimizing missed opportunities in order to reap greater benefits (Equation [2]).[4] The minimization of missed opportunities necessitates justification, which explains the Principal's attempts to show that power relationships refer to a common good.

$$\begin{cases} \max EU_{\text{Principal}} \\ \min (U'_I - \bar{U}'), U'_I > \bar{U}' > 0, \end{cases} \quad [2]$$

where $\bar{U}'$ is the Agent's expected utility from entering into a power relationship, U'_I is what the Agent would potentially (counterfactually[5]) gain if he/she maximized his/her expected utility, given the set of constraints imposed by the Principal.

II. "Mechanics" of Domination by Virtue of a Constellation of Interests

In exercising power based on a constellation of interests, the Principal seeks justification for a very particular kind of reasonable choice.[6] This choice is made neither between the best and the second best options (as neoclassical economic theory assumes) nor even between the satisfactory and the less satisfactory options (as advocates of the theory of bounded rationality argue). The minimization of missed opportunities has several common features—including embeddedness in power relationships—with a selection between the worst and the second worst,[7] but it is not reduced to the latter and should be considered as a distinct model of choice. In a sense, differences between the worst and next to worst choices mirror those between maximizing behavior and bounded rationality: maximizing behavior and the choice between the worst and the second worst refer to *absolute*—yet opposite—yardsticks, whereas bounded rationality and the minimization of missed opportunities derive from *relative*—yet again opposite—criteria.[8]

It is worth noting that bounded rationality can derive both from individual decision-making (Figure 6.1) and power relationships (Figure 6.2). As for the latter, the Principal offers an employment contract to the Agent. The Principal sets the level of satisfaction for the Agent ($\bar{U}$), which falls short of the optimum, whereas he/she continues to maximize his/her utility. In other words, the Principal acts according to the model of optimizing while the behavior of the Agent can be better understood in terms of satisficing. The employment contract enables the Principal to choose a particular task to perform, x, in such a way as to maximize the associated satisfaction; the Agent performs x and, in exchange, gets a fixed salary, w (Simon, 1951, p. 299). In what follows, only bounded rationality as a by-product of an employment contract is considered.

It might seem that the minimization of missed opportunities shares several common features with coercion, or the forced choice between the worst and the second worst, so the reader may wonder whether there is a point in looking for a new concept while an old and popular one exists. For instance, James Coleman offers a broad and all-encompassing definition of power relationships backed by coercion: "The exchange is a somewhat special one in that the superordinate agrees to withhold an action that would make the subordinate worse off in return for the subordinate's obeying the superordinate" (1990, p. 71).

Coercion refers to the pain and deprivation of the Agent (his/her payoff necessarily has a negative value) whereas, in the case of domination by virtue of a constellation of interests, the payoff has a positive value (if its value is negative, then domination by virtue of a constellation of interests should be considered as a special case of coercion). In other words, the Agent always loses if coerced, whereas he/she misses opportunities to gain more—in relative terms—if subjected to domination by virtue of a constellation of interests (Figure 6.3). "Those with power are transacting with agents who receive rents and hence are not indifferent between the current transaction and their next-best alternative" (Bowles & Gintis, 2008, p. 568).

There is also a need to differentiate two middle-range models of choice: the principle of satisficing and the minimization of missed opportunities. Sets of choices deriving from these two models might partly or completely overlap. They are mapped separately for the sake of graphic demonstration. It should be noted, however, that even if the two sets completely overlap, the logic of choice remains different. In

Figure 6.3
Four Models of Choice Resulting from Power Relationships Compared

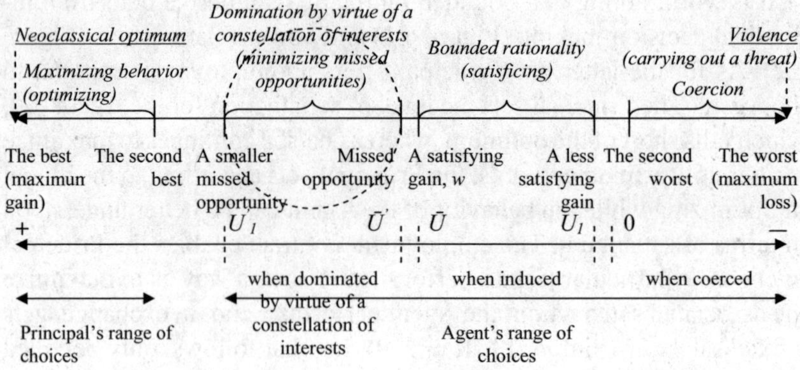

Neoclassical optimum	Domination by virtue of a constellation of interests	Bounded rationality	Violence
Maximizing behavior (optimizing)	(minimizing missed opportunities)	(satisficing)	(carrying out a threat) Coercion

| The best (maximum gain) + | The second best | A smaller missed opportunity U_1 | Missed opportunity $\bar{U}'$ | A satisfying gain, w $\bar{U}$ | A less satisfying gain | The second worst U_1 | The worst (maximum loss) 0 − |

- when dominated by virtue of a constellation of interests
- when induced
- when coerced

Principal's range of choices ← → Agent's range of choices

the model of satisficing, the point of reference ($\bar{U}$) is located at the left end, whereas in the model of domination by virtue of a constellation of interests the point of reference ($\bar{U}'$) moves to the right end. In the former case, the Agent moves *towards* the point of reference keeping in mind what he/she would gain from accepting power; in the latter he/she moves *from* it thinking about missed opportunities in the case of disobedience.

It appears that the behavior at the two extreme points of the continuum does not contradict the usual assumptions of *homo œconomicus* with regard to who is supposed to maximize utility (optimizing) or minimize pain (coercion). However, a caveat should be recognized: the model of optimizing helps predict only the behavior of the Principal. The model of coercion that finds its best expression in the principle "purse or life" is better at catching the interactive dimension of power: the Principal sets the limits within which the Agent can choose.[9] The Principal attempts to achieve his/her optimum at the extreme left of the continuum by forcing the Agent to move in the opposite direction.

As in the cases of satisficing and coercion, two points of reference in the situation of domination by virtue of a constellation of interests, a missed opportunity and a smaller (relative to the first) missed opportunity, are set for the Agent by the Principal.[10] Monopolistic domination has several features in common with using threats in the nonzero-sum, mixed-motives game (both players can win, but the gain is unevenly distributed): one of the parties controls the other's choices by binding his or her own choices. "A strategic move is *one that influences the other person's choice*, in a manner *favorable to one's self,* by affecting the other person's expectations on how one's self will behave" (Schelling, 1960, p. 160; emphasis added).[11] The Agent cannot pay back in the Principal's coin: the latter does not consider threats by the former credible because of the Agent's placement on the "long side" of the market, i.e., because the Agent lacks structural advantages. The Principal's power has both components, structural and strategic (see also Section I of Chapter 5).

One can further develop the model by assuming that the final outcome is subject to bargaining *after* the initial conditions are set by the Principal. In other words, the maximization of the Principal's gain produces his or her drift into *ex post* opportunism (this concept is discussed in more detail in Saussier, 2005, pp. 76-82). *Ex post* opportunism explains attempts to redefine the values of U'_1 and $\bar{U}'$ after the Agent agreed on them and transferred the right to control. Unforeseen contingencies and the impossibility of perfectly assessing the difficulty of the task assigned to the Agent increase the room for maneuvering (Kreps, 1990a, pp. 111-123).

The Principal defines the range of possible outcomes, i.e., the Agent's missed opportunity $\bar{U}'$ (what he or she is going to miss without accepting power relationships) and the smaller missed opportunity U'_1 (Figure 6.4), and then tries to narrow the range of choices available to the latter by moving U'_1 to the right (U'_2). U'_n then approaches $\bar{U}'$. The Principal has more degrees of freedom in changing U'_n than $\bar{U}'$ because the value of the latter depends on total benefits from better coordination of actions with the help of power relationships.

The Agent also might behave opportunistically, for instance, in the form of shirking, and neutralize the Principal's attempts to move U'_1 to the right. In the final account, the Principal and the Agent find themselves in the situation of bargaining with a first-mover advantage (the former moves first by setting the initial limits of the latter's choice).

Figure 6.4
Principal's Ex Post Opportunism

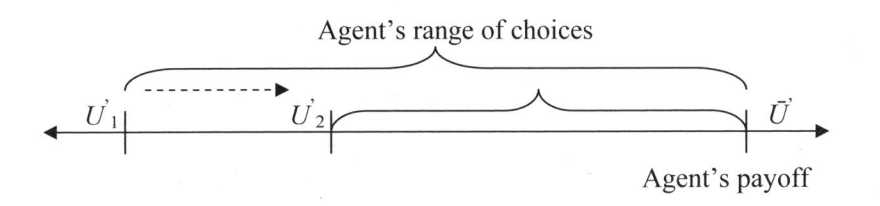

Agent's range of choices

U'_1 ----------> U'_2 $\bar{U}'$

Agent's payoff

Here domination by virtue of a constellation of interests includes elements of bargaining power as the capacity of a party in the transaction to appropriate a larger share of the joint surplus resulting from it. Power relationships, as was shown above, contribute to fixing coordination failures and, hence, generate a surplus. The distribution of this surplus gives rise to conflicts and tensions as to the proportions of sharing it between the transacting parties (Serrano, 2008). The conflicts tend to be especially intense if both parties try to maximize their respective utilities.[12] However, if one of the parties, the Principal, manages to get the second, the Agent, to minimize missed opportunities, conflicts become less intense. In fact, they arise only if the Principal behaves opportunistically, as specified above. Again, domination by virtue of a constellation of interests shall be considered a generic concept with regard to bargaining power that refers only to a particular and limited aspect of the former.

The bargaining between the Principal and the Agent has several features of a game about splitting a particular amount of money between two players with one notable exception: in this game, no party has a structural advantage such as the "short side" of the market.[13] Each can claim as large a share as they wish, yet they receive it only if their sum does not exceed the initial amount (Schelling, 1960, p. 57; Kreps, 1990b, pp. 116-120; Kagel & Roth, 1995, p. 286). Laboratory gaming-simulation shows that the players pay attention not only to pecuniary considerations; their choices also have a moral dimension (the sense of the fairness of the proposed split and the willingness to avoid feeling like a dupe). There is no single outcome of the bargaining between the Principal and the Agent; each of the plural outcomes refers to particular values and norms shared by both of them.[14]

At this point, the neoclassical approach, which ignores aspects related to justification, reaches its limits. Neoclassical theory and its core element, a utility-maximization model, allows for analyzing some, yet not all, aspects and dimensions of domination by virtue of a constellation of interests. First, power relationships in this particular context call for justification. Second, the internal dynamics of domination by virtue of a constellation of interests, namely *ex ante* and *ex post* bargaining, strengthen the need for justification. The model of rational choice appears to be a necessary but insufficient condition for understanding this form of power.

What arguments help to justify domination by virtue of a constellation of interests? If both interacting parties can win—the Principal in absolute terms (he/she tends to act along the lines of maximizing behavior) and the Agent in relative terms (he/she has not lost all opportunities to be better off)—power relationships are potentially *justifiable* in terms of a presumable commonality of interests or a "common good." The common good derives from the willingness of the Principal and the Agent to enter into a relationship and takes the form of a rent (joint surplus) to be shared between them.[15] This justification has a utilitarian character, which does not mean that there are no other principles endorsed by both the Principal and the Agent. The study of non-utilitarian justifications for domination by virtue of a constellation of interests, nevertheless, is beyond the scope of this chapter.

Rent can be attributed to variations in natural resource quality (agricultural land, ore, oil, gas and so forth), to positive effects of cooperation resulting from both the division of labor (Adam Smith)[16] and associational gains of teamwork[17] or to monopoly profits resulting from restrictions on competition. For instance, Clifford Gaddy and Barry Ickes define the former type of rent as "the revenue received from sale of the resource minus the cost of producing it" (2005, p. 560). The latter type is usually called protection rent "accruing to those customers [Agents] who drew effective protection [offered by the Principal] against outside competitors" (Tilly, 1985, p. 175). Rent might also derive from barriers erected by the Principal not against outside competitors, as in the case of protection rent, but against the Agent (administrative barriers restricting the Agent's access to the law as a coordination device). Then, the former stimulates the latter's obedience by lowering administrative barriers or completely removing them on a case-by-case basis (Figure 6.5). In other words, rent can result from controlling access either to rare resources or to a transaction, a field (see Subsection I.5 of Chapter 5).

Figure 6.5
Sources of Rent Shared by the Principal and the Agent

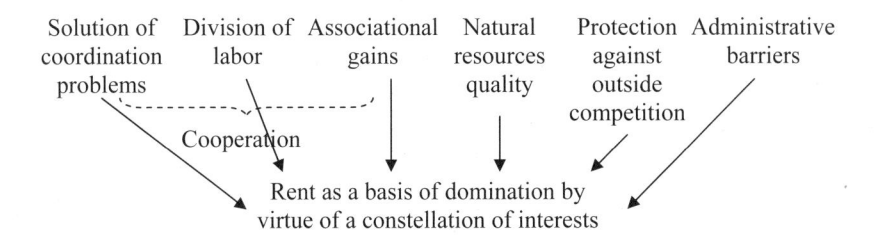

Solution of coordination problems — Division of labor — Associational gains → Cooperation — Natural resources quality — Protection against outside competition — Administrative barriers → Rent as a basis of domination by virtue of a constellation of interests

III. Empirical Evidence: Minimizing Missed Opportunities in Russia

Developments in Russia since the start of market reforms in the early 1990s provide rich illustrations for the proposed analysis. They took especially manifest forms between 1999 and 2008, during the period of rapid economic growth. Namely, relationships between the government (represented by office holders with their particular group and individual interests) and businesses have several elements of domination by virtue of a constellation of interests. This means, in particular, that one of the major conditions for success of a business enterprise in Russia consists in accepting the domination of office holders, who then assume the role of the Principal. The Russian state extracts rent based on a variety of sources ranging from control over natural resources, chiefly oil and gas, to control of access to the national and regional markets.

Estimations show that oil and gas rents accounted for over 40 percent of Russia's GDP in 1981; their share in 2005 was about 25 percent (Gaddy & Ickes, 2005, p. 562). When world oil prices are high, the Russian economy is booming. It is estimated that Russia's oil and natural gas revenues provide as much as 40 percent of the national government's budget and 55 percent of export earnings (US Energy Information Administration, 2005). Between 1999 and 2008, the annual GDP growth rate of the Russian economy did not dip below 5 percent and sporadically (10.7 percent in 2000) reached a two-digit level, which makes it attractive for investors, both domestic and foreign (Table 5.3).

However, access to this potentially lucrative market is granted exclusively to those businesspeople who accept only a fraction of potential profits and acknowledge domination of office holders by virtue of a constellation of interests at different levels in the state hierarchy, starting with local and municipal and moving up to federal. Although a formal employment relationship emerges only in the case of (re-) nationalization, power relationships nevertheless exist and take less formal and manifest forms. Domination by virtue of a constellation of interests allows office holders to assume the role of the Principal without changing the formal ownership structure (or changing it only in exceptional cases). The Agent (the owner of a particular business) shares his or her profit with the Principal, both formally and informally, so as not to lose all opportunities to make it. "To avoid losing all their wealth, the owners of resource companies shared some of their rent ... as a means of guaranteeing that they could keep the rest" (Gaddy & Ickes, 2005, p. 570; see also Gaddy,

2004, pp. 350-351). The value of $\bar{U}'$ varies in function of investment opportunities in other industries/regions/countries and the business's mobility (from zero-profit in the case of small businesses to the average payback in other international markets for big foreign investors). The Agent's actual share (U'_I) falls short of the maximal profit by 3 percent to 10 percent (in exceptional cases—by a half).

Federal Law 57-FZ "On foreign investments into economic enterprises of strategic importance for the state security and defense" enacted on April 29, 2008 represents a good example of domination of office holders by virtue of a constellation of interests at work. The law is intended to regulate the access of foreign direct investors to the national market, more specifically—to a number of key industries. Their list is telling (Article 6): it includes mining, the oil and gas industry as well as natural and other monopolies (firms that have a dominant position in telecommunications). In other words, a state body established exclusively for this purpose (Articles 2^3 and 4^1) controls access to both natural resources as the key source of wealth in Russia and to the field of transactions characterized by significant structural biases. Access is granted under a number of conditions (Article 12) varying from the obligation to avoid layoffs during a specified period of time to the implementation of a business plan that in turn has to be approved by the state body in charge of "gate keeping" (Federal Antimonopoly Service). The state is transformed here into a "gatekeeper" deciding who is to be admitted into the field, mining or market, under which conditions and at what price (see also Sections I and II of Chapter 5).[18]

Relationships between state officials and "home grown" business people are structured in a similar manner. In order to enter the market, one has to buy an "entry ticket." By buying it, one loses less than when remaining outside the field of interactions (and especially when challenging the gatekeeper's domination). While remaining directly disengaged from the ownership of businesses, the gatekeeper nevertheless dominates them.

The empirical evidence results from two series of qualitative interviews, "A" and "B," whose parameters are outlined in Section V of the Introduction and the Appendix. The codebook for content analysis contains the entry "Constellation of interests." The definition of this code reads: "Power limited by competitive markets (both national and international). In the opposite case—when not limited by market competition—power is embedded in monopolistic market structures" (Table 6.1). In other words, a fragment was coded in this manner in two cases: when

Table 6.1
Coding Frequency for "Constellation of Interests", Sets "A" and "B"

	Set "A"		Set "B"	
Total count	112		30	
No. of cases	50		18	
% of cases	78.1		41.9	
N of words	8286		1979	
% of words	1.9		1.1	
Tag	Enabling	Constraining	Enabling	Constraining
Tag count	85[†]	19	22	2
% of Total count	75.9	17	73.3	7
No. of cases with the tag	37[♠]	15	12	2
% of cases coded "Constellation of interests"	74	30	66.7	11.1

Legend: † The tags "Enabling" and "constraining" were not inserted in all fragments coded "Constellation by interests," so they do not add up to the total count. ♠ Some cases (transcripts) contain several fragments coded "Constellation of interests," some of them with the tag "Enabling," some other with the tag "Constraining." Hence, the sum of the numbers of cases with the tags can exceed the number of cases with the code "Constellation of interests."

the competitive market limits the discretion of power holders (with an addition tag "Constraining") and when distorted market structures, e.g., as a result of the entry control, contribute to strengthening their domination (with an additional tag "Enabling"). The frequency of the latter tag, in terms of both of its count and the number of cases (transcripts), far exceeds that of the former, which confirms that, instead of limiting power, the market underpins it in the Russian case. In the following, the principal emphasis is placed on the "Enabling" tag illustrating the idea of domination by virtue of a constellation of interests.

> "Does one want to establish a monopoly? No other country in the world has such a big number of small firms as Russia. An individual [state official], in exchange of a significant amount of money, issues a document allowing the concentration of a half of the cement industry in hands of one person" (19A).

> "Businesses get problems if they cannot reach an agreement with the executive power or if they don't accept a subaltern position and try to set their own rules" (36A).

"Businesses tend to concentrate around local, regional and federal budgets and to appropriate their shares (*raspil*) together with the new Russian *nomenklatura*. The price of the entry ticket to these markets is quite high" (6B).

"The [telecommunication] companies want to restrict access to the Russian market for alternative mobile network operators. It's clear-cut. They want to keep the existing contracts under which they get licenses almost for free, even taking into consideration bribes. If they were to buy the licenses at a more or less honest auction, they would have to pay much more" (45A).

Domination by virtue of a constellation of interests involves a particular form of profit sharing and redistribution. Russians call it *otkaty* (kickbacks), which means paying back a share of profit after making it. Kickbacks differ from forms of corruption that *precede* making profit and involve *advancing* money; the latter can be compared with buying a "ticket" to make profit. The connection between the size of profits and the price of the "ticket" is less direct (many unforeseen factors can influence the final outcome). Thus, kickbacks seem appropriate for sharing rent on the basis of minimizing the Agent's missed opportunities: their ratio to the profit is determined *ex ante*, their actual amount—*ex post*, when the total size of profits is known.

"Let's consider a big investment project with the participation of foreign investors, say the construction of S. Z. [a business center]. There is one group of state servants from power ministries that has worked with the Chinese, and they lobby for the project. However, there is a competing group whose area of specialization has been Germany and the Scandinavian countries since the Soviet times. They find it interesting that a Scandinavian investor went with someone with whom they could easily find a common language and who would pay them *otkaty*" (46A).

The "10 percent" rule of sharing profits is enforced at the federal level as well as at the regional levels, even in the case of relatively small-scale research projects funded by government agencies. If one claims to get something more than U'_1 ($\bar{U}'$ plus a "bonus"), then the state officials do everything to lower the level of profitability below $\bar{U}'$, eventually by deploying extralegal strategies.

"We observe collaboration and cooperation [between the regional administration and business], without it a business would leave the region, they wouldn't work here. [It can happen] if [the regional administration] starts to create obstacles for the business. I think they're not stupid over there, in the regional administration. They carefully assess the capacities of every enterprise. In other words, *how much they can get from it without making it bankrupt*" (43A, emphasis added).

The term "*otkat*" becomes increasingly popular in the discourse about the state service, which may suggest the spread of the underlying practice, i.e., domination by virtue of a constellation of interests. It gains ground compared with a more conventional one, *vziatka*, or bribe (and more "neutral" with regard to various techniques for imposing will). If, in set "A," the latter term appears still more frequent, the former prevails in set "B" (Table 6.2).[19] Representatives of the younger generation of state servants and experts—those in their forties and below—tend to use the term "*otkat*" more actively than their more senior colleagues.[20] This seems to confirm the relatively recent nature of the underlying phenomena.

> "*I've heard that starting with a particular level in the hierarchy, bribes (vziatki) are less commonly used and all "normal people" work through kickbacks (otkaty). I would agree with this. At least I've got a very similar impression*" (30A).

Rent secured by virtue of a constellation of interests can be used for a variety of purposes ranging from large-scale "national projects"—which provide for making their sources of financing non-transparent and, hence, uncontrollable—to paying extra cash to the technical staff of the office to increase their motivation, and meeting certain personal and "status" needs of state servants.

> "There is an oil company S. The state bought it from Mr. X. But he got only a half of the total amount, at best. He didn't touch the rest. There is a good idea [related to the so-called national projects]. But financing it through the [federal] budget would be too straightforward; any theft would then be too obvious" (44A).

> "[In exchange,] business is required to participate in politics at the regional level, to financially support the [ruling party] Edinaia Rossiia" (36B).

The existence of a non-empty set of outcomes that satisfy both the Principal and the Agent (any outcome above $\bar{U}$ but below the profit minus *otkat*) lets the former *justify* power relationships in terms of a common good. Interviews show that several stakeholders attempt to offer a

Table 6.2
Relative Frequency for Otkaty and Vziatki

	Set "A"			Set "B"		
	Count	Cases	% of Cases	Count	Cases	% of Cases
otkat*	46	14	21.9	8	4	9.3
vziatk*	107	38	59.4	4	4	9.3

Legend: * Refers to a "wild card," i.e., to any character or a combination of characters.

justification for the existing configuration of relationships between state servants and private businesses. The control of access to natural resources and/or to the market field enables the former to speak in terms of a rent or a joint surplus to be shared, the nature of which differs significantly from that discovered by Smith.

> "If you make a promotion for a businessman ... and he offers you an expensive gift after making significant profits.... I realize that it's against the law and I'm telling you amoral things, but if he pays a holiday package for your family when the state does not offer you an opportunity to be able to pay for yourself, I won't refuse. It's not about corruption, it's rather about lobbying—in the good sense of this term" (31A).

> "As a matter of fact, I was one of the founders of your business. You bake bread with Mr. Pancaker [after I put both of you in contact], make money. Pancaker sells more flour and that also makes money. Yet your common and successful business started only because I suggested to you both how to find each other. If you hadn't initially contacted me, you wouldn't have reached Pancaker and nothing would have happened" (39A).

Despite the fact that businesses maintain their formal independence from the state, they enter into a power relationship. The Agent's unilateral dependency on the state official takes three empirically verifiable forms: (i) the latter has far more influence over setting the rules of the game (the principle of minimization of missed opportunities resulting from the control of access and its parameters, U'_I and $\bar{U}'$); (ii) only the latter can enforce the rules and corresponding rights and obligations; and (iii) the latter tends to avoid taking on any binding obligations (the Principal tends to get U'_I as close to $\bar{U}'$ as possible) while keeping a close eye on the obligations imposed on the former.

> "Everything that concerns the [compulsory] financing of social projects [when a company is forced to make additional contributions to them in exchange for the right to continue doing business] represents payments additional to regular taxes.[21] They are decided on the basis of a mutual agreement. However, problems can arise.... The firm fulfills its promises, but the regional administration wants more than that" (43A).

> "[The partnership between the state and businesses] should be based on the equality of the parties. However, I fail to understand how this equality can be achieved if only one party drafts all the documents, whereas the other simply obeys. If a business accepts this, they say—I'm a subaltern, you're a boss. But nevertheless we form a state-private partnership" (36A).

Of the three forms of enforcement in contracts—self-enforced, enforced by one of the parties and enforced by a third party (North, 1990, pp. 34-35)—only the second is possible since not all (if any) clauses of such deals are put in writing and, after all, the state is itself the supreme guarantor (see Section I of Chapter 4). The Agent's only leverage consists in deciding to quit (the "exit" strategy) and in accepting $\bar{U}$. If one takes sunk costs into consideration, its value can be close to zero or even negative. The dominant hardly considers such threats credible. In other words, by implicitly or explicitly agreeing to minimize missed opportunities, the Agent also contributes to the reproduction of domination by virtue of a constellation of interests.

> "Do they [the state officials] consider this an obligation? Well, in their speeches that may be the case. 'The people expect from us.' It's a very common expression in their milieu: 'the people expect from us,' 'the business expects from us'.... On the other hand, I don't believe that the business has any leverage to enforce [these obligations]' (45A).

Conclusion

Sub-optimal outcomes derive from particularities of individual decision-making; they are also generated in the process of interaction. Power relationships help to solve some coordination problems yet they lead to sub-optimal outcomes, at least for the Agent. This chapter explores the model of choice embedded in a particular technique for imposing will, namely domination by virtue of a constellation of interests. It has been argued that this model cannot be reduced to optimizing, satisficing or coercion. The Principal acts according to the principles of maximizing behavior, whereas the Agent minimizes missed opportunities. Asymmetries proper to all forms of power relationships coupled with problems related to bargaining about the exact amount of missed opportunities add a moral dimension to relationships between the Principal and the Agent. References to a common good, i.e., a rent to be shared by the Principal and the Agent, provide some grounds for justification.

The Russian case clearly illustrates the logic of extracting and sharing rents as a driving force of domination by virtue of a constellation of interests. The state officials in this country use a variety of sources of rents, ranging from restricted access to natural resources to restricted access to the market field. As long as the Agent does not miss all opportunities to make profit, which seems easily attainable when economic growth is fueled by high hydrocarbon prices, domination by virtue of a constellation of interests is justified in terms of a common good. However, the sustainability of power relationships in the long run raises many doubts: a less appropriate conjuncture would contribute to making the Agent's payoff negative and, hence, to debunking the myth of a community of interests shared by the Principal and the Agent. The Principal might then resort to techniques of coercion that leave much less room for justification. The economic crisis that started in the second half of 2008 provides a good opportunity for testing this assumption (for some applications of the proposed approach to the 2008 crisis, see also Section V of the Conclusion).

Notes

1. Namely if, in the situation of multiple equilibria, the market is "locked in" a suboptimal one (Weil, 1989); or market failures prevent the production of public goods (for a list of market failures, see Wolf, 1988).
2. The terms "Principal" and "Agent" are employed here exclusively in the context of power relationship. Such interactions represent a subset of a larger set of relationships in which one person, an agent, "is employed to do an act on behalf of another called the principal, so that as a rule the principal himself becomes bound" (Munro, 1987, p. 966). Interactions between a lawyer and a client, for example, represent an instance of Principal-Agent relationship but do not include elements of domination as outlined above.
3. Average costs of production achieve their minimum if there is a single supplier in an industry.
4. The minimization of missed opportunities can be opposed to their maximization. Niklas Luhmann argues that trust may involve the latter as the expression of freedom and uncertainty associated with trust: the higher the temptation to behave contrary to what is expected, the more solid grounds for the emergence of trust. "It must be possible for the partner to abuse the trust; indeed it must not merely be possible for him to do so but he must also have a considerable interest in doing so ... [trust] must present itself as a sort of missed opportunity" (1979, p. 42). The opposition of the minimization and maximization of missed opportunities further confirms the complementarity/substitutability of trust and power as mechanisms of coordination.
5. Steven Lukes (2005, pp. 43-44) invites us to think counterfactually to analyze power.
6. The model of rational choice refers to the task of optimization whereas reasonable choice derives from a more encompassing category of common sense and necessitates that one takes into consideration reasonable options and strategies (Garfinkel, 1967, pp. 100-105).
7. In terms of game theory, the choice between the worst and the second worst involves the *Minimax* strategy. It consists in minimizing the maximum possible loss. For example, in the zero-sum game of power (see Table in Endnote 19, Chapter 2), the *Minimax* strategy also leads to the upper left outcome (0, 0), but its "mechanics" differ from that of Nash equilibrium. The first party considers the worst that can happen to him or her if the second party chooses the strategy "Impose will" (-1) or "Do not impose will" (0). In both cases, the former has good reasons for opting for "Imposing will." Similar considerations explain the second party's preference for "Imposing will," and the combination of these strategies will produce (0, 0). It should nevertheless be noted that game theory ignores non-utilitarian motives in human behavior and for this reason does not help catch all aspects of domination by virtue of a constellation of interests.
8. Samuel Bowles and Herbert Gintis conceptualize the employment relationship in a manner having "elective affinity" with the approach developed here. Namely, they

argue that the Agent accepts the Principal's control because the former "receives a rent: the present value of the job exceeds the next-best alternative (job search)" (2008, p. 568). This means that the Agent has fewer opportunities by rejecting the Principal's power than by accepting it. They further generalize this reasoning to a number of other transactions, e.g., between bank and borrower or between seller and buyer if one of the parties—usually the bank and the seller—has a structural advantage because of their placement on the "short side of a non-clearing market" (Ibid).

9. The list of available options is not impressive: the Agent has to choose between the worst and the second worst, i.e., the lesser of two evils.

10. Domination by virtue of a constellation of interests has to be clearly differentiated from the concept of market power widely used in neoclassical economics. Market power implies a monopolist's capacity to set price above marginal costs, and to transform him or herself from a price-taker into a price-maker. Aspects related to interactions between the monopolist and his or her counterpart appear hidden and mediated by market price. Market power refers to an empirically observable outcome of domination by virtue of a constellation of interests. The latter concept "unveils" how the former derives from a particular combination of structural and strategic components of power in interactions at the micro-level.

11. In contrast to non-cooperative games, power relationships allow for making binding agreements. Thus, the Principal can influence the Agent's choices in a manner favorable to him- or herself by manipulating the latter's incentive structure (see Dowding, 1996, pp. 5-8), i.e., not only in an indirect manner, but also in a direct one.

12. The bargaining between two parties involved in a Coasean conflict about negative externalities caused by the activities of one of them illustrates the point perfectly. Both parties can gain by trading the right to produce harmful effects. However, as each of them tries to get the maximum share of the joint surplus, this places the prospects of making a deal in jeopardy. Experimental economics provides some supporting evidence: the parties reach an agreement only if at least one of them fails to maximize. "To the extent that the sharing behavior indicates that either the subjects were failing to profit maximize or were maximizing interdependent utility functions which might violate one of the axioms of the Coase theorem, our results cannot be taken to verify the theorem" (Hoffman & Spitzer, 1982, p. 93; see also Cooter, 1987; Oleinik 2008e). Thus, a Coasean conflict embedded in power relationships has an easier solution.

13. The situation of bilateral monopoly (Friedman, 1987) lies close to the assumptions on which the game of splitting the money is based. The structural advantages of one of the transacting parties are nullified by those of the other, which makes the process of bargaining problematic and costly (see the previous endnote). The recurrent conflicts over gas supplies between Russia and Ukraine can be interpreted in terms of the bargaining game under conditions of bilateral monopoly: Ukraine has a virtual monopoly over the transit infrastructure, whereas Russia controls the unique gas fields (Oleinik, 2009d). If transactions between the parties do not involve power relationships, their conflict only grows more intense as they try to behave according to the principle of maximizing.

14. David Kerps defines his concept of corporate culture structuring relations between the Principal and the Agent in these terms: it is "some sort of principle or rule that has wide (preferably universal) applicability and that is simple enough to be interpreted by all concerned" (1990a, p. 93).

15. This makes a link with discussions about assumptions of the economics of abundance: "abundance is the antithesis of scarcity. Abundance means that everyone

[including the subordinate] has adequate health care, nutrition, education, transportation, recreation, housing, self-expression, and personal security" (Peach & Dugger, 2006, p. 693).

16. In terms of the new institutional economics, both variations in natural resource quality and the division of labor take the form of specific assets. Specific assets cannot be easily redeployed outside their actual combination without a substantial loss in their value (Ménard, 2005a, p. 55). For instance, variations in natural resource quality contribute to the development of site specificity and physical specificity if special equipment is needed for processing crude oil with particular characteristics. From this point of view, monopolistic domination has several elements in common with power relationships within hybrid forms.

17. "Increased productivity among members of the group who feel a sense of responsibility to do their fair share as members of a group" lies at the origin of associational gains (Williamson, 1975, p. 44).

18. A sketch of this thesis was first outlined in an Op-Ed article (Oleinik, 2008g) that caused fierce polemics (Fadeev, 2008, Oleinik, 2008h). Once again, it should be noted that the access control works under the assumption that the economy is growing, i.e., foreign investors are interested in "getting in" (especially in 2005-2007). This may explain that the law was "put on hold" at the time of crisis that started in the second half of 2008: instead of trying to "get in," foreign investors started to "get out" (see graph below).

Graph Net Capital Export/Import by Private Sector, Based on the Balance of Payments, 1994-2008, US$ Billion

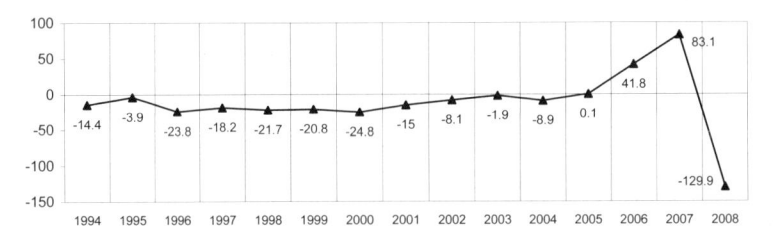

Source: The Central Bank of the Russian Federation, retrieved from http://www.cbr.ru/eng/statistics/credit_statistics/print.asp?file=capital_e.htm

19. The questions and comments of the interviewer were excluded from content analysis.

20. **Table Relative Frequencies of the Words "*Otkat*" and "*Vziatka*," by Age Groups, %**

Age\Word	under 30	31-40	41-50	51-60	over 61	Chi square	P (2-tails)
otkat*	0	43.5	52.2	2.2	2.2	20.112	0.001
vziatk*	5.6	30.8	31.8	27.1	4.7	7.210	0.205

Legend: * refers to a "wild card," i.e., to any character or a combination of characters

21. Gaddy and Ickes call them informal taxes (2005, p. 566).

7

Doing Business in a Russian Region: Controlling Access to the Field

Introduction

Rent represents a core building block in neoclassical economic theory. Broadly defined, rent equals profit—total revenues minus opportunity costs—which makes it the chief purpose of economic activities. "Rent is that part of the payment to an owner of resources over and above that which those resources could command in any alternative use" (Buchanan, 1980, p. 3). Various models of economic action—maximizing, satisficing behavior and the minimization of missed opportunities (see Chapter 6)—all imply that the actor appropriates some rent. However, a simple search in the Google database suggests that the relative importance of different forms of rent depends on the institutional environment. The expressions "administrative rent" and "resource rents" can be found with the relative frequencies of 2.2 to 1 in Russian-language documents whereas their ratio appears completely reversed in English-language documents (1 to 34.5).[1]

Resource rent derives naturally from the control of access to the resource enabled by well specified and properly enforced property rights. Administrative rent has another origin: it results from various barriers and restrictions imposed on transactions. This kind of rent, for instance, "refers to all income obtained from trade restrictions" (Colander, 1984, p. 8). Emphasis shifts from controlling access to the rare resource to controlling access to the transaction, to the field (see Figure 5.1).

Neoclassical economists acknowledged the existence of administrative rent relatively recently, in the late 1970s—early 1980s, with the help of the theory of public choice and, more specifically, the theories of rent-seeking and directly-unproductive activities, DUP. Economic sociologists do not use this concept very actively, yet they may make a contribution to its further development—by embedding it in the field of transactions (Chapter 5). The present chapter is intended to demonstrate the significant opportunities available in this connection.

At a first glance, the Russian economy seen through the lens of rent represents a puzzle. On the one hand, it is one of the world's richest economies in terms of natural resources. Resource rent may be operationalized as the share of a country's gross national income derived from the depletion of energy resources (crude oil, natural gas, and coal), other mineral resources (such as diamonds or metal ores), and forest resources, all measured annually as a percentage ranging from 0 percent to 100 percent (Ulfelder, 2007, p. 1002). The World Bank includes a measure of the depletion of energy resources in its World Development Indicators, which is updated on a regular basis. Energy depletion equals the product of the physical quantities of oil, natural gas and coal extracted and unit resource rents as the difference between market prices for energy resources and the costs of their extraction and distribution. The average value of energy depletion for the Russian Federation calculated for the decade of 1995-2005 (including periods of both low and high market prices) equals 27, or 4.3 times the mean value (M=6.3, σ=15) for 173 countries (World Bank, 2007). Expressed in standardized Z-values (units of standard deviation), this equals 1.37, which brings Russia into the top 20 wealthiest countries in terms of energy resources. Russia's dependence on resource rents has taken especially manifest forms since the second half of the 1990s. Gaddy (2004, p. 347) observes a strong association between world oil prices and Russia's economic growth.

On the other hand, the outcomes of the above-mentioned Google search indicate that, in Russian public and academic discourse, administrative rent attracts relatively more attention than resource rent. This may be interpreted as an indication that the scope of the control of access to the field extends far beyond the oil and gas industry. Techniques of "not letting in" the field tend to be widespread in all Russian regions, however poor in natural resources they are, and touch a wide rage of businesses, ranging from small enterprises to large corporations. The purpose of this chapter is to explore various configurations of the control of access to the field and link them to administrative rent. Chapters 3 and 5 outlined the core principles of the strategy of domination by "not letting in." In this chapter, the strategy of "not letting in" is further deconstructed and analyzed in depth. In particular, it focuses on how a field with clearly identifiable boundaries emerges through interactions between government and businesses.

The actor with a comparative advantage in drawing boundaries (e.g., the state, see Section II of Chapter 5) achieves the "enclosure" of the field and, consequently, produces structural conditions suitable for strengthening a dominant position. More specifically, A, a business, gets access to the field in exchange either for the payment of some "entrance fees" to C, the state (the "entry ticket" represents a form of appropriation of administrative rent), and/or for the acceptance of rules set by C (they are embedded in formal and informal institutions) and/or for the submission to orders issued by C. As long as A's interests consists in entering the field and A gains something even after C has appropriated a part of the rent from a better coordination or a deeper division of labor, C dominates A by virtue of a constellation of their interests. In other words, administrative rent corresponds to a particular manifestation of domination by virtue of a constellation of interests derived from the strategy of controlling access to the field but does not exhaust all the possible outcomes.

The chapter is organized as follows. Section I discusses boundaries delimiting various fields of interactions: informational, legal, territorial and market. Section II explains the choice of a particular Russian region for an in-depth case study. The methodology of triangulating the results of qualitative and quantitative studies of the same case is applied in Section III to demonstrate the importance of the strategy of "not letting in" for the continuous reproduction of the model of power relationships prevailing in the region. Outcomes of both qualitative and quantitative content analyses of in-depth interviews (within-method triangulation; see also the Methodological Appendix) are compared with those of a series of econometric tests (between-method triangulation). Section IV attempts to generalize the study of the strategy of "not letting in" beyond the scope of a particular, however representative, region.

I. Variety of Fields: An Overview

Since interactions take place in various spheres of everyday activities, instead of speaking of the field of interactions, one should rather assume their plurality. Everyday language does not necessarily label them in a uniform manner, yet such expressions as "information field," "legal field," "market field" are neither rare nor language-specific.[2] Academic discussions help define these fields more carefully and make sense of them.

I.1 Information Field

The information field is probably the form of field most frequently mentioned in public discourse. The theory of conventions provides some analytical tools suitable for theorizing about the field of interactions in general and the information field in particular (Boltanski & Thévenot, 1991; Thévenot et al., 2005). Seen in a "conventionalist" perspective, the field has institutional boundaries: access is open to anyone who accepts particular "rules of the game" and criteria of worth. The most successful players climb up the internal hierarchy of the field and earn the privilege to enforce norms and criteria of worth making coordination possible. This means that access to the field appears conditional to the acceptance of domination on the part of those at the top of the field's hierarchy.

The information field, or *le monde de l'opinion publique*, gratifies those actors who can attract the attention of the mass media and remain in its focus as long as possible. "The beings can reach a superior status only under the condition that they become visible" (Boltanski & Thévenot, 1991, p. 228). Celebrities dominate this field and control access to it by setting and enforcing criteria of what is worth the mass media's attention.

Nevertheless, the state and its representatives, office holders, may also try to have a say in the control of access to the information field.[3] For instance, they may give privileged treatment—exclusive interviews and news—to the members of media whose agendas have some elective affinity with their own priorities (Wilson, 2005, 65 ff.). In the same manner, members of the media with a "wrong" agenda do not get access to exclusive news, which complicates the task of keeping or increasing their audiences. State representatives dominate the mass media by virtue of a constellation of their interests when providing exclusive information in a highly selective manner.

I.2 Legal Field

If the theory of conventions emphasizes informal institutional boundaries—norms and criteria of worth—the study of the legal field calls for paying particular attention to formal institutions and mechanisms of their enforcement. By defining what is legal and what is not, lawmakers draw clear boundaries around the legal field. In order to be admitted into the field, the actor must "fine tune" his or her preferences to those set by the law and must accept the domination of lawmakers, lawyers and law enforcement agents. Everything depends on the parameters of the legal norms: if they correspond to the interests of most actors, access cannot be highly selective, which also narrows the room for dominant actors' discretionary behavior. The opposite happens if legal norms reflect the partisan interests of particular actors or groups. In this respect, Hernando de Soto (2005, p. 132) differentiates "good" laws from "bad" ones: "A law is 'good' if it guarantees and promotes economic efficiency and 'bad' if it impedes or disrupts it." According to him, the prevalence of "bad" laws lies at the origin of institutional exclusion and of a large extralegal sector in developing and post-socialist countries because such laws complicate the task of "getting in" and of relying on the law and formal property rights in the coordination of activities.

To solve the problem of the extralegal sector, De Soto (2000) proposes the strategy of legalizing informal norms that serve to increase the number of "good" laws at the expense of "bad" laws: informal norms spontaneously developed by ordinary people by definition correspond to their interests. However, he mostly relies on benevolent and "enlightened" lawmakers and law enforcement agents ignoring the fact that "widening" the gates leading into the legal field undermines their dominant position.[4]

De Soto's logic also implies that actors realize the advantages of obeying "good" laws: they facilitate coordination and, hence, transform into a source of rent (for example, by reducing transaction costs). Yet, actors do not always perceive the law in this way. First, they may become accustomed to bypassing it. "There is no reason to expect that an entrepreneur who has broken a 'bad' law, such as one that imposes a uselessly difficult set of requirements to get a permit, will not later break a 'good' law that requires the payment to the government of sales or income taxes" (Thoumi, 1995, p. 95). Second, an advanced level of interdependence in the actors' behavior must be achieved prior to their realization of the beneficial effects of the law. "It is only when the members of a society become conscious that they depend on one another to act in a certain way that law emerges" (Yaney, 1973, p. 14). In other words, domination by granting conditional access to the legal field works only under particular historical conditions.

I.3 Territorial Field

The concept of territoriality introduced in Chapter 5 refers to a spatially delimited field of interactions. In this case, the enclosure of the field is achieved with the help of spatial boundaries. The field itself represents nothing other than an area in physical, geographical space. However, the shape of its boundaries depends less on physical characteristics (altitude, relief, etc.) than on the requirements of domination. In this sense, territoriality means domination that is embedded in physical space, "a spatial strategy to affect, influence, or control resources and people, by controlling area" (Sack, 1986, p. 1).

Why would A be interested in entering a particular area even at the price of accepting additional conditions set by C? It is worthwhile to differentiating three possible figures of constellating interests of those who would like to get into the territorial field (A) and those who keep the gate (C). First, if actors perceive a particular area as a natural meeting place, a "focal point" for finding counterparts, contract-making appears more complicated and costly—in terms of transaction costs—outside this area (Subsection III.2 of Chapter 5). This configuration enables C to extract administrative rent by letting A in under certain conditions.

Second, if an area contains deposits of natural resources (or simply has relatively abundant rare resources with limited mobility, i.e., site-specific assets), then A can hardly obtain access to the rare resources without entering the area. Two types of access control—to a resource and to a field—then tend to overlap (Figure 5.1). The barriers erected around the area's perimeter reinforce property rights and *vice versa*. Such a configuration creates favorable conditions for the appropriation of both resource rent and administrative rent.

Third, the overlap between the two types of access control lessens if an area is characterized by rapid socio-economic growth fueled by resource rents. A may be interested in entering the region to obtain a slice of this growing "pie" (the Gross Regional Product, GRP) even without trying to acquire property rights over the resources that serve to drive growth (e.g., a company servicing a mining firm). Under such conditions, C extracts administrative rent directly and indirectly—resource rent (the former includes a portion of the latter).

I.4 Market Field

Neoclassical economic theory has a strong record of measuring the outcomes of monopolistic domination. Monopoly and related forms (monopsony, oligopoly) emerge as a result of restricting access to a market that is not necessarily localized in space. Barriers taken into consideration by neoclassical economists—barriers to entry and barriers to exit—are essentially economic in nature (cf. institutional, symbolical and spatial barriers outlined in Table 5.1). They derive from particular strategies of pricing (e.g., predatory pricing) and the dynamics of costs (economies of scale, sunk costs, etc.). Monopolistic pricing causes a net loss of welfare conventionally measured as Harberger's triangle (gains from an exchange at a higher than competitive price appropriated neither by the monopolist nor by its counterpart).

The theories of rent-seeking and directly unproductive activities further extend and correct the neoclassical model of monopoly. Gordon Tullock, in particular, argues that the loss caused by monopoly exceeds the scope of Harberger's triangle because the rent appropriated as a result of monopolistic pricing is normally spent on establishing a monopoly and on creating other conditions necessary for extracting rent, i.e., in an unproductive manner. Tullock's rectangle (DECA on Figure 7.1, triangle ACB corresponds to Harberger's triangle) refers to the cost of "the activity of getting a monopoly or getting some other government favor" (Tullock, 1984, p. 224; see also Buchanan, 1980, p. 8; Tullock, 2005, pp. 92-93).

The introduction of the government into the model of monopoly paves the way for considering other than purely economic barriers (quotas, permissions, licenses, patents and so forth). It is also in keeping with the differentiation between a gatekeeper and a dominant actor in the field

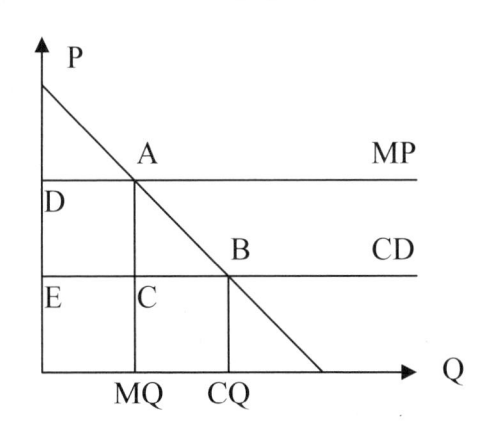

Figure 7.1
Neoclassical Model of Monopoly: Standard and Extended

Source: Tullock, 2005, pp. 92-93. MP refers to a monopolistic price, MQ—to a monopolistic quantity, CQ—to a competitive quantity, CD—to a competitive demand.

introduced in Subection I.5 of Chapter 5. The gatekeeper, C, creates favorable conditions for monopolist A by restricting access to the field for actors of the same type in exchange for a part of A's monopolistic rent. A, in turn, dominates B whose access to the field turns out to be unrestricted or restricted to a lesser degree, which maintains competition among B-type actors.

Nevertheless, the neoclassical interpretation of market power does not address a number of issues related to monopolistic domination. First, it usually acknowledges the active role of only a would-be monopolist. A presumably takes initiatives and offers bribes (paid out of A's expected or actual monopolistic rent) and the other stimuli to C in order to establish or strengthen a dominant position in the market field. State capture and influence are mentioned in this regard. In the case of the latter, A relies "on its own superiority in terms of its market share, production magnitude, property rights, privileged access to resources and its connections with officials at different levels of the government" (Guo & Hu, 2004, p. 267), in the former—exclusively on C's gatekeeping capacities. C's interest in domination using the privilege of keeping the gate to the field tends to be overlooked. To bridge the conceptual gap, Yong Guo and Angang Hu (2004, p. 271) introduce the notion of administrative monopoly as "a type of monopoly maintained by administrative power, to which various government departments resort so as to ensure a monopolistic status for interests of their own or of a particular sector or local enterprises affiliated with them."

Second, the neoclassical account focuses on individual decision-making, not on aspects emerging in the process of interactions between C, A and B. What emerges is domination by virtue of a constellation of the interests of these three actors. Each of them gains something from transacting with the others, yet the gains are distributed highly unevenly: C appropriates the lion's share, A—a significant part of them, B gets marginally more than when not entering the field. Of the three, only C maximizes profit/utility, whereas A and B minimize missed opportunities.[5]

Ignorance of the issues related to domination by virtue of a constellation of interests prevents the in-depth assessment of interconnections between corruption—narrowly defined as the use of public office for private gains—and the control of access to the market field. The common perception of rent-seeking as a source of corruption (Galitsky & Levin, 2007, p. 25) tells only a part of the story. On the one hand, corruption is intended to reduce the asymmetries inherent in power relationships and their particular form, domination. A monopoly condition makes rent extraction possible, but does not necessarily involve any form of rent sharing and redistribution. "Without bribery, the subordinate could not utilize the power of his superior and ... therefore, could not become a basis for the development of practical relationships of mutual dependence between superior and subordinate" (Yaney, 1973, p. 26). Viewed from this angle, A bribes C not only to restrict access of its competitors to the field, but also to reduce asymmetries in the relationships between A and C caused by privileges associated with the function of gatekeeping. Thus, bribery corresponds to interests of both C (who appropriates a part of the administrative rent through it) and A, while making them "constellate." Who takes initiatives and who bribes whom then becomes less relevant: both can.

On the other hand, an administrative rent is not necessarily appropriated uniquely in the form of bribes, C may spend a part of it in public interests too. When discussing practices of creating and capturing administrative rent in China, Tak-Wing Ngo mentions (2008, p. 30) "the dual facets of rent-creation as a legitimate government action and as a source of corruption." Namely, administrative rent can transform into a policy instrument to guide the technology transfers necessary for the development of the national or regional industry (Ibid, p. 35), national and regional development projects (Ibid, p. 42) etc. If this is the case, B, the key "utility donor," receives back a portion of the rent extracted by A and subsequently redistributed by C.

Third, the neoclassical account of monopoly appears to be disconnected from the explanation of the formation of the regional and national markets (they presumably emerge in a spontaneous manner). Karl Polanyi (1957, Ch. 5) challenges this view by insisting that, if the regional market can emerge spontaneously, the national market necessitates the involvement of the "visible hand" of the state. The analysis of administrative rent through the lens of domination by virtue of a constellation of interests highlights an alternative path in the formation of the national or regional market. Both national and regional markets may be a product of C's "visible hand." They may result from the enclosure of the market field corresponding to interests of C and A: this allows them to extract, share and redistribute rent.[6] In the final analysis, the enclosure serves to transform the market as a set of exchanges between equals into a field of power and domination (see Chapter 5).

However, empirical studies of the market embedded in a territory confront substantial challenges. The regional dimension of the market field, or, to put it differently, the market dimension of the territorial field accounts for difficulties in differentiating between the two fields with the help of empirical analysis (see Section III below). The frontier between the two fields appears blurred.

II. Case Study: Selecting the Case, Methods of Analysis, and Sources of Information

There are several rationales for the choice of the region as a unit of analysis when making an empirical study of the enclosure of the four fields. It seems desirable since one of the fields, territorial, is embedded in geographical space, and the other, market, may have a spatial dimension. This choice also helps maintain a reasonable level of compatibility with respect to the data, especially statistical. Statistical data are never perfect, especially in the post-Soviet countries (Herrera, 2006), yet within the same country statistical figures tend to have a similar bias, or, to express the same idea in more technical terms, measurement error.

A good candidate for the in-depth case study should have the following characteristics:

i. this region should have abundant natural resources: resource rent represents a significant part of rents captured in Russia;
ii. it should have a strong leader able to carry out the enclosure of the field(s), the key condition for appropriating administrative rent;
iii. in the other dimensions (population, GRP, etc.) it should be close to the Russian average.

A region located in Siberia meets all these criteria. In 2007, Region S.—it will be referred to in this manner—produced 57.8 percent of a basic energy resource in Russia (Federal State Statistics Service, 2008a). Its production has been growing steadily since the 1940s, except in the first half of the 1990s (Figure 7.2). The dynamics of its world price since the late 1980s follows the pattern of other energy resources: a downward trend in the 1990s, then a surge in the early 2000s (Figure 7.3). Expressed in standardized Z-values, the amount of the aggregate resource rent[7] produced in S. equals 1.23, which places it in a relative position within Russia comparable to that occupied by this country on an international scale.

For the past thirteen years, the region has been governed by a strong leader, one of the few regional leaders whose influence exceeds the scope of a particular territory: his name is consistently included in the federal list of politicians whom Russians trust the most (Figure 7.4). This al-

Doing Business in a Russian Region 209

Figure 7.2
Energy Resource Production in Region S., million tons, 1940-2005

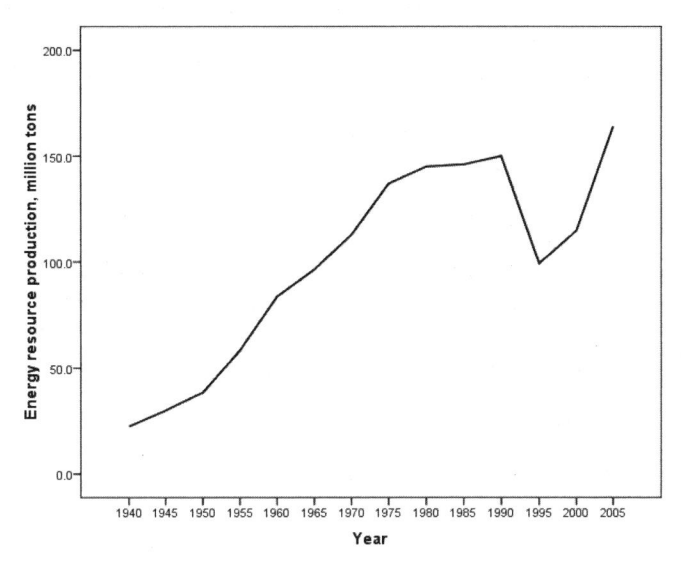

Source: Kemerovostat, 2008, pp. 182-183

Figure 7.3
World Price for the Energy Resource, current US $ per ton

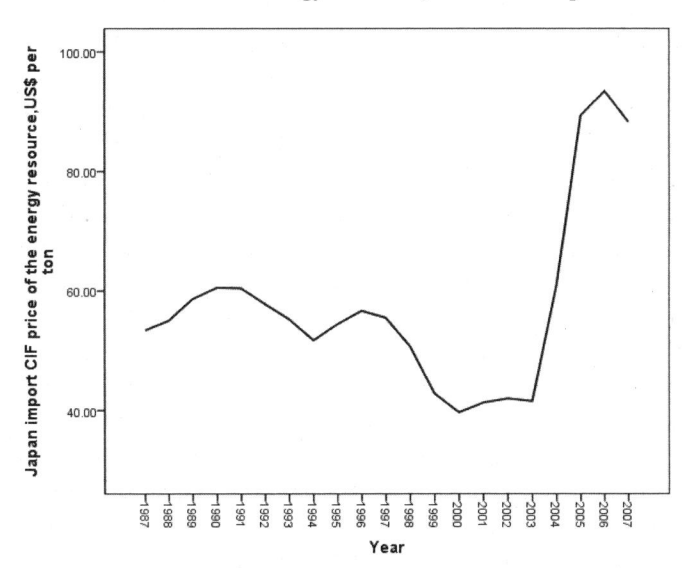

Source: British Petroleum, 2008.

Figure 7.4
Name 5-6 Politicians You Trust the Most, the Score of the Governor of Region S., %, 2000-2008

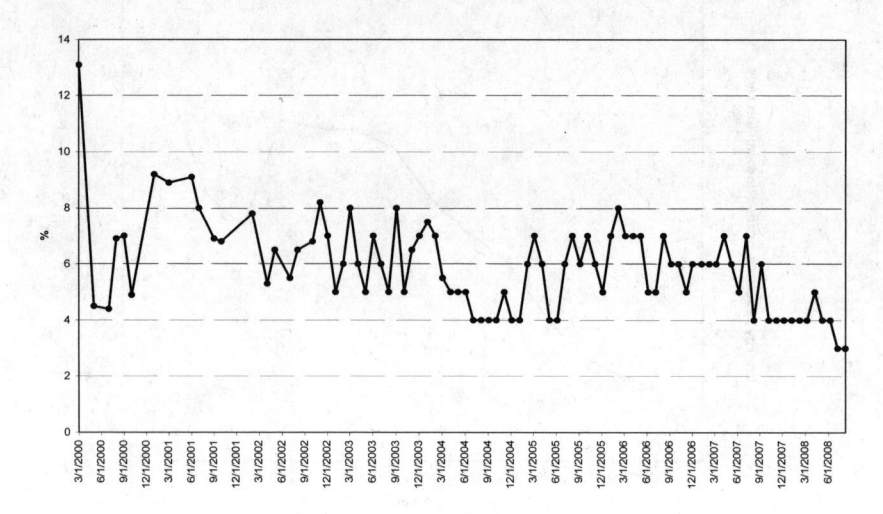

Source: regular surveys conducted on a representative sample by the Levada-Centre, retrieved from http://www.levada.ru/politiki.html.

lows the governor of S. to have his own agenda and to carry out his own policies even during a time when the so-called "vertical of power" is growing stronger, i.e., hierarchical control over regional administrative bodies is being tightened (see Subsection II [a1] of Chapter 8). Despite the significant contribution that Region S. has made both to the Soviet and the Russian economies, not all its leaders were similarly influential in the past (Konovalov, 2004). The governor of S. can be considered among a few "outliers" in this regard not only among S.'s past leaders, but among leaders of the other Siberian regions as well (Konovalov, 2006).

Region S. lies close to the average for the Russian Federation on most other dimensions. The Z-value for its GRP per head in 2007 equals -0.02 (μ=121,134.6 Russian Rubles, RUR, σ=101,940.8), 0.65—for its total population (μ=1,775,110, σ=1,617,821), 0.26—for the total monthly income per head (μ=10,436.5 RUR, σ=4,883.6) and 0.12—for the total value of fixed assets located in Region S. (μ=755,916.5 million RUR, σ=1,352,542.4; Federal State Statistics Service, 2008a).[8] Last but not least, the attention of the non-local media to the regional government and administration of S. also falls within one Z-score of the mean frequency of mentions. A search conducted in the LexisNexis database including materials published in major world periodicals in English between January 1, 2005 and January 1, 2009 shows that Region S. is mentioned 494 times, 37.2 percent of them—in connection with the regional government and administration, 5.7 percent—in connection with enterprises acting in S. The mean frequency with which the regional administration is mentioned for a random sample of 25 regions is 45.9 percent ($\sigma=12.25$), that with which the businesses are mentioned—6.3 percent ($\sigma=4.92$).[9]

A combination of, on the one hand, the outstanding features of Region S. with regard to the potential for capturing rent and, on the other hand, the region's close to average socio-economic parameters makes it an almost perfect "critical case" (see also Section I of the Introduction). Case studies usually involve the use of multiple available sources of both qualitative and quantitative data. As for sources of qualitative data, two series of in-depth semi-structured qualitative interviews were conducted in Region S. in 2006-2008. The sample of the first of them (N=17) includes middle- (bureau—*otdely*—and department heads) and top-level (former vice-governors and governors) state officials at the regional level. These interviews were conducted as part of a wider research project, the parameters of which are outlined in Section V of the Introduction and the Appendix. The sample deriving from the second project (N=9) comprises businesspeople representing small, medium-size and large enterprises in Region S.[10] Despite the fact that the focuses of the two projects and, accordingly, their interview guides, differ, both of them produced data that is highly relevant to the discussion of possible figures of constellation of *C*'s, *A*'s and *B*'s interests. The official statistics produced by the Federal State Statistics Service (2008a) and its regional branch are the principal source of the quantitative data.

The plurality of sources prompts the triangulation of research methods. Two versions of triangulation are actually applied (Jick, 1979; see the Methodological Appendix for more details): "within method" (the use of multiple techniques within a given method) and "between methods" (the use of two or more distinct methods). The latter method necessitates some form of "quantification" of the qualitative data in order to make the data in the two formats compatible and comparable. Such quantification is achieved with the help of a content analysis computer program QDA Miner. Content analysis was carried out on a merged set "C" (N=26: 12 middle-level office holders, 4 top-level office-holders and 10 businesspeople) comprising interviews originated from the two above-mentioned projects.

III. Empirical Evidence: Region S. as a Field of Domination

The analysis of the primary (qualitative before quantification) and secondary (quantitative) data has a double objective: first, to compare the relative scope of access control in the four fields (information, legal, territorial and market) and, second, to emphasize a particular form of domination, namely domination by virtue of a constellation of interests, emerging as a result.

III.1 Model of Measurement and Its Testing

Anticipating difficulties with the operationalization of such independent variables as the types of access control, a list of possible indicators corresponding to each of them was drawn up. In all, it includes 11 indicators for three independent variables (standard econometric considerations account for their selection), namely "Capital," "Labor" and "Human capital," and 30 indicators for four dependent variables, namely [the control of access to] "Information field," "Legal field," "Territorial field" and "Market field." Figure 7.5 summarizes the expected patterns of relationships between them in the form of a model of measurement.

The inclusion of a particular indicator has either a theoretical or a practical rationale. For instance, retail trade turnover (a cause-indicator) arguably refers to consumer purchasing power multiplied by consumer power expressed in numbers. An interview suggested the interpretation of the percentage of firms making losses in the total number of firms as an effect-indicator for the control of access to the territorial field:

> "When I was transferred to Moscow, there was no single enterprise bankrupt in [Region S.]. I repeat: no single one. In just six months there were sixty, if one counts only large enterprises" (17C).

The interlocutor alludes to significant changes in the rules of the game that occurred after his departure from the highest regional office: the enclosure of the territorial field necessitates that those who managed to "get into" the field before it started and consider their current status as granted shall be "kicked out," including by means of forced bankruptcy (see Subsection III.2 for more illustrations).

In a similar manner, the other interlocutor refers to the Internet as a source of reliable and free information over which state bodies and other

Figure 7.5
Model of Measurement

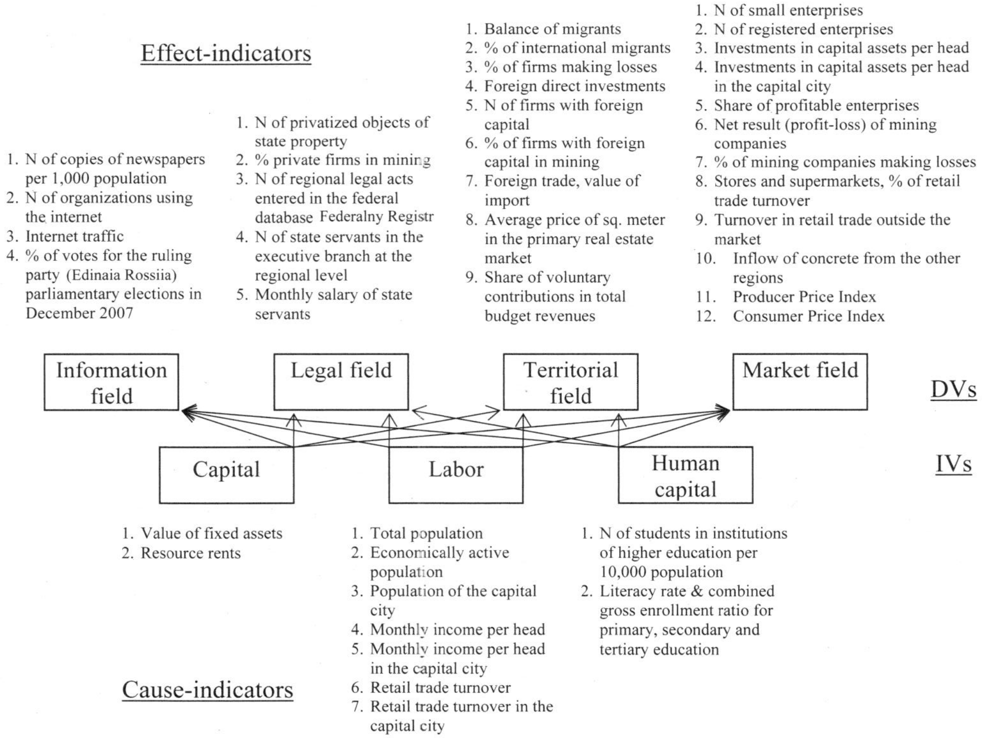

Effect-indicators

Information field
1. N of copies of newspapers per 1,000 population
2. N of organizations using the internet
3. Internet traffic
4. % of votes for the ruling party (Edinaia Rossiia) parliamentary elections in December 2007

Legal field
1. N of privatized objects of state property
2. % private firms in mining
3. N of regional legal acts entered in the federal database Federalny Registr
4. N of state servants in the executive branch at the regional level
5. Monthly salary of state servants

Territorial field
1. Balance of migrants
2. % of international migrants
3. % of firms making losses
4. Foreign direct investments
5. N of firms with foreign capital
6. % of firms with foreign capital in mining
7. Foreign trade, value of import
8. Average price of sq. meter in the primary real estate market
9. Share of voluntary contributions in total budget revenues

Market field
1. N of small enterprises
2. N of registered enterprises
3. Investments in capital assets per head
4. Investments in capital assets per head in the capital city
5. Share of profitable enterprises
6. Net result (profit-loss) of mining companies
7. % of mining companies making losses
8. Stores and supermarkets, % of retail trade turnover
9. Turnover in retail trade outside the market
10. Inflow of concrete from the other regions
11. Producer Price Index
12. Consumer Price Index

DVs

IVs

[Diagram: Information field, Capital, Legal field, Labor, Territorial field, Human capital, Market field]

Cause-indicators

Capital
1. Value of fixed assets
2. Resource rents

Labor
1. Total population
2. Economically active population
3. Population of the capital city
4. Monthly income per head
5. Monthly income per head in the capital city
6. Retail trade turnover
7. Retail trade turnover in the capital city

Human capital
1. N of students in institutions of higher education per 10,000 population
2. Literacy rate & combined gross enrollment ratio for primary, secondary and tertiary education

official organizations have very limited control. This reasoning explains the inclusion of the variable "Internet traffic" in the list of effect-indicators for the control of access to the information field.

> "I don't see any point in listening to them [representatives of the state-sponsored regional chamber of commerce and industry].... I'll use my computer to search for the information on the web instead. I'll get some answers for free whereas in this organization there is nothing but bureaucracy with no free entry, exit, no response whatsoever" (22C).

Publications in the Russian mass media (and the interview 19A with an official from the Federal Antimonopoly Service, FAS, organized in the framework of the wider research project) lead to the idea of using the inflow volume of concrete as an effect-indicator for the control of access to the market field. A high concentration ratio characterizes the cement industry in Russia, and particularly in Region S. that produced 5.8 percent of the total output in 2007 (Federal State Statistics Service, 2008c).[11]

Several indicators refer to the capital city as the unit of analysis instead of the region. As a rule, the situation in the capital city of a region has the same features as that in the region as a whole.[12] Along with increasing and diversifying the list of indicators, this serves to increase the reliability of the quantitative analysis while minimizing the risk of Type I error (the risk of rejecting the null hypothesis when it is true).[13] After inspecting the shape of the distribution of cause- and effect-indicators, a decision was made to apply a log transformation to a significant number of them. As a result, all the variables included in the measurement model have a distribution that does not significantly violate the assumption of normality.

Instead of discussing each empirical test separately, which would take too much space, they can be usefully summarized with the help of meta-analysis. "A meta-analysis is simply a systematic review that uses quantitative techniques to summarize quantitative results" (Vogt, 2007, p. 306). A simple form of meta-analysis used here consists in presenting the results of several multiple regressions using the measurement model as a set of guidelines for making sense of them. In all, 30 multiple regressions were run: four—for [the control of access to] the "Information field," four—for the "Legal field," eight—for the "Territorial field" and 14—for the "Market field" (plus three additional tests involving the other dependent variables: the GRP, the Human Development Index and the Budget Balance: Surplus/Deficit).

Each time the expected count—calculated with the help of the multiple regression equation—was compared with the observed count. To reject H_0 (the null hypothesis stating that there is no relationship between the variables included in the equation) either the latter has to exceed the former or *vice versa*—in keeping with the underlying rationale. For instance, the expected volume of foreign trade except with countries that are members of the Commonwealth of the Independent States (the former Soviet Union without the Baltic States) in 2007 can be calculated using the following equation:

$$Foreign\_trade_{Expected} = -7.786 - 0.089 \times Lg10(Resource\_Rents + 1) + 0.95 \times Lg10(Retail\_trade) + 1.199 \times Lg10(GRP)$$

The model accounts for about 70 percent of the variance in the volume of foreign trade among Russian regions ($R=0.834$, $R^2=0.696$ and the adjusted $R^2=0.684$). The overall regression is statistically significant[14] $F(3, 76)=57.87$, $p<0.001$. The variables "Resource_Rents," "Retail_trade" and "GRP" all appear to be significant predictors of the dependent variable with $t(79)=-2.714$, $p=0.008$; $t(79)=8.704$, $p<0.001$ and $t(79)=5.245$, $p<0.001$ correspondingly. Complete results for the multiple regression are presented in Table 7.1. The expected count (2.95) largely exceeds the observed count for Region S. (2.53). This means that, without the restrictions associated with the control of access to the market, the volume of foreign trade—after the log transformation—would be about 17 percent higher.

Table 7.1
Results of Standard Multiple Regression to Predict the Volume of Foreign Trade (Y) from Resource Rents (X_1), Retail Trade Turnover (X_2) and GRP (X_3)

	Variable	Mean	Standard deviation	B	Beta	Significance
Y	Lg10 (Foreign trade)	2.508	0.776			
	Intercept (Constant)			-7.786		<0.001
X_1	Lg10 (Resource rents)	4.866	1.538	-0.089	-0.176	0.008
X_2	Lg10 (Retail trade turnover)	4.839	0.506	0.95	0.619	<0.001
X_3	Lg10 (GRP)	5.113	0.242	1.199	0.374	<0.001

The econometric test also does not rule out the fact that the volume of inflow of cement, the other effect-indicator for the control of access to the market field, is associated with such independent variables as "Fixed assets" and "GRP." The predictive equation is as follows:

$$Inflow_{Expected} = -2.207 + 1.912 \times Lg10(Assets) - 1.298 \times Lg10(GRP)$$

The quality of the model is poorer than in the previous case: it accounts for only about 42 percent of the variance ($R=0.647$, $R^2=0.419$ and the adjusted $R^2=0.403$; see Table 7.2). Nevertheless, the overall regression is statistically significant $F(2, 73)=26.31$, $p<0.001$. Without the control of access to the regional market, more cement produced in the other regions (2.44 compared with 1.35 after the log transformation) would be consumed by B-type businesses in Region S. This case also highlights the difficulties associated with the task of clearly differentiating the market field from the territorial field. The regional administration has a limited ableness (see Subsection I.2 of Chapter 5) to control access to the national cement market. The scope of its control of access to the market field is limited by the administrative boundaries of Region S. Thus, the discrepancy between the expected and the observed counts may be attributed to the control of access either to the market field or to the territorial field or to both.

Table 7.3 contains summary outcomes of 30 econometric tests. Overall, it provides a rather mixed picture. Only tests concerning the control of access to the information field appear consistent and positive: they

Table 7.2
Results of Standard Multiple Regression to Predict Inflow of Cement (Y) from Fixed Assets (X_1) and GRP (X_2)

	Variable	Mean	Standard deviation	B	Beta	Significance
Y	Lg10 (Inflow of cement)	1.996	0.934			
	Intercept (Constant)			-2.207		0.229
X_1	Lg10 (Fixed assets)	5.62	0.451	1.912	0.839	<0.001
X_2	Lg10 (GRP)	5.113	0.242	-1.298	-0.328	0.012

Table 7.3
Meta-Analysis of Outcomes of 30 Multiple Regressions

Field	N of effect-indicators	N of statistically significant tests	Inconclusive: expected count equals observed count‡	Fail to reject the null hypothesis, H_0	Reject H_0	Ratio Reject / N of tests
Information	4	4	0	0	4 (2)	1
Legal	5	4	0	3 (1)†	1 (1)	0.25
Territorial	9	8	0	4 (2)	4 (1)	0.5
Market	13	14♣	3 (3)	4 (2)	7 (3)	0.5
Other DVs	3	3	0	1	2 (1)	0.67

Legend: ‡ The expected count exactly equals the observed count. Because of the log transformation—it tends to "compress" the magnitude of the variation—the equality of the counts after rounding can be considered a separate category. † The number of tests with large effect sizes is reported in brackets (out of the total number of tests in this cell). The effect size—R^2 in the case of multiple regressions—is considered large if it equals or exceeds 0.8 (Warner, 2008, pp. 107, 353-355). ♣ The two units of analysis are involved, the region and the capital city.

all suggest rejecting the null hypothesis. As for the control of access to the legal field, three out of four tests show that the null hypothesis cannot be rejected. To explain this outcome, one should keep in mind the timeframe for conducting the interviews—they coincided with the period of increased hierarchical control in relationships between federal and regional administrative bodies, especially in law making.

> "We have to react immediately to any requests to make our regional legal acts, orders conform to the federal laws. The control in this area has increased without leaving much room for maneuvering" (8C).

The outcomes of the tests for the control of access to the territorial field were evenly split, whereas most of those for the control of access to the market field cannot rule out its existence in Region S. Nevertheless, because of an eventual overlap between these two types of access control, a finer analysis carried out with the help of a more extensive list of effect-indicators may be needed. It is worth mentioning that, among the independent variables, the two indicators of purchasing power appear to be the strongest predictors: they are entered in 12 models in all—far more frequently than any other predictors. This further confirms the importance of analyzing the field of retail trade in order to understand how access control works (see Subsections III.1 and III.2 of Chapter 5).

III.2 Content Analysis of Qualitative Interviews

The full version of the codebook (see the Appendix) comprises 55 codes. The original model (see the Methodological Appendix) for triangulating the results of the three types of content analysis—qualitative coding, content analysis with the help of a dictionary based on substitution (a number of words and expressions is associated with each qualitative code) and quantitative content analysis (co-occurrence of words)—indicates a high level of reliability in attributing qualitative codes. All Pearson's coefficients of correlation between the outcomes of the three types of contents analysis exceed 0.7 (Figure 7.6). However, only 15 codes forming three categories—"Domination by virtue of a constellation of interests" (4 codes), "Techniques for imposing will" (7 codes), "Power in its pure form" (4 codes), and a stand-alone code "Constellation of interests" (see Section III of Chapter 6)—were selected for analysis in this subsection. The first category (codes [The control of access to the] "Information field," "Legal field," "Territorial field" and "Market field") and the stand-alone code appear especially relevant because they serve to triangulate "between methods," namely the econometric models with the content analysis.

The four codes included in the category "Domination by virtue of a constellation of interests" highlight means by which it can be achieved. Control of access enables C, the regional administration, to secure dominant positions in various fields that it manages to "enclose." There are two categories of actors admitted to a field: As who have a competitive edge because of various privileges granted to them by C (e.g., their restricted number) in exchange for accepting C's supremacy and Bs who do not

Figure 7.6
Path-Model for Content Analysis of Interviews Conducted in Region S.

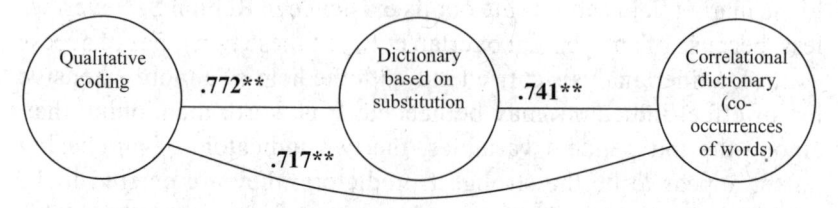

Qualitative coding —.772**— Dictionary based on substitution —.741**— Correlational dictionary (co-occurrences of words)

.717**

Legend: The level of statistical significance (** for correlations significant at the 0.001 level) is indicated for the sake of reference: the non-random character of the sample of transcripts makes statistical inferences meaningless. In this case, the values of the Pearson correlation coefficients have a purely descriptive meaning.

have any privileges but still gain something from entering the field. *A*'s payment for admitting him or her to the field does not necessarily take a monetary form (e.g., a share of *A*'s monopolistic profits). *A*'s major obligation, a "debt of honor," consists in contributing to strengthening *C*'s domination: financially, ideologically, structurally (by furthering the "bias of the system," see Section III of Chapter 2) and so forth.

III.2.1 Information Field. In the case of the information field *C* "trades" *A*'s access to public attention for the latter's willingness to promote *C*'s cause and to help *C* build an even more positive reputation (that can be converted, for example, into electoral votes). Controlling access to the information field works with regard to the mass media—through practices of the so called "selective accreditation"—and the news or actors covered by them—mostly through self-censorship as an expression of "anticipated reactions": "[*A*]'s acts based on his anticipations of [*C*]'s reaction to them" (Wrong, 1980, p. 8).

> "Let's assume that there exists an unwanted journalist, a journalist with whom I was not able to make a deal. For instance, a journalist who keeps picturing me in a bad light. I organize a press conference…. How can I not to let this asshole in? And I still need to get a large attendance, to promote the event as actively as possible. I can simply say that accreditation is needed. The unwanted journalists will be then told: 'Sorry, no places are left' or 'Sorry, you applied too late'" (9C).

> "I don't recall where—on the web or in a newspaper, but [this project] was actively promoted. Maybe on the [regional] TV—the information about it was made available because the administration was interested in intensifying public interest in the project" (14C).

> "They should show that a particular organization, a farmer or a small entrepreneur or anyone else had presented an idea, it was carefully considered and realized. We helped in this endeavor, look at the outcome. No way. You can only see a top administrator who distributes [resources] and praises himself: look, how much money I redistributed" (22C).

III.2.2 Legal Field. Control of access to the legal field refers to the practices of defining what is legal, extra-legal or criminal, at *C*'s discretion. The access control tools range from various kinds of certificates, *spravkas*, necessary for the official recognition of various kinds of everyday situations (e.g., that a certain X. does indeed live at a particular address) to permits or licenses required from businesspeople in particular industries such as mining, retail trade, real estate, the service sector, etc. Contrary to De Soto's assumptions, state representatives may be interested in keeping them as a means for recognizing the legal status of only a "docile" business, organization or individual.

"An old lady comes in—I need a certificate that in 1994 a particular municipal enterprise was transformed into a small private firm. We send her to the archive knowing that she will never find it. Yet, the decision at stake is whether she will get a pension or not" (2C).

"The Duma [Russian Parliament] eliminated the option 'Against all' in voting ballots. What does this mean? Particular candidates will get a green light whereas the others will see their documents [for the registration] rejected" (10C).

"I'm familiar with licensing alcohol products. One can get a license for retail trade relatively easily, for wholesale trade—with far more problems. They impose very high requirements for excise warehouses. You would think they store diamonds, not alcohol. There must be licensed guards, a customs' office, several computers and so forth. In short, the highest degree of idiocy. The problem must be solved in some way—just don't forget to bring an envelope [with cash]" (19C).

III.2.3 Territorial Field. When attributing the "Territorial field" codes emphasis was placed on the embeddedness of domination in geographical, physical space. The administrative borders of the municipality, region then transform into resources of power, i.e., boundaries of the territorial field. This transformation produces a drift into the extension of administrative borders as the materialization of an increased scope of domination.[15]

Keeping in mind the difficulties of distinguishing the market field from the territorial field, it was decided to apply the code "Territorial field" only to these fragments that contained manifest references to the control of access to interactions in physical space, including the lease and sublease of municipal and regional property. An example of the control of access to the territorial field can be found in the restrictions—imposed with the help of a Region S. law dated April 2008—on unaccompanied appearances of minors in the street and other public spaces between 10:00 p.m. and 6:00 a.m.[16] Instead of trying to restrict particular activities of the minors (drinking, gambling, loitering, prostitution), the administration decided to limit their movements to private spaces (see also Subsection I.5 of Chapter 5).

"When you travel from [the capital city of Region S.] to [the capital city of a neighboring region], there is a no man's land everywhere. Yet if you set up a pavilion, they [the regional administration] will immediately impose a tribute" (19C).

"Lease rates are subject to discretionary interpretation. They are published, their range is known, say, from 0.5 to 15. Using these rates, the same space for lease can be assessed at 2 rubles or 10 rubles per square meter. It can be leased for 10 years or for one year only" (18C).

"There have been so many tragedies in the administration, you know, especially among former vice-governors. They can hardly find a decent job in the region. Remember former vice-governors and where they work now—those who left after a scandal: either in Moscow, or in private business or simply stay at home. Very few work in the region" (10C).

Region S. first introduced—in the late 1990s—a path-breaking practice of signing agreements of socio-economic cooperation between the regional administration and all more or less significant businesses (ten years later this practice prevails in many other Russian regions). In fact, without accepting the terms of this agreement whose essence consists in the obligation to support—financially and by all other available means—the administration's initiatives, a particular business can hardly "get into" the region. If the business declining the terms of the agreement is of local origin, then the administration tries to kick it out by organizing endless checks or compliance controls, by refusing to renew licenses and permits and so on.

> "These agreements are common. This measure is, of course, forced and not entirely legal. Yet it has become a kind of tradition here. People from the other regional administrations come to learn how it works" (8C).
>
> "Everyone is aware that the region needs it. Enterprises work in this territory. We create a reputation for them, after all. They realize that we'll treat them differently if they refuse [to sign the agreement]" (4C).
>
> "No businessperson will accept it out of good will. It's a hidden form of coercion. But can one proceed in any other way? They don't give you a license next time, they will let your direct competitor in. You realize that you cannot afford losing this spot. And you start making sacrifices, paying for your being here" (1C).
>
> "[The governor] can use ecological,[17] sanitary, fire protection considerations as a lever against [these who do not sign the agreement], as well as the issues related to taxes etc. There have been many [businesspeople] like this—he kicked all of them out" (16C).

III.2.4 Market Field. The attribution of the "Market field" codes derives from the assumption that the boundaries of the field are other than geographical: financial and institutional, including social (membership in a particular social group or network as a condition for accessing it[18]). The restricted access to the market field naturally produces a drift toward monopolization. Administrative rent in its most common interpretation represents nothing other than profits shared between C, the gatekeeper, and A, an actor with a competitive edge, as a result of restricting access to the market field of A's competitors. The administration in Region S. manages to enclose the market field, on the one hand, by erecting various barriers against unwelcome participants in auctions that it organizes and, on the other hand, granting privileges and tax exemptions to selected businesses.

"As for businesses, they can get privileges, tax exemptions, simplified procedures, in general terms—their demands are treated well by the administration" (13C).

"Let's assume there are two to three enterprises that produce something (milk, meat, it does not really matter) and there exist federal and regional programs for development and support. If our administration chooses a particular enterprise and offers any kind of support to it, the two other immediately find themselves at disadvantage.... If an enterprise in our region does not see a green light, it has either to accept a merger or go bankrupt" (20C).

"There is a certain Regional Insurance Company. It's called regional! Enterprises receive letters from the administration stating that they should buy insurance only from this company. A clear and strong signal for them, isn't it?" (21C).

The case of retail trade is worth mentioning separately as it shows how various market barriers can overlap. At the first level, the role of gatekeeper is performed by the large retailer (C) that controls the access of producers (A) and customers (B) to their meeting place. However, the access of large retailers to the consumer goods market can be restricted by the administration (it has the power to regulate the consumer market) that appropriates the function of gatekeeping at a higher level (C'; see Subsection III.2 of Chapter 5). In other words, the administration restricts competition among the large retailers (capturing a share of the resulting administrative rent in exchange), whereas the large retailer in turn limits competition among producers (also capturing a share of the administrative rent emerging at this level). Region S. is the home of a large retailer, K., and also the market that other retailers are keen to enter, e.g., L.

"A narrow circle of entrepreneurs receive preferable treatment. All the others are considered competitors that have to be eliminated by any available means. N., a vice-governor in the regional administration, helped K. a lot" (19C).

"I think that, in a city like [the capital city of S.] in the West there would be no more than 130 stores.... As of today, we've got about 1,000-1,200.... They correspondingly have very high operating costs.... All these considerations are relevant to the question as to the necessity of administrative barriers" (26C).

"Initially I did not know anyone at L. We had spent about a year getting into the chain; we were introduced by someone.... *How did L. enter [the regional market]?* I tell you that they succeeded only after entering a local power group, after learning how to live together" (22C).[19]

III.2.5 Associations between Various Forms of Access Control. Various forms of entry control are differentiated analytically, whereas in practice they not only coexist but also reinforce one another. For instance, controlling access to the information field can strengthen access to the market field.

"A tender is often won by the one who knows about it. An insignificant advantage in the access to the information, the closeness to sources of information ensures a significant competitive edge" (14C).

A closer inspection of coding co-occurrences shows particularly strong associations between the following pairs of codes (they tend to co-occur more often than the other pairs controlling for the factor of randomness): "Market field" and "Legal field," "Territorial field" and "Market field," "Legal field" and "Territorial field" (Table 7.4). The overlap between the market field and the territorial field appears particularly revealing as it provides some support for the conceptualization of the regional market as the market field embedded in the territorial field. Geographical and administrative boundaries maintained by the regional administration strengthen barriers to entry and to exit, a central element of the market field and *vice versa*.

"This hampers normal competition, the normal price formation, the normal supply of human and material resources. For instance, the location of the enterprise conditions its access to raw materials. Taken all together, this creates such an uneven competitive environment that one dies off whereas the other survives against all rules and principles. The latter produces a more expensive product at a higher cost. However, it sells it everywhere. We buy it and then call all this capitalism. There is nothing in common with capitalism! The market means that there is a third one who chooses between you and me, not that we arrange everything between us instead of being chosen" (22C).

"The support [provided by the regional administration] can be used in the interests of the region. However, many entrepreneurs view this support—it can take not only pecuniary forms—as a condition for capturing administrative rent only" (15C).

When exploring coding co-occurrences with the help of a dendrogram and a 3-D map it appears that the "Constellation of interests" code has the attributes of a centroid.[20] The "Constellation of interests" code is located right in the center of the 3-D map of coding co-occurrences (Figure 7.7). On a similar map derived from the content analysis of interviews carried out in the framework of the wider research project (Set "A," N=47, excluding those conducted in Region S.; not reproduced), this code is also located close to the center, which may indicate a valid character of the finding. The other proof of its validity consists in a high Pearson's coefficient of correlation value, 0.652 at p=0.006, between Jaccard's coefficients of similarity between the qualitative codes calculated for the sets "A" and "C" (Table 7.5).

Table 7.4
Sequences of Codes, Controlling for Chance Co-Occurrences at α=0.1

Code A	Code B	Freq A	Freq B	Freq (B|A)	% of A	Freq (A|B)	% of B	% Events	z	Prob.
Market field	Legal field	60	47	12	20.0	12	25.5	24.5	4.224	0.0004
Constellation of interests	Market field	62	60	17	27.4	14	23.3	23.3	3.325	0.0027
No feedback	Force_physical violence	40	27	4	10.0	4	14.8	23.5	3.708	0.0067
Structural bias	Force_physical violence	34	27	4	11.8	4	14.8	22.2	3.551	0.0083
Coercion	Positive incentives	53	24	5	9.4	5	20.8	15.6	3.277	0.0094
End-in-itself	Structural bias	19	34	3	15.8	3	8.8	33.3	3.521	0.0128
Structural bias	Structural bias	34	34	4	11.8	4	11.8	22.2	2.967	0.0183
Manipulation	Informational field	16	12	2	12.5	2	16.7	18.2	3.766	0.0206
Symbolic violence	Positive incentives	16	24	1	6.3	2	8.3	25.0	2.973	0.0402
Territorial field	Market field	73	60	12	16.4	11	18.3	17.2	1.816	0.0611
Territorial field	Coercion	73	53	10	13.7	10	18.9	15.6	1.818	0.0626
Asymmetrical	Symbolic violence	79	16	3	3.8	3	18.8	8.8	2.17	0.0658
Asymmetrical	Manipulation	79	16	3	3.8	3	18.8	8.8	2.17	0.0658
Market field	Constellation of interests	60	62	11	18.3	9	14.5	18.4	1.756	0.0712
Legal field	Constellation of interests	47	62	8	17.0	8	12.9	19.0	1.769	0.0723
Legal field	Territorial field	47	73	9	19.1	9	12.3	21.4	1.744	0.0725
Territorial field	Constellation of interests	73	62	12	16.4	11	17.7	17.2	1.7	0.0737
Market field	Territorial field	60	73	10	16.7	10	13.7	20.4	1.668	0.0794

Legend: Code A is the first code in a sequence, code B—the second. The two codes are allowed to overlap, but not to be separated by any other code. "Events" in the ninth column of the table refers to the total number of code sequences that have been identified. To get Z-values (the tenth column) one needs to compare the observed frequency of a code sequence to the expected frequency (calculated on the basis of a random distribution of code sequences "weighted" by their share in the number of "events"). The author thanks Normand Péladeau of Provalis Research for help in interpreting these variables as they are not routinely calculated in QDA Miner. The level of α is set at 0.1, which is acceptable for explorative research.

A comparison of coding frequencies in the two sets of interviews also suggests a number of important observations. Out of the 15 codes of particular relevance for the present discussion, four occur substantially more frequently in the "C" set of interviews conducted in Region S. (Table 7.6). For instance, the "Territorial field" code occurs almost seven times, the "Market field" code—almost four times, the "Constel-

Doing Business in a Russian Region 225

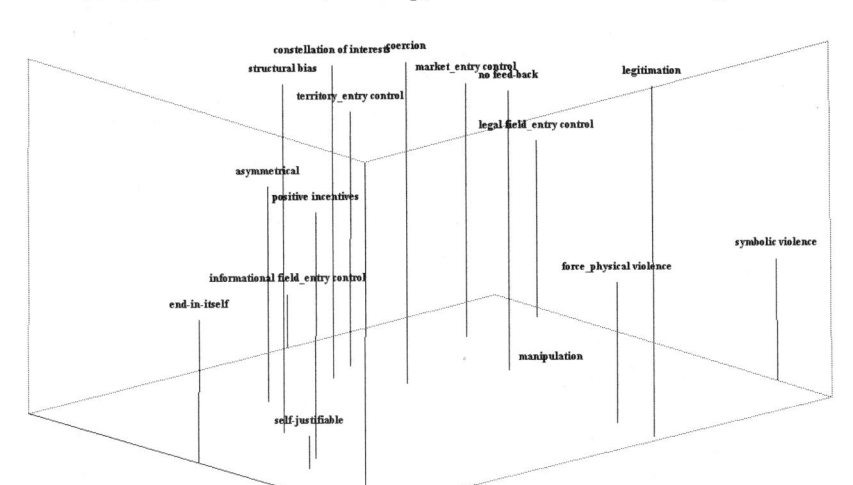

Figure 7.7
Co-Occurrence of Codes, 3-D Map, Interviews Conducted in Region S.

Table 7.5
Jaccard's Coefficients of Similarity with the Code "Constellation of Interests"

Code	Interviews in Region S. (N=26), Set "C"	Interviews in the other regions (N=47), Set "A"
Coercion	0.87	0.545
Territorial field	0.8	0.486
Asymmetrical	0.72	0.739
Market field	0.68	0.474
No feed-back	0.667	0.585
Legal field	0.52	0.475
Structural bias	0.5	0.595
Positive incentives	0.44	0.574
End-in-itself	0.435	0.295
Informational field	0.391	0.378
Self-justifiable	0.364	0.381
Manipulation	0.292	0.474
Force_physical violence	0.292	0.475
Symbolic violence	0.217	0.564
Legitimation	0.217	0.308

Table 7.6
Codebook for Content Analysis, Selected Codes

Category	Code	Region S.; Set "C" Count	Region S.; Set "C" % Codes	Other regions; Set "A" Count	Other regions; Set "A" % Codes	Region S.; Set "C" Cases	Region S.; Set "C" % Cases	Other regions; Set "A" Cases	Other regions; Set "A" % Cases	Region S.; Set "C" Nb Words	Region S.; Set "C" % Words	Other regions; Set "A" Nb Words	Other regions; Set "A" % Words
[Domination] by virtue of a constellation of interests	Constellation of interests*	62	4.6	76	1.9	22	84.6	34	72.3	5129	4.1	5472	1.6
	Information field	12	0.9	27	0.7	10	38.5	17	36.2	969	0.8	1032	0.3
	Legal field	47	3.5	62	1.6	16	61.5	25	53.2	3319	2.6	3196	0.9
	Market field	60	4.5	49	1.2	20	76.9	22	46.8	3755	3.0	2367	0.7
	Territorial field	73	5.5	32	0.8	23	88.5	21	44.7	5009	4.0	1597	0.5
Power in its pure form	Asymmetrical	79	5.9	179	4.6	21	80.8	46	97.9	3188	2.5	5724	1.7
	End-in-itself	19	1.4	32	0.8	11	42.3	23	48.9	555	0.4	894	0.3
	No feedback	40	3.0	63	1.6	18	69.2	31	66.0	1616	1.3	2530	0.7
	Self-justifiable	14	1.0	46	1.2	8	30.8	24	51.1	592	0.5	1261	0.4
Repertoire of techniques for imposing will	Coercion	53	4.0	88	2.2	21	80.8	34	72.3	2020	1.6	2897	0.8
	Force_physical violence	27	2.0	47	1.2	9	34.6	25	53.2	928	0.7	1776	0.5
	Legitimation	7	0.5	26	0.7	6	23.1	17	36.2	250	0.2	1022	0.3
	Manipulation	16	1.2	47	1.2	9	34.6	22	46.8	730	0.6	2224	0.7
	Positive incentives	24	1.8	120	3.1	14	53.8	40	85.1	693	0.6	3912	1.1
	Structural bias	34	2.5	82	2.1	14	53.8	33	70.2	1361	1.1	3487	1.0
	Symbolic violence	16	1.2	55	1.4	6	23.1	27	57.4	849	0.7	1994	0.6

Legend: * Power embedded in monopolistic structures of the market. Focus on the outcome: how interests of *C* and *A* constellate as a result.

lation of interests" code—2.4 times, the "Legal field" code—2.2 times more frequently. One possible interpretation consists in a particularly heavy reliance of the regional administration, *C*, on controlling access to the regional market as a strategy for reproducing and strengthening its dominance. *A*, businesses allowed to enter the market, accept the status quo because of a competitive edge that *C* creates for them in exchange for a share of the administrative rent and their support of a wide—and not specified *ex ante*—range of *C*'s policies and initiatives.

Thus, the initial assumption that accounts for the choice of Region S. for the case study finds confirmation in the outcomes of the content analysis. The results of the econometric models (Table 7.3) at least do not rule out the proposed reading of *C*'s domination embedded in the regional market. However, an apparent inconsistency exists in this regard: the spread of the control of access to the information field in Region S. seems to be confirmed quantitatively but not qualitatively (the frequency of the corresponding code does not differ in the two sets of interviews). This may be due to manipulation (see Section III of Chapter 2) whose objective consists precisely in making A and B believe that C does not distort the flow of information: the frequency of the "Manipulation" code exceeds that of the "Information field" code.

III.2.6 Securing B's Compliance: How Administrative Rent Is Spent. Thus far, a constellation of C's and A's interests has remained the focus of attention. B, the ordinary person who buys goods and services from A at a higher price, has no interest in challenging C's domination either. The high visibility of the governor of S., who personifies C in this region, at the federal level was mentioned earlier. He has even more intense popular support at the regional level: before the elections of the governors were abolished in December 2004, the governor won two consecutive elections by a wide margin with 95 percent of the votes in 1997 and 93.5 percent of the votes in 2001. Hence, it is worthwhile to shed more light on the reasons for B's acceptance of A's and C's domination.

Controlling access to the regional market serves to capture administrative rent (although C's domination has other manifestations as well, the existence of a constellation of B's and C's interests will be demonstrated by referring to this aspect). A part of it remains in hands of A, whereas C receives the rest. How does C spend administrative rent? On the one hand, C acts in the interests of the population of Region S. and its socio-economic development as they are perceived by C. The existence of such "benevolent" spending of administrative rent means that B receives a portion of it back—after it passes through A's and C's hands. On the other hand, C spends administrative rent in its own particularistic interests (Figure 7.8). These range from investments in projects that do not have any other value than the reproduction of C's domination to corruption and embezzlement in more or less sophisticated forms.

> "[The money] can be spent on sponsoring various projects that otherwise should be financed from the budget, yet they don't get funded. For instance, on building playgrounds for kids, nursing homes etc. Such projects have to be financed from the budget but then suddenly they decide to build them at the expense of businesses" (22C).
>
> "Businesspeople, who sublease [the regional and municipal property], are well integrated in the administrative system. The money generated here serves the needs of the administration, the private needs of its representatives" (18C).

These excerpts show that a portion of the administrative rent partly replaces budget expenditures, partly complements them. A reasonable question arises: why does the regional administration not simply increase

Figure 7.8
Distribution of Administrative Rent between *A*, *B*, and *C*

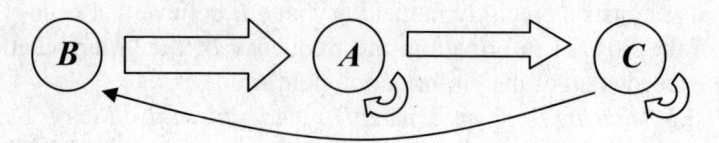

regional and local taxes instead? Revenues from taxation are much more tightly controlled by outsiders, e.g. the federal government. In other words, the key advantage of relying on administrative rent instead of taxes consists in increasing *C*'s room for maneuvering and reducing the transparency of transfers of wealth. This enables *C* and only *C* to decide the parameters for dividing the captured administrative rent between "benevolent" and "corrupt" uses.

> "The existing practice of extracting additional resources from the businesses has an explanation: in this way the regional administration manages to make their flow less transparent and not subject to accounting, unlike budget resources that are closely monitored. One can hardly move the money from one category of expenditures to the other. Here representatives of the regional administration even succeed in putting a portion of the additional resources in their pockets" (25C).

This caveat should be kept in mind when assessing the amount of the administrative rent extracted in Region S.: figures of official statistics capture only the tip of the iceberg. The portion of the administrative rent that is actually entered in account books falls into the "Other revenues" category of the regional budget.

> "The practice of co-financing is widely used at the regional, the municipal levels. The budget has a particular category, 'Other revenues,' which accumulates these additional resources. *What is its share in the total revenues?* Approximately 24-25% of the total" (10C).

According to official figures, the resources accumulated under this category[21] represented 1.8 percent of the total income of the Region S. budget in 2006 compared with 0.5 percent in the consolidated budget of the Russian Federation (an aggregate of all the regional budgets). In 2007, these figures were 1.3 percent and 0.35 percent correspondingly.[22] The fact that these figures depart from the estimate given by the insider, a member of the regional legislature, (24 percent versus 1.8 percent) further confirms the non-transparent character of the flow of administrative rent. The divergence between the figures in the regional budget and in the consolidated budget once again indicates the greater ability of the regional administration of S. to enclose the regional market and capture administrative rent. As for the portion of the administrative rent appropriated by *C*, the collected data do not suffice to estimate it with a high level of precision. For instance, the total amount of rent generated in China's monopoly sectors in the second half of the 1990s is estimated at 1.7-2.7 percent of the GDP (Guo & Hu, 2004, p. 276). In Region S., the portion of the administrative rent officially captured by *C* represented 0.24 percent of the GRP in 2006. Using the rough ratio of 1 to 10 between the officially and the unofficially captured parts of the administrative rent, one arrives at an estimate of the portion of the administrative rent appropriated by *C* as 2.4 percent of the GRP.

In the final account, *B* receives only a small fraction of the administrative rent that he or she mostly pays for. Nevertheless, the fact that *B* receives something either in the form of private (e.g., small increases in scholarships, pensions) or public (e.g., renovated facades and pavements) goods—in the other regions *B* may get nothing—leads him or her to give full support to *C*'s dominance. A political regime with elements of populism emerges out of domination by virtue of a constellation of *A*'s, *B*'s and *C*'s interests. Compared with populist regimes in several Latin American countries (Touraine, 1988), this populism has an even stronger "market" component because of its deep embeddedness in the regional market.

IV. Generalizing Practices of Access Control

Practices of the access control spread beyond borders of Region S.: they are imitated by representatives of the other regions but also appreciated at the federal level. The national market as the solid link between the market field and the territorial field then substitutes for the regional market as a driving engine of domination. Region S. has broken a new path followed by the others (Oleinik, 2008c).

The federal government actively uses the control of access to the market field in the oil and gas industry, the key generator of resource rent in the Russian economy. Administrative rent is to be entered into calculation as well as a result of a high concentration ratio in this industry (see Table 8.3). Foreign investors can obtain access to Russian energy resources only if they accept conditions set by the gatekeeper at the federal level (see Section III of Chapter 6). Russian oil and gas companies are no exception either: they must share resource and administrative rents with *C* (Gaddy & Ickes, 2005, pp. 564-567). *C* tends to impose the same principles not only on investors but also on customers of Russian energy resources, using the position of the largest supplier of natural gas to the European Union as a lever (see Section II of the Introduction).

While access control techniques work better in circumstances of economic growth, they can be adapted and adjusted to a shrinking economy as well. As the state—not only in Russia but also in the West—then becomes the quasi-unique source of affordable credits and other resources necessary for the survival of businesses, its representatives can impose several conditions on loan applicants (see also Scott, 2001, p. 72 and Section V of the Conclusion). In Region S., such conditions include the transparency of the applicant's internal accounting for the regional administration. The knowledge of insider information opens the way for more effective strategies for capturing and distributing rent: C becomes aware of A's $\bar{U}'$ (see Figures 6.3 and 6.4). The federal government adapted very similar practices of imposing conditions on loan applicants when the financial crisis did not leave them alternative options: businesses must make all insider information available to government officials.[23]

> "Many enterprises would like to be given preference. The competitions [organized by the regional administration] provide them with preferences. So, to apply, the enterprise must be fully transparent. We must know everything about it—taxes, costs, price formation. The competition allows for establishing a direct contact between the enterprise and the administration" (8C).

Both continuity and change characterize the emerging model of domination by virtue of a constellation of interests: this contributes to the reproduction of power in its pure form in the new institutional environment and by using new techniques for imposing will. The institutional change—the spread of techniques of the access control underlying domination by virtue of a constellation of interests—results from the activities of institutional entrepreneurs (cf. Davis & North, 1970), office holders who assume the role of C. Incremental changes in the institutional environment underlying domination by virtue of a constellation of interests then transform into a "structural bias" that allow it to reproduce with minimal human agency. However, at the early stages of the institutional change, strategic components of power (see Subsection I.4 of Chapter 5) prevail over structural ones.

Who are these institutional entrepreneurs in Region S.? It is common to assume continuity between the Soviet and the post-Soviet power elites (see Section IV of the Introduction, Conclusion of Chapter 3). The governor of S. indeed started his political and administrative career during the Soviet time (as of 2010, he is in his sixties). However, office holders in Region S. tend to be slightly younger than their counterparts in the other regions and at the federal level. This relative youthfulness takes especially manifest forms if the employees of the regional and municipal bodies are counted: 56.7 percent of state representatives in 2007 are 40 years old or younger. This means that they started their professional careers after the fall of the Soviet Union (Table 7.7).

Interviews with representatives of this age group also contain more frequent references to the control of access to the territorial field (Table 7.8). All this suggests that the task of enclosing the territorial and the national market necessitates skills and know-how that could hardly have been learned in the Soviet institutional environment. It can be fully ac-

Table 7.7
Composition of the State Service at the Regional Level, by Age Groups, % of Total, on January 1, 2002 and January 1, 2007

Year, unit of analysis	30 and younger	31-40	41-50	51-60	61 and older
2002, the Russian Federation (n=153,256)	19.4	21.4	34.1	22.5	2.5
2002, Region S. (n=8,996)	23.8	25.6	33.1	15.9	1.6
2007, the Russian Federation (n=204,935)	21.2	24.4	27.8	24.6	1.9
2007, Region S. (n=9,325)	25.5	23.7	27.1	22.3	1.4
2007, Region S.: including those employed at regional and municipal bodies (n=18,551)	32.3	24.4	25.1	17.4	0.8

Source: Kemerovostat, 2008, pp. 26-27; Federal State Statistics Service, 2008b, Table 2; Gosudarstvenny komitet, 2002, p. 128.

Table 7.8
Cross-Tabulation Forms of the Entry Control (Dictionary Based On Substitution By Age, Selected Codes, %

	<30	31-40	41-50	51-60	61+	Chi^2	P (2-tails)
Territorial field	11.5	14.2	3.9	13.0	4.0	31.319	0.000
Information field	0	5.9	0	1.5	0	23.667	0.000
Market field	0.8	1.2	0	2.5	0	14.564	0.012

Legend: The code "Legal field" is not shown because differences between age groups do not attain a level of statistical significance.

complished by representatives of the new generations of state servants who thus revive power in its pure form by using innovative techniques: old wine in a new bottle.

Conclusion

The case study of Region S. helps us better understand how domination by virtue of a constellation of interests works and why A, businesses, and B, the general population, accept the control to access exercised by C, the regional administration. It further develops insights into the theory of public choice and the theory of rent-seeking and DUP by shifting focus from individual decision-making and the aggregation of individual choices through neoclassical macro-economic models (i.e., via the price mechanism) to interactions. Domination derives from interactions between A, B and C and a particular resulting constellation of interests.

The transaction is a unit of analysis in the institutional economics in the traditions of Thorstein Veblen and John Commons. They and their followers also highlight links between transactions and power: "the four economic issues arising out of that unit of activity, the bargaining transaction, are competition, discrimination, economic power and working rules" (Commons, 1931, p. 653). However, the proposed approach extends the scope of the concept of transaction and underlines its trilateral rather than bilateral nature.

In practical terms, this means that, in order to minimize missed opportunities, businesses have to accept a subjacent position with regard to C, the actor that controls the gate to the field. The ideology of free enterprise and the business ethics adapted to the open market appear inappropriate and even counter-productive when transacting in the market field. One must be prepared to transfer a part of the administrative and resource rent to C not only through official channels such as taxation, but also through non-transparent schemes that occasionally involve corruption.

> "I play according these rules, but consider them damnable. I simply don't have any other choice. I consider my behavior damnable because I feel morally handicapped, I feel unable to achieve anything using legal means. I feel guilty because I'd prefer to do it in a right way, I'd like to sleep without nightmares—and I can't" (22C).

It has also been shown that rent-seeking represents only a particular case of a broader phenomenon. Rent-seeking activities occur in the market environment, more precisely in the market field as the enclosed market. Domination by virtue of a constellation of interests may emerge in any field of interactions as the enclosed area of transacting actors: the information field, the territorial field, the legal field and so forth. Not only pecuniary interests can constellate and produce the drift into power and domination. For instance, the interest in getting into the information field can be explained by the desire to remain in the public eye, to gain recognition. This does not involve maximizing utility or profit (if the sphere of public opinion lives according to its own rules of the game). In other words, the theory of public choice studies a particular manifestation of domination by virtue of a constellation of interests in the market field.

The scope of domination through the market extends far beyond the administrative boundaries of Region S. It structures interactions in all key industries and spheres of activities in Russia. It can also be observed in several other countries. China's institutional system has many features of domination by virtue of a constellation of interests in the market field (Ngo, 2008; Guo & Hu, 2004). The same generally appears true as far as countries of "catch-up" modernization are concerned (Oleinik, 2006b): the state plays a leading role in the economic development of the "latecomers" namely by regulating access to the national market. The protectionist policies that are widespread in these countries highlight the highly ambiguous status of the market. While acknowledging its importance as an engine of socio-economic growth, state representatives tend to enclose the market field, to capture rents and to reproduce their domination on this basis.

Notes

1. The search was carried out on March 26, 2009 using Google.Ru and Google.Com search engines respectively.
2. The search using Google.Ru, Google.Com and Google.Fr conducted on March 29, 2009 shows that ratios of frequencies with which the four expressions are found in documents in Russian, English, and French appear comparable:

    Table Ratios of Frequencies with which the Four Fields Are Mentioned Web-Based Documents in Russian, English and French

Key word	Russian	English	French
Информационное поле / Information field / Champ d'information	138	197	47
Правовое поле / Legal field / Champ de la loi	97	71	43
Региональное поле / Territorial field / Champ territorial	2	1	19
Рыночное поле / Market field / Champ marchand	1	25	1

3. By doing so they undermine the autonomy of the functional subsystems, a core principle of a modern, "complex" society.
4. De Soto (2005, Chapters 6 & 7) blames the heritage of mercantilism in Latin America for the spread of "bad" laws. Instead, they can reasonably be deduced from the desire of state representatives to strengthen their dominant positions by shaping the boundaries of the legal field and making access to it conditional.

5. A would maximize its profit/utility only if there were no transfer of monopolistic rent to C; see Chapter 6.
6. The history of mercantilism in Medieval France (Ekelund & Tollison, 1984) as well as practices of establishing regional monopolies in present-day China illustrate this path. For instance, regional monopolies in China "work in two ways: (1) restricting market access of goods from the outside; and (2) limiting out-flow of local goods, raw materials and technologies" (Guo & Hu, 2004, p. 273).
7. The aggregate resource rent at the regional level was calculated on the basis of the official data for 2007 (Federal State Statistics Service, 2008a) using the following formula: Coal production multiplied by coal prices for industry plus Oil production multiplied by world oil (Urals) price plus Natural gas production multiplied by European natural gas price plus Timber production multiplied by prices for Russian timber.
8. 68.26 percent of cases lie within the distance of plus/minus one Z score from the mean if they are distributed normally. The city of Moscow, the other subject of the Russian Federation, would be a clear outlier on all the dimensions under consideration. Its Z-score for natural resource rent equals -3.16, 3.65—for the GRP per head, 5.37—for population and 6.46—for the value of fixed assets.
9. The search was carried out on March 24, 2009 using the name of the region as a key word. Needless to say that a similar search in the database containing documents published in Russian periodicals, e.g., the Integrum mediabank, would produce more valid results. Unfortunately, the author does not have access to it. It is worth mentioning that during the five years under consideration there was no change in the highest regional office in Region S. Such changes tend to be associated with more frequent mentions of the regional administration (M_{change}=48.28 against $M_{no\ change}$=41; however outcomes of the t-test for mean differences appear statistically not significant, or only marginally acceptable for explorative research).
10. The preliminary of outcomes of this project are published in a separate article (Kurbatova & Aparina, 2008). In all, 24 in-depth interviews were carried out, but only nine of them are actually used in the present study. The author expresses his gratitude to Dr. Natalia Aparina for making transcripts of these interviews available for a secondary analysis.
11. The governor of S. in 2007 attempted to kick one of the largest businesses in the industry out of the market appealing to the negative externalities (pollution) caused by its operations. However, the FAS interpreted these policies differently viewing them as undue restriction of competition. As of November 2008, the FAS laid criminal charges (under Article 178 "Prevention, restriction or elimination of competition" of the Criminal Code of the Russian Federation) against the regional administration and the governor in person.
12. The only caveat in regard to Region S. consists in the fact that it has two large cities of a similar size and socio-economic importance. Such a "duopolistic" structure characterizes few Russian regions. However, this observation does not undermine the above-formulated principle of "elective affinity" between the institutional environment of the region and that of its capital city. In fact, several interlocutors emphasized that S.'s governor and the capital city's mayor represent an almost perfect match. "Let's take a simple example—the city of W. [the capital city of a neighboring region]. I've been in the downtown there. There are garbage, empty bottles, and mud everywhere. My folks tell me: if R. [S.'s governor] and G. [mayor of S.'s capital city] took control over there, they would kill half of their administration" (10C).
13. "When multiple significance tests are performed, the probability that there will be at least one instance of Type I error in the set of decisions goes up as a function of

the number of tests that are performed; this is called inflated risk of Type I error" (Warner, 2008, p. 1016). The introduction of the second unit of analysis having very similar characteristics with the first one makes possible the use of two datasets instead of one to test the same model of measurement.

14. The notion of statistical significance appears inappropriate because the analysis refers to the total population. However, the level of statistical significance is used to eliminate week associations in descriptive (as opposed to inferential) statistics.
15. In the 1940s and 1950s the regional administration undertook several attempts to expand administrative borders at the expense of the neighboring regions (Konovalov, 2004, pp. 78, 182).
16. The legitimacy of this act from the point of view of the federal legislation was challenged by the *Prokuratura* in November 2008, which serves an additional proof of the above mentioned restrictions on the ability of the regional administrations to control access to the legal field (see *Kommersant*, No 207 [4024] from 14.11.2008, p. 6).
17. As in the case of the cement producer considered above.
18. See Kurbatova & Aparina, 2008 on how social boundaries work in Region S.
19. This interview perfectly illustrates the access control at the two levels: the interlocutor, producer of a consumer good, had a difficult time when trying to get it accepted by the retailer L. However, the retailer L. also had problems when entering the market.
20. See the Methodological Appendix for more details on the procedure for finding the centroid.
21. Code 2 07 00000 00 0000 000 in the Russian budgeting system.
22. The following sources are used to calculate these figures: Law of the [Region S.] No 64-OZ from 4.6.2007 "On the approval of the report about the execution of the regional budget in 2006"; Law of the [region S.] No 33-OZ from 5.6.2008 "On the execution of the regional budget in 2007"; Report on the execution of the consolidated budget of the Russian Federation and of the state off-budget funds in 2006 retrieved from http://www.roskazna.ru/store/reports_file204.zip; Report on the execution of the consolidated budget of the Russian Federation and of the state off-budget funds in 2007 retrieved from http://www.roskazna.ru/store/reports_file355.zip.
23. Despite the danger of going bankrupt without government loans, the Russian business elite considered this requirement too constraining and leading toward losing control over their own businesses (see *Kommersant*, No 10 [4065] from 22.1.2009, p. 1).

8

Existing and Potential Constraints Limiting State Servants' Opportunism

Introduction

Classical studies of bureaucracy carried out in Western countries derive from the assumption that their subject does not significantly differ from other socio-professional groups. This allows applying standard research methods. For instance, Michel Crozier (1963) builds his analysis of the bureaucratic milieu in France on two case studies. Neither factual questions nor questions about values and beliefs seem problematic. The latter type contains especially valuable information if one probes into intentions and justifications for their actions developed by actors vested in power (see Section V of Chapter 2).

Yet, the present state of our knowledge about the inner life of Russian office holders does not allow us to proceed directly: the design of the most recent studies (Kryshtanovskaya, 2005; Institut Sotsiologii RAN, 2005; Brym & Gimpelson, 2004; Federal'naia i regional'naia elita Rossii, 2004) included neither in-depth interviews with office holders themselves nor participant observation, probably as a result of the extreme insularity of this milieu and the corresponding difficulties in obtaining access to it. The task of gaining access to a closed milieu is a necessary yet insufficient condition for understanding its constitution. A high risk of double thinking, i.e., "an adherence *demonstrated publicly* to the ideas and norms which are accepted in society and which *may not correspond with* the internal convictions of individuals and *even contradict* their actual conduct" (Klopin, 1994, p. 70; emphasis added), potentially questions the validity of data collected through in-depth interviews and questionnaires.[1] The next to worst strategy would be to rely on secondary data, or to collect the data through participant observation. However, this prevents collecting data relevant for studying the inner world of research subjects, namely their intentions and justifications.

Another option consists of asking indirect, projective and vignette questions by presenting the respondent with several scenarios of his/her behavior in an imaginable situation. This manner of proceeding has an important advantage: it allows inquiring into intentions and justifications by asking the respondent to justify his/her eventual actions in a "critical situation." The critical character of the situation means that there are several socially acceptable justifications for the same act. With the variable of social approval/disapproval controlled, the respondent's choice reveals his or her preferences. A study of business people presumably involved in extralegal activities incorporated this research methodology (Oleinik et al., 2005).

Still another alternative, also imperfect, involves adapting a "black box" approach common in economic sciences. The researcher does not venture to look inside the black box of the phenomenon under investigation because of the lack of information. He or she nevertheless aims at analyzing factors influencing processes inside the black box. For instance, the firm was treated as a black box, or a "shadowy figure," before the path-breaking analysis of its internal processes by Ronald Coase (1988). The input and the output were known, as well as the situation in the market, yet the mere transformation of the former into the latter remained obscure.

If projected onto studies of bureaucracy, the black box approach suggests that the researcher avoids making any heroic assumptions with regard to office holders' values, interests and intentions. One "soft" assumption consists in attributing self-interested behavior to office holders: if one does not have enough reasons for assuming their interest in the commonwealth (this word can hardly even be translated into Russian), then presumably they might behave opportunistically (see Subsection IV [IIc] of Chapter 2). Opportunism can take two forms: group (seeking narrow group interests) and individual. In order to elaborate on this assumption, or refute it, one needs to study factors that could limit office holders' opportunism. The more we know about these factors, the narrower the "shadowy" area that remains outside the reach of our understanding. In the final analysis, it might appear that office holders do care about the common good—if there is no room for behaving opportunistically.

On paper, in societies with regularly held elections office holders play the role of the Agent who is expected to act in interests of the Principal, namely the general population. The picture becomes a bit more complicated after differentiating between elected officials and bureaucrats, namely professional office holders. The general population is the Principal in relationships with elected officials and political appointees who, in turn, assume this role with regard to professional bureaucrats (Figure 8.1). The risk of opportunism exists at each level of Principal-Agent relationships (see also Section I of Chapter 6); elected officials tend to "forget" promises made at the time of elections, professional bureaucrats tend to "shirk," to reduce their zeal to a minimum while carrying out the agenda provided by elected officials. "The central concern is how the Principal can best motivate the Agent to perform as the Principal would prefer, taking into account the difficulties in monitoring the Agent's activities" (Sappington, 1991, p. 45).

Several studies of government and governance include the assumption of the drift of office holders into opportunism. Marissa Golden (2000) considers the Reagan administration, for instance, a "success story" of elected officials who managed to increase the level of bureaucratic compliance. Paul Gregory (1990) focuses on the Principal-Agent problem and a limited range of its solutions in the Soviet institutional environment.[2] More recently, Jan-Hinrik Meyer-Sahling (2004; 2006) emphasizes the Principal-Agent problem in relationships between electors and elected officials in Eastern Europe, especially the tendency of the latter to exercise political discretion over personnel policy.

The research question can be formulated in the following way: under what constraints did holders of offices in governmental bodies act in Russia in 2004-2008? Constraints embedded in the institutional environment, as Anthony Giddens (1984, p. 169) points out, are a double-edged sword: they limit the actor's freedom and let him or her pursue individual and group interests more successfully. "Structure is always both enabling and constraining." The net balance between enabling and constraining, nevertheless, varies from one individual or collective actor

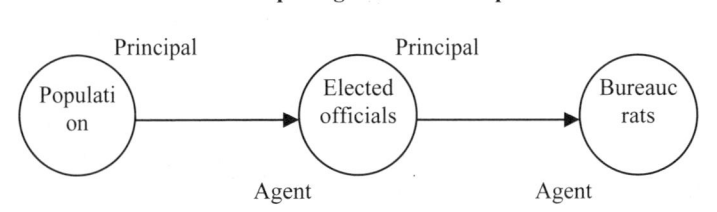

Figure 8.1
Principal-Agent Relationships

Population → Elected officials → Bureaucrats
(Principal) (Agent/Principal) (Agent)

to another. Some of them are more able than others to transform institutions into a partisan weapon by shaping them according to group and individual preferences. They manage not only to mobilize the "bias of the system" but also to produce and strengthen it. For others, the balance is less favorable: institutions constrain their actions rather than help in achieving their objectives.

Constraints do not remain invariable over time because they are reproduced and changed by actors aiming at changing the net balance in their favor. The changing configuration of constraints has taken especially manifest forms in the case of Russia since the start of reforms in the second half of the 1980s. Dynamic aspects lie beyond the scope of the present chapter (cf. Chapter 4), tasked with providing a snapshot of the situation in the milieu of the Russian state service during the period from 2004 to 2008.

Different balances of enabling and constraining influences result in particular configurations of power relationships, i.e., they determine an actor's capacity to impose his or her will on other actors. The focus on factors limiting office holders' opportunism also helps to collect additional empirical data relevant to the study of Russian power. More specifically, the lack of constraints under which office holders act creates favorable conditions for the transformation of power into an end-it-itself and strengthen the self-justifiable character of their power (see Subsections II.1 and II.2 of Chapter 3). The structural analysis of constraints complements the content analysis of the office holders' discourse provided in the Introduction, Chapters 3, 4, 6 and 7 as a source of information about the model of power prevailing in Russia. This "between methods" triangulation further increases the validity and reliability of reported outcomes.

In what follows I refer to two types of sources. First, I use secondary quantitative data collected mostly by international organizations such as Transparency International or the World Bank. Second, I use primary qualitative data, transcripts of in-depth semi-structured interviews from set "A" (see Section V of the Introduction and the Appendix). So, the subject of the analysis can be defined as a configuration of constraints which office holders in Russian government bodies at the federal and regional levels acted under in 2004-2008.

In Section I, I outline potential constraints of office holders' opportunism. This list derives from a taxonomy of power relationships constructed in Chapter 2 with the help of mechanisms for imposing will as a differentiating criterion. A tentative assessment of the hardness of these constraints in Russia of the mid-2000s is provided in Section II on the basis of the primary data (compared with the secondary data). The concept of hardness of constraints, initially borrowed by János Kornai (1980, Vol. A, pp. 25-26; Vol. B, pp. 561-565) from mathematical programming, indicates the degree to which certain obstacles or conditions restrict activities and limit the number of choices available, in our case to office holders. Soft constraints create conditions favorable for the production and reproduction of power in its pure form. The issues of strengthening the constraints are discussed in the Conclusion.

I. Constraints Limiting the Office Holders' Opportunism

A number of scholars distinguish forms of power as a function of the source of the subordinate's submission to the power holder; they highlight vehicles for imposing will—force, coercion, manipulation and so forth (Wrong, 1980, Ch. 2; Ledyaev, 1997, Ch. 12; Scott, 2001, Ch. 1). The approach focusing on techniques for imposing will seems appropriate for studying the degrees of freedom available to power holders. Techniques for imposing will appear both enabling and constraining. On the one side, they provide the power holder with a toolbox for imposing his or her will. In the case of the state service, one can then speak of political technologies. On the other side, a set of available techniques defines what is feasible and places limits on the power holder's potentially boundless desires. For instance, physical force can be used to support claims to power if obedience is achieved through the creation of physical obstacles restricting the freedom of another. At the same time, one force can counterbalance the other force and so limit the scope of the latter.

A taxonomy of power relationships can be proposed using as a differentiating criterion the techniques for exercising control and imposing will; it derives from the discussion of various forms of power in Section III of Chapter 2. It can easily be adapted for the purposes of an inquiry into the constraints of power by listing countervailing factors limiting the scope of uses of a particular technique (Figure 8.2).

In the proposed taxonomy of power relationships, a set of potential constraints corresponds to each of the nine techniques for imposing will that have been identified. This helps to systematize the existing and potential constraints of office holders' discretion (Table 8.1). The fourth column contains a tentative assessment of the hardness of each constraint that refers to the discussion in Section II. The measure of the hardness varies from 0 (absolutely soft constraint that enables the discretionary

Figure 8.2
Taxonomy of Power Relationships

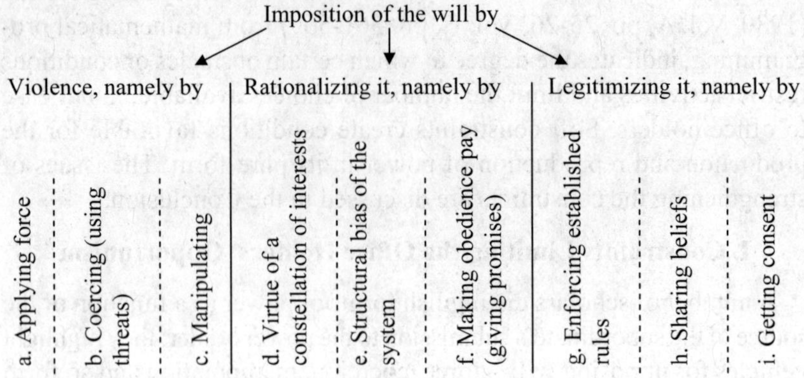

Imposition of the will by

- Violence, namely by
  - a. Applying force
  - b. Coercing (using threats)
- Rationalizing it, namely by
  - c. Manipulating
  - d. Virtue of a constellation of interests
  - e. Structural bias of the system
  - f. Making obedience pay (giving promises)
- Legitimizing it, namely by
  - g. Enforcing established rules
  - h. Sharing beliefs
  - i. Getting consent

behavior of office holders) to 1 (absolutely hard constraint that leaves no room for discretion).

The measure of the hardness equals the ratio of the number of "constraining" tags attributed to fragments of interviews coded in a particular manner to that of "enabling" tags attributed to segments with the same code (see also Section III of Chapter 6 on how the tags are attributed). The second reported measure of hardness (in brackets) has the total frequency of the particular code in its denominator. It differs from the first one because some fragments do not allow for a clear differentiation of the enabling and constraining effects. This calculation seems to be more relevant for answering the research question as to whether the existing constrains effectively limit office holders' opportunism. The codebook for qualitative content analysis originally included 55 codes (see the Appendix), but only 17 codes corresponding to the techniques for imposing will inform the analysis offered in this chapter (Table 8.2). A dictionary based on substitution with entries corresponding to each qualitative code complements the qualitative content analysis. Reported results were checked for their reliability and validity using the model of triangulation described in the Methodological Appendix.

II. Tentative Assessment of the Hardness of Constraints

[a1] Hierarchical control operates within the state service. It helps to reduce the scope of the discretionary behavior of individual office holders or small groups ("teams") and coalitions of state servants, but it has only a limited impact on the scope of the discretion of office holders

Constraints Limiting State Servants' Opportunism 243

Table 8.1
Configuration of the Constraints That Can Limit Office Holder's Discretion

Mechanism of imposing will	Corresponding constraints	Level at which these constraints act	Hardness in Russia, 2004-8[†]
a. Applying force	a1. Hierarchical control	Group	0.78 (0.67)
	a2. Peer control[*]	Group	0.88 (0.7)
	a3. Other groups struggling for power	National	0.56 (0.56)
	a4. Balance of powers	International	0.82 (0.71)
b. Coercing (threats)	b1. Brinkmanship	International	n.a.
	b2. Limited war	National/Intern.	n.a.
c. Manipulating	c1. Freedom of the press	National/Intern.	0.45 (0.39)
d. By virtue of a constellation of interests	d1. Market competitiveness	National/Intern.	0.18 (0.17)
	d2. Dependence of the economy on international markets	International	n.a.
e. Structural bias of the system	e1. Non-specific assets	National/Intern.	n.a.
	e2. Counter-hegemony	National/Intern.	n.a.
f. Making obedience pay (promises)	f1. Private property enforcement	National	0.12 (0.11)
g. Enforcing established rules	g1. Bureaucratic traditions and regulations	Group	0.78 (0.45)
	g2. Rule of law	National	0.48 (0.44)
h. Sharing beliefs	h1. Divine command (religion)[*]	National	1.00 (0.17)
	h2. Tradition[*]	National	0.54 (0.36)
	h3. Natural law	National	n.a.
	h4. Scientific doctrine	Group/National	0.75 (0.56)
	h5. *Volonté générale*	National	0.78 (0.45)
i. Getting consent	i1. Charisma[*]	National	0.48 (0.39)
	i2. Freedom of elections	National	0.65 (0.51)
	Resources		0.55 (0.48)
	Administrative reform		0.44 (0.26)
	Mean for 17 constraints		0.6 (0.45)

Legend: (*)—Constraints embodied mostly in informal institutions; (†)—A tentative evaluation based on the content analysis of 64 interviews, it varies from 0 (this factor only contributes to increasing the room for office holders' discretion) to 1 (a hard constraint limiting the scope of the discretionary behavior); cells referring to factors that tend to constrain discretionary behavior (the value of the second measure exceeds 0.5) are shadowed.

as a whole group (the third column of Table 8.1 contains information as to the level at which a particular type of constraint can be imposed). Since the end of the 1990s, policies intended to "strengthen the vertical of power" have led to more efficient hierarchical control *within* the state service. The measure of the hardness, 0.78 (0.67), indicates a moderately strong constraining effect on the part of these policies as far as the opportunism of individuals and small groups is concerned. "The Russian

Table 8.2
Codebook "Constraints of Office Holders' Opportunism" for Content Analysis

Category	Code	Count	% Codes	Cases	% Cases	Nb Words	% Words
constraints	Administrative reform	53	1.1	31	48.4	3443	0.8
constraints	Charisma	26	0.5	18	28.1	1375	0.3
constraints	Constellation of interests	112	2.3	50	78.1	8344	2.0
constraints	Elections	39	0.8	19	29.7	3583	0.8
constraints	Ideology	45	0.9	25	39.1	1988	0.5
constraints	International	56	1.1	29	45.3	2437	0.6
constraints	Law	129	2.6	42	65.6	8027	1.9
constraints	Peer-control	40	0.8	24	37.5	1730	0.4
constraints	Popular protests	41	0.8	21	32.8	3417	0.8
constraints	Press	39	0.8	18	28.1	3305	0.8
constraints	Private property	36	0.7	21	32.8	2563	0.6
constraints	Regulations	124	2.5	55	85.9	6414	1.5
constraints	Religion	6	0.1	6	9.4	208	0.0
constraints	Resources	118	2.4	40	62.5	6826	1.6
constraints	Rivals	18	0.4	12	18.8	938	0.2
constraints	Traditions	58	1.2	36	56.3	2744	0.6
constraints	Vertical of power	154	3.2	57	89.1	7984	1.9

state under Putin is more responsible to its population, but not more accountable" (Cook, 2006, p. 144).[3] The contrast is especially sharp with regard to the situation of the 1990s when office holders were not closely monitored by their superiors.

> "They [office holders] do feel responsible, bear a responsibility to the ugly mechanism of the state, at least the people of my generation do. Our predecessors, apparently, did not. They managed to get away with so much! Sometimes they solicited us to do some foolish things too. They're like fools as far as I'm concerned. You'd be prosecuted immediately! They don't understand this: 'Come on, we went far further than this'" (13A).
>
> "There are no such things as bribery in most manifest forms because everyone watches 'Criminal Russia' [a TV show on criminal investigations] and is aware of possible provocations" (6A).

Hierarchical control operates in a "top-bottom" manner, originating from the highest administrative body, the Presidential Executive Office. This office occupies a very special place in the system of governance. Despite its name (which suggests a link with the executive branch of power), it does not fit the usual division of power into the executive, the legislative and the judicial branches. All other offices, regardless of their formal status, occupy a subjacent place with regard to the Presidential Executive Office (Figure 8.3[4]), the embodiment of Supreme Power.

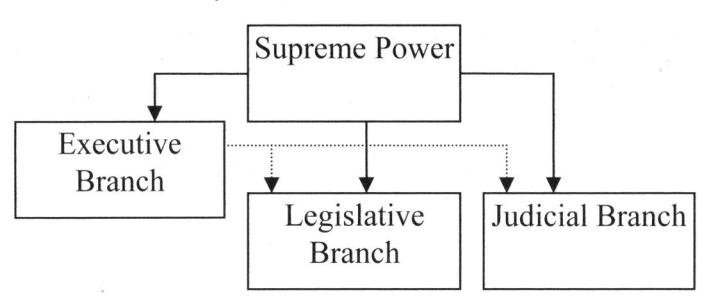

**Figure 8.3
Hierarchy of the Branches of Power in Russia**

```
                    ┌──────────────────┐
                    │  Supreme Power   │
          ┌─────────┤                  ├─────────┐
          │         └────────┬─────────┘         │
          ▼                  ▼                   ▼
   ┌─────────────┐    ┌─────────────┐    ┌─────────────┐
   │  Executive  │    │ Legislative │    │   Judicial  │
   │   Branch    │    │   Branch    │    │   Branch    │
   └─────────────┘    └─────────────┘    └─────────────┘
```

"The Parliament, the government and the court are nothing else than executive branches of this Power" (Pivovarov, 2006a, p. 147; see also Kryshtanovskaya, 2005, p. 217). An expert who works for the Presidential Executive Office actually confirms this assessment:

"You know, the Presidential Executive Office and the President.... They're not a part of the executive power, they're more than that. They're the supreme power. *If I follow you, if one looks for the body that controls how most important decisions are made and implemented, it is*.... The Presidential Executive Office and the President, correct" (47A).

Compared with the Soviet system of hierarchical control, the current situation nevertheless seems far inferior. In the former instance, subordinates' room for maneuvering was narrower and disciplinary sanctions—more severe.

"The minister in his industry commanded everyone, from Moscow down to the last rank-and-file worker. All his orders were immediately executed. Now it's not the same.... There was a very rigid structure and any discretionary behavior was immediately prosecuted" (52A).

Systems of e-governance could potentially facilitate the task of monitoring and control by reducing associated costs. This is especially true as far as A2A (Administration to Administration) systems allow monitoring the circulation of electronic documents and the execution of orders (for an overview of different systems of e-governance see Peristeras & Tsekos, 2004). The eventuality of increasing control explains several cases of resistance to the introduction of centralized computer systems for the circulation of documents in some post-socialist countries.[5]

Negative sanctions are never enough to induce office holders to behave in a less discretionary way. Negative sanctions can reduce the space for discretionary behavior, but do not simultaneously prevent subordinates from behaving in this manner as long as that space does not completely disappear, which is possible only at the price of prohibitive costs for monitoring and control. This is why the efficiency of hierarchical control falls short of the maximum both in relative—compared with the Soviet period—and absolute terms.

> "In the sphere where I'm competent to judge, vertical power exists only in a negative sense. [Superiors] have enough prerogatives to prevent [inferiors] from doing what [the former] don't want [the latter] to do. But [superiors'] prerogatives aren't enough to motivate inferiors to proceed in a way preferable for superiors" (45A).

[a2] Mechanisms of control might also be embedded in horizontal structures. Peer groups can limit their members' individual discretion by imposing and enforcing group norms. Then instead of playing his or her own "game" (pursuing narrowly defined self-interests) the member of a "team" contributes to the group's well-being (see Subsection VI.3 of the Introduction). Mechanisms of peer control have the same potential flaw as hierarchy: in the best case, they contribute to reducing the scope of an individual's lust for power while tending to be counter-productive as far as various forms of group discretionary behavior are concerned. In the best case, peer control contributes to the transformation of non-systematic bribe taking into systematic and organized one.

The interviews suggest that peer-control functions in the world of Russian office holders and constrains individual opportunism moderately-strongly, the measure of the hardness equals 0.88 (0.7). For instance, the hiring procedure for state service often involves a "background check": calls to the applicant's previous places of work and informal talks with his or her previous colleagues.

> "I'd say the following: if I hire someone, I always call a few of his previous places of work. I always find an acquaintance over there who can characterize him" (37A).

> "[We pay attention to] first, the formal testimonials from the previous place of work and, second, informal talks with his superiors or workmates—who interacted with him on a daily basis" (33A).

In some situations, peer control reinforces the drift into power in its pure form and extends the scope of the group of subordinates by taking control over fellow—yet less influential—office holders. In other words, one group within the state service intends to strengthen its domination at the expense of not only ordinary citizens, but other groups of office holders as well. Peer control not only appears useless in fighting against such forms of power lust, it changes into one of the driving forces of power lust by contributing to group cohesion. Anecdotal evidence indicates that a number of groups with strong internal cohesion struggle for domination in the Russian state service and, hence, Russian society as a whole: the Moscow group and the Peter (St. Petersburg) group.

> "[The Moscow group] is built on the basis of personal loyalty one has demonstrated during previous work together. *How long would it take to build a good reputation?* Just the time needed to learn how to share [illicit profits] with your superiors. As soon as they see you can do it well—they accept you as a new member of their clan" (44A).

> "If people from Peter come [to power], this means that the government is going to be populated by people from this city" (5A).

[a3] The violence potential at the disposal of a group or an individual who controls the state can potentially be counter-balanced by the violence potential of other groups and individuals struggling for power. Charles Tilly (1985, p. 183) sees the *differentia specifica* of the state in "eliminating or neutralizing their [the former group's] rivals inside ... the territories in which they have clear and continuous priority as wielders of force." The groups currently vested with power have been successful so far in eliminating potential challengers or reducing the amount of resources at their disposal, which seriously undermines challengers' violence potential. The list of eliminated challengers includes the group of so-called oligarchs—businessmen who made their fortunes during the 1990s (some of the members of this group have been sent to jail, others have been forced into exile), groups of former sportsmen that "produce, promote, and sell private protection" (Gambetta, 1993, p. 1) and controlled a number of government bodies at the regional and federal levels in the 1990s (Volkov, 2002), and traditional organized crime (Oleinik, 2003) whose representatives also had some political aspirations. None of these groups had any interest in building a modern civil service. Nevertheless, their mere existence put limits on office holders' discretion. From this perspective, their elimination has increased the room for behaving opportunistically.

Conflicts between the "ruling" groups have a constraining effect: they play the role of checks and balances with regard to one another.[6] However, compared with the second half of the 1990s these conflicts have become less intense:

> "There was more truthful information [at that time]. One group shed some light on the true face of the other, in reaction to the fact that Luzhkov [the mayor of the

city of Moscow, head of the Moscow group] was attacked and the public learned something new about him" (49A).

One group that still represents a danger for power holders is their former colleagues: members of the groups that were in power in the 1990s but have since lost it. They are dangerous because they know the state machinery well from inside and still have sympathizers at various levels of the state hierarchy. Conflict between members of the current and previous political elites inevitably emerges in Russia at the time of every succession to the "throne" (Klyuchevsky, 1958, pp. 211-212; Pivovarov & Fursov, 1998).

> "They [power holders] don't fear the elections, they do fear succession to power, which is quite different. For this reason, for instance, they react so anxiously to Kasyanov [the former prime minister]. He is close to them; they understand the seriousness of his aspirations.... Kasyanov and Voloshin [the former head of the Presidential Executive Office] are friends. The latter is really fearsome, I worked for him. There is also Khodorkovsky [one of the oligarchs, former head of the Yukos, currently in jail], he [Voloshin] also worked with Khodorkovsky.... They [power holders] fear people like Kasyanov, Khodorkovsky or Berezovsky [the other oligarch, currently in forced exile in the UK], because they know these people and understand them" (42A).

[a4] Geopolitical theory provides us with some useful insights with regard to counterbalancing the violence potential of the group vested with state power and its rivals outside national borders. In Tilly's terminology, war making implies a continuous comparison of the violence potential on an international scale. Randall Collins (1995) argues that geopolitical theory appeared to be a very efficient tool for predicting the collapse of the Soviet Union as a result of its over-expansion and geographic location in the middle of an inland region. The last war that the Soviet Union pursued on foreign soil—the invasion of Afghanistan (1979-1989)—ended in defeat on the eve of its fall. The fall of the Soviet Union contributed to the strengthening of the unipolar character of international relations and their restructuring around a country with the largest violence potential, i.e., the United States (Centre for Study of Globalization and Regionalization, 2004). It should be noted that since then the Russian Federation, the key successor to the Soviet Union, has faced few significant threats to its security at the international level (Colton, 2006, p. 8). References to a larger power limit the scope of office holders' discretion in more or less "peripheral" states. According to the informants' opinion, this constraint tends to be one of the hardest: 0.82 (0.71).

"The power ministries group, at least those members who work for FSB [Federal Counterintelligence Service], yet this particular subculture progressively spreads to the rest of this group.... They have fears of the West inherited from the past. If they keep their money in off-shores, this gives Western intelligence services a lever over them. This is dangerous, non patriotic and terrible" (50A).

There exists an unexpected and unusual channel of international influence, namely the fact that the children of many top Russian officials study and live abroad, in the United Kingdom, in the US, and other Western countries. Thus, these children play a double role: on the other hand, they are "hostages" in a figurative sense and, on the other hand, they are potential "agents" of Western influence, also in a figurative sense.

"I know great many state servants whose kids study abroad, in the US, in England" (43A).

"There is a good tradition for sending kids to study in England. There is also the other tradition: some of the state servants whose kids finish their studies and can find a job over there are strongly encouraged to stay *over there*" (45A; emphasis added).

[b1] Some strategies help to significantly reduce the need to rely on physical or psychic violence, making force a support "of the last resort." The first of these strategies, brinkmanship, "is the deliberate creation of a recognizable risk of war, a risk that one does not completely control" (Schelling, 1960, p. 193). In terms of contemporary politics, pressure applied to the group vested in power from outside the country may be as efficient, if not more efficient, in limiting the scope of its discretionary behavior as a more obvious confrontation.

For various reasons (one group will be outlined briefly in [d2]), just the opposite happens in Russia of the mid-2000s. A number of representatives of the industrially developed states concentrated in the Western hemisphere express support for the Russian power elite (this takes especially obvious forms in the cases of Gerhard Schröeder, the former German chancellor, and Silvio Berlusconi, the Italian prime minister; see Section IV of the Conclusion) and prefer to "close their eyes" to the potential dangers associated with power in its pure form in national as well as international affairs. Being representatives of modern states, they are expected to demonstrate that their support has a legitimate character and not only to refer to pragmatic considerations (e.g., the need for diversifying energy supplies). To solve this dilemma "they [may] act in ways that keep themselves intentionally uninformed. They do not go looking for evidence" (Bandura, 1990, p. 189) of the perverse effects of the reliance on the representatives of power in its pure form.

[b2] The other strategy for playing with threats instead of applying force consists in substituting a small-scale, limited war for a full-scale war. "One of the functions of limited war ... is to pose the deliberate risk of all-out war, in order to intimidate the enemy and to make pursuit of his limited objectives intolerably risky to him" (Schelling, 1960, p. 193). The strategy of limited confrontation can be used within national boundaries and in international relations, by both rivals of the dominant group and the dominant group itself. Limited confrontation, or confrontation with regard to particular policy issues, helps reduce the scope of the dominant group's discretionary behavior only when applied by its rivals. In the Russian case, the strategy has been used more often by the group vested in power to achieve the opposite ends, i.e., to increase the scope of discretionary behavior.

The two Chechen wars (December 1994—May 1996, August 1999 onward) illustrate this point. It is well documented that the first of the two wars resulted from a struggle (potentially large-scale, i.e., civil war) with internal rivals of the group—the Yeltsin "family"—then vested in power. "According to Oleg Lobov, secretary of the Security Council of the Russian Federation, 'we need a small victorious war, as in Haiti, to raise the president's ratings'" (Tishkov, 2004, p. 127). Yet the wars have had important "side-effects." In particular, they contributed to the spread of terrorism and turned into a long-lasting military conflict whose scope can hardly be considered "small."

> "There [in the power elite] are widespread concerns and fears about the situation in Chechnya and the neighboring regions" (42A).

Furthermore, the wars fuelled some criticism from the part of external rivals. This criticism has not been intense enough to be considered an example of limited confrontation: international pressure has not produced significant changes in Russian policies in Chechnya so far.

If lost, a limited war may have a beneficial effect by transforming into a powerful incentive to mobilize efforts, including those of office holders, around the task of modernization. Such post-war periods appears associated with less discretionary behavior on the part of office holders. "Modernization caused by a military defeat ... represents a typical pattern of development through mobilization" (Gaman-Gultivina, 2006, p. 180).

[c1] Freedom of the press, if it exists, prevents the group vested in power from controlling information flows and distorting them for the purposes of manipulation. Reporters Without Borders (RWB), an interna-

tional non-governmental organization, regularly releases press freedom indexes in most countries of the world. Every kind of violation directly affecting journalists (such as murders, imprisonment, physical attacks and threats) and news media (censorship, confiscation of issues, searches and harassment) are enumerated in these indexes. The Russian score systematically lies in the first quartile of the list, i.e., in the bottom 25 percent (Figure 8.4). This score remained virtually unchanged in 2008 compared with 2002, and is around 48 (the zero-score corresponds to perfect freedom, the highest score—it usually amounts approximately to 100—to the lack thereof). Only four post-Soviet countries have a consistently poorer record: Turkmenistan, Uzbekistan, Belarus, and Azerbaijan.

Emphasis is placed on distorting information flows rather than on limiting them. Distortions contribute to the creation of a virtual world shaped according to the desires and interests of the group vested in power. "The key to 'virtual politics' is that authority is invented; political technologists stage the basic mythology of the state" (Wilson, 2005, p. xvi). It is worth noting that the task of manufacturing misinformation has always been one of the specialties of Soviet and Russian intelligence services (Albats, 2004, p. 30). They have elaborated numerous technologies of manipulation.

Figure 8.4
Press Freedom Score for Russia, Reporters Without Borders version, 2002-2008

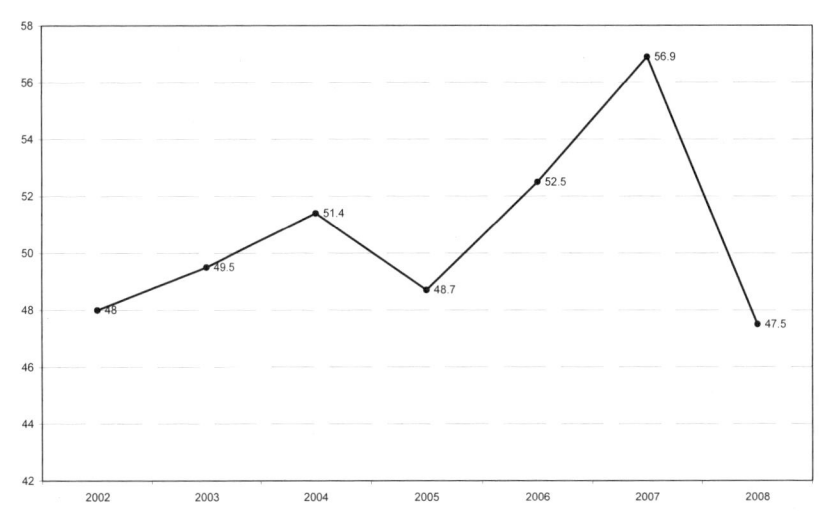

Source: Reporters Without Borders, retrieved from http://www.rsf.org/article.php3?id_article=29031.

"If a ministry is often subject to journalist investigations, it means they've got a bad PR specialist who is not doing his job well" (3A).

"The bureaucracy relies on hiding the information, sometimes temporarily, or, on the contrary, on its selective release" (30A).

Control is tighter over TV and relatively looser over the printed press. Criticisms of particular government policies do not necessarily cause the censors to feel anxious, as long as the model of power relationships as a whole remains unquestioned. The availability of the international press reduces the scope of conscious distortions in information flows.

"In some cases one can use publications in Financial Times as leverage. I know of several examples when Gazprom and some government bodies changed their decisions as a result of bad publicity in the West" (45A).

According to our experts' evaluations, control over the printed press seems tighter at the regional level and there are fewer alternative sources of information. At this level, the group vested in power often manages to turn the mass media into an additional mechanism for reproducing power in its pure form. Thus, the assessment in Table 8.1, 0.45 (0.39), a soft constraint, corresponds only to the federal press. At the regional level, this may well be even more "enabling" at the office holder's discretion.

"Speaking of [Region S.], the press does not influence the decision-making process. The regional authorities put all the mass media under control, none of them can be considered as oppositional. Even X. [a newspaper known for its independent editorial policies in the 1990s] has become much less critical.... What surprises me is that in public opinion, well, in the opinion of the political elite the leaders of the regions [with relatively tight control over the mass media] are weak. They've got an image of not being able to influence" (43A).

Russia does not figure on the RWB "watch list" of censorship practices on the Internet (Reporters Without Borders, 2004). However, the absence of apparent restrictions on the RuNet does not preclude use of the above-mentioned technologies of manipulation. The virtual discourse appears saturated with voices whose origins are hardly identifiable and independency—highly questionable (e.g., the same political technologist can run several Internet sites, which creates an impression of pluralism).

"No way to get reliable information. I was surfing on the net yesterday and found an interesting article on the situation in Yakutia. I know all the guys whose names are mentioned well and realize what is going on in reality. One group is struggling with the other for power. Yet it is pictured as a crime scene, the policemen make an arrest, etc. A commoner is happy: justice is rendered and corruption—punished. This has nothing to do with the real situation. If one was involved in siphoning budget moneys before, now other people will do the same. The latter will spend their previously accumulated incomes on buying freedom out. The people are happy: look,—they prosecuted a criminal! Good job, the policemen!" (36A).

[d1] The task of measuring power by virtue of a constellation of interests and its limits in the market requires references to macro-economic data. Economists assume that the closer the market is to the situation of perfect competition, the less room there is for any of the competitors to influence market price and extract rent, and vice versa. Such indicators as concentration ratio (the share of the x largest firms in total output) provide us with a rough estimate of the strength of power by virtue of a constellation of interests. For instance, if values of CR_4 lie in the range of 25-50 percent (the four largest firms produce between 25 percent and 50 percent of the total output in an industry), then each of these four firms has some market power and forms a loose oligopoly. Values above 50 percent would seem to indicate a tight oligopoly. The closer the values are to 100 percent, the closer the situation of monopoly is and the stronger market power is.[7]

At first sight, the situation in key Russian industries in the first few years after the new millennium was not so serious as to speak about monopolistic capitalism. Only in three industries out of ten, ferrous metallurgy (38.9 percent), the fuel industry (32.8 percent) and non-ferrous metallurgy (31.8 percent), the CR_4 value suggests the existence of a loose oligopoly in 2004 (Federal State Statistics Service, 2006a, p. 74).[8] However, a closer look at the industry in which the lion's share of the Russian GDP is produced, oil and natural gas, provides a completely different picture. The natural gas industry is monopolized by Gazprom, whereas the oil industry has the characteristics of a very tight oligopoly (Table 8.3).[9]

The non-competitive organization of industries gives business owners an important lever in pursuing their individual and group interests. These interests have an important political dimension: distortions in the structure of competition generated in the market can be protected and even strengthened by political intervention. In these conditions, the question as to who owns a business protected from competitive pressures becomes of secondary importance. The state can extract rent either directly, through ownership of such businesses, or indirectly, in the form of administrative rent captured as a result of domination by virtue of a constellation of interests (see Chapters 5, 6 and 7).

Table 8.3
Concentration Ratios in the Russian Oil Industry, 2004-2008, %

	2004	2005	2006	2007♦	2008♦
CR_3	52.3	50.5	50.9	52.9	57.6
CR_4	65.3	64.1	64.5	66.1	70.5
CR_6	78.2	76.5	76.6	83.2	87.2
CR_8	87.7	86.9	86	88.5	92.5

Source: Calculated by the author on the basis of the official data of the Central Dispatching Office of the Fuel and Energy Complex (TsDU TEK; retrieved from http://about.onlinebroker.ru/news.asp?news_id=110106.10&pg=2; http://analit.onlinebroker.ru/stock/intraday.asp?news_id=100107.11&pg=10; and http://analit.onlinebroker.ru/stock/company.asp?pg=2&em_id=10000&news_id=050208.3); the list of the eight biggest oil companies includes Lukoil, Rosneft, TNK-BP, Surgutneftegaz, Gazpromneft [former Sibneft], Tatneft, Slavneft and Yukos). ♦ Data for January only.

As of 2007, the Russian government controls 50.002 percent of Gazprom capital (Gazprom, 2007, p. 80) directly. The state officially controls three of the eight largest oil companies, Rosneft, Gazpromneft, and Slavneft. All other key players act under the indirect yet tight control of office holders. One of the means of this control consists in the state monopoly on pipelines. Office holders turn the monopolistic structure of the oil and gas industry into a means to strengthen their hold on power. Consequently, a strongly enabling role of this factor [d1], 0.18 (0.17), comes as no surprise.

> "All oil companies are far from being saints. They pump more oil than official statistics show. They're encouraged to pump more, sell more, and then ... *share the profits*? No, the moneys go to Edinaia Rossiia [the United Russia, the party that controls the federal and most regional parliaments]. It has a special budget. Up to 3 million tons of undeclared crude oil [annually[10]] are handled through a special firm that ships it by pipelines, sells it and transfers the money to the budget of Edinaia Rossiia. These moneys do not show up in any official budgets" (44A).

> "As far as the oil and gas industry is concerned, all significant businesses are in fact under tight state control. They are managed by different clans in the [Presidential] Executive Office" (3A).

[d2] Another potential constraint of power in its pure form derives from international markets. The more an economy is open to international trade, the fewer chances there are for office holders to control the options available to the subordinate and extract a rent with the help of protectionist policies intended to enclose the national market. Yet openness (measured, for instance, by the size of trade barriers) can play both a constraining and enabling role with regard to the eventual opportunism of

office holders. Their hold on the industry with one of the largest deposits of hydrocarbons in the world puts top Russian officials in a privileged position in international affairs and limits external pressures on them (see [b1]). They consistently decline any attempts to soften their quasi-monopoly over supplies of natural gas to Western Europe. For example, since 2000, the Russian government has been refusing to sign the Energy Charter Protocol on Transit that is intended to promote competition as a way to "ensure secure, efficient, uninterrupted and unimpeded Transit" of energy and to grant non-discriminatory access to transit facilities to all potential suppliers of hydrocarbons (Energy Charter, 2007, Art. 2^1 & 8^4).

The degree of economic dependence on international markets seems to better predict the behavior of state officials. If the state enjoys a dominant position in the international market, which is the case of Russia at least in the European market for natural gas, the more open such an economy is, and the greater the opportunities of office holders for extracting rent and converting it into a resource for strengthening power in its pure form. This explains the continuous lobbying for Russia's admission to the World Trade Organization by state officials.

[e1] If the system has a structural bias then one of the interacting parties has significantly more degrees of freedom than the other. This can result from the possession of specific assets. Economists call an asset specific if it has a limited "redeployability," i.e., in any other combination it will yield less. The owner of the specific asset tends to behave opportunistically: he or she threatens to withdraw it if the counterparts do not increase his or her share in the net profit, quasi-rent. On the contrary, the less specific the assets, the more equal the repertoire of choices available to interacting parties and, hence, their bargaining power (see Section II of Chapter 6).

Asset specificity takes several forms. One of them consists in physical specificity, if production requires a specific technological design or specific inputs. Physical specificity influences the structure of the international market for crude oil. In fact, there are several segments of this market on which particular types of crude oil containing different quantities of sulfur are traded: Brent (a blend of crude oil from the North Sea and North Africa), West Texas Intermediate and Sour (WTI/WTS), Dubai, Iranian Light and Heavy, Urals (a blend of crude oil from Russia), and so forth. The level of sulfur determines the specifications of the equipment to be installed at oil refineries. This produces a "lock-in" effect: after adjusting the equipment for a particular type of crude oil it becomes costly to adapt it to another type. Long-term customers of Urals crude oil then have a weak bargaining position with the Russian government who controls oil exports.[11]

[e2] The structural bias of the system can also take the form of hegemony (see Subsection IV [IIIe] of Chapter 2). It involves the evaluation of submission in terms of minimizing missed opportunities that, unlike domination by virtue of a constellation of interests in the market, does not necessarily take a pecuniary form in this case (cf. Chapter 6). In contrast to coercion, when the subordinate minimizes eventual losses, in the case of hegemony he or she expects some positive benefits. According to his or her perception of gains, he or she would be relatively better off by not challenging the power holder and incurring relative (not necessarily absolute!) losses in the opposite case.

The situation in Region S. (see Chapter 7), where several fields—information, legal territorial and market—are enclosed, illustrates the point. Businesses can work in the region and make profits as long as they accept the rules of the game set by the regional administration. Profit-making appears conditioned by the acceptance of the status quo. In this situation, businesses cannot maximize profit because they are required to spend a part of it on various programs implemented by the regional administration—along with paying regular taxes. However, if they do not accept these rules of the game, businesses are pushed out of the region.

> "Only those who take care of interests of the region can work here.... If you're an efficient owner and understand interests of the region—go work, good luck on it. If you don't—expect problems.... Here businesses have no choice but to be socially responsible. If they aren't, they'll lose their place" (48A).

[f1] If the market approaches the conditions of perfect competition, then justification of office holders' power becomes possible primarily in terms of the exchange of public services in return for taxes. Subordinate economic agents, economists argue, are especially interested in establishing and enforcing exclusive property rights by the state because well-defined and protected property rights help to reduce uncertainty in interactions, create incentives for a more efficient use of resources and avoid the "tragedy of the commons," i.e., overexploitation of open access resources (Eggertsson, 1990, pp. 84-91, Ch. 8 & 9). "The creation of an infrastructure designed to specify and enforce a body of property rights entails the delegation of power to agents of the ruler" (North, 1981, p. 25). As a result, a constraint of the dominant's discretion emerges: the

subordinate considers power relationships acceptable as long as the dominant commits him/herself to respect and protect property rights. In this situation, obedience does pay because it allows the individual to accumulate wealth and gain power over material objects.

The commitment of Russian office holders to keep their promises to respect property rights raised serious doubts in the past and continues to seem problematic now. The institution of property rights in its existing form strongly enables office holders' discretion, 0.12 (0.11), instead of limiting it. Property rights are granted and enforced in a selective and conditional manner, in exchange for the owner's acceptance of office holders' domination. This suggests that power embedded in property, power-property, a key element of patrimonial power (Section I of Chapter 3), continues to play a significant role along with the more recent addition to the repertoire of techniques for imposing will, namely domination by virtue of a constellation of interests.

> "Private property? It depends on the meaning you attribute to this term. It's a highly relative category" (63A).
>
> "Business got the starting capital from the state and society. Now it's time to get it back" (11A).
>
> "Those businesses that try to behave more or less honestly, well, to the extent that that is possible in Russia, they are the least protected.... The one who has more administrative resource, personal connections, can easily challenge outcomes of the privatization even in the cases when everything had been legal, appropriate to the law of that day" (3A).

A series of empirical studies shows that violations of property rights committed by the office holders represent the major obstacle to doing business in Russia in the early part of this decade (Frye, 2004). Clifford Gaddy and Barry Ickes (2005, pp. 572-574) argue that insecure property rights induce owners of resources to maximize short-term gains at the expense of long-term profits. In the oil industry, for instance, this leads towards the depletion of old oil fields and underinvestment in new explorations.

The Heritage Foundation assesses the security of property rights in a comparative perspective while calculating its annual "Index of Economic Freedom." A negative trend can be observed in the Russian case: the level of protection and enforcement of property rights by the government went down from 50 (on a scale of 1-100, where 1 refers to completely unprotected property rights, 100—to fully protected) in 1995-2001 to 30 in 2002-2008 and even 25 in 2009 (Figure 8.5).

Figure 8.5
Index of Economic Freedom in Russia, "Property rights" component, Heritage Foundation version, 1995-2009

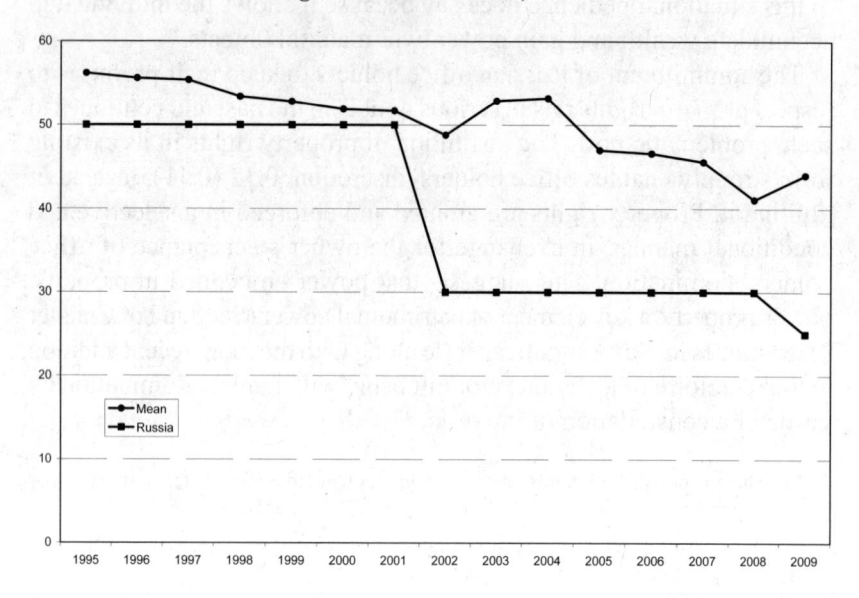

Source: The Heritage Foundation, retrieved from http://www.heritage.org/index/excel/ DownloadRawData.xls. "Mean" refers to the sample mean (N=183 in 2009).

The Yukos case—the forced redistribution of property rights as a result of criminal charges brought by state prosecutors against the owners of the largest Russian oil company, Mikhail Khodorkovsky and Platon Lebedev—indicates that the dangers of expropriation are especially high in the oil and natural gas industry due to its importance for the reproduction of power in its pure form. The two businessmen were arrested in October 2003; in September 2005 the tribunal found them guilty of tax evasion, fraud and a number of other economic crimes and sentenced everyone to eight years in jail (the economic aspects of the case are discussed in more detail in Oleinik, 2005d). In the end, the key assets of Yukos were redistributed in favor of the state-controlled firm Rosneft. The former company has lost its leadership in the oil industry (it pumped the eightieth largest volume of crude oil in 2006), whereas the latter changed from an outsider (ranked eighth among the eight largest oil companies in 2004) to the leader (ranking first in 2008; the volume of pumped crude oil increased by 245 percent between 2004 and 2005). The belief that "the assault on Yukos has thus far been unique, both in form and content" (Weinthal & Luong, 2006, p. 245) ignores the reputation of the Russian government with regard to using violence inherited from the Soviet predecessor. If the business community interprets a single exemplary prosecution as a credible threat then state officials manage to increase the room for discretionary behavior even without carrying out the threat on a regular basis (Schelling, 1960, Ch. 5)!

[g1] Long-lasting bureaucratic traditions exist in Russia (Ryavec, 2003), but they contain very few, if any, elements of rational decision-making. This continuity of power in its pure form however is not easily decipherable: the forms of office holders' discretion and techniques for imposing will change repeatedly. An external observer gets the impression that no rules of decision-making exist at all and there is no point in guessing the outcomes of administrative deliberations. The lack of written job descriptions and specifications of document circulation further complicates the task of predicting the behavior of office holders.

> "We attempted to work out regulations, algorithms for decision-making: if yes then one thing, if no then else. This reduces the impact of the human factor.... Now we've got all of them although at the beginning there was no single regulation. Not only in our [federal] service, nowhere [in government offices]" (37A).

Since the adoption of a program for reforming the state service in 2003—the outcomes of the administrative reform in the mid-2000s will be also discussed in Section I of the Conclusion—the number of regulations has increased, as well as their impact on everyday behavior of office holders. Several informants mention the efficiency of regulations in constraining opportunism, even if in many cases their effect appears ambiguous. The measure of the hardness, 0.78 (0.45), reflects this.

> "From a formal point of view, we act on the basis of regulations issued by the [federal] government and the ministry. There is almost no room for maneuvering: no one will allow us to prepare a document that falls outside the scope of our competence" (2A).

> "I know all my job descriptions by heart. My service functions in the frameworks set by the Monitoring and control division of the Presidential Executive Office, any single paragraph is carefully spelled out. Taking into consideration our specificity, we must follow what the law dictates" (12A).

> "There is a strict rule that any written complaint must be answered within 30 days. If you fail to do so, there will automatically be no bonus" (13A, interview 52A corroborates this point).

Nevertheless, the constraining role of written regulations tends to be stronger at the lowest levels of the hierarchy, while their impact appears minor at the top.

"As long as you're at the bottom of the ladder, you must follow your job description very closely. Once a certain level is reached, you can start to use personal connections" (19A).

The lack of the continuity of "rationalistic" bureaucratic traditions can be attributed to a high turnover at the lowest layer of the Russian state service (from the entry-level positions of specialists up to associate heads of bureaus) combined with limited opportunities for vertical mobility and promotion to the middle- and highest layers in the hierarchy (the former comprises heads of bureaus and associate heads of departments, the latter—heads of departments, associate ministers and ministers).[12] They naturally have only short-term objectives concerning a career in the state service: to establish useful connections, to acquire particular know-how before applying for a job in the private sector in 3-4 years.

"A maverick, somebody who is not well-connected, can reach at best the level of the head of a bureau. No chance to go further regardless of his qualities and efforts.... At the lowest level the turnover is extremely high.... People come, for example, to learn basic accounting and then leave..." (53A).

"Young people stay at the ministry for a couple of years only, which is just enough to make contacts and to find a well-paid job. They don't have any long-term plans in regard to the state service. As a result, there is the endless fluctuation of executives, it is not good for the industry. I've been working at this department for one year. Turnover has been one-third" (2A).

An attempt was recently undertaken to establish new administrative traditions. Presidential decree No. 885 on the General principles of professional behavior of state servants enacted on August 12, 2004 outlines a set of moral standards, including a top priority of the rights of the individual and citizen: respect for the law; impartiality; the need to avoid conflict of interest, etc. (Grazhdan, 2005, pp. 117-118). The decree does not specify any mechanism for enforcing these principles; instead it states that they are only voluntary.[13] Thus, there is a high risk that these moral standards will be ignored in everyday life, as often happened with standards imposed from the top down in the past (Shlapentokh, 1989, pp. 18-50). The true "moral code" of the state service includes quite different ethical prescriptions and imperatives: pragmatism as a terminal value;[14] obedience to superiors coupled with ignorance of inferiors, *Them*, and so forth.

"It seems to me that this [bureaucratic] culture is characterized by an incredible flexibility, the complete absence of values, any extrinsic criteria for judging behavior" (45A).

"The only thing that unites the state servants is the love for Franklin [on US dollars]. Nothing else" (44A).

[g2] A rich body of both quantitative and qualitative data suggests that the legal framework does not place strict limits on the behavior of office holders in Russia. For instance, Transparency International (TI) studies the perception of corruption in the public and political sectors in a comparative perspective on an annual basis. The Russian score has never been high, i.e., experts and business people, both resident and non-resident, do not consider the rule of law efficiently enforced (Figure 8.6).

It is worth noting that the scores of some other post-Soviet countries, namely the Baltic States, do show a significant variability and progress towards a more law-bound civil service (for instance, the score of Estonia has improved from 5.7 in 1998 to 6.6 in 2008). Only six post-Soviet states had lower scores in 2008: Uzbekistan, Belarus, Tajikistan, Azerbaijan, Turkmenistan, and Kyrgyzstan.

Our expert interviews confirm the loose character of the constraint related to the rule of law but help make the picture more nuanced. The

Figure 8.6
Corruption Perception Index for Russia, Transparency International version, 1996-2008

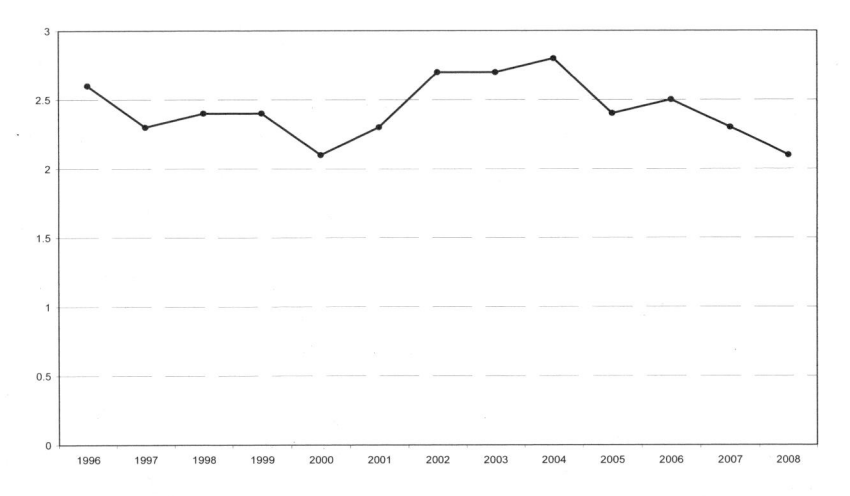

Source: Transparency International, retrieved from http://www.transparency.org/policy_research/surveys_indices/cpi. 0 refers to an absolutely corrupt government, 10—to an absolutely transparent one.

low- and middle-ranked office holders adhere to the letter of the law, which can be verified and enforced relatively easily with the help of tight hierarchical control [a1]. The task of hierarchically monitoring their adherence to the principles and general meaning of the law appears less feasible.

> "The law does not count a lot, only the letter of the law. A decision has to adhere to the letter of the law, only to the letter, I'm afraid, not to its meaning" (45A).

> "Let's consider the request of information made by a MP. What really matters here is to send an answer before the deadline [set by the law]. We write the answer: Dear NN, as per your request we inform you that we do not have such information about X. Regards, date and signature. Formally speaking, the procedure was respected, the deadline wasn't missed" (36A).

Subordinates—ordinary Russians—have a very limited capacity to enforce the law from below. The number of litigations with office holders is a less telling indicator than the ratio of the cases that have been won. New opportunities related to submitting a case to the European Court of Human Rights increase the chances of success, yet the procedure is too time consuming and costly to result in any radical changes in the situation (Oleinik, 2007b, pp. 312-314).[15]

> "I know several such cases [litigations with office holders]. Sometimes they can be successful enough. But such cases represent at best 10-15% of their total number" (46A).

The law constrains top office holders to an even lesser degree. They do not necessarily feel constrained even by the letter of the law: the scope of their power allows them to reshape the law, selectively applying and transforming it into a weapon. The law then should be considered "as a form or dimension of social power" (Turk, 1976, p. 276). Instead of violating the law when it puts limits on office holders' discretion, they prefer to reshape it according to their wishes by enacting new laws and revoking old ones. This can be done either through substituting decrees (issued by the executive) for laws, as in the 1990s, or by keeping the legislative under control of the executive. Top state executives in the current situation can do both: the ratio of the number of enacted laws to that of decrees in 2000-2003 has increased compared to 1996-1999, yet insignificantly (1.23 against 1.04; see Remington, 2006, pp. 276-277); the executive holds a majority in the Russian parliament through the proxy, the party *Edinaia Rossiia*.

> "In this country every group of office holders [that attains power] practically rewrites all laws" (3A).

The law is selectively enforced in respect of the enemies of top office holders who consider themselves above the law. All these considerations explain an enabling rather than a constraining role of the law: 0.48 (0.44).

> "Everything goes according to the Franko principle:[16] 'For my friends, anything, for my enemies, the law.' The legal constraint is tight only in this sense" (42A).

[h1] In tsarist Russia religious faith was included in the repertoire of constraints on the ruler's discretion, at least at the discursive level, as reflected in the concept of *samoderzhavie* (Subsection I.3 of Chapter 4). When defining power, Vladimir Dal' (1955) mentions that "great authority derives from God. Any authority derives from God. Any authority reports to God" (see also Pobedonostsev, 1965, p. 253 quoted in Subsection II.1 of Chapter 3).

During Soviet times, the state, namely the KGB, controlled all key appointments at the highest layers of the church hierarchy (Albats, 1994, pp. 43-47; Voslensky, 1984, p. 75). More recently, the increased economic dependence of the Orthodox Church on the state (Mitrokhin, 2000) prevents it from taking a more or less critical stance on issues related to state administration. The corrected score of religious faith indicates its failure to constrain opportunism: 0.16 (the uncorrected score 1.00 only means that the unique "constraining" tag is not matched by any "enabling" tag, yet there are several coded fragments with no tag attached).

[h2] Traditions that exist at the level of the nation as a whole are functionally different from state service traditions. The latter refers to the enforcement of established rules, the former to a set of beliefs shared by both the dominant and the subordinate. Nevertheless, in the Russian case there is significant discontinuity in national traditions. Russians rank traditions rather low (usually the last or the next to last of eleven proposed alternatives) while speaking about their order of priorities, the constitution of an ideal society in Russia and that of the actual society, the resources and the conditions that they consider important for achieving their goals and so forth (Oleinik, 2003, pp. 165-166).

The results of a "Public Opinion" Foundation (*FOM*) survey conducted in 2002 on sources of shame and pride in the Russian national consciousness provides us with a more colorful picture of the discontinuity. The term "great divide" seems appropriate indeed: Russians appear extremely ambivalent with regard to the history of their country in general and its different periods in particular (Table 8.4). The period before the 1917 revolution gets 11.7 percent of votes: it was mentioned

Table 8.4
Sources of Pride and Shame in Russian History, % of Respondents Who Mentioned Them

	The 2000s	The 1990s	The 1960-1980s	Stalinism	Before 1917
Sources of pride			Exploration of space (14) Achievements in sports (9)	Victory in WWII (41) Recovery after WWII (2)	The rule of Peter the Great and other events (9)
			The Soviet Union (13) Strong state (4) Achievements in science (4) Military-industrial complex (3)		
Sources of shame		The rule of Yeltsin and other events (10)	The rule of Gorbachev (3) The war in Afghanistan (6) The rule of Khrushchev (1) The rule of Brezhnev (1)	Stalinism (18) Revolutionary violence (4)	Slavery and other events (2)
			Communism (3)		
			Undue behavior of the country leaders (2)		
			Poverty (2)		
			The lack of respect for ordinary people (1)		

Source: FOM—"Public Opinion" Foundation, retrieved from http://bd.fom.ru/report/cat/man/shame_pride/d020608; N=1,500 in 44 regions of the Russian Federation.

by 9 percent of the respondents as a source of pride and by 2.7 percent—as a source of shame.[17] 80.2 percent of respondents mentioned Stalinism (+56/-24.2), 49.2 percent—the post-Stalin period (+35/-14.2), 11.7 percent—the 1990s (all of them in a negative sense). Besides the 1990s (the negative perception of traditions associated with this period of time has a consensual character), all the other periods of time give rise to extremely ambivalent feelings. Thus, traditions are of little help in finding a set of beliefs shared by most Russians independently of their position in the state hierarchy.

It is worth noticing that a negative tradition—the lack of respect for the individual—was attributed to all periods in Russian history. Only a small fraction of respondents made this observation. Most Russians in the early 1990s endorsed the tradition of "hierarchical egalitarianism": they used to reject only those inequalities that did not derive from established power (Levada, 1993, p. 40).

[h3] The doctrine of natural law that would suggest considering basic rights as entailed by the nature of the world and the nature of human beings is deeply entrenched in the European school of thought, especially during the Age of Enlightenment (Arnaud, 1999, p. 199). This does not

seem to play any significant role in the Russian context in general and in the context of the Russian state service in particular.

[h4] A scientific doctrine popular among both office holders and ordinary people can reduce the scope of the discretionary behavior of the former group: their power enjoys legitimacy as long as they act in accordance with scientific prescriptions. "Scientific communism" is a well-known example but not the only one: according to some scholars, the rise of early capitalism in England was due to a large extent to the popularity of the writings of Adam Smith, Jeremy Bentham and Joseph Townsend among members of some groups in the English population and their representatives in the parliament as well as a particular configuration of powers in the parliament (Polanyi, 1957, Ch. 10; North, 1981, pp. 156 ff.).

The content analysis of interviews produced a paradoxical—at first sight—result. The moral and ideological convictions inherited from the Soviet period have a constraining effect on the opportunism of office holders. A relatively high score for the scientific doctrine, 0.75 (0.56), derives mainly from references to the behavior of senior office holders who started their career in the early 1980s or even earlier.

"A philosophy like the one that existed during the Soviet time is needed. It could integrate the society and set objectives, targets and means for achieving them for every single state servant" (62A).

"A new motivation should be found. We have to start with what we had in this country, with these people—we all had a different motivation" (40A).

"The group of professionals who were formed during the Soviet time is progressively disappearing. The ministry indeed could be proud of them, they saved it many times" (2A).

Referring to a scientific doctrine to justify power relationships produces the rule of experts. It is worth discussing subtle yet important differences between the rule of experts and rational bureaucracy. First, rational bureaucracy is "value-free," it derives from respect for technical rules and procedures in decision-making (for this reason rational bureaucracy is compatible, according to Weber, with quite diverse political regimes), whereas the behavior of experts can be better described in terms of value-based rationality. If bureaucrats are bound by procedures, experts are bound by the ideology embedded in a scientific doctrine. Second, experts do not necessarily commit themselves to the office and consider their job—sometimes temporary—as a vocation. Yet, Weber (1968, p. 958) places the vocation of office holder (*Beruf*) in the center of his analysis of bureaucracy.

In the context of domination by virtue of a constellation of interests, the services of a special kind of experts, technocrats, appear in high demand.[18] The technocrat is "a policymaker who is motivated to pursue the objectives postulated by traditional *normative* economic analysis" (Rose & Mishler, 1995, p. 16; emphasis in the original). Not surprisingly, the rule of experts was considered the most popular alternative to democracy in most Eastern European and post-Soviet countries in the mid-1990s.[19]

Most of technocrats were recruited in the 1990s when the rhetoric of capitalist domination took its most obvious forms. Their mere presence makes the state service more predictable on the basis of rational calculations.

> "I was hired through competition; I was a complete stranger who had no ideas about the functions of the state servant. I advanced quickly and I was not the only one. There existed a special procedure for supporting smart young people" (13A).
>
> "Unlike many of my fellows, I don't believe in total corruption. There are ... people with whom one can easily speak the professional language and solve problems in the best interests dictated by their job" (42A).

[h5] Referendums and initiatives serve to make the abstract notion of *volonté générale* operational and concrete. "Referendum means that laws and resolutions made by representatives must be submitted to the people for acceptance or rejection.... Initiative means that people have the right not only to vote on proposals but also to *initiate* the enactment of new laws or constitutional amendments, and alter or abolish old ones, if a certain number of people so request" (Brenner, 1994, p. 155, emphasis in the original).

According to Russian law, citizens and their groups do not have the right to initiate the enactment of new laws (cf. 51.4 percent of 216 amendments voted in Switzerland between 1874 and 1985 were popular initiatives; Ibid, p. 156). The Constitution of the Russian Federation specifies the list of subjects entitled to take initiatives; it includes the president, the upper house of the parliament, members of the upper and lower houses of the parliament, the government, and the regional parliaments in the subjects of the Federation (Article 104). The right of the Constitutional Court, the Supreme Court and the Supreme Commerce Court to initiate new laws is limited to their jurisdictions.

On the other hand, Russians citizens can ask to have a referendum held on an important issue. The first law of the Russian Federation on referendum was enacted on October 16, 1990; the second on October

10, 1995 and the third on June 28, 2004 (the last version is currently in force). Each consecutive version of the law made the task of holding a referendum more difficult. To hold a referendum, the group of citizens who propose it has to get approval from a number of other citizens. The first law set this minimal requirement at the level of 10 million (Article 10) without establishing any requirements with regard to their place of residence. The second law (Article 8) increased the level to 20 million and stated that they should represent at least 10 regions of the Russian Federation (out of 88). Article 14[1] of the third law does not change the minimum number of signatures but adds that they must be collected in at least 40 regions (not more than 50,000 in each). It goes without saying that these developments narrow the scope of collective action from below. The need for large-scale coordination and organization implies that only proposals supported by the power elite have good chances of success.

> "Decisions were initiated from below under the Gorbachev rule and at the very beginning of the Yeltsin rule. After 1993, well, even earlier, after 1992, one should forget about this" (46A).

> "Popular protests played a very important role. In the 1990s they were common and had a broad, sometimes extreme scope. When miners, for instance, blocked the traffic on the Trans-Siberian railroad.... This had an impact" (49A).

The language of political technologies and administrative resources progressively takes the place of references—real or spurious—to the common will in political discourse. From this perspective the common will does not and cannot exist, it is simply a fiction, an empty abstraction. The population then transforms into a meaningless aggregate subject to manipulation by different organized groups, mainly by groups vested in power. "Almost every significant political force, and some insignificant ones, is subject to political manipulation" (Wilson, 2005, p. 38). From the point of view of office holders, mass protests can be anything but spontaneous; they assume that all mass actions are staged—either by themselves or by groups trying to challenge their power.

> "Anyone who has money or power can stage public activities. Government bodies or pressures groups often inspire different 'public' initiatives and proposals in order to lobby their own interests" (48A).

Nevertheless, a number of large-scale mass protests that happened in the second half of the 2000s, namely the protests against the monetization of privileges of senior people in the first half of 2005 and the

Butovo protests in the summer 2006 (inhabitants of a Moscow suburb protested against the mass construction of new buildings in their area, similar protests subsequently spread well beyond the region of Moscow), instilled anxiety in many office holders. They account for a relatively high score of *volonté générale*, 0.78 (0.45).

> "Let's take the most recent case with the monetization of privileges, when people went down the street and the state had no choice but to significantly increase social spending" (52A).

> "We are also victims of this monetization. Everything went from the top, we, state servants, just take the order and start to calculate revenues, expenses etc. Then it appears that nothing works, a big blow for us. We start to re-calculate everything, in other words, these events turned to be a double evil: the people got irritated, whereas we did the job twice…" (20A).

> "For us, when we say 'people,' we mean the population who went down in Butovo…. They deserve some respect" (59A).

[i1] The adjective "charismatic" applies to "the bearers of specific gifts of body and mind that [are] considered 'supernatural'" (Weber, 1968, p. 1112). The requirement that a charismatic leader has to possess these qualities and, furthermore, that they be recognized as such and acclaimed by the subordinate potentially limits the room for discretionary behavior.

In the Russian case, causal relationships apparently work the other way around: power in its pure form provides access to mechanisms of imposing will, for instance, manipulation, that helps to persuade the subordinate of the dominant's supernatural qualities. Attempts to emphasize their sexuality—as a quality valuable during the election period—with the help of particular political technologies illustrate this point (Oleinik, 2010). From the point of view of informants, charisma has an enabling effect with regard to the opportunism of office holders, especially at the highest levels of the hierarchy (where there are more conditions for manipulation): 0.48 (0.39).

On the other hand, because charisma allows its bearer to have an independent source of legitimate power, it cannot be tolerated among low- and middle-ranked office holders. In this perspective, the Russian state service does not look exceptional:

> "Charisma is really harmful, because of potential competition. This is one of the worst qualities of the office holder" (42A).

[i2] Free and competitive elections held on a regular basis are often considered the single most efficient constraint on the discretion of the

power elite. At least the "export" version of democracy promoted by international organizations and Western governments often takes a "realistic" form: it is relatively easy to organize formally free elections and have them monitored by external observers. At the same time, if formally free elections are not complemented and reinforced by other constraints of power in its pure form, there is a high risk of discrepancy between the form and the content. This is why "realistic" democracy often turns into plebiscitarian autocracy (see Rose, Mishler & Munro, 2006, Ch. 1 and Section III of Chapter 2). Formally free elections are not enough to place hard constraints on the power elite: they are a necessary yet insufficient condition for achieving this result. The concept of guided democracy as its distorted or inverted—to use Marxist terms—form provides us with some useful insights in this respect. It means that "the organization of patronage within established vertical relationships ensures that the exercise of electoral choice by subordinate classes poses no threat to the dominant powers within society or state" (Beetham, 1991, p. 174).

The task of "guiding" democracy calls for so-called administrative resources as means for influencing voter's choices. The list of administrative recourses used in Russia, in particular, includes command-order methods (bosses demand their subordinates to vote for a particular party or candidate and apply administrative sanctions to those who do not obey); manipulation of election results (electoral fraud) and candidates' personal information (*kompromat*); budget financing for electoral projects supported by power holders; turning lights and heating in flats on and off at will (i.e., sending a signal that the level of comfort depends on voters' support for a particular party or candidate), and so forth (Wilson, 2005, Ch. 4; Ledeneva, 2006, Ch. 3). "Staged" political initiatives (see [h5]) also contribute to producing electoral results desirable for groups vested in power.

> "Non-governmental organizations are our tool during elections" (59A).

The score of elections, 0.65 (0.51), indicates their inconclusive impact although this does, however, lean toward the constraining effect. This means that efforts to make elections completely guided are successful, but there is still some work—from the point of view of office holders—to be done.

> "I won't mention political parties—they don't have any influence except during the election period" (59A).

"I worked at a polling station—not as an observer, just as a representative of the [regional] administration, a technical representative so to speak: how to place polling booths, how to fly flags.... I swear that there was absolutely no manipulation in counting votes" (7A).[20]

Freedom House has been evaluating political rights and civil liberties throughout the world since the early 1970s. The results of its annual surveys provide a framework for judging the degree to which elections in a particular country are free *and* fair. Freedom House uses two indexes, one for political rights[21] and another one for civil liberties.[22] The combination of two indexes gives a good approximation of both the freedom and fairness of elections. In contrast to many other post-Soviet countries, namely the Baltic States, Russia has not shown any progress since its independence in 1991. On the contrary, this country sees its score declining from 3.0 (a partially free political system) in 1992 to 5.5 (a system that is not free) in 2005-2008, below the score of the Soviet Union before its fall (4.5 in 1990; see Figure 8.7). In 2008, only four out of 15 post-Soviet states, namely Azerbaijan, Turkmenistan, Uzbekistan and Belarus had a lower score than Russia.

Figure 8.7
Status of Freedom in Russia, Freedom House version, 1991-2008

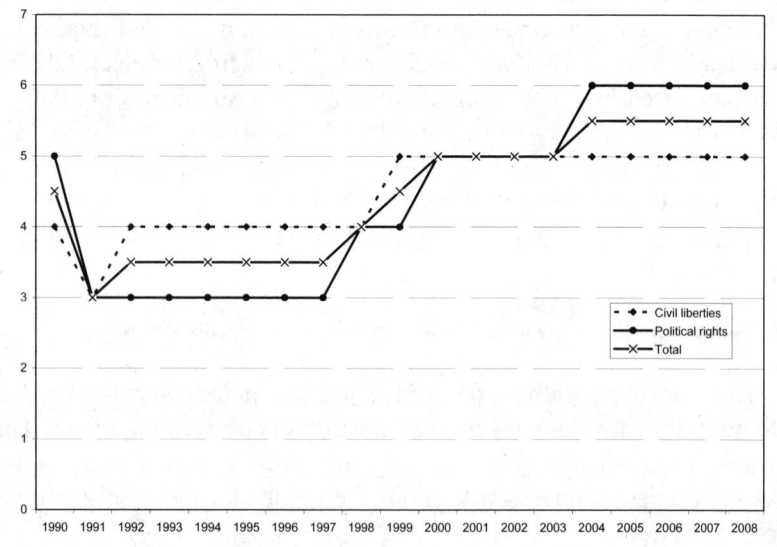

Source: The Freedom House, retrieved from http://www.freedomhouse.org/uploads/fiw09/CompHistData/FIW_AllScores_Countries.xls. The 1990 score refers to the Soviet Union. A free country has a rank between 1 and 2.5; a partially free one—between 3 and 5; one that is not free—5.5 and below.

Conclusion

The study of the existing constraints of power enables us to test the hypothesis about the character of power in a particular institutional context, namely in post-Soviet Russia. The lack of constraints or their loose character means that one cannot rule out the hypothesis of office holders' opportunistic behavior. As long as the more comprehensive information about values and everyday behavior of individuals and groups vested in power remains unavailable, we can assume that the model power in its pure form prevails in the Russian institutional context.

In the present situation the tentative assessment of elements of the institutional environment shows that most of them *enable* office holders' pursuit of individual and group interests rather than *constrain* them. The potential constraints appear quite weak: the mean uncorrected score for 17 items equals 0.6 and 0.45 in its corrected version. On average, the institutional environment under which office holders act leans toward facilitating their opportunistic behavior. Six elements of the institutional environment have a constraining effect (if measured with the help of the corrected score), eleven—an enabling effect.

The overall picture can be hardly described in the words of Ivan Karamazov, a character of Fedor Dostoevsky, as "everything is permitted." Individual opportunism appears constrained at least by three factors: peer-control, hierarchical control and ideology/scientific doctrine. At the same time, the state service as a whole acts under a much softer set of constraints, especially those at the top of the ladder. Their behavior can well be described as "fearless," meaning that they do not have anything to be afraid of. The observation of Nikolai Karamzin (1991, p. 102) that "fearlessness is one of the biggest evils of our time related to the state" may still be true. At least ordinary Russians—56.9 percent of them (N=1,500, 2005)—explain the inefficiency of the state service exactly in terms of their fearlessness in face of punishment for eventual wrongdoings (Sedova, 2006, p. 17).

What actors may be interested in strengthening the institutional constraints listed in Table 8.1? Office holders themselves can hardly do this job: interests of actors vested in power in its pure form are structured in such a way that their major ambition and *Beruf* consists in its continuous reproduction. Interviews suggest that administrative reform entrusted to office holders failed to limit the scope of opportunistic behavior (the score equals to 0.44 [0.26]; see also Section I of the Conclusion).

"Administrative reform was needed only for one thing—to help the supreme power, the team of the new president, to concentrate all controls in their hands.... This objective is achieved.... As far as state management is concerned, there was no such objective, apparently" (3A).

"The key objective of administrative reform consisted in a very decent idea ... What do we have as an outcome? Divide and rule" (58A).

The abundance of resources further limits office holders' interest in genuinely reforming the system of governance. As long as they can extract resource and administrative rents (see Chapter 7), reproduce and strengthen their dominant positions, no changes seem desirable from their point of view. What is even more surprising, ordinary Russians think in a similar manner and connect their support for the political regime to the—positive in 2000-2008—economic dynamics at the macro-level: "evaluations of the current national economy had an exceptionally strong influence on support for the current regime" (Rose, Mishler & Munro, 2006, p. 164). As all interviews were organized within this timeframe, they tend to emphasize an enabling role of resources, the score of this factor is 0.55 (0.48).[23] The constraining impact is often mentioned at the regional level and when discussing the material situation of the "workhorses," office holders at the lowest levels of the hierarchy (up to the bureau head).

"The country simply has been living off the oil bonanza since 1999—nothing happens" (36A).

"I compare the achievements we had in the 1990s—not because it's my personal accomplishment, but keeping in mind several breakthroughs in building the infrastructure—and what exists now, where there are far more resources. One could pave roads with gold, one could build golden airports, the level of life should have been completely different! Yet, these resources are not sufficient. There is not enough money. Theft and embezzlement are everywhere, throughout country" (62A).

The actors at the international level—Western governments and corporations, international organizations and social movements—have limited leverage to influence the situation, even if they decide to do so (an unlikely possibility). In fact, they can influence the severity of only a few constraints: [a4], [b1], [b2] and [c1], to a lesser degree—[d1] and [d2]. Their constraining impact appears to be the most significant in absolute terms, 0.82 (0.71), but limited to the international level only. Furthermore, hopes for changes induced from above paradoxically further the logic of power in its pure form because they derive from the implicit assumption that "the person over whom power is exercised is not usually as important as other power-holders" (Arthur Stinchcombe cited in Tilly, 1985, p. 171).

Much more ought to be done from below. However, the proposed reasoning leads to an apparent contradiction: if power in its pure form is embedded in existing institutional structures, how one can expect individuals and groups who act within these same structures to challenge it? To avoid this contradiction, we need to question deterministic assumptions with respect of human behavior. To what degree is human behavior determined by external constraints embodied, for instance, in institutions and to what degree can the actor go beyond institutionally prescribed roles? This age-old sociological question, which has not yet been answered in a satisfactory manner, appears relevant in the context of post-Soviet transformations. No changes from below are imaginable if we stay within the limits of purely reactive and deterministic models of human behavior. The history of modern countries teaches us that determinism is not absolute, and only the continuous struggles of collective actors representing the interests of subordinates for limiting the scope of power elites' discretionary behavior produced a configuration of power relationships usually associated with modernity. In other words, "popular resistance to war making and state making made a difference" (Tilly, 1985, p. 183; see also Pipes, 2000, pp. 146-158). A crucial difference, one may be willing to add. "Power never limits itself and voluntarily abandons its drift into expansion, only civil resistance may do the job" (Makarenko, 1998, pp. 281-282).

The other condition under which an escape from the vicious circle of institutionally embedded power becomes possible consists in convincing social and economic actors that other configurations of power relationships may be far more attractive for them. Yet, unfortunately, social surveys show that most Russians simply do not believe that any alternative to the current political regime is feasible. "Since those with a preference for an alternative regime are a minority, most Russians appear resigned to accept it as 'the only regime in town'" (Rose, Mishler & Munro, 2004, p. 204).

Notes

1. Similar problems are encountered in studies of organized crime. The higher the probability that research subjects are involved in behavior subject to public disapproval, the higher the risk of distortions due to double thinking.
2. He highlights Principal-Agent relationships in interactions between three levels of decision-making: high-level decision-makers, those who assist them and those who implement and are held responsible for the instructions of high-level decision makers (see Section VI of the Introduction). The general population is not included in this structure.

3. Prof. Peter Solomon (University of Toronto) suggested that the word "responsive" seems more appropriate in this context.
4. Section IV of the Introduction and Section I of Chapter 4 outline the position of supreme power with regard to the state service composed of three braches of power. As for the internal hierarchy of the braches of power, the full explanation of the subjacent place of the legislative and judicial branches in relationships with the executive branch would require a separate study. An insider, the former associate federal minister makes the following assessment: "Well, everything is clear, in the current situation the state equals the executive power. Because the judicial, legislative powers... The judicial power, for instance, is in a deep crisis, it is corrupted as a result" (36A).
5. For instance, Bulgarian customs officials did everything to postpone the installation of a new computerized system in the first half of the 1990s, presumably because it would have reduced their room for maneuvering in collecting border taxes and fees and, hence, opportunities to take bribes. I am grateful for this example to Prof. Rumen Gechev, former deputy prime minister and minister of economic development of Bulgaria (1995-1997).
6. Eva Etzioni-Halevy defends a similar thesis. She insists that the relative autonomy of elites "from each other, and the relative autonomy of some other elites from the elites of the state and the government ... is ... an important requirement for democracy" (1993, p. 101).
7. On the concept of market power in comparison with that of domination by virtue of a constellation of interests in the market, see Section II of Chapter 6.
8. But if one uses alternative indicators, for example, the share of the total industrial output produced by the 200 largest Russian firms, there is clear evidence that the concentration has been rising since the second half of the 1990s, with the exception of 2001 and 2002. The value of this indicator increased from 35 percent in 1996 up to 58 percent, the historical maximum for the post-Soviet period, in 2003: data of the Rating Agency "Expert RA" retrieved from http://raexpert.ru/researches/ and the personal communication of Prof. Svetlana Avdasheva, the State University—the Higher School of Economics. The author is indebted to Prof. Avdasheva for providing him with this data.
9. A more precise estimate can be obtained if links within vertically integrated groups are taken into consideration. Not all links in these groups have a formal and transparent character. As a result, a formally independent unit may appear to be embedded in a vertically integrated group. For instance, CR_3 in the oil industry calculated according to the Federal State Statistics Service in 2003 was 32.5 percent, whereas its adjusted value was significantly higher: 51.2 percent (see Avdasheva, Alimova & Yusupova, 2005).
10. In 2005 Russia produced in total 470.2 million tons of crude oil.
11. For instance, the fact that the only Bulgarian oil refinery located in Bourgas has been using Urals crude oil indicates that some of the choices of the Bulgarian government are conditioned by the position taken by the Russian government. I am indebted for this case to Prof. Gechev.
12. 70 percent of those who start their professional career in the state service do not expect to reach a position higher than the head of a bureau in the end (Gimpelson & Magun, 2004, pp. 18-19).
13. Breaching them is not among the reasons for dismissing an office holder, see Articles 33 and 37 of the Federal Law on the Civil Service in the Russian Federation enacted on July 24, 2004.
14. The contradiction in this formulation is only apparent, taking into consideration the particularities of domination by virtue of a constellation of interests.

15. According to Luzius Wildhaber, the chairman of the European Court of Human Rights, Russia came in first in the number of complaints in 2005 (approximately 20 percent of all complaints originate in this country) and this number keeps growing, see *Kommersant*, No. 202 from October 27, 2006, p. 3.
16. Most probably the source means Óscar R. Benavides, the Peruvian dictator in the 1930s.
17. If a characteristic was attributed to a longer period of time, for instance, "the lack of respect for ordinary people," then the percentage of votes was divided by the number of periods covered.
18. The technocrats in the Russian case are represented by the group of the "liberals" in the power elite and sub-elite (see Subsection VI.2 of the Introduction).
19. The idea of the rule of experts, for instance, was endorsed by 56 percent of Romanians and 90 percent of Slovaks (Ibid).
20. This witness only demonstrates the absence of the use of administrative resources in the most manifest forms. Office holders in region S. to which the informant refers secure voters' support using techniques of domination by virtue of a constellation of interests (see Subsection III.2.6 of Chapter 7).
21. It includes a series of questions as to whether there exist fair electoral laws, equal campaigning opportunities, fair polling, and honest tabulation of ballots; there is a significant opposition vote, *de facto* opposition power, and a realistic possibility for the opposition to increase its support or gain power through elections; the people have the right to organize in different political parties or other competitive political groupings of their choice, and the system is open to the rise and fall of these competing parties or groupings, and so forth.
22. It refers to freedom of expression and beliefs, associational, organizational and individual rights, the rule of law.
23. The crisis that started in the second half of 2008 without any doubt changes the perception of the impact of resources.

9

Conclusion: Impossible Change?

Numerous attempts have been made to reshape the Russian institutional landscape both in the past as well as more recently, during the period covered in this book. They have taken the form of revolutions and reforms, both small- and large-scale. The best institutional and organizational designs developed through the experience of other countries have served as models in these endeavors.[1] Efforts to change the situation by creating original designs "from scratch," without regard for foreign templates and blueprints, have not lacked either: from time to time, Russia played the role of an institutional "exporter," such as, for instance, after World War II with regard to Eastern European countries (Douglass, 1972).

I. Dashed Hopes

The term "post-socialist reforms" is used as a generic name for a large number of policies intended to produce political, economic and social changes in the former socialist countries of Eastern Europe and the Soviet Union. At the early stages of post-socialist reforms their expected outcomes appeared very promising and clear-cut: the market would substitute for a centrally planned economy; democracy for a single party political system; and an "open" society for a "small" society.[2] The projection of these expected outcomes into the reality of the early 1990s explains a "teleological," in Wladimir Andreff's term (1993, p. 11), orientation of reforms at that time: the point of departure was believed to count less than the point of arrival. The idea of a simultaneous movement along three vectors—political (leading to full-fledged democracy), economic (leading to the full-fledged market) and social (leading to the "open" society)—summarizes the initial design of post-socialist reforms.

However, in the second half of the 1990s it became evident that the movement along the three axes would be more difficult than expected and, nearly a decade later, reforms still have not produced the desired outcomes. In fact, in several countries, namely successors to the Soviet Union (with a notable exception of the Baltic states), reforms "went awry" and significantly deviated from the linear trajectory. The divergent paths of post-socialist countries (e.g., "success stories" of Poland, Slovenia and the Czech Republic) called for theoretical explanations and corresponding adjustments in the design of reforms.

It turned out that issues related to institutions and institutional changes had been neglected in the initial blueprints of reforms. The neglect of institutions can be compared with giving cards (or, better, tokens, title deeds and paper money in the Monopoly board game) to players without telling them the rules of the game and reaching an agreement in regard to their enforcement. The key novelty reflected in a new consensus among Western advisers and financial sponsors of post-socialist reforms consisted in "bringing institutions back in." In the economic sphere emphasis has shifted from macro-economic stabilization, price and trade liberalization and mass privatization to the case-by-case privatization of residual state property, start-up development and institution-building (Andreff, 2003, pp. 15-21).

Being vested in the monopoly of the legitimate use of violence, the state has a comparative advantage in enforcing norms and rules and, by doing so, in maintaining order. Hence, the introduction of new norms calls for reforming the state apparatus: state servants should be motivated to implement new rules and possess qualifications for overseeing their implementation and enforcement. That being the case, administrative reform becomes a centerpiece of post-socialist transformations: it creates favorable conditions for successfully implementing all other "partial" policies.

In the late 1990s, administrative reform became a top item on the agenda of reforms in Russia: movement in all other spheres is now believed to be conditioned by progress, or the lack thereof, in reforming the state apparatus. The president initiated work on the federal program for reforming the state service in August 2001. It was promulgated in November 2002 and its temporal scope covered the period 2003-2005. In 2003, the president issued a decree intended to implement the program.

A strategy of administrative reform for 2006-2008 was adapted by the Russian government in 2005.[3]

The officially declared aim of administrative reform consists in modernizing the state service and making it more compact and effective. The effectiveness of power has two dimensions: the effectiveness of the very power relationship and the effectiveness of management (see Section II of Chapter 2). Judged according to the first criterion, the effectiveness of power, administrative reform can be considered a success. In 2006-2008, the number of Russians who appear ready to accept unconditional submission to the will of the individual vested in power increased markedly, compared with the situation of the mid-nineties: 43 percent in 2008 compared with 33 percent in 1995 (Table 9.1).

However, achievements assessed with the help of the second criterion, the effectiveness of management, tend to be far less obvious, if they exist at all. Even indicators chosen by designers of administrative reform[4] suggest total failure. One of them, the Transparency International Corruption Perception Index reached an all-time low in 2008 (Figure 8.6). Two others, "Government effectiveness" and "Regulatory quality"[5] from a set of indicators regularly calculated by the World Bank on the basis of a series of surveys of businesspeople and experts, show a downward trend as well, after peaking in 2003-2004 (Figure 9.1).

Table 9.1
Can There Be, in Your Opinion, Situations When the People Need a Strong and Authoritative Leader, an "Iron Hand"?

	November 1989	September 1994	July 1995	September 1996	March 2006	March 2007	July 2008
Our people need an "iron hand" all the time	25	35	33	37	42	45	43
There are situations (such as now) when it is necessary to give all the power to one person	16	23	27	32	31	29	29
It should never be possible for one person to get full power	44	23	24	18	20	18	18
Difficult to answer	16	18	15	13	8	8	10
N	1,500	3,000	3,000	2,500	1,600	1,600	1,500

Source: Obshchestvennoe mnenie—2008, 2008, p. 28.

Figure 9.1
Quality of Governance in Russia, World Bank version, 1996-2008

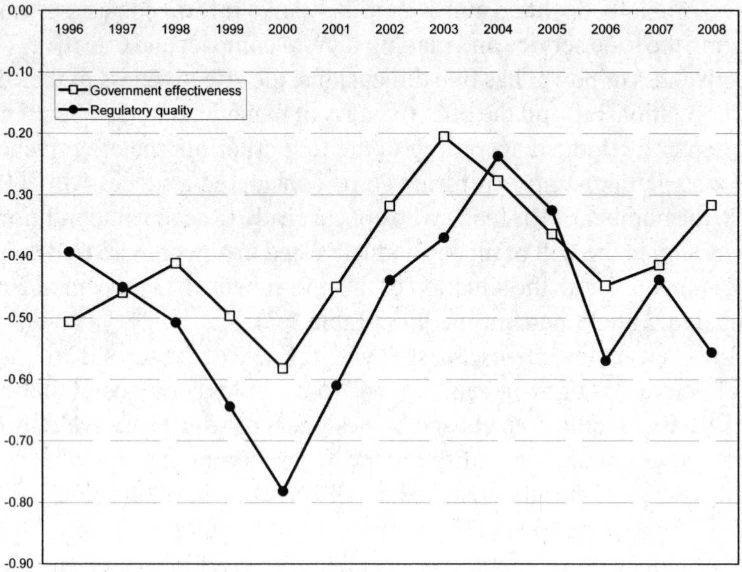

Source: The Worldwide Governance Indicators Project by the World Bank, retrieved from http://info.worldbank.org/governance/wgi/pdf/wgidataset.xls.
Legend: Values of both indicators vary from –2.5 (the lowest relative score) to +2.5 (the highest one). Both indicators are built on the basis of regular surveys conducted on a sample of experts and businesspeople. Since the surveys were not carried out in 1997, 1999 and 2001, means of the preceding and the following years are substituted for values of the indicators in these years.

The success of the first dimension of administrative reform only confirms the continuous reproduction of the prevailing model of power relationships, Russian power (Chapter 3). This implies power as an end in itself, as opposed to power as a means to achieve another end that has an instrumental nature (see the third dimension of the taxonomy of power introduced in Section V of Chapter 2). Power having a terminal value does not absolutely need to produce anything other than the fact of unconditional obedience. At the same time, unconditional obedience undermines the subordinate's initiative and, thus, complicates the achievement of practical results. A sergeant in the army may manage to get recruits to obey all his orders, however nonsensical they may seem to them, but only at the price of destroying grounds for genuine cooperation.[6]

It follows that the success of the first dimension and the failure of the second represent two sides of the same coin: one cannot increase effectiveness of management without depriving power of its character as a terminal value. The continuity of Russian power hampers attempts to boost effectiveness of management, as hypothesized in the Introduction. Administrative reform failed because it did not touch upon the core principles of Russian power.

In this context it is hardly surprising that an absolute majority of respondents in a pilot survey carried out by the "Public Opinion" Foundation (*FOM*) on representative samples in four regions of Russia in October 2003, after the official and widely publicized launch of administrative reform, declared that they knew nothing about it.[7] The chosen design of administrative reform excludes any meaningful involvement of the population because the latter would contradict the essence of the prevailing model of power.

A triple-layer design seems appropriate for comprehensive administrative reform (Figure 9.2). Its first layer corresponds to particular administrative processes, documents and policies, for instance, programs of electronic governance (e-governance). At the second layer administrative reform deals with the state apparatus as a whole. The question of how e-governance fits current patterns of interaction between office holders illustrates the new focus. The third layer refers to a prevailing

Figure 9.2
A Triple-Layer Design of Administrative Reform

Particular administrative processes and policies

State apparatus as a whole

Prevailing model of power

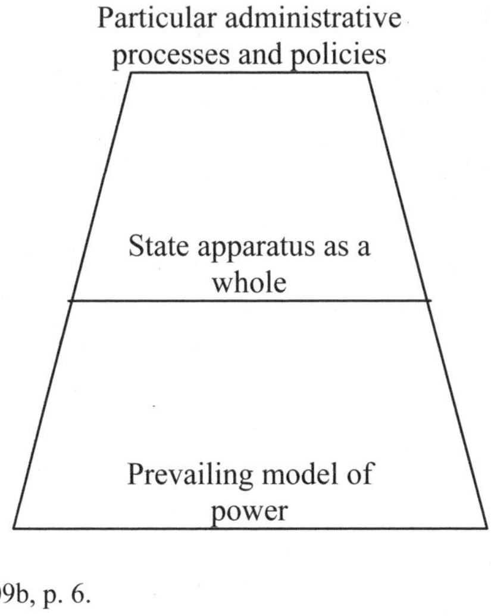

Source: Oleinik, 2009b, p. 6.

model of power in which the state apparatus is embedded. Issues of the compatibility or incompatibility of e-governance with this model emerge at this stage of reform.

However, even if the design of administrative reform had been more ambitious and touched upon the third, deepest, layer, there would be still no guarantee that the model of power underlying the state service changes. The October 1917 revolution was intended to radically reshape the institutional environment in Russia: its rhetoric against czarism helped mobilize large masses of ordinary people. In the final account, the prevailing model of power kept reproducing and even strengthening, nevertheless. The October 1917 revolution did not alter the path of Russian institutional evolution, as shown in Subsection IV.8 of Chapter 4.

II. Shining Path[8]

The phenomenon of path-dependence has several alternative explanations varying from emphasis on a difficult switch from an institution to alternative ones once the number of its "users" exceeds a certain limit to the assumption that shared mental models prevent the emergence of alternative concepts and, thus, restrict the range of things that individuals are capable of doing by the use of words and sentences (see Section II of Chapter 4). Path-dependence in the Russian case involves the stability over time of two types of habituses, in the terms of Pierre Bourdieu,[9] or sets, in the terms of Dmitrii Uznadze,[10] or habits of thought, in the terms of Thorstein Veblen.[11] The first underlies domination, the second—submission. Both people who interiorize the habitus/set/habit of thought of domination and those who acquire the habitus/set/habit of thought of submission tend to take the existing power relationships for granted, without questioning them. Russian power appears to be embedded in these habituses/sets/habits of thought at the infra-individual level. These "plot-genes" of Russian power make its unconscious reproduction possible.

However, the mechanism for transmitting and reproducing the prevailing model of power would not work smoothly under extremely variable external conditions without conscious actions, especially, but not exclusively, on the part of people vested in power. Path-dependence as a combination of continuity and adaptability calls for recognizing that habituses/sets/habits of thought influence and shape interests lying closer to conscious and deliberate actions. "Not ideas, but material and ideal interests, directly govern men's conduct. Yet very frequently the 'world images' that have been created by 'ideas' have, like switchmen, determined the tracks along which action has been pushed by the dynamics of interest" (Weber, 1946, p. 280; see also Swedberg, 2003, pp. 1-5).

The period of time from 1999 to 2008 considered in the book provide an opportunity to take a closer look at how the reproduction of the habitus/set/habit of thought underlying domination under new conditions, namely the transition towards a full-scale market economy, necessitates deliberate actions on the part of individuals and groups vested in power. Adaptation to new conditions represents a serious challenge, similar to that faced in the aftermath of the October 1917 revolution. At the very outset, outcomes appeared far from certain.

The challenge was successfully met as a result on an important institutional innovation, namely the emergence of a power triad as a key configuration of power relationships. The power triad composed of C, who controls access to the market (supreme power and its lieutenants), A, who consequently acquires the status of a monopolist (businesses) and B (the rest of the population), who gains only compared with the situation when no market exists, lays the groundwork for domination of, on the one hand, C over A and B and, on the other hand, A over B, by virtue of a constellation of their interests in the market (see more in Chapters 5 and 7). A's, B's and C's interests tend to be structured within the power triad in such a manner that they reproduce the underlying patterns of domination (for C and, to a lesser extent, A) and submission (for B and, to a lesser extent, A). In the final account, the emerging market transforms into a weapon in the hands of C and, to a lesser extend, A.[12]

Some additional considerations with regard to origins of path-dependence were not discussed in the book in depth, but deserve exploration in further research. They refer to processes both at the national and international levels. An under-explored source of path-dependence existing within the Russian institutional system derives from the congruence of models of power structuring relationships at the micro- (within the family or a group of personally known people, for instance), meso- (within a network or a firm) and macro- (in politics) levels. An under-explored source of path-dependence originating in international relations consists in negative convergence between Russian power and the model of power embodied in the power elites of some Western countries.

III. Congruence of Power in Everyday Life and Politics

A modern institutional system involves a double differentiation. On the one hand, various functional subsystems—economy, society, politics, science, technology and so forth—acquire autonomy from each other. "The functional differentiation of sub-systems and, in particular, the divorce between politics and religion, or between the economy and politics, and the formation of the worlds of science, art and private life, are indeed preconditions for modernization" (Touraine, 1995, p. 202; see also Turner, 2000; Boltanski & Thévenot, 1991; Walzer, 1983; Luhmann, 1979).

On the other hand, the spheres of public and private life become clearly separated, with the former being transformed into a place where the individual plays easily recognizable and "decipherable" by the generalized Other roles, and the latter—into a place where he or she can organize things and relationships at will and basically remain him- or herself. In a sense, privacy offers a "shelter" from social, political and economic forces outside their control. "Private life is regarded as a sort of a peculiar refuge, where one may hide from unexpected blows on the part of a new social and economic order" (Khlopin, 1994, pp. 75-78).[13] Some scholars further argue that the opposition between action "in private" and that "in public" does not catch all possible regimes of social action and introduce a third, intermediate one. Action oriented by a common plan or project refers to the "felicitous exercise of the will by an individual endowed with autonomy and capable of projecting herself successfully into the future" (Thévenot, 2007, p. 417; see also Thévenot et al., 2005, pp. 35-40; Boltanski & Thévenot, 2000).

It follows that a modern institutional system has a complex structure: it includes several regimes of social action and, furthermore, the regime of interactions "in public" implies several autonomous subsystems. Power is present in all elements of this complex structure. For instance, each functional subsystem has its own principles of stratification that underlie various positions or "states" (*états*). Higher states enable those who reach them to have more influence than the others, to make decisions having major consequences (Boltanski & Thévenot, 1991, p. 99). In a similar vein, Michael Walzer suggests that modernity does not mean "simple equality" in the distribution of resources. By putting forward the concept of "complex equality" he acknowledges inequalities existing within each functional system and wants only to prevent their convertibility: "no social good X should be distributed to men and women who possess other good Y merely because they possess Y and without regard to the meaning of X" (Walzer, 1983, p. 20). In other words, a differentiated system has multiple centers of power, whereas a non-differentiated system—only one.

The question as to whether in a particular society, say Russian, there exist various independent centers of power has both theoretical and practical significance. At the theoretical level, the existence of multiple independent centers of power and power elites serves an additional demonstration of its modern character. It also helps refute the hypothesis about the closeness of the prevailing model of power to power in its pure form because the latter implies monopolization of power regardless of the sphere of activity (see Subsection II.4 of Chapter 3). At the practical level, multiple centers of power play the role of "checks and balances" that limit the scope of the discretionary behavior of individuals and groups vested in power (see also Subsection III [a3] of Chapter 8). Moreover, the multiplicity of centers of power makes criteria for regulating access to power less uniform, which leaves the door open for changing the institutional path by providing viable alternatives.

These aspects were not given attention in the present book and call for further research. For, instance, a rough estimate for the degree of monopolization of centers of power in various spheres can be obtained by comparing lists of the most influential people in each of them. The larger the overlap, the less separated the sources of power in functional subsystems tend to be.[14] The outcomes of previous research indicate a low degree of autonomy of functional subsystems in Russia (Oleinik, 2003), which provides an additional reason to support the thesis about the existence of a unique center of power (supreme power).

The other differentiation associated with modernity prompts comparisons between power relationships structuring interactions at the registers of familiar ("in private"), normal and justifiable ("in public") action. Is there any similarity in patterns of coordination through power in the family, in the firm, in the university, in politics—to list just a few examples corresponding to the various registers? There may be no direct convertibility of power between the family and the university even in societies without strong traditions of academic freedom (i.e., with no autonomy of academia as a functional subsystem). But does this necessarily mean that the head of the family exercises his or her power over other family members differently than the university professor when he or she interacts with students? These questions clearly refer to the first dimension of the taxonomy of power outlined in Section III of Chapter 2. Of all the three dimensions of power, this one has been least incorporated in the discussion throughout the book because of the principal focus on supreme power situated at the register of justifiable action as the finest expression of power in its pure form.

This under-explored dimension of power nevertheless has important implications with respect to the overall stability of the institutional system. Harry Eckstein (1966, p. 234) postulates that "a government will tend to be stable if its authority pattern is congruent with the other authority patterns of the society of which it is a part." In terms of the above-mentioned example, the stability of the political power results from its congruence with the power of the family head and that of university professor. Eckstein is not alone in promoting this view. Advocates of economic democracy, i.e., the implementation of democratic principles within the firm, use similar arguments. "The common individual must take experience of democratic self-government in his everyday life if he is to learn to participate meaningfully in the democratic governance of civil society" (Putterman, 1988, p. 260; see also Dahl, 1985).

How congruent do power relationships corresponding to different registers have to be? Robert Dahl defends a radical position: to be sustainable, the principles of democratic governance must apply at all layers of the institutional system. Very few countries, if any, actually meet this requirement. "In all democratic countries some kinds of organizations are explicitly and even legally governed by systems of non-democratic authority: business firms, for example" (Dahl, 1990, p. 1). Eckstein's position appears more moderate in this regard: he admits that the degree of congruence may weaken in the more distant segments, for instance, within the family (the private sphere).[15]

The task of confronting two alternative hypotheses, the first stating that the stability of the institutional systems involves the congruence of power relationships at all its layers and the second assuming that the process of modernization undermines such congruence, calls for further empirical research. However, one can tentatively assume that congruence between models of power relationships at various levels of the institutional organization in Russia does indeed exist, yet it has a rather authoritarian character. In other words, the people vested in supreme power, the boss of a firm, a university professor, the head of a family and even an intimate partner—because sexual relationships are permeated by power too (Foucault, 1984a; 1984b; 1976)—all of them may be involved in reproducing the same prevalent model of power, Russian power. If so, such congruence then transforms into an important factor of path-dependence observed in the history of this country (see also Chapter 4).

IV. Negative Convergence between Russia and the West

When discussing path-dependence, exogenous influences also need careful consideration. External shocks represent a serious challenge to the stability of the institutional system because they often lead to reforms or revolutions: the defeat in the Napoleonic wars stimulated reforms in southwestern Germany at the start of the nineteenth century, the defeat in the Crimean War contributed to the "Great reforms" of the 1860s in Russia (Zweynert, 2009; see also Subsection II [b2] of Chapter 8).

The other important mechanism for "internalizing" external influences consists of institutional transfers. Relative "latecomers" in the process of modernization tend to imitate institutional patterns of more successful—primarily in military and economic terms—countries-"leaders" associated with the West and, more recently, with the United States (Badie, 2000, Ch. 3; Oleinik, 2006b). The latter countries play the role of a trendsetter for the former. The Western model shows, at least *in potentia*, an alternative to the path shaping the evolution of "latecomers."

Since the second half of the twentieth century, a growing number of common trends have been characterizing developments in both Western countries and countries that embody less effective—in terms of their military and economic performance—institutional models, including Russia. Examples of convergence in various spheres abound (Oleinik, 2008a); they range from the practices of doing business without reference to the law or ethical principles[16] to similar military experiences.[17] Convergent trends in the evolution of models of power prevailing in the United States and Russia respectively deserve principal attention.

Most developed countries in the West, including the United States, cannot escape a worldwide decline in the level of generalized trust that has been documented with the help of the World Values Survey data since the early 1980s (Table 2.1). This trend results in placing greater emphasis on power when coordinating social actions at the expense of the other coordination devices, trust and convention. Describing the practices of contract making in the US business in the early 1960s, Stewart Macaulay (1963, p. 61) noticed that "disputes are frequently settled without reference to the contract or potential or actual legal sanctions." Not so in the 1990s. The reliance on procedures of legal enforcement, i.e., on the state as a guarantor of last resort, rapidly replaced word of honor not only in business, but also in everyday life. Francis Fukuyama (1996, p. 311) ascertains the growing readiness of Americans to sue: "the increase in litigation means that fewer disputes are capable of being resolved informally... For negotiation to work, each party must have some degree of belief in the other's good intentions." As for Russia, the decline in the level of trust takes even more manifest forms, which strengthens the features of a power-centered society (see Section I of the Introduction).

Institutional systems in Russia and the United States may become more similar, yet this similarity does not necessarily improve their performance and effectiveness. Wladimir Andreff (1992, pp. 70-71) describes the trends outlined above in terms of negative convergence: "if congruence is negative convergence which selects only severest problems of both systems, this implies *a priori* that efficient economic processes, institutions and regulations may yield degenerating results, and also *a priori* that mistaken processes, institutions and regulations may generate unexpectedly efficient outcomes." The intensifying reliance on power serves to maintain order (hence an "efficient outcome") at the price of extinguishing trust and convention (hence a "mistaken process").

There are no comprehensive studies of the "internal mechanics" of negative convergence.[18] This may, arguably, both result from internal factors[19] and emerge in the process of interactions between the power elites of "negatively convergent" countries. The latter mechanism of "contamination" seems particularly interesting because of its embeddedness in institutional transfers.

Interactions between the power elites of countries involved in institutional transfers, both as "exporters" and "importers," are commonly considered a one-way process of reproducing institutional patters existing in most developed countries in the rest of the world (cf. Oleinik, 2008a). However, social action, in this case—between the power elites—always implies mutual adaptation and adjustments, even when the parties involved possess unequal power: Herbert Simon (1953, p. 503) reminds us that, for every action, there is an opposite reaction. This means that, while power-holders in Russia attempt to replicate the institutional models of the countries-"leaders," the Western power elites may learn from their Russian counterparts patterns of behavior consistent with the model of power prevailing in this country. At least, without such learning of "basics of Russian power" the parties simply would not understand each other, which prevents making the adjustments necessary for action in concert.

The process of learning takes either direct or indirect forms. Direct contacts between members of the power elites in Russia and the West did not stop even during the Cold War, after the fall of the Soviet Union their intensity significantly increased because of the active use of Western blueprints during the early stages of reforms. Not surprisingly, the people who were most actively involved in consulting Russian decision-makers also appeared to be among those who learned the local rules of the game quickly.[20]

Two Western political leaders and self-proclaimed friends of the Russian Establishment, former chancellor of Germany Gerhard Schröeder[21] and Italian Prime Minister Silvio Berlusconi, showed themselves to be such apt learners that independent observers started comparing their behavior to that of Russian leaders. This "strange" congruence inspired the Italian Nobel prize winner, novelist Dario Fo, to write a piece *L'anomalo bicefalo* (2003) about a fictitious situation of transplanting the Russian president's brain into the head of the Italian prime minister. It is worth noting that these members of the Western power elite demonstrated a strong inclination toward the "office holder entrenchment," an outcome of the transformation of power into an end in itself. Both of them initially refused to acknowledge their defeats in the 2005 elections and leave office (Berlusconi managed to return to the highest executive office in 2008). The temptation to be good learners when interacting with members of the Russian power elite presumably derives from the attractiveness and *"charmes discrètes"* of power in its pure form. Compared with a "modest" and limited authority subject to numerous constraints that a leader possesses in conditions of full-fledged democracy (on differences between "power" and "authority", see the Introduction to Chapter 3 and Part II of Chapter 2), Russian power ensures many more degrees of freedom, which eventually paves the way to discretion and opportunism (see Chapter 8).

Indirect learning also takes place. Instead of unmediated personal contacts between members of the power elites, it results from the involvement of actors in a particular game, which necessarily restricts the range of alternative strategies available to them. In other words, the parameters of the situation, the "game," prompt specific behavioral patterns, such as when cheating becomes an unavoidable element of some card games. Thomas Schelling argues that rules of the Cold War "game" dictated a particular behavior to the antagonists involved in it, namely the Soviet Union and the United States. For instance, both of them preferred to rely on violent techniques for imposing will by staging limited—as opposed to all-out—wars and maintaining significant arsenals of nuclear and conventional arms because in the context of the Cold War "'disarmament' in the literal sense ... could produce instability rather than stability" (Schelling, 1960, p. 240).

The situation on the market for hydrocarbons, oil and natural gas, represents another example of indirect learning. Members of the Russian power elite use existing imperfections of its structure to their advantage and consciously strengthen them (see Section II of the Introduction). European consumers confront a strong, with elements of a tight oligopoly and a loose monopoly, position on the part of few large Russian oil-companies[22] and Gazprom, the largest producer of natural gas in the world.[23]

In face of a significant structural bias favoring the Russian power elites, which closely control exports of hydrocarbons (see Subsection II [d1] of Chapter 8), and taking into consideration the common knowledge that these biases could be used as a weapon (as during disputes over gas supplies between Russia and the Ukraine in January 2006 and March 2008) a rational response of the European power elites consists in consolidating their positions and creating a kind of counter-monopoly of final consumers. This involves closer government regulation of the domestic markets of European countries, including measures for controlling access to this market, and more intense government interventions. The drift into monopolization, as the present book shows, creates conditions favorable for the transformation of the market into a weapon, this time in the hand of the European power elites.

The question as to whether the process of learning has gone too far and the model of power that the Western power elites embody does not differ significantly from Russian power anymore calls for further comparative research. Despite quite opposite starting points in their evolution, some similarities do indeed exist,[24] especially after Russian power started to reproduce itself through the market, a core element of the institutional architecture in the West. However, much work still remains to be done with regard to comparing various nation-specific models of power relationships and empirically measuring the degree of their eventual convergence.

V. The 2008 Crisis: A Test for Resistance to Temptations

The global crisis that started in the second half of 2008 represents another situation with substantial risk for transforming the market into a weapon in the hands of power holders. Even if, in Adam Ferguson's words, the crisis is "the result of human action, but not the execution of human design" (paraphrased in Hayek, 1967, p. 96), it involves a series of structural biases that create numerous opportunities for profiting from them and converting them into a resource for strengthening the market power of particular businesses. Furthermore, government interventions intended to bridge structural gaps also offer a multitude of occasions for strengthening power with their help, the power of office holders and that of selected businesses. The latter configuration seems particularly relevant in the context of the present discussion because it serves to test the explanatory potential of the power triad consisting of C (the state), A (selected businesses) and B (the rest of the population) (see more about the power triad in Subsection I.5 of Chapter 5).

Access control to the market makes sense when actors find it more profitable to enter the market than to remain outside of it. In other words, actors find more opportunities for making profits/increasing their utilities on the market with controlled access than in other places. The crisis means that economic actors lose money instead of making it. At first glance, C has no chance to capitalize on his or her position as a "gatekeeper" within the power triad during the crisis: As rush toward the exit instead of lining up at the entrance to the market. If this were confirmed, such reasoning would limit the applicability of the approach developed in this book mainly to the periods of sustainable economic growth (see also Section III of Chapter 6).

The unusually sharp forms of the structural biases taking place during the crisis call for government interventions—in Russia as well as in the West and China, this rising world power (the junction of power and the market takes in this country very manifest forms too, see Subsections I.4, III.2.6 and Conclusion of Chapter 7). And contemporary governments, in contrast to their counterparts at the time of the Great Depression of the 1930s, appear better prepared and more willing to intervene in the market play by providing financial assistance and much needed investments. If access control to the market loses its relative importance during the crisis, access control to funds distributed by government may eventually take place taking into consideration the fact that access to government subventions and loans becomes a matter of life and death for most businesses.

The power triad may emerge as a result of the transformation of the distribution of public funds into a particular field of domination with clear boundaries and the control of access. All As want to get into the field, but only a few succeed because of the scarcity of the funds and barriers erected by C, Bs are better off if some businesses survive and provide them with jobs—no one has an interest in a total collapse—even if most funds are taken from their pockets, C eventually transforms the role of a distributor of public funds into a resource for strengthening its power. A new constellation of C's, A's and B's interests emerges.

A brief discussion of the American Recovery and Reinvestment Act of 2009 illustrates the thesis that no country is immune to this new configuration of the power triad. At least, several sections of this Act do not prevent the possible drift into transforming the distribution of public funds into a weapon in the hands of office holders charged with this function. The Act is intended to regulate government spending and tax credits totaling, at the federal level, about eight hundred billion US dollars, or approximately 5.5 percent of GDP in current dollars (US$14,441.4 billion in 2008[25]). The authors of the Act devote significant attention to issues of public accountability and transparency in using these funds. For instance, the Recovery Accountability and Transparency Board was established "to conduct oversight of covered funds to prevent fraud, waste, and abuse" (Section 1521).[26] However, the question of facilitating access to the money and especially that of preventing the eventual discretion of office holders in their distribution are not addressed in an explicit manner.

First, all public funds are channeled through the existing system of government bodies. Section 3(b) stipulates that "the President and the heads of Federal departments and agencies shall manage and expend the funds made available in this Act." The Act does not contain special provisions in respect of lobbying and other elements of the "business as usual" and their impact on the distribution of public funds in interests of a "selected few" As. The Memorandum "Ensuring Responsible Spending of Recovery Act Funds" sent by President Obama to the Heads of Executive Departments and Agencies on March 20, 2009 does too little to exclude all considerations but the merit of an application when allocating the funds.[27]

Second, the provision on the mandatory use of American iron, steel and manufactured goods in all projects benefiting from the funds appropriated under the Act appears particularly controversial (Section 1605 also labeled "Buy American"). On the one hand, it introduces elements of protectionist policies, even if they are accompanied by the promise that they "shall be applied in a manner consistent with United States obligations under international agreements" (Subsection 1605d). Protectionist policies, as indicated in Section II of Chapter 5, pave the way to domination by virtue of a constellation of interests in the market. On the other hand, this provision also leaves the door for office holders' discretion open, thus facilitating their eventual transformation into "gatekeepers" within the power triad, Cs. This enables the head of a Federal department or agency to waive the "buy American" requirement under certain conditions (Subsection 1605b). At least, it is not excluded that some non-American suppliers (*A*s) are admitted to the national market characterized by less severe competition (i.e., a structural bias) in exchange for their actions in the interests of those who have the right to wave the requirement (*C*s), whatever form *C*s' interests could take. Taxpayers (*B*s) gain something compared with the alternative situation with no Act because some jobs are still created.

Content analysis of publications in the mass media confirms that access to the funds made available under the Act (i) varies across different groups of businesses and (ii) in some cases has a problematic character. Both LexisNexis Academic and Google show a higher frequency of references to carmakers in the context of "access to bailout funds," followed by those to banks and insurers.[28] Not all financial institutions appear equally eligible for funds, however. Only those registered as banks can get access to the funds, which prompted some of them, such as American Express, initially a credit- and charge-card company, to change their organizational form (associated transaction costs shall be included in the price of their "entry ticket;" see also Subsection I.5 of Chapter 5). There are also sharp divides between large and small banks, as well as regionally and nationally operating ones.[29]

The insufficient attention to issues of access to bailout funds can potentially undermine the spirit of public accountability and transparency intended for the Act by its authors from the Obama administration. This shortcoming does not necessarily result from "ill will" of office holders seeking an additional opportunity to strengthen and extend their power. It may be attributed as well to an insufficient theoretical understanding of conditions under which government intervention transforms from a means to restore order into an end in itself.

VI. Back to Marx and Keynes or Beyond Them?

The 2008 crisis led to a growing disappointment with the ideal of the free, unregulated market and the neoclassical policies of *laissez-faire*. It prompts a kind of revival of Karl Marx' ideas and, particularly, those of John Maynard Keynes. The recent rise in the popularity of the first can be attributed to his criticism of the capitalistic system as a whole, its inherent instability and immoral character (titles with accusation of Wall Street's "greed" make headlines even in the mainstream mass media). The second laid the theoretical groundwork for justifying government intervention in the functioning of the market. Paul Krugman (2009, p. 190) insists in this respect that "John Maynard Keynes … is now more relevant than ever." The search for references to Marx and Keynes in discussions of the crisis in the printed mass media confirms this observation: during just the first year of the crisis that started in the second half of 2008 their number has increased more than two-fold compared to the period covering the twenty-five previous years (Table 9.2).

The revival of Marxism and Keynesianism, nevertheless, does not imply any theoretical breakthrough or even a persuasive reply to criticisms that were addressed to these approaches previously. For instance, neither advocates of Keynesianism nor their neoclassical critics take the arguments of each other seriously. Krugman admits that "[Keynesians], who had comforted themselves with the belief that the great divide in macroeconomics was narrowing, were shocked to realize that [neoclassical] economists hadn't been listening at all."[30] He himself seems not willing to make steps toward rapprochement and argues against the introduction into Keynesian models of the assumption of rational choice, as a response of New Keynesians to criticisms put forward by neoclassical economists:[31] "standard New Keynesian models left no room for a crisis like the one we're having, because those models generally accepted the efficient-market view of the financial sector."

When discussing government intervention, several elements of criticism put forward by neoclassical economists remain unanswered. It would be simply unwise to recognize the authentic Keynesianism as "the only plausible game in town," as Krugman suggests, without carefully addressing them. Monetarist critics of Keynes (Milton Friedman and his followers) "strongly question whether discretionary policy—given the

Table 9.2
Number of Co-Occurrences of References to Karl Marx and John Maynard Keynes with the Word "Financial Crisis" in Major US and World English-Language Publications

Keyword / Period	Marx / Marx!	Keynes / Keynes!
October 8, 2007—October 8, 2009	61 / 88	108 / 231
Before October 8, 2007 (the databank covers the period since the early 1980s)	24 / 74	49 / 102

Source: LexisNexis Academic.
Legend: the parameters of the search are set in such a manner that the words "financial crisis" and Marx or Keynes co-occur in the same paragraph (using the operator "W/50"). An exclamation mark (!) truncates a word to find all the words made by adding letters to the end of it. For example, Marx! refers to variations on the term Marx such as Marxism, Marxist, Marxian etc.

state of existing or future knowledge of macroeconomic processes—can ever create stability" (Ekelund & Hébert, 2007, p. 505). Upon closer inspection it appears that this objection has two dimensions. On the one hand, do the office holders responsible for defining the parameters of government intervention have sufficient cognitive capacities to take into consideration all relevant factors and to foresee all possible consequences (Simon, 1978; see also Section I of Chapter 6)? On the other hand, do the office holders act in the public interest or, alternatively, do their individual or group interests overrule all other considerations (see the Introduction to Chapter 8)? The latter aspect brings us back to the core argument of this book.

Even perfect—on paper—designs of economic institutions and policies often fail to do justice to problems related to the drift of office holders into opportunism: instead of making these institutions work in the public interest, they tend to convert them into a resource for strengthening their grasp on power (in various forms ranging from the office holder's entrenchment to the transformation of the market into a weapon). When discussing the model of market socialism, which also offers a recipe for dealing with the inherent instability of the market, Joseph Stiglitz (1994, p. 15) reasonably asks "Do bureaucrats have the incentives to carry out the prescriptions provided by the advocates of market socialism?"

The institutional environment of a (post)socialist country without any doubt differs from that in a country with developed democratic institutions, especially with regard to the configuration of constraints under which elected officials and office holders act. Yet, even in the latter case, a proper response of office holders to the various needs expressed by elected officials and, through them, by society, should not be taken for granted. Not all American presidents, whatever ambitious plans they had to serve the public good, managed to ensure a satisfactory level of response on the part of office holders.[32]

To summarize, neither the return to Keynes nor to Marx nor to any previous theory guarantees an adequate answer to the challenges of the 2008 crisis. One could gain some insights from inquiring into the origin of power in its pure form, for example, in the Russian case, because such inquiry helps ensure a better understanding of the dangers (strengths are researched relatively well) of government intervention into the market play. The most serious of them consists in using existing and emerging structural biases to the office holder's advantage by transforming the market into a weapon in their hands. This book represents a contribution toward building a general theory addressing the challenges of the situation in which, on the one side, government intervention appears inescapable but, on the other side, it could only increase society's dependence on power as a mechanism of coordination and, furthermore, make the exercise of power by office holders even more independent from it. Some key elements of the theoretical edifice are still missing, namely the complete specification of conditions, first of all—institutional, under which the market becomes a mechanism for strengthening power instead of being a liberating force[33]—as several generations of classical and neoclassical economists used to believe.

The capacity of social scientists—institutional economists, political sociologists and analytical philosophers—to meet these challenges depends in turn on the institutional organization of science. Its current state complicates communication between scholars, especially across divides between various small groups of scholars linked by personal relationships, schools of thought and disciplines (Oleinik, 2009c). This issue, nevertheless, has to be the object of a separate study.

Notes

1. Institutional transfers, or efforts intended to replicate institutional and organizational structures that initially emerged abroad, in a different institutional environment, have recently attracted considerable attention of Russian scholars (Oleinik, 2006b; Oleinik, 2002a; Kleiner, 2001; Polterovich, 2001).
2. Characterized by a sharp differentiation between *Us* and *Them*, lack of control over everyday violence, the personification of relationships, and a blurred border between the private and public spheres (see also Subsection VI.3 of the Introduction).
3. Poruchenie Prezidenta Rossiiskoi Federatsii ot 15.8.2001 "O razrabotke Programmy reformirovaniia gosudarstvennoi sluzhby" [Order of the President of the Russian Federation from 15.8.2001 about the preparation of a program for reforming the state service]; Ukaz Prezidenta Rossiiskoi Federatsii ot 19.11.2002 No. 1336 "O federal'noi programme 'Reformirovanie gosudarstvennoi sluzhby Rossiiskoi Federatsii (2003-2005)'" [Decree of the President of the Russian Federation from 19.11.2002 on the federal program for reforming the state service of the Russian Federation (2003-2005)]; Ukaz Prezidenta Rossiiskoi Federatsii ot 23.7.2003 No. 824 "O merah po provedeniiu administrativnoi reformy v 2003-2004 godakh" [Decree of the President of the Russian Federation from 23.7.2003 on means of carrying out administrative reform in 2003-2004]; Rasporiazhenie pravitel'stva Rossiiskoi Federatsii ot 25.10.2005 No. 1789-p "O kontseptsii administrativnoi reformy v Rossiiskoi Federatsii v 2006-2008 godakh" [Direction of the government of the Russian Federation from 25.10.2005 on the program of administrative reform in the Russian Federation in 2006-2008].
4. Rasporiazhenie pravitel'stva Rossiiskoi Federatsii ot 25.10.2005 No. 1789-p, Annex.
5. Government effectiveness refers to the quality of public services, the quality of the civil service and its degree of independence from political pressures, the quality of policy formulation and implementation, and the credibility of the government's

commitment to such policies. Regulatory quality refers to the ability of the government to formulate and implement sound policies and regulations that permit and promote private sector development.
6. Practices of *dedovshchina* common in the Soviet and post-Soviet military perfectly illustrates this point. The *dedovshchina* involves the unconditional submission of conscripts and "freshmen" to more senior soldiers—regardless of their official rank—and sometimes takes very humiliating forms (Sieca-Kozlowski & Daucé, 2006). Humiliating orders, however, undermine any prospects for genuine cooperation necessary, for example, in action. Not surprisingly, the Russian-Georgian confrontation in South Ossetia in August 2008 ended up with a few cases of desertion from Russian ranks caused by the *dedovshchina*.
7. Fifty-three percent in the Chuvash Republic, 52 percent in the region of Krasnoyarsk, 50 percent in the region of Samara and 47 percent in the region of Saratov.
8. Shining Path is the English translation for *Sendero Luminoso*, a guerrilla movement in Peru oriented against the power elites in that country and capitalist imperialism. It was particularly active and violent in the 1980s and early 1990s.
9. See Section III of the Introduction and Subsection I.2 of Chapter 5.
10. Set refers to "an initial, fundamental reaction to a situation where there is a problem to be considered and solved" (Uznadze, 1966, p. 10). In contrast to the concept of habitus, the theory of set, first, derives from numerous experiments and, second, implies a more limited capacity for reactivation in other contexts. The last characteristic makes the set more flexible and prone to dynamic adaptation than habitus (a more comprehensive comparison of the two concepts can be found in Oleinik, 2003, pp. 27-31). These important breakthroughs, nevertheless, appear to be achieved at the expense of attention to links between psychological structures and the institutional environment.
11. Habit of thought, like habitus, involves strong connections between the individual- and institutional-level phenomena. Individual habits, according to Veblen, tend to be associated with particular patterns of interactions, like conspicuous consumption (see the Introduction, Endnote 26) or invidious comparison proper to capitalist competition. In the most general terms, a "heightened facility of expression in a given direction ... is called habit" (Veblen, 1939, p. 106).
12. It is worth highlighting the substantial differences between the approach in terms of the power triad and a "capture" theory of regulation popular in neoclassical economic literature. Both theories acknowledge a leading role of interests of actors involved in market transactions. For instance, the "capture" theory of regulation "is based upon self-interested motives of demanders and suppliers" of state regulation (Ekelund & Hébert, 2007, p. 549; see also Tullock, 2005; Subsection I.4 of Chapter 7). Their interests lead them to seek various restrictions and barriers that distort market structure. In the terms introduced above, C refers to a supplier, A and B—to demanders. Nevertheless, first, the approach proposed in this book links interests to underlying habituses/sets/habits of thought instead of assuming their exogenous character. Second, in contrast to the "capture" theory, no assumption of C's neutrality is made (C plays a passive role because the regulator is "captured" either by A or B in function of particular circumstances). The priority of reproducing and strengthening the existing model of power guides C's actions who takes initiatives when distorting market structure. Third, C's neutrality seems possible only in conditions of a democratic political process, which implies perfectly free and competitive elections, whereas the power triad may emerge in a variety of institutional contexts ranging from a power-centered society to all kinds of imperfect, or "realist" democracy (see Section III of Chapter 2).

298 Market as a Weapon

13. The definition of the private and public spheres, like most other concepts in the social sciences, has a contested character (see also Introduction to Chapter 2). For instance, Jürgen Habermas sees a key distinctive feature of the public sphere in particularities of discourse and "communicative action" in this realm: "more than anything else, it is criticism that characterizes the life of the public sphere" (Broman, 1998, p. 129; see also Stewart, 2001, Ch. 5).
14. For the region considered in-depth in Chapter 7, a simple comparison of two lists of most influential people, in politics and in the economic sphere, indicates a significant overlap: out of 32 most economically influential people 17 represent regional political leaders and top office holders, out of 29 most politically influential people 7 represent business. 21 individuals out of 61, 34.4 percent, secure a place on both lists simultaneously (*Samye vliiatel'nye ljudi Rossii*, 2004, pp. 358-361).
15. "Government will be stable … if a high degree of resemblance exists in patterns adjacent to government and one finds throughout the more distant segments a marked departure from functionally appropriate patterns for the sake of imitating the governmental pattern or extensive imitation of the governmental pattern in ritual practices" (Eckstein, 1966, p. 240). The question as to how to define and, especially, measure the degree of congruence represents a separate issue. Eckstein (1966, pp. 236-239) mentions two forms of congruence: identity and isomorphic patterns (gradual resemblance). Several other approaches also focus on structural and functional similarities lying at the origin of congruence (Oleinik, 2002a).
16. This drift is best illustrated by the accounting scandals involving Enron and WorldCom in 2001-2002 in the United States whereas "business according to understanding", i.e., informal and sometimes criminal norms, prevailed in Russia in the 1990s (Oleinik, 2002b).
17. Russia in Chechnya since the first half of the 1990s, the United States in Iraq and Afghanistan (on the last case, see Oleinik, 2008b).
18. For instance, Andreff (1992, p. 72) illustrates how it works referring to the mathematical concept of congruence.
19. E.g., similar problems at a particular stage of technological development—problems of a "risk society" (Beck, 1992)—prompt similar solutions.
20. The story of Andrei Shleifer, a professor of economics at Harvard, represents a case in point. A leading specialist on issues of privatization (Boycko, Shleifer & Vishny, 1995), Shleifer used his insider's knowledge as a key consultant of the Russian government when investing on the Russian stock market and thus violating terms of the contract with the US Agency for International Development (*The Harvard Crimson* from July 29, 2005; retrieved from http://www.thecrimson.com/article.aspx?ref=508343). This example illustrates the learning how to do business without reference to the law or ethical principles.
21. As of the end of 2009, Schröeder is chair of the Shareholders' Committee of Nord Stream AG, the project of a pipeline in which Russian state-owned company Gazprom has a 51 percent majority stake.
22. In 2006, 33 percent of the European Union's imports of crude oil came from Russia, whereas OPEC countries supplied 38 percent (European Commission, 2008, p. 7).
23. Russia had a 42 percent share of the EU's imports of natural gas in 2006, whereas the second largest supplier, Norway, had a 24 percent share (Ibid).
24. For instance, Richard Pipes (2000) strongly opposes Russian historical path to that of England, whereas Vladimir Putin feels free to draw parallels between his power-sharing arrangement with Dmitry Medvedev, his successor to the highest office, and that of Tony Blair, prime minister of the United Kingdom between 1997 and 2007, with Gordon Brown, who assumed the highest executive office in 2007 and

occupied it till 2010 without confirming his mandate by an election (see Endnote 19 of the Introduction). Whether Putin is right or wrong concerning the substance of his comparison necessitates a careful comparative research using the most recent empirical data.

25. Data of the Bureau of Economic Analysis, the US Department of Commerce, retrieved from http://www.bea.gov/national/xls/gdplev.xls.
26. An official website, www.recovery.gov was created in order to help taxpayers track their money spent under the Act "from below."
27. Section 3 of the Memorandum requires, namely, that all communications with registered lobbyists concerning applications for the funds made available under the Act must be in writing and have to be subsequently posted on the Recovery website. The Memorandum does not apply to the tax-related provisions of the Act. Moreover, the Memorandum does not apply to non-lobbyist employees of lobbyist employers.
28. Carmakers are mentioned in 50 percent of major US and world English-language publications retrieved using the key sentence "access to bailout funds" with the help of LexisNexis Academic on October 7, 2009 (N=10). The Google search with identical parameters produces a similar picture: 36.4 percent of the references concern carmakers, 26.1 percent—banks and 20.5 percent—insurers (N=88).
29. Similar policies in Japan in the late 1990s induced the process of concentration in the banking industry because regional banks did not get access to the bailout funds, which only amplified structural biases favoring the "selected few" (Herbener, Jeffrey M. [1999], The Rise and Fall of the Japanese Miracle, *Mises Daily* from September 20; retrieved from http://mises.org/story/298).
30. Krugman, Paul, How Did Economists Get It So Wrong?, *The New York Times* from September 6, 2009; retrieved from http://www.nytimes.com/2009/09/06/magazine/06Economic-t.html.
31. Keynes (1936) in Chapter 12 of his *General Theory of Employment, Interest and Money* compares the stock market with newspaper beauty contests and describes it in terms of "animal spirits" that have very little in common with rational considerations. In contrast, the Introduction and Chapter 5 consider how one can find a compromise between the model of rational choice and some theories that exclude the assumption of rationality.
32. Among rather rare exceptions, scholars mention "Reagan's administrative presidency [that] structured incentives in a way that altered bureaucrats' self-interest calculations and led to a great deal of bureaucratic compliance" (Golden, 2000, p. 23).
33. From traditional ties, from slavery, even from the danger of death: "the market for the redemption of prisoners of war saved many human lives, diminished their sufferings, and generally decreased the brutality of war" (Frey & Buhofer, 1986, p. 739).

10

Methodological Appendix: Mixing Quantitative and Qualitative Content Analysis

Introduction: The Text as a Key Source of Information in the Humanities and Social Sciences

Although the subject matter of the natural sciences—the objective reality—can be studied directly, the humanities and social sciences deal with the reality *as we perceive it* in essentially indirect manners. For instance, Max Weber (1968, p. 4) sees the specific purpose of sociology in discovering the subjective meaning attached to social action. The external observer discovers a subjective meaning attributed by the actor only indirectly, by studying traces that his or her actions leave on material objects, visual images, texts, pieces of art and so forth.

The text, whether it is an official document, a novel, the transcript of an interview or a personal diary, is a key source of information about the subjective perceptions and justifications elaborated by the actor so that the other interacting parties correctly interpret and "decipher" his or her intentions. Highlighting this fact, Vladimir Bibler considers the text to be *the* key source of information in the humanities. The humanities scholar "does not deal with an empirical subject, but with a *possible*, *assumed* subject as he represents himself in his other being—in the *text*" (Bibler, 1991, p. 72; emphasis in the original; see also Lotman, 1990, pp. 2-4).

Viewed from this perspective, the relevance of content analysis goes far beyond narrowly defined boundaries of semiotics, hermeneutics, linguistics, and a few other disciplines in the humanities and social sciences. Content analysis then transforms into a key methodological tool of humanitarian and social inquiries. The fact that there exist highly heterogeneous techniques of content analysis commonly producing divergent outcomes makes such status of content analysis questionable. The main dividing line lies between qualitative content analysis with its stronghold in semiotics and quantitative content analysis, which is widely used by linguists. The present appendix focuses on discussing possible solutions for dealing with the instability and divergence of the outcomes of content analysis that undermine its methodological value and status.

Marilyn White and Emily Marsh (2006) usefully summarize key distinctions between the qualitative and quantitative versions of content analysis. Namely, they point out their different ontological and epistemological roots: quantitative analysis is positivist in its orientation whereas qualitative analysis is "interpretativist"; the first is "objectivist" whereas the second—"constructivist." Quantitative content analysis relies on techniques of random sampling and highly standardized coding schemes. Purposeful samples and "grounded" coding schemes tend to dominate in qualitative content analysis. Because of this, qualitative content analysis is criticized for its highly subjective character and difficulties with controlling the impact of the coder's personality, his or her particular background, interests and even mood at the moment of coding. Criticisms of quantitative content analysis refer to another logic: they suggest that the exclusive reliance on frequencies and probabilities makes the humanities and social sciences a province of the natural sciences and places their own project in jeopardy.

The existence of two alternative approaches within quantitative content analysis further complicates the situation. On one hand, the correlational tradition heavily emphasizes co-occurrences of words; it classifies words in function of their co-occurrence with other words. On the other hand, the substitution tradition implies that classifications of words derive not from simple co-occurrences but from *ad-hoc* dictionaries built by the researcher to test particular hypotheses and theories. Correlated words form "themes" in the former case and "categories" in the latter. "These two traditions [do] not stand easily for a team photograph" (Hogenraad et al., 2003, p. 222). Figure 10.1 shows a simple taxonomy of divergent approaches in content analysis.

Calls for finding a middle ground and overcoming existing oppositions are not uncommon. For instance, Eco (1990, p. x) urges qualitative content analysts to introduce "into the study of literary texts the methods of linguistic structuralism, semiotic, of Information Theory, cybernetics

Figure 10.1
Traditions in Content Analysis

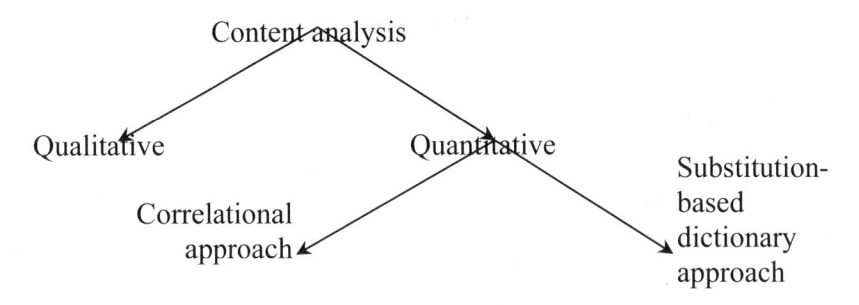

```
                Content analysis
                /             \
         Qualitative         Quantitative
                            /           \
         Correlational                Substitution-
         approach                     based
                                      dictionary
                                      approach
```

and mathematical-statistical analysis." In other words, his idea involves combining semiotics with methods of quantitative content analysis. Ermakov et al. (2004) use methods of both qualitative and quantitative (the correlational approach) content analysis when inquiring into the image of power in Russian culture and the impact of a particular model of power observed in this country on linguistic structures. However, qualitative and quantitative methods are rarely used concurrently and applied to the same text, which complicates the task of comparing their results. An original methodology for confronting outcomes of qualitative and quantitative content analyses is outlined in what follows and tested on two different sets of texts.

Section I discusses various issues in the reliability and validity of different forms of triangulation applied to content analysis. It helps formulate two research questions as to how to measure the reliability and validity of alternative analyses of the same text. Path-models for various forms of content analysis of the same text are outlined in Section II. Section III describes the two sets of texts—transcripts of in-depth unstructured and semi-structured interviews carried out in the framework of two separate research projects—used for testing the path-model empirically. Section IV presents outcomes of a series of empirical tests performed with the help of software programs for content analysis QDA Miner version 2.0.8 and WordStat version 5.1.12. Some directions for further developments are proposed in the Conclusion.

I. Reliability and Validity of Various Forms of Triangulation

Practices of combining different methods of research, including in the field of content analysis, are commonly referred to as triangulation. The idea of triangulation and its forms (Jick, 1979)—"within method" (the use of multiple techniques within a given method) and "between methods" (the use of two or more distinct methods to analyze the same data)—seems easy to grasp. However, in practice, the task of integrating multiple methods, cross-checking the reliability and validity of their outcomes represents a serious challenge. "There is little evidence in the literature to suggest how different research methods might be integrated" (Gray & Densten, 1998, p. 420).

The key problem lies in finding a common denominator for qualitative and quantitative data without which meaningful comparisons of the outcomes of "between methods" triangulation are hardly possible. How can the data be converted from one format to the other, how can it be translated without losing much information? Jick (1979, p. 609) argues in favor of converting the numerical data into a format suitable for qualitative analysis: "Qualitative data and analysis function as the glue that cements the interpretation of multi-method results." However, this approach makes replication extremely difficult, even virtually impossible. Further, there is no way to assess the reliability of triangulation and its outcomes. Similarly to the case of field-notes and accounts written by an anthropologist about his or her journey to an exotic and distant country, the perception of the outcomes of triangulation with a qualitative denominator depends on the personal reputation of their author (Geertz, 1988). They may be deemed valid if the scholar appears trustworthy, but hardly reliable because of his or her unique personality and reputation.

The search for a quantitative denominator has pitfalls as well. It may involve a significant loss of qualitative information when converting it into a numerical form. Most software programs for content analysis allow for *either* its qualitative version *or* its quantitative version, which prevents the retrieval of output in a compatible numerical format. In the best case, the question about reliability, i.e., "whether the results of a study are repeatable" (Bryman, 2004, p. 28), is answered *separately* for qualitative and quantitative content analyses of the same text. Reliability of quantitative content analysis involves recounting words and their clusters, themes and categories, using various software programs and different hardware.[1]

The reliability of qualitative coding is conventionally measured with the help of inter-coder agreement coefficients. They range from simple percent agreement $PA_O = \frac{Total\ A's}{n}$, where A refers to the number of units for which the coders agree and n—to the total number of coded units, to more sophisticated coefficients that allow for the discounting of high levels of agreement due to chance. Their list includes Cohen's *kappa*, Scott's *pi* and Krippendorff's *alpha* (Neuendorf, 2002, pp. 153-158; Warner, 2008, pp. 833-834). Of these three, Cohen's *kappa* $\kappa = \frac{PA_O - PA_E}{1 - PA_E}$, where PA_E refers to the chance level of agreement, is most widely used. An inter-coder agreement coefficient exceeding 0.7 suggests an acceptable level of reliability (Gray & Densten, 1998, p. 423).

The assessment of the reliability of qualitative coding requires time and substantial human resources. Budget constraints limit the scope of involving at least one additional coder, let alone several, especially in the case of doctoral research. Concurrent qualitative content analyses also appear very time consuming as, along with the time required for multiple readings by each coder, the coders also need to get together—often several times—and discuss common coding policies and their application.

The task is further complicated by the necessity to assess the reliability of triangulation, or the joint reliability of qualitative and quantitative content analyses of the same text. Strategies for assessing it are neither known nor have they been empirically tested. This prompts the first research question addressed here as to *how can the reliability of triangulation be measured, both "within method" and "between method," in content analysis*. An ideal algorithm should also satisfy the criterion of efficiency by saving time and human resources, which makes the research question more specific: "How can the reliability of triangulation be measured in a reasonable amount of time?"

The situation for assessing the validity of content analysis presents even more challenges. "Validity is concerned with the integrity of the conclusions that are generated from a piece of research" (Bryman, 2004, p. 73). A repeatedly observed character of patterns of themes and categories does not guarantee that they accurately tap the meaning of the text. In fact, the text does not necessarily have a unique meaning. Lotman (1990, Ch. 3) differentiates two types of the text: logical and rhetorical. The purpose of the former lies in conveying the author's message—single and unambiguous. A valid content analysis should then catch and "decipher" this message as accurately as possible. The rhetorical text, on the contrary, is intended to prompt discussions and various interpretations. Bakhtin's (1979) concept of "polyphonic novel"[2] containing a plurality of "voices" with their own "truths" along with the author's concept clearly corresponds to this type of the text. The validity of the outcomes of content analysis, then, has to be judged with respect to a particular position and "readings" chosen by the coder.

The two traditions in quantitative content analysis allow for switching positions in keeping with the type of the text. The correlational tradition appears appropriate for analyzing the logical text. This approach allows for a "representational" reading. The substitution tradition fits the spirit of the rhetorical texts with multiple readings that it prompts. "When a researcher understands texts representationally, they are used to identify their sources' intended meanings. When a researcher understands texts instrumentally, they are interpreted in terms of the researcher's theory" (Roberts, 2000, p. 262). This citation highlights ambiguities with identifying the exact type of the analyzed text: in some case it can be classified either in one category or in the other. Nevertheless, the structure of the text can be considered a proxy for its type: "The less structured the text, the more structuring and categorizing must be the analysis" (Hogenaraad et al., 2003, p. 226). A textbook chapter conveys a unique message about knowledge accumulated in a particular field, which calls for a representational reading. Table 10.1 summarizes possible combinations of the type of text and the type of its reading. Qualitative analysis—as a result of its subjective component—has some "elective affinity" with instrumental reading.

The existence of multiple points of reference—the author's intention, the readers' interests—turns into an advantage when triangulating outcomes of qualitative and quantitative content analysis. "The [convergent] validity of a measure ought to be gauged by comparing it to measures of the same concept developed through other methods" (Bryman, 2004, p. 73). This explains the second research question addressed here, namely *how to measure validity of triangulation, both "within method" and*

Table 10.1
Type of Content Analysis in Keeping with the Type of the Text and the Type of the Reading

		Type of reading	
		Representational	Instrumental
Type of text	Logical	Correlational tradition of quantitative content analysis	Substitution tradition of quantitative content analysis (*ex ante* built dictionaries); qualitative content analysis
	Rhetorical	Substitution tradition of quantitative content analysis (*ex post* built dictionaries); qualitative content analysis	Qualitative content analysis

"between method," in content analysis simultaneously controlling the reference point.

II. Path-Models for Content Analysis

A series of path-models help address the issues of reliability and validity in content analysis. They derive from the idea of mapping the outcomes of quantitative and qualitative content analyses of the same text and quantitatively measuring the strength of the relationship between different points on this map. Content analysis of a logical text can be visualized with the help of a path starting at a point corresponding to the text's intended meaning (Figure 10.2). In quantitative terms, this point can be described by a vector of themes, or clusters of co-occurring words: $T = \langle t_1, t_2, t_3 ... t_n \rangle$. The correlational approach in quantitative content analysis serves to specify its parameters. The end point of the path is represented by a constellation of qualitative codes $Q = \langle q_1, q_2, q_3 ... q_n \rangle$. These codes are attributed by the reader (coder) in his or her attempts to decipher the original meaning of the text conveyed by the author. The path goes through a middle point, a vector of categories $C = \langle c_1, c_2, c_3 ... c_n \rangle$. C's parameters refer to frequencies of particular entries in the *ad hoc* dictionary based on substitution. When creating an entry, the reader again thinks about the author's original meaning. The fact that the themes, the categories and the qualitative codes all have the same purpose of conveying the author's intentions makes quantitative relationships between vectors *T*, *C* and *Q* meaningful.

Content analysis of the rhetorical texts involves changing the start point. In this case, the path starts from a constellation of qualitative codes $Q_j = \langle q_{1j}, q_{2j}, q_{3j} ... q_{nj} \rangle$ attributed in keeping with a particular reader's interests and theories. Since, usually, there is no single reader but rather several (*j*=1...m) readers,[3] it is worth speaking about the paths in the plural. Even the same reader can adapt divergent approaches to the same text and read it from various perspectives. All paths lead to the same end point, the text, even if they highlight different parts of it and, hence,

Figure 10.2
Path-Model for Content Analysis of the Logical Text

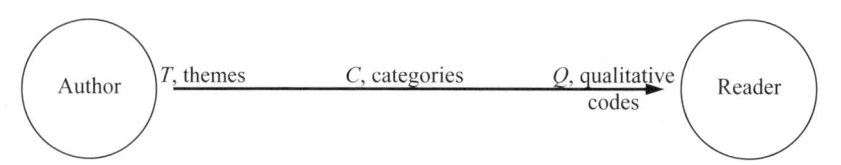

Author — *T*, themes — *C*, categories — *Q*, qualitative codes → Reader

different parts of vector T. Each of these paths goes through a particular middle point whose exact position can be located with the help of vector $C_j = \langle c_{1j}, c_{2j}, c_{3j}...c_{nj} \rangle$. However, categories in the dictionary based on substitution this time derive from a reader's interests and theories instead of the author's.[4] In the final account, the path model for analyzing the rhetorical text resembles a spark (Figure 10.3).

It is legitimate to ask how strongly vectors located on a particular path are associated. Furthermore, links between vectors at the same level of the path model, e.g., between all vectors of categories C or between all vectors of qualitative codes Q, can also be explored. However, the interpretation of associations will depend on the research question. If reliability is at stake, then one set of associations counts; if validity—the other. The basic path model has to be adjusted accordingly.

II.1 Assessing Reliability of Content Analysis

In this case, reliability refers to uniformity and consistency in coding texts using a specific frame of analysis: either the author's perspective or the reader's. If a single reader codes a series of texts, the degree of reliability of his or her content analysis can be assessed without involving additional coders and training them to apply the same set of criteria. The principal emphasis shall be placed on measuring associations between

Figure 10.3
Path-Model for Content Analysis of the Rhetorical Text

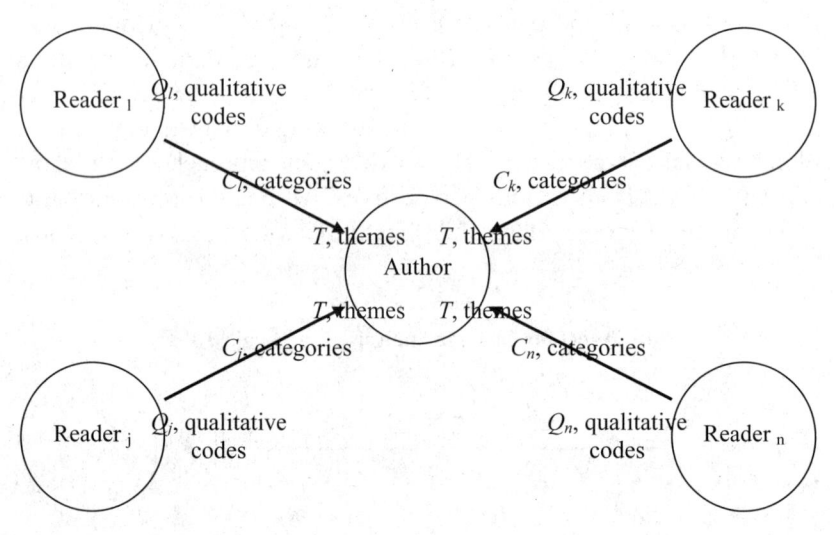

vectors *T*, *C* and *Q* lying on the same path while using text as the unit of analysis.

Each of the points on the path can be represented in a matrix form (Table 10.2). Rows in these matrices correspond to cases (texts), columns—to variables (themes in matrix *T*, categories in matrix *C* and qualitatively coded segments in matrix *Q*). Cell values then contain the information about the presence or absence of a particular theme, category or code in a given text or their frequencies. Distances between rows or columns—depending on the choice of the unit of analysis—can be measured by means of factor analysis.[5] Factor analysis, a data reduction technique, offers additional opportunities for exploring patterns of relationships between units of analysis, as will be shown in the Conclusion.

At this stage, only one element of factor analysis, the use of the cosine of the angle between two vectors to measure the distance between them, is used. "The cosine is a measure of the angle between two *t*-dimensional object vectors when the vectors are considered as ordinary vectors in a space of *t* dimensions" (Salton & McGill, 1983, p. 203). The cosine coefficient of similarity

$$SIM_{Cos}(text_i, text_j) = \frac{\sum_{k=1}^{t}(VAR_k \times VAR_k)}{\sqrt{\left(\sum_{k=1}^{t}VAR_k^2 \times \sum_{k=1}^{t}VAR_k^2\right)}}$$

accounts for the length of the text: a short one can still be compared with a long one (Grossman & Frieder, 2004, p. 19). The frequency with which a variable VAR_k occurs can be weighted by the inverse frequency of the texts containing it $TF * IDF = VAR_k \times \log\left(\frac{N}{n_k}\right)$, where *N* is the total number of texts, *n*—the number of texts containing VAR_k, in order to increase the precision of the instrument (Salton & McGill, 1983, p. 62; Grossman & Frieder, 2004, p. 2).

A reliable content analysis implies a high level of congruence between matrices *T*, *C* and *Q*. In other words, a particular text occupies a

Table 10.2
Matrix Representation of Vectors

	Variable₁	Variable₂	…	Variableⱼ
Text₁				
Text₂				
…				
Textᵢ				

similar position in all of them with respect to the other texts as a result of consistency in identifying themes and categories and in attributing qualitative codes provided that the categories and qualitative codes derive from the same perspective (the author's or a reader's). In this case, triangulation serves to assess a reader's consistency in qualitative coding across texts that he or she coded, with themes and categories serving as "yardsticks" against which qualitative codes are judged. Coding patterns are compared across texts, not across readers. If the values of the cosine coefficient for the same text in matrices T, C and Q are associated, then content analysis produces reliable outcomes.

The list of possible measures of association, congruence, between the matrices includes the Pearson correlation coefficient r between raw values of the cosine coefficients and Spearman's rank correlation coefficient rho. If the latter is chosen, the texts have to be rank-ordered according to the degree of their similarity. This option involves a significant loss of information, which is particularly visible when the sample of analyzed texts is small. The Pearson correlation coefficient does not have this shortcoming.

The calculation of partial correlation coefficients, for instance, between matrices T and Q, also makes sense. This serves to control the impact of the dictionary based on substitution that lies at the origin of matrix C and answer the question as to whether it can be considered a confounding variable, an intervening variable or a source of spuriousness.

Two strategies exist in regard to selecting the *centroid*, or the vector selected as the origin for the purpose of comparisons. In principle, "the choice of point selected as origin does not affect the result" (Basilevsky, 1994, p. 283). However, measurement errors and even minor inconsistencies in coding may affect the overall result when changing the centroid. To minimize the impact of non-systematic inconsistencies and errors, one of vectors with the highest similarity index in a matrix shall be chosen as the centroid. For rhetorical texts, matrix Q seems appropriate for identifying the centroid that will be used for calculating the cosine coefficients in matrices T and C as well; for the logical texts—matrices C or T. The other related problem consists in deciding whether one or several centroids are to be selected for multiple readings of a set of rhetorical texts. "Pure" rhetorical texts call for the latter option, "mixed" cases (rhetorical texts with some elements of logical texts) make it possible to select just one centroid.

To summarize, the assessment of reliability of the within (quantitative) method triangulation involves calculating the Pearson coefficients of correlation between the cosine coefficients of similarity of cases in matrices T and C. Reliability of the between (qualitative and quantitative) methods of triangulation can be gauged by calculating the Pearson coefficients of correlation between the cosine coefficients of similarity of cases in matrices and C and Q and partial correlation coefficients—in matrices T and Q. Triangulation carried out in a reliable manner, in turn, suggests that outcomes of qualitative and quantitative content analyses are also reliable.

II.2 Assessing Validity of Content Analysis

If words and text fragments are consistently placed in the same theme, category or qualitative code, another question arises: do these measures adequately tap the author's or the reader's concepts? To address this question, the degree of the validity of content analysis needs to be gauged. This can be done after making a few adjustments and corrections in the path model outlined above. First, the unit of analysis is no longer the case, but the variable (theme, category or qualitative code).[6] It helps see whether similar constellations of qualitative codes and categories characterize similar texts. Second, validity means congruence in the distribution of themes, categories and qualitative codes. Equal distances separate, on one side, two given qualitative codes in matrix Q and, on the other side, two corresponding categories in matrix C if both qualitative codes and categories in the dictionary based on substitution derive from the same underlying concepts. This involves calculating the cosine coefficients of similarity between themes, categories and qualitative codes and then cross-correlating these coefficients.

The valid within (quantitative) method of content analysis implies that values of the cosine coefficients of similarity between variables in matrices T and C are correlated. This is possible, when the dictionary based on substitution does not corrupt the original language of the text. A strong correlation between the values of the cosine coefficients of similarity between variables in matrices Q, C and T indicates the validity of the between (qualitative and quantitative) method of content analysis. Finally, the validity of triangulation increases one's confidence in the validity of the outcomes of qualitative and quantitative analyses. Valid triangulation conditions the convergent validity of the categories and qualitative codes used in content analysis. The latter serves as the criterion indicator for the former and *vice versa*.

II.3 Criteria for Assessing the Path Model

Several criteria have to be kept in mind when evaluating the proposed path model. First, there is a systematic measurement error when relying on the values of the Pearson correlation coefficients to assess the degree of congruence between the cosine coefficients in the three matrices (except between matrices T and C). In fact, the values of the Pearson correlation coefficients depend not only on the degree of the reliability and validity of content analysis, but also on the inherent differences between qualitative and quantitative content analyses. For instance, qualitative coding can have different levels of "depth," ranging from taking the text at face value (manifest qualitative coding) to reading "between lines" (latent qualitative coding). Quantitative coding has far fewer degrees of freedom in this respect. Consequently, one can predict stronger correlations between the cosine coefficients of similarity for matrices T and C (both refer to quantitative content analysis) than for matrices C and Q (because matrix Q contains the outcomes of qualitative content analysis).

Conventionally calculated inter-coder agreement coefficients provide a yardstick for assessing the values of the Person correlation coefficients for matrices Q and C, as well as Q and T. Inter-coder agreement coefficients arguably account for possible variation in the levels of depth in qualitative content analysis. Thus, the Person correlation coefficients can be "standardized' to the level of agreement deemed acceptable for the purpose of assessing the reliability of content analysis.[7] In fact, in this case, the Person correlation coefficient is nothing other than a particular inter-coder agreement coefficient calculated for the same coder at different moments in time (i.e., there is a kind of multiplication of his or her self in time). For instance, if the value of the inter-coder agreement coefficient deemed acceptable is 0.8, then a Person correlation coefficient for matrices Q and C equal to 0.6 in fact suggests a stronger association—and the degree of reliability of results—in the order of 0.75 ($r = \dfrac{0.6}{0.8}$; i.e., one controls for the particularities of qualitative content analysis).

Second, the dictionary based on substitution and, thus, matrix C, can be built either *ex ante* or *ex post* qualitative content analysis—with rather different outcomes. The *ex ante* built dictionaries have the following flaw: "it lifts the words out of context" (Hogenraad et al., 2003, p. 225). This flaw brings matrix C closer to matrix T by increasing the strength of the association between them and farther from matrix Q by weakening the strength of their association. The *ex post* built dictionaries have the opposite effect on the path-model: entries in them are contextualized and "customized" to a particular text subject to content analysis. In other words, the *ex ante* dictionary contains words and phrases suitable for describing concepts in general, whereas the *ex post* dictionary shows how these concepts are described by a given author or group of authors.

Third, long texts tend to deflate the values of the cosine coefficients of similarity. Long vectors in which they are transformed include many variables. As a result, the probability of a perfect fit between long vectors decreases (Salton & McGill, 1983, p. 203).

III. Description of the Data: Content Analysis of In-Depth Interviews

The path model was empirically tested on two sets of in-depth qualitative interviews with state representatives and experts on the issues of state service in the Russian Federation. In one case, interviews were more structured than in the other, which allows applying the path model to the content analysis of various types of texts. The interviews were conducted within the framework of two separate research projects, by two independent research teams, each containing several interviewers (see Section V of the Introduction). Although both studies focused on the power elite, they addressed different research questions: (i) what are the key characteristics of a particular model of power relationships that structures interactions within Russia's power elite and between its members and ordinary men and women (the "Bureaucrats" project); (ii) whether members of Russia's power elite play a stabilizing or destabilizing role in socio-economic development (the "Crisis" project). Here as everywhere in the book, the set of interviews conducted in the framework of the "Bureaucrats" project is referred to as set "A" and the other one, carried out in the framework of the "Crisis" project, set "B." Table 10.3 summarizes their principal parameters.

The two sets of transcripts represent a good fit for testing the path model. First, the transcripts represent a highly diversified collection of texts. As the mean standard deviations suggest, their length varies significantly (more—in set "A", less—in set "B"). If the proposed strategy of triangulation works under these conditions, one could safely assume that it will perform better when applied to less heterogeneous sets, such as summaries of scientific articles (analyzed in Hogenaraad et al., 2003) or texts of small ads published in newspapers.

Table 10.3
Parameters of Two Sets of Interviews Subjected to Content Analysis

	Set "A"	Set "B"
Period of time	2006-2008	2005
Type of qualitative interviews	Semi-structured	Unstructured
Total number of interviews	64	43
Total number of words	284,124	148,292
Mean number of characters	35,062	22,998
Standard deviation for Mean number of characters	22,515	8,091

Second, transcripts of in-depth interviews can be read in an instrumental as well as in a representational manner. Structured interviews have two "authors": the interviewee and the interviewer, who produces the interview guide. After conducting and transcribing the interview, the interviewer transforms into the reader attributing codes and creating entries in the dictionary based on substitution. In other words, the format of the qualitative interview provides a rare opportunity for switching from the author's position to the reader's and, consequently, from a representative reading to an instrumental one. Multiple readings of the same text further allow for assessing how close it lies to the logical and rhetorical formats. This can potentially be done by comparing the strength of associations between matrices T, C and Q lying on various axes of the spark-type path-model. If the values of the Pearson correlation coefficients in one set substantially exceed the corresponding values in the others, it would indicate a rhetorical nature of the text.

For that reason, the content of both sets of transcripts was analyzed from multiple perspectives, i.e., using multiple "frames." The "crisis" framework (a codebook containing descriptions of thirteen qualitative codes grouped under three headings: "instability," "stabilizing factors" and "destabilizing factors" plus a dictionary based on substitution with a similar structure; see Subsection III.3 of the Appendix) is derived as closely as possible from the interview guide for set "B": this refers to the "author's perspective" in this case. However, the "crisis" framework was also used in the content analysis of set "A" where it represented a "reader's perspective"—one of several. *Vice versa*, the "bureaucrats" frame (a codebook with forty-one qualitative codes grouped under five headings: "business," "constitution," "constraints," "critical situation" and "hour-glass society" plus a dictionary based on substitution with a similar structure; see Subsection III.1 of the Appendix) suggests a representational reading of set "A" and an instrumental reading of set "B." A third frame, "power" (a codebook consisting of fifteen qualitative codes grouped under three headings: "power in a pure form," "techniques for imposing will" and "domination by virtue of a constellation of interests" plus a corresponding dictionary based on substitution; see Subsection III.2 of the Appendix), lies closer to the research questions explored in the "bureaucrats" project, but provides a new perspective for reading the transcripts. In the end, the content of each transcript was analyzed using the three frameworks outlined above.

The dictionaries based on substitution derive from a combination of the *ex ante* and the *ex post* techniques for building them (see Section IV of the Appendix). At the first stage, a list of words and phrases that presumably fit each code from the codebook was prepared. Then, after the qualitative content analysis was carried out, they were contextualized and "fine-tuned" using particular expressions frequently found in the transcripts. Thus, instead of containing samples of ordinary and "plain" language, the dictionaries index a particular language spoken by the Russian state servants and experts interviewed. The comparison of the number of words classified under the three dictionaries based on substitution suggests that they have a very similar "categorizing" power with a slightly better grasp of meaningful expressions in set "B" (Table 10.4; questions and remarks made by the interviewers were excluded from analysis).

Two modules of a software program, QDA Miner and WordStat, can be used to perform all forms of content analysis in virtually any language (Russian in this case) without spending much time and resources on converting the data sets when switching from qualitative to quantitative content analysis and to retrieve outcomes in a compatible format. These two modules can be used to produce the T, C and Q matrices. The values of the coefficients of similarity between the vectors[8] were exported into SPSS version 16.0 to calculate the coefficients of correlation (this also can be done using a third module of the software program for content

Table 10.4
N of Words Categorized under the Dictionaries Based on Substitution

	Set "A"		Set "B"	
	Count	%	Count	%
Total word count	284,349	100	148,369	100
N of words categorized under the "bureaucrats" dictionary	26,192	9.2	19,446	13.1
N of words categorized under the "crisis" dictionary	26,427	9.3	19,294	13
N of words categorized under the "power" dictionary	21,918	7.7	16,010	10.8

analysis, SimStat). Only one person—the author—was involved in coding fragments of the interviews and building the dictionaries based on substitution.

IV. Discussion: On the Plurality of Readings

Several iterations in attributing qualitative coding appeared necessary to achieve a satisfactory—at least moderately so—strength of associations between matrices Q, C and T (the Pearson coefficient of correlation exceeding .25 or .3125 on the scale "standardized" to 0.8). Depending on the particular set of interviews and the framework applied in a specific reading, the desired outcome was achieved after 2 to 4 iterations. In other words, each of 107 transcripts was read and coded ten times on average, which took more than six months of work in all (not counting the time spent on transcribing, the initial reading, developing and improving the interview guides). Furthermore, fragments of various transcripts coded in a similar manner were also retrieved and re-read "across transcripts," in order to ensure consistency in qualitative coding. This amount of time far exceeds that necessary to process a purely quantitative data set, but certainly falls short of the time budget required for content analysis by a group of coders. It also seems affordable for a PhD student working on his or her thesis.

As a result of the arguably rhetorical nature of the analyzed texts, matrix Q was used to identify the centroid. Two versions of the path model for assessing the reliability of the content analysis were tested both on set "A" and set "B": with a single centroid identified through the path of the "original" reading (the "bureaucrats" framework for the set "A," the "crisis" framework for set "B") and with three centroids identified for each path.

The values of the Pearson correlations between the cosine coefficients of similarity in matrices lying on the same path correspond to the pattern predicted in Subsection II.1 (Figure 10.4). Associations between matrices T_i and C_i (the within method triangulation) tend to be stronger than between, matrices C_i and Q_i, on the one hand, and matrices T_i and Q_i (the between methods triangulation), on the other. Association only between two matrices, C_1 and Q_1 (one pair out of eight), suggests that a further improvement in qualitative coding using the "crisis" codebook may be desirable.

It also makes sense to calculate coefficients of the partial correlation between the cosine coefficients of similarity in matrices T_i and Q_i and compare them with the Pearson coefficients of correlation. This serves

Methodological Appendix 317

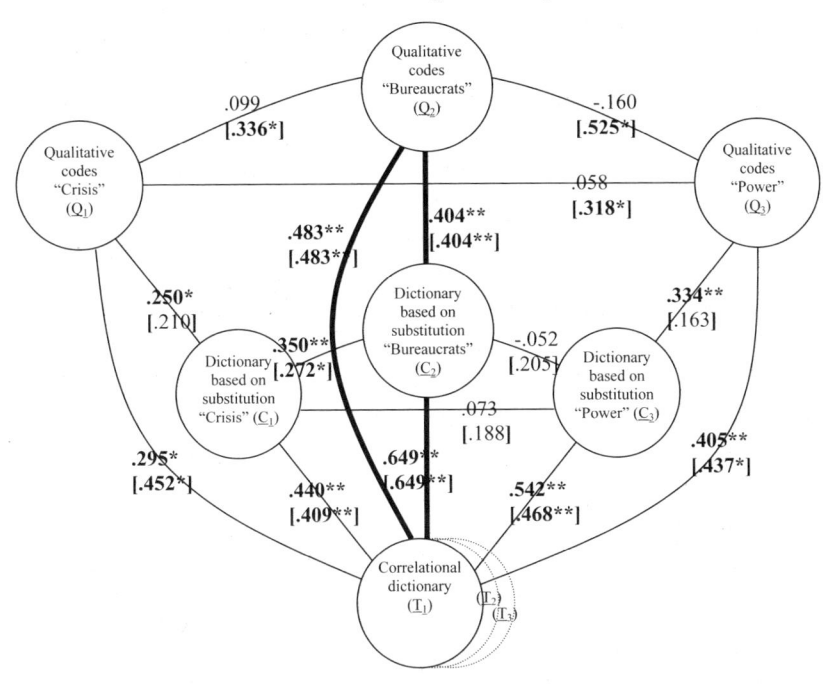

**Figure 10.4
Path Model for Assessing Reliability, Set "A"**

Legend: Moderate-strong correlations are indicated in bold. The level of statistical significance (* for correlations significant at the .05 level, ** for correlations significant at the 0.001 level) is indicated for the sake of reference: the non-random character of the sample of transcripts makes statistical inferences meaningless. In this case, the values of the Pearson correlation coefficients have a purely descriptive meaning. The strength of association between matrices for the case of a single centroid—from the "bureaucrats" framework (from matrix Q_2)—is indicated in square brackets. The path that refers to the "original" ("bureaucrats") framework is indicated by thick lines.

to control for C_i, i.e., for the impact of the substitution tradition of quantitative content analysis. In all three cases, the correlation decreases, but does not drop significantly: $r_{T1Q1.C1}=.213$ (cf. $r_1=.295$), $r_{T2Q2.C2}=.317$ (cf. $r_2=.483$) and $r_{T3Q3.C3}=.283$ (cf. $r_3=.405$). This means that the dictionary based on substitution partially mediates the association between matrices T and Q (Warner, 2008, pp. 407-409). This further supports the logic underpinning the path model: matrix C lies "halfway" between T and Q yet has a dynamic of its own. The substitution tradition of quantitative content analysis, if it combines the *ex ante* and *ex post* techniques for building dictionaries, represents a "hybrid" form combining elements of the representational quantitative analysis and qualitative coding in such a manner that it acquires a unique identity.[9]

The values of Spearman's rank correlation coefficients for the same path model are predictably lower than the corresponding values of the Pearson correlation coefficient because of the loss of information. In fact, a moderately strong association between them characterizes set "A" ($r=.666$), which may indicate that the loss of information has a consistent character.

It is worthwhile to discuss the relationships between matrices of the same type, e.g., between C_1, C_2 and C_3, or between Q_1, Q_2 and Q_3, with a single centroid in triangulation (the values of the Pearson correlation coefficients are indicated in square brackets in Figure 10.4). Out of six pairs, only two (C_2 and C_3, C_1 and C_3) do not show at least a moderate strength of association. Association along the diametral paths suggests either that the "author's message" "overpowers" the alternative readings, or a pattern that may emerge by chance in relationships between any long vectors. "[It was found] that more documents judged to be relevant actually were found in longer documents. The reason for this might be that a longer document simply has more opportunity to have some components that are indeed relevant to a given query" (Grossman & Frieder, 2004, p. 19). The regularity formulated above may well apply to the case under consideration: two particular transcripts, with especially significant word counts, when read from different angles, tend to appear close to each other because of their richness in relevant information. In the same vein, short transcripts appear close to each other independently of the content analysis framework because of their lack of relevant information.

A pair-wise comparison of the Pearson coefficients of correlation for, on one hand, the path model with a single centroid, and, on the other hand, one with three centroids, may help in assessing a possible impact of the relative power of the author's message, even if the text does not seem to be the most appropriate unit of analysis compared with the variable. When using the text as the unit of analysis, the impact of the author's message can be measured only indirectly: the closer the content analysis framework is to the author's intentions, the more consistent its outcomes. The observed pattern, weaker associations between matrices T_i and C_i, C_i and Q_i, and stronger association between matrices T_i and Q_i lying on the same "non-original" path,[10] provide some further evidence confirming the relative strength of the author's message. After all, the "bureaucrats"—"original"—path shows the strongest associations in the path model with a single centroid. Yet even this additional evidence does not serve to rule out the alternative explanations, as the discussion below demonstrates.

The path model for assessing content analysis reliability was also tested on set "B" of transcripts with different—to some extent—parameters. Some results were completely replicated, while others were not. Practically all measurements referring to narrowly defined reliability confirm their precision. Associations along all the paths, including the one corresponding to the "original" framework for this set (the "crisis" framework), appear either moderate or strong, which suggests a higher level of content analysis reliability in this case compared with the previous one (Figure 10.5). The values of the coefficients of the partial correlations also show very similar patterns consistent with the interpretation proposed above: $r_{T1Q1.C1}=.293$ (cf. $r_1=.319$), $r_{T2Q2.C2}=.282$ (cf. $r_2=.544$) and $r_{T3Q3.C3}=.230$ (cf. $r_3=.343$).

The loss of information when relying on Spearman's rank correlation coefficients in this case seems to be even more substantial and less consistent along various paths. The Pearson correlation coefficient be-

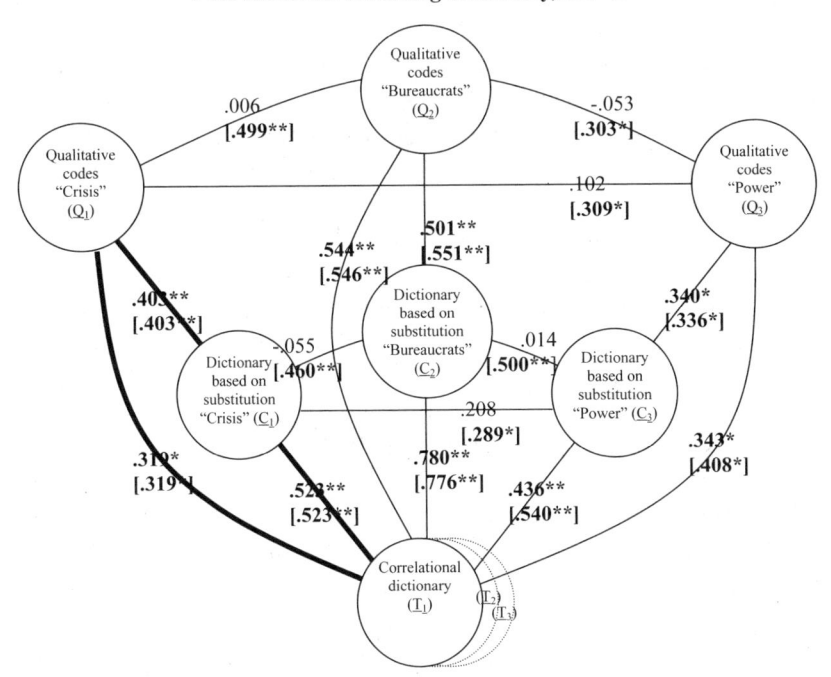

Figure 10.5
Path Model for Assessing Reliability, Set "B"

tween pairs of measures (r and rho) gauging the strength of association between the same pairs of matrices is close to zero. This may be due to a more substantial similarity (indicated by the mean Pearson correlation coefficient standard deviation) between texts in this set. As a result, there are more cases with the same rank. A small size of the "population" (15 pairs of the correlation coefficients) makes it impossible to draw too far-reaching conclusions: samples with N=30 or less should be considered with extreme caution (Warner, 2008, p. 269).

However, simple references to the size of the sample do not serve to explain a different pattern of associations along the diametral paths. In fact, the "original" path does not show the strongest associations in the path model with a single centroid. Furthermore, the "alternative" frameworks (the "bureaucrats" and the "power") serve to strengthen the associations between matrices lying on the corresponding paths contrary to the outcomes of the content analysis of set "A." As there is less variability in the word count of the transcripts, the impact of the length of the vectors may be less significant in set "B." Thus, the observed differences may be due to a less structured character of interviews in this case: non-structured texts prompt multiple readings. As office holders and experts were the principal interviewees in set "B" as well, the "bureaucrats" framework may well appear more appropriate despite being "non-original."

Two empirical tests of the path model for assessing content analysis validity—one done on set "A," the other one on set "B"—served to collect additional evidence with respect to assessing the relative strength of the author's message. In this test, the variable (qualitative code or category in the dictionary based on substitution) is used as a unit of analysis. Two caveats have to be made before the outcomes of the tests are discussed. First, restricted options in QDA Miner and WordStat with respect to using themes as the unit of analysis resulted in the exclusion of matrix T from the path model for assessing the validity of the content analysis. For a similar reason, it includes the Jaccard coefficients of similarity instead of the cosine coefficients, which makes the path model less precise. Second, because of the small size of the populations (n=13 in the "crisis" framework for content analysis, n=41 in the "bureaucrats" framework and n=15 in the "power" framework) the interpretation of the values of the Pearson coefficients of correlations between the Jaccard coefficients of similarity between variables calls for extreme caution.

Associations between all matrices show a consistent pattern: there are moderate to strong correlations (r ranging from .616 to .892) between the

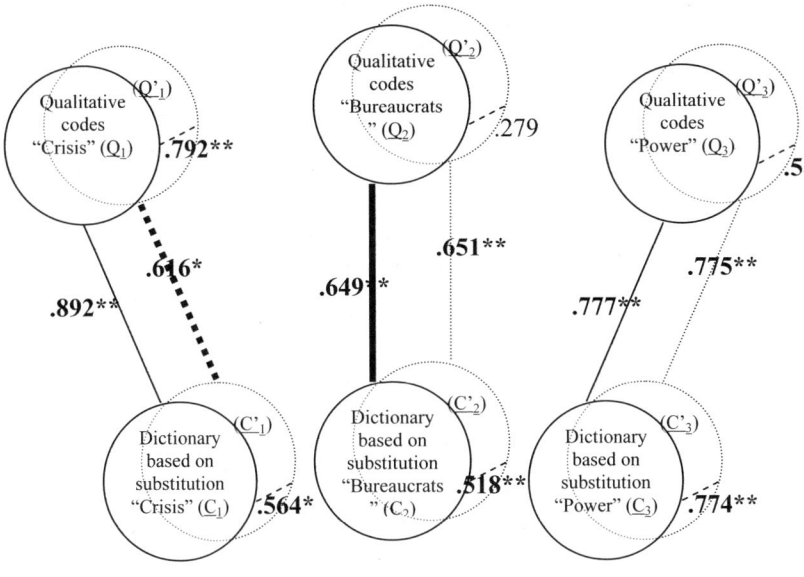

Figure 10.6
Path Model for Assessing Validity

[Path diagram showing relationships between qualitative codes and dictionary-based substitution codes for "Crisis" (Q_1, C_1), "Bureaucrats" (Q_2, C_2), and "Power" (Q_3, C_3), with corresponding primed variables (Q'_1, Q'_2, Q'_3, C'_1, C'_2, C'_3). Path coefficients: .792**, .279, .775**, .616*, .651**, .5, .892**, .649**, .777**, .564*, .518**, .774**]

Legend: The upper path model refers to set "A," the lower—to set "B." The paths that refer to the "original" ("bureaucrats" and "crisis" correspondingly) frameworks are indicated by thick lines. The "power holders" code (heading "destabilizing factors") is the centroid in the "crisis" framework, the "vertical of power" code (heading "constraints")—in the "bureaucrats" framework, the "asymmetrical" code (heading "power in a pure form")—in the "power" framework.

Jaccard coefficients of similarity in matrices C_i and Q_i lying along all the three paths. There is no substantial difference in this regard between set "A" and set "B." The observed pattern suggests that the outcomes of the content analysis have a valid character: qualitative codes co-occur with categories corresponding to them. To weaken the effect of the smallness of the population, the two frameworks, "bureaucrats" and "power" were merged (the fact that both refer to the issues of power and actors vested in it can justify such operation). The association between matrices C and Q remained moderate: $r=.676$ in set "A," $r=.579$ in set "B" (n=56).

A moderate association between the constellation of qualitative codes in set "A," on the one hand, and that in set "B" (this refers to "horizontal" links in Figure 10.6, e.g., between Q_i and Q'_i), on the other appears relevant to the task of comparing the relative strength of various perspectives, the author's and the reader's. Certain congruence also characterizes the constellations of quantitative categories in the two sets.

Out of six correlations of this type, only one ($r=0.279$) is rather weak. This provides some support for the idea about a plurality of possible readings of the same text. Namely, transcripts of semi-structured and unstructured interviews allow a variety of their readings and interpretations. The transcripts included in set "A" are relatively more structured, yet the level of precision of the path model does not make it possible to determine if the "bureaucrats" framework for reading it is any better than the "crisis" one. This calls for a discussion of further improvements in the model and techniques for testing it.

Conclusions

A first, rather straightforward, direction for further improvements in the path model lies in comparing its outcomes when only one reader performs the content analysis and when a team of coders simultaneously applies a single analytical framework. This strategy serves to compare measurements of reliability derived from two independent sources: the "within method" of triangulation for team coding and a combination of the "within method" and "between methods" of triangulation for the path model.

Second, the path model should ideally be tested on two divergent sets of texts: on the one hand, highly structured, purely "logical" texts (e.g., abstracts of scientific articles) and, on the other hand, completely unstructured, purely "rhetorical" (e.g., poems or transcripts of unstructured interviews). This approach serves to compare the two perspectives, the author's and the reader's, in a more direct manner. The theory predicts that the more structured the text is, the narrower its reading will be. However, the level of precision achieved with respect to the path model does not make it possible to clearly distinguish the unstructured interviews from the semi-structured interviews in this regard (a reliable measure of structuration also seems desirable).

Third, the precision of the path model can be improved by making the option of calculating the cosine coefficient of similarity available in the content analysis programs. Reliance on the Jaccard coefficient of similarity when triangulating results of qualitative content analysis leads to the consideration solely of co-occurrences but not frequencies or *TF*IDF*. Further, the other relevant improvement involves changing the way in which the cosine coefficient of similarity is calculated. The standard formula does not take into account the mean distance separating two codes or categories. In practice, this means that vectors with two codes lying close to each other and with the same codes separated by a long text will be considered highly similar, which reduces the precision in gauging congruence between matrices, especially when matrix *T*—the longest one—is involved. Alternatively, one can introduce "dummy variables" to measure distances between codes or categories in average units (expressed in the number of words, for example) of codes or categories. Let us assume the mean length of coded segments in the text is *N* words, which gives us the value of the unit of the dummy variable. Then the mean distance between two variables can also be expressed in *k* dummy variables $k = \dfrac{mean\,dist.}{N}$. As a result, the conventional matrix form transforms into a matrix with dummy variables corresponding to distances between each pair of variables (Table 10.5), i.e., cell values for "regular" variables refer to their frequencies, cell values for "dummy variables"—to "frequencies" as mean distances between them expressed in *N*. Thus, to each variable a number of dummy variables measuring distances from it to all other variables shall be added.

Last but not least, the path model for assessing the validity of content analysis potentially has another application—the search for latent qualitative codes. As mentioned in Subsection II.1, distances between units of analysis, texts or variables, are measured with the help of factor analysis—at least of some of its elements. A further step can be taken. Factor analysis as a data reduction technique services to indicate if the observed constellation of qualitative codes can be described by referring to a few "latent qualitative codes" analogous to factors or principal components. The cosine coefficient of similarity gauges the angle between a vector and a factor (or principal component) instead of a pair of vectors. Factors can then be viewed as axes that permit the mapping of the vectorial space. If found, such "latent qualitative codes" would have the same meaning as headings in the codebook for qualitative content analysis—higher-level concepts from which qualitative codes

Table 10.5
Matrix for Calculating the Cosine Coefficient of Similarity with Dummy Variables

	$Variable_1$	Dummy $variable_{12}$	Dummy $variable_{13}$	Dummy $variable_{1j}$	...	$Variable_2$	...	$Variable_j$
$Text_1$								
$Text_2$								
...								
$Text_i$								

can de deduced. Jacques Derrida's (1967) call for discovering rules of "arch-writing" (*archi-écriture*) and the preoccupation of specialists in semiotics with discovering links between the sign and the signified justify the proposed introduction of latent qualitative analysis. It will also fit in well with the general imperative of triangulation because of its elective affinity with latent semantic analysis.

Very preliminary outcomes of the search for techniques appropriate to latent qualitative analysis do not look discouraging. Before qualitative codes were attributed, they were grouped under various headings. If latent codes exist, then codes from the same heading should be expected to appear close to each other—closer than to codes from the other headings. An empirical test using the merged framework "bureaucrats" plus "power" and set "A" partially confirms this prediction, despite the remaining imperfections of the path model. For instance, the mean distance to the centroid "asymmetrical" for all codes under the "structural" heading ($M=.62$, $SD=.17$) significantly exceeds that for all codes under the "constraints" heading ($M=.47$, $SD=.23$; $t(30)=2.19$, $p=.037$).[11] A similar *t*-test for independent samples carried out on the "crisis" set differentiates three headings. The mean distance of the codes under the "techniques for imposing will" heading ($M=.51$, $SD=.14$) from the centroid differs from that of both the "structural" heading ($M=.25$, $SD=.17$; $t(24)=-4.18$, $p<.001$) and the "constraints" heading ($M=.3$, $SD=.19$; $t(26)=-3.39$, $p=.002$). In other words, when triangulating the grouping of codes done before conducting the qualitative content analysis and *ex post* clusters of qualitative codes, some congruence can be found. Needless to say, more sophisticated techniques for identifying latent codes should be found and tested in order to make latent qualitative analysis operational.

Notes

1. Sometimes these multiple runs are not without problems. For instance, in the process of working on this text the author used two computers. To his great surprise, despite using the same content analysis software program, they initially produced slightly divergent results when calculating frequencies of categories. After the intervention of the software producer's representative, who made some adjustments in the algorithm for retrieving words, the problem was solved and both computers started to produce identical output.
2. He refers to Dostoevsky's novels as an example.
3. Even if, according to some accounts, about 25 percent of papers published in academic journals are never cited at all (Salton & McGill, 1983, p. 247), they were nevertheless read by the editors, peer-reviewers and close colleagues and friends of their authors.
4. In terms introduced by Skinner (2002a, p. 93), categories C refer to "meaning$_3$" and codes Q—to "meaning$_2$." Skinner's "meaning$_1$" differs from the interpretation

of co-occurrences *T* proposed here: according to him, they are independent of both the author's and the reader's intentions and represent the "the arbitrariness of the sign" (Derrida, 1967, p. 74).
5. The assessment of reliability calls for *Q*-mode of factor analysis, whereas the choice of the variable as the unit of analysis necessitates *R*-mode (Basilevsky, 1994, pp. 278-282).
6. This paves the way for the *R*-mode of factor analysis.
7. This fruitful idea was initially suggested by Normand Péladeau of Provalis Research in a personal communication dated April 11 and 13, 2008.
8. Unfortunately, the version of WordStat used calculates only the Jaccard coefficient of similarity (Salton & McGill, 1983, p. 203) for matrix *Q*. It does not affect the meaningfulness of using the Pearson coefficients of correlation to gauge congruence between the matrixes, yet it certainly decreases the precision—reliability and validity—of the qualitative content analysis. The Jaccard coefficient takes into account the occurrence of a code, not its frequency in a particular text.
9. This can be compared with the "hybrid" (long-term contracting, for instance) form identified in economic and managerial sciences: it combines elements of the "firm" (a hierarchical organization) and the "market" and has its own unique identity (Ménard, 2005b).
10. Relatively strong associations between matrixes Q_i, Q_j and Q_k and, as a result, stronger associations in the path model with a single centroid between T_i and Q_i, may be due to the use of the Jaccard coefficient of similarity in matrixes *Q* (see Endnote 8).
11. As in previous cases, outcomes should be interpreted in a descriptive rather than inferential manner. Probabilities are indicated for the sake of reference, "as if" they referred to a random sample.

Appendix

I. Lists of Respondents

I.1 Set "A"

#	Gender	Age	Status	Place	Year
1A	Male	41-50	Bureau head, regional legislature	St. Petersburg	2006
2A	Female	31-40	Bureau head, federal ministry	Moscow	2006
3A	Male	41-50	Bureau head, federal agency	Moscow	2006
4A	Male	31-40	Bureau head, federal ministry	Moscow	2006
5A	Male	41-50	Bureau head, regional administration	Kemerovo	2006
6A	Female	31-40	Bureau head, federal ministry	Moscow	2007
7A	Male	<30	Bureau head, regional administration	Kemerovo	2008
8A	Female	31-40	Bureau head, federal ministry	Moscow	2008
9A	Male	41-50	Bureau head, federal ministry	Moscow	2008
10A	Male	31-40	Bureau head, federal government	Moscow	2008
11A	Male	41-50	Bureau head, federal service	Moscow	2008
12A	Male	51-60	Head of a unit, Presidential Executive Office	Moscow	2008
13A	Male	31-40	Bureau head, federal ministry	Moscow	2006
14A	Female	31-40	Bureau head, regional administration	Kemerovo	2008
15A	Female	51-60	Bureau head, regional administration	Moscow	2008
16A	Male	31-40	Associate bureau head, Presidential Executive Office	Moscow	2008
17A	Female	51-60	Bureau head, Presidential Executive Office	Moscow	2008
18A	Female	<30	Associate head of a unit, Presidential Executive Office	Moscow	2008
19A	Male	<30	Associate department head, federal service	Moscow	2006
20A	Male	51-60	Associate department head, regional administration	St. Petersburg	2006
21A	Female	51-60	Associate department head, regional administration	Kemerovo	2006
22A	Male	31-40	Associate department head, regional branch of a federal service	St. Petersburg	2006
23A	Male	61+	Associate department head, Presidential Executive Office	Moscow	2007
24A	Female	31-40	Associate department head, federal ministry	Moscow	2007
25A	Male	61+	Associate department head, regional administration	Kemerovo	2008

26A	Male	51-60	Associate department head, federal ministry	Moscow	2008
27A	Female	31-40	Associate department head, regional administration	Kemerovo	2008
28A	Male	41-50	Associate department head, regional administration	Kemerovo	2008
29A	Female	41-50	Department head, regional administration	Kemerovo	2006
30A	Male	31-40	Former department head, federal ministry	Moscow	2006
31A	Female	41-50	Department head, Presidential Executive Office	Moscow	2007
32A	Male	31-40	Department head, Presidential Executive Office	Moscow	2007
33A	Male	61+	Former department head and ambassador, federal ministry	Moscow	2007
34A	Male	41-50	Department head, Presidential Executive Office	Moscow	2008
35A	Male	51-60	Former senior official, Presidential Executive Office	Moscow	2006
36A	Male	31-40	Former associate federal minister	Moscow	2006
37A	Male	41-50	Associate head, federal service	Moscow	2006
38A	Male	41-50	Senior official, Presidential Executive Office	Moscow	2007
39A	Male	41-50	Head of the regional branch of a federal service	St. Petersburg	2007
40A	Male	41-50	Senior official, Presidential Executive Office	Moscow	2007
41A	Male	31-40	Associate head, office of the regional administration in Moscow	Moscow	2008
42A	Male	31-40	Expert, GR-specialist	Moscow	2006
43A	Female	31-40	Expert, head of the PR-department of a large corporation	Kemerovo	2006
44A	Male	41-50	Expert, business	Moscow	2006
45A	Female	41-50	Expert, university professor and adviser	Moscow	2006
46A	Male	41-50	Expert, journalist and activist	St. Petersburg	2006
47A	Male	41-50	Expert, adviser to the Presidential Executive Office	Moscow	2006
48A	Male	51-60	Expert, member of the regional legislature	Kemerovo	2006
49A	Male	41-50	Expert, former adviser to the Presidential Executive Office	Moscow	2006
50A	Male	31-40	Expert, former adviser to the office of the Associate Prime Minister	Moscow	2006
51A	Male	31-40	Expert, university professor and adviser	Moscow	2008
52A	Male	61+	Associate bureau head, federal ministry	Moscow	2006
53A	Male	41-50	Associate bureau head, federal ministry	Moscow	2006

54A	Male	<30	Associate bureau head, regional administration	Kemerovo	2008
55A	Female	<30	PR-specialist, regional administration	Kemerovo	2008
56A	Female	41-50	Associate bureau head, regional administration	Kemerovo	2008
57A	Male	<30	Associate bureau head, regional administration	Kemerovo	2008
58A	Male	51-60	Former vice-governor	Moscow	2006
59A	Male	51-60	Vice-governor	Moscow	2006
60A	Male	41-50	Former vice-governor	Kemerovo	2006
61A	Male	61+	Former governor	Kemerovo	2006
62A	Male	51-60	Former governor	Moscow	2007
63A	Female	41-50	Vice-governor	Moscow	2008
64A	Male	51-60	Member of the Council of Federation (upper chamber of the parliament)	Moscow	2008

I.2 Set "B" (All Interviews Conducted in Moscow in 2005)

#	Gender	Age	Status
1B	Male	51-60	Expert, leader of a non-governmental organization, NGO
2B	Male	61+	Expert, member of a Council at the Presidential Executive Office
3B	Female	51-60	Expert, head of a research center
4B	Female	61+	Expert, adviser to a federal service
5B	Male	51-60	Expert, adviser to the Presidential Executive Office
6B	Male	61+	Expert, former senior official, Presidential Executive Office
7B	Male	61+	Expert, member of the Russian Academy of Sciences
8B	Female	61+	Expert, leader of a NGO
9B	Male	61+	Expert, head of a research center
10B	Male	61+	Expert, GR-specialist
11B	Male	61+	Expert, president of a NGO
12B	Male	41-50	Expert, associate head of a research center
13B	Male	51-60	Expert, former associate federal minister
14B	Male	61+	Expert, consultant
15B	Male	41-50	CEO, medium-size enterprise
16B	Male	51-60	Managing director, large investment company
17B	Female	41-50	Senior manager, large corporation
18B	Female	51-60	Director, medium-size enterprise
19B	Male	51-60	Senior manager, large corporation
20B	Male	41-50	Financial director, large corporation
21B	Male	41-50	Director, publishing house
22B	Male	51-60	Director, medium-size company
23B	Male	41-50	Former associate federal minister
24B	Male	41-50	Associate federal minister
25B	Male	41-50	Associate federal minister

26B	Female	61+	Former associate federal minister
27B	Male	41-50	Department head, federal ministry
28B	Male	51-60	Associate department head, federal ministry
29B	Male	51-60	Associate federal minister
30B	Male	41-50	Head, federal service
31B	Male	51-60	Member of Parliament
32B	Male	41-50	Member of Parliament
33B	Male	51-60	Member of Parliament, former head of a federal service
34B	Male	51-60	Member of the regional legislature
35B	Male	51-60	Member of the regional legislature
36B	Male	61+	Member of Parliament
37B	Male	51-60	Member of Parliament
38B	Male	51-60	Member of the regional legislature
39B	Male	41-50	Member of the regional legislature, leader of a political party
40B	Male	51-60	Member of Parliament
41B	Male	51-60	Member of the regional legislature
42B	Male	51-60	Member of Parliament
43B	Female	51-60	Former federal minister, former leader of a political party

I.3 Set "C" (All Interviews Conducted in Region S.)

#	Gender	Age	Status	Year
1C	Male	51-60	Bureau head, regional administration	2006
2C	Male	<30	Bureau head, administration of the capital city	2008
3C	Female	31-40	Bureau head, regional administration	2008
4C	Female	51-60	Associate department head, regional administration	2006
5C	Male	61+	Associate department head, regional administration	2008
6C	Female	31-40	Associate department head, regional administration	2008
7C	Male	41-50	Associate department head, regional administration	2008
8C	Female	41-50	Department head, regional administration	2006
9C	Female	31-40	Press-secretary, large corporation	2006
10C	Male	51-60	Member of the regional legislature, associate head of a committee	2006
11C	Male	<30	Associate bureau head, regional administration	2008
12C	Female	<30	Associate bureau head, regional administration	2008
13C	Female	41-50	Associate bureau head, regional administration	2008
14C	Male	<30	Associate bureau head, regional administration	2008
15C	Male	41-50	Former vice-governor, now teaches at university	2006
16C	Male	61+	Former governor, now the head of a non-profit foundation	2006
17C	Male	51-60	Former governor, now doing business in another region	2007
18C	Male	51-60	Senior manager, large enterprise, experience with working for the regional administration	2006

19C	Male	41-50	Owner, medium-size business, former member of the regional legislature	2006
20C	Female	41-50	Owner, medium-size business	2008
21C	Male	51-60	Senior manager, medium-size company	2007
22C	Male	51-60	Senior manager, medium-size enterprise, food industry	2008
23C	Male	41-50	Associate director, medium-size enterprise	2006
24C	Male	31-40	Owner, small business	2006
25C	Male	41-50	Owner of a small business, real estate	2006
26C	Male	31-40	Senior manager of a supermarket chain	2006

II. Interview Guide

A. Personal experience working in the state service

1. If you do not mind, a few words about your professional career. How did you start working in the state service? What considerations played a role?
2. When considering an applicant for a job, how much attention is paid to his/her educational credentials? What education can be considered an asset for a state servant (social sciences, engineering, natural sciences)? Why?
3. Would you like to leave the state service, if an opportunity arises? If so, what considerations would lead to such decision: salary, vocation, rapid career advancement, other (please specify)?

One often hears the expression "team work."

4. Does the state service imply teamwork? Who normally makes up a team: a boss and his associates, a group united by common ideological values, something else? Where do teams come from? Have you heard of the notion of "bench" (*skameika*)? If so, how does it differ from a team?

In the 1990s, it was quite common to hire one's close relatives to work together in a private firm, in the state service.

5. What do you think about working in the state service together with close relatives? For what reasons? Is there any difference with friends and acquaintances in this respect?

Let us imagine the following unlikely situation. As a result of lay-offs, a state servant loses his or her job.

6. Can he or she count on the support of his or her former colleagues in the search for a new job? Where will the new job most likely be found?
7. What should the state servant be afraid of?

8. Is it appropriate to speak about trust in the context of the state service? Who can be trusted these days?
9. How has the circle of your connections changed since you started to work in the state service? Who forms it, along with your immediate colleagues?

You mentioned [the name of the most senior state official mentioned by the respondent].

10. If you needed to reach this person, how many intermediate links would be used?
11. What kind of future do you see for your child? Is it worth it to send him/her to an ordinary high school, university (as opposed to those for the elite)? What life priorities you would suggest for your child?

B. Decision-making procedures in government bodies

It is usually expected that state servants are guided by state interests.

12. What do you associate with the notion of "state interests"?
13. Louis XIV reportedly said, "I am the state." In today's Russia, the state is who [pause] or what?
14. Do you have a job description? How closely does it regulate what you actually do?
15. Who initiates decisions most frequently: your superiors, yourself or your subordinates?
16. What would you say about initiatives that come from the population and businesses in general: do they help or hamper your work?

Many actors try to predict the actions and decisions of state servants: journalists, business people, and experts. Unfortunately, predictions seldom appear accurate.

17. What motives does one have to take into consideration in the behavior of state servants in order to make accurate predictions? The desire to get promoted, the desire to increase the scope of power of a particular government body, personal or group material gain, something else?

One of the objectives of administrative reform consists in clearly delimiting the circle of individuals who make key decisions.

18. Could you please comment on this?
19. How would you describe the role that the bureau heads (*nachal'niki otdelov*) perform in the overall functioning of the state service?

One often hears about strengthening the vertical of power as a means to increase subordinates' responsiveness.

20. Does the vertical of power work? Decisions made at which level of the hierarchy are implemented the most adequately?
21. How can subordinates be motivated to work harder? Do positive or negative incentives work better?
22. How much freedom do you have in making decisions? What could prevent you from making the most appropriate, from your point of view, decision? Conflicts of interest with superiors, conflict of interests within a team, existing traditions of the state service, public opinion, something else?
23. Could you please compare today's procedure for decision-making with that in use in the 1990s? What about the procedure for decision-making that existed during the Soviet period?

C. Fight against corruption

The fact that corruption penetrates the state service is widely acknowledged. On the other hand, lobbying is widespread in the Western countries.

24. Would you be able to differentiate among three phenomena: the use of informal contacts, lobbying and corruption?

Gavriil Popov, the former mayor of the city of Moscow, once insisted that a bribe is nothing more than a particular payment for a service provided by the state servant.

25. Can you comment on this please?

D. Relationships between the state and business

Let us talk now about the particularities of relationships between the state and businesses in Russia.

26. Do businesses need any support and, if so, in what form? What can they offer in exchange?
27. What does the expression "socially responsible business" mean for you? What strategies for raising the additional resources needed for the development of this country or a particular region do you consider the most effective?

Agreements about socio-economic partnerships in which businesses assume additional obligations in exchange for lowering barriers to their development are common these days in many regions in Russia.

28. Could you please comment on these practices? What interest does a business have entering into such "partnership" with the regional administration?
29. How often, according to your estimates, do state servants leave the state service to take up jobs in the private sector? What about the movement in the opposite direction?

Power and money tend to be interconnected.

30. What lies at the origin of the other: money or power?
31. How sustainable are the tendencies towards stabilization that have been observed in the economy and society? Immediately after the 1998 crisis, business people started to include decisions made by the government in the list of *force majeure* events. Do you have any comments on this?

III. Codebooks

III.1 Bureaucrats

Category	Code	Description
business	budget	Dividing the pie: getting a share in the budget as a strategy for doing business.
business	foots	How to "attach foots" to a document (*pridelat' nogi*): who is involved, what are the interests of the parties involved?
business	kickbacks	Practices related to kickbacks (*otkaty*): whether there is a "normal" level of kickbacks, what are their forms (cash vs. something else) and scope.
business	networks	Networking: stable connections between businesses and the state service. Government relations (GR) and how they work.
business	revolving doors	Movements of people from the private sector to the state service and vice versa. When people decide to change office and for what reasons.
Constitution	commonwealth	Definition of the common good (in contrast to private good). Commonwealth in the British sense.
constitution	conflicts of interest	How do they emerge between different groups in the bureaucracy, what are their sources, how are they handled?
constitution	consolation	Different practices related to consolation and sign-off (*soglasovanie*) in relationships between different offices and bureaus. How it is achieved, who takes part in the process, formal and informal practices, etc.
constitution	functional	Capacities of an office holder to perform particular functions. His/her functional usefulness or the lack thereof (not decision making). Sphere of power.
constitution	generations	Different generations in the state service, relationships between them, including conflicts.
constitution	information flows	How information flows are organized: sources of information, what is considered to be reliable information, etc.
constitution	layers	Layers that exist within the state service and what their respective functions are, areas of initiative, prerogatives, etc. E.g., the level of the bureau (*otdel*) head vs. specialists, etc. Who makes decisions (cf. Who governs?). Scope of power.
constitution	kinship	The role of kinship ties in the state service. Relationships between close relatives if both of them work for the state (description, not evaluation cf. kinship as a critical situation).

cont.

constitution	other_teams	Teams in forms other than benches and teams narrowly defined: corporations, *esprit de corps*, *zemliachestva*, etc.
constitution	power institutions	The role played by power institutions (the FSB, the police, etc.) and their influence. Their relationships with other government bodies.
constitution	president administration	Everything related to the Presidential Executive Office: the scope of its power, control, etc. Relationships with other government bodies.
constitution	promotion	How office holders are promoted. How great are their chances of moving up to higher layers in the hierarchy? Are there limits to movements through the ranks?
constitution	teams	Teams and "benches" within the state service: their purpose, the role of leaders, internal structure and composition.
constitution	trust	Issues of trust: whether office holders trust each other, the scope of trust.
constitution	vocation	Is a bureaucratic career considered a vocation, *Beruf* (in M. Weber's terms)? "Entrance into an office, including one in the private economy, is considered an acceptance of a specific duty of fealty to the purpose of the office in return for the grant of a secure existence."
constraints	administrative reform	Evaluations of the outcomes of administrative reform.
constraints	charisma	Whether personal charisma (exceptional qualities) is required in order to hold an office? How are people with higher than average capacities regarded by fellow office holders?
constraints	constellation of interests	Power limited by competitive markets (both national and international). In the opposite case—if power is not limited by market competition—can we speak about power embedded in a monopolistic industrial organization (e.g., using oil and gas supplies as leverage and a means to increase the room for maneuvering)?
constraints	elections	Elections as a potential constraint. What does the respondent think about elections and their impact on his/her everyday business?
constraints	ideology	Ideology, scientific doctrine as a possible constraint.
constraints	international	Constraints of office holders' opportunism generated in international affairs, e.g., limits imposed by elites in more powerful states.
constraints	law	Law as a potential constraint. How the law is perceived by office holders? Do they consider legal requirements a must?

cont.

constraints	peer-control	Control exercised by colleagues, i.e., fellow office holders (in contrast to the control exercised by superiors).
constraints	popular protests	Popular protests and demonstrations as potential constraints. What does the respondent think about the cases of manifest expressions of disapproval by the population (e.g., monetization, Butovo, etc.)?
constraints	press	The mass media (newspapers, TV, etc.) as a potential constraint on the optimism of office holders. Limits of their influence.
constraints	private property	Whether private property is respected and protected against violations (which would limit the discretion of power holders). Alternatively, do we observe the phenomenon of "power-property"?
constraints	regulations	Internal regulations and routines as potential constraints, including written "regulations" and job descriptions.
constraints	religion	Perception of religion and whether religious beliefs place limits on the discretion of office holders.
constraints	resources	Availability of financial and other material resources as a constraint on the discretion of office holders.
constraints	rivals	Other groups struggling for power placing constraints on the discretion of office holders.
constraints	traditions	Traditions existing within the state service and in the society as a whole as a potential constraint (the belief in the sanctity of age-old traditions, in M. Weber's terms).
constraints	vertical of power	Hierarchical control and the strengthening of the "vertical of power"; how efficient is it, what are recent tendencies in limiting individual opportunism in this manner?
critical situations	relatives	Justifications for working or not working with close relatives.
critical situations	why trust	Reasons for trusting or not trusting people.
hour-glass	information exchanges	Information flows between the state service and society (cf. code "Information flows") is attributed to the description of internal information flows). E.g., what information is made available to the public, how is it distorted or reframed?
hour-glass	us/them	*Us* versus *Them*: whether office holders view themselves as different from the rest of the population and, if so, in what way. Perception of the population and their requests.

III.2 Power

Category	Code	Description
by virtue of a constellation of interests	informational field_entry control	The control of entry to the information field: selective accreditation of the mass media, who is allowed to appear on TV, who gets access to the public sphere and under which conditions.
by virtue of a constellation of interests	legal field_entry control	The control of entry to the legal field: who is admitted to the *pravovoe pole* and under which conditions (e.g., conditions of legalization)? Everything related to obtaining permits, licenses and *spravkas*.
by virtue of a constellation of interests	market_entry control	The control of entry to the market: the market here is a field not localized in space. How are participants at auctions selected, entry barriers that neoclassical economic theory discusses. Monopolies (resulting from various barriers) as opposed to natural monopolies (resulting from a particular shape of the supply curve).
by virtue of a constellation of interests	territory_entry control	The control of entry to a territory (local, regional market). The idea of geographical boundaries is expressed well. The market localized in space includes practices of lease and sublease.
power in a pure form	asymmetrical	Asymmetry in the distribution of rights and obligations. References to the vertical of power if the asymmetry is highlighted (e.g., all initiatives come from the top).
power in a pure form	end in itself	Power as a means to strengthen / reproduce itself.
power in a pure form	no feedback	The lack of feedback loops in relationships between the dominant and the subordinate. How power holders do not listen to those who are subject to their control.
power in a pure form	self-justifiable	No references to superior principles. Situations in which power holders do not feel obliged to justify their actions and decisions.
repertoire of techniques for imposing will	coercion	Making threats: instances when the subordinate has a choice between the worst and the second worst: if you don't do something, negative sanctions will follow.
repertoire of techniques for imposing will	force_physical violence	The actual application of force as a way to get things done. Killings, prison (note: "not letting out"), pressure. Restricting freedom and narrowing the room for maneuvering.

cont.

repertoire of techniques for imposing will	legitimation	Authority as power justified by references to a superior principle (law, traditions…).
repertoire of techniques for imposing will	manipulation	Restricting / distorting the information flow in such a way that the subordinate is not aware that he/she is acting in the principal's interests. Various types of political technologies.
repertoire of techniques for imposing will	positive incentives	Monetary and other pecuniary incentives as to how to get the subordinate motivated. Includes corruption as a way of getting things done.
repertoire of techniques for imposing will	structural bias	Situations in which the subordinate's choices are restricted structurally, by the existing rules of the game. "*A* may exercise power over *B* by getting him to do what he does not want to do, but he also exercises power over him by influencing, shaping or determining his very wants" (Lukes). Natural monopolies as opposed to the other monopolies.
repertoire of techniques for imposing will	symbolic violence	The imposition of a particular worldview, the power of labeling. Education if the creation of a particular mind set is emphasized.

III.3 Crisis

Category	Code	Description
Destabilizing factors	administrative reform	Administrative reform as a destabilizing, disruptive force (it produced a mess in decision-making).
Destabilizing factors	deficit of ideas	The inability to produce new ideas, strategies despite the need for them. This includes national ideas, ideology that could unite people.
Destabilizing factors	economy / infrastructure	Poor state of the economy (infrastructure, inflation, low investments, need for restructuring, fiscal policy favoring the oil and gas industry only, *ZKKh*).
Destabilizing factors	popular protests	Popular protests: real and potential for them. Riots, mass demonstrations, etc. as destabilizing and disruptive forces.
Destabilizing factors	power holders	Actions of those vested in power as a destabilizing factor: a low level of professionalism, self-interested behavior at the expense of the common good (including corruption), negative selection, business-like mind-set, the lack of responsibility, internal conflicts, conflicts between generations.
Destabilizing factors	succession	Unresolved problems of succession. Changes in the highest office as a destabilizing factor. Also instability due to the arrival of a new chief.
Destabilizing factors	vertical of power	Side-effects of the vertical of power: excessive role of the person at the top, unresolved problems as to how to motivate subordinates, no feedback in the state apparatus (but not in the state - society interface), no reliable mechanism for implementing decisions.
Instability	risk	Future events whose probabilities can—at least potentially—be assessed and calculated. There should be a quantitative assessment.
Instability	uncertainty	Future events as unpredictable and impossible to calculate. The idea that no one knows what could happen tomorrow (capital flight as a possible outcome).
Stabilizing factors	enlightened bureaucrats	Reformers who want to change the system for the better. To be a good professional is not enough, a professional with a strategic, "enlightened" vision.
Stabilizing factors	manipulation	Control over the mass media, policies concerning their accreditation to create the image of stability, prosperity. Falsifications during elections. Manipulation at the micro-level is not considered here.
Stabilizing factors	popular support	High level of trust in the president, public support for his policies. Popular political leaders in general.
Stabilizing factors	resource rents	Resource rents as a factor of stabilization (in the opposite sense they are coded as "Economy / Infrastructure").

IV. Dictionaries Based on Substitution

IV.1 Bureaucrats

Budget
- Stealing from the budget: *вор* AND государств* /S; *вор* AND бюджет* /S
- Interest in the budget: бюдж* AND интерес /S
- пилит*; пилят; распил*

Foots
- Pushing a document: продвиж* AND документ* /S; продвиж* AND иде* /S
- Document turnover: прохожден* AND *скор* /S; прохожден* AND *быстр* /S
- ногами; ноги

Kickbacks
- взятк*; взяточн*; вымога*; занес*; занос*; коньяк*; коррупц*; крыш*; откат*; подкуп*; рэкет*

Networks
- State service and business: бизн* AND чиновн* /S; бизн* AND власт* /S
- Useful connections: связ* AND бизн* /S
- *лоббирова*; GR*; аффилир*; джиар*; лоббист*; тусовк*

Revolving doors
- Landing area (a job in the private sector expected after leaving the state service): запасн* AND аэродр* /S
- Revolving doors: крутящ* AND двер* /S
- Migration 1: бизнес* AND *служб* /S
- Migration 2: чиновн* AND бизнес* /S
- Establishing connections: нараб* AND связи /S

Commonwealth
- State's interest: *государствен* AND интерес* /S; *государствен* AND иде* /S
- Regional interest: интерес* AND территор* /S; интерес* AND регион* /S
- Public interest: интерес* AND общ* /S; интерес* AND национальн* /S
- государствен*_мышлен*; государствен*_подход*; государственност*; общ*_благ*; общ*_дел*

Conflict of interest
- Sphere of interest: интерес* AND затр* /S; интерес* AND заде* /S
- Conflict of interest: интерес* AND конфликт* /S; интерес* AND противореч* /S
- Conflict situation: конфликт* AND ситуац* /S
- Opposition: противостоян* AND мэр* /D; противостоян* AND чекист* /D
- Divide and rule: раздел* AND властв* /S
- интриг*

Consolation
- визирова*; компромис*; консенсус*; согласит*; согласов*; согласу*

Functional
- *профессионал*; квалифиц*; компетент*; специалист*; технар*; функционал*

Generations
- генераци*; когорт*; молодеж*; поколен*; средн*_возраст*

Information flows
- Information exchange: обмен* AND информац* /S
- Speaking common language: язык* AND одн* /S
- President's address: презид* AND послан* /S
- Mailing list: спис* AND рассыл* /S
- Telephone book: телеф* AND справочн* /S
- инициатив*; отслежива*

Kinship
- Family members: родствен* AND устр* /S
- Дьяченко; жена; кумовст*; мам*; муж; пап*; семьей; семья; супруг*; сын*

Layers
- Layers: на AND уровн* /S
- Center: центр* AND власт* /S
- законодател*_власт*; исполнит*_власт*; компетенц*; муницип*; регион*_власт*; регион*_уровн*; статус*; федеральн*

Other teams
- Acquaintances: круг* AND общен* /S
- Informal connections: неформ* AND связ* /S; неформ* AND мероприят* /S
- землячеств*; корпорац*; обойм*; питер*; солидарн*

Power institutions
- Special services: силов* AND ведомств* /S; силов* AND служб* /S
- *прокур*; арми*; военн*; кгб*; мвд*; милиц*; силовик*; спецслужб*; фсб*

President administration
- Presidential executive office: президент* AND администр* /S; президент* AND власт* /S
- кремл*

Promotion
- Appointment: назначен* AND должност* /S
- Promotion: повышен* AND служб* /S
- Higher status: повы* AND статус* /S
- Moving through the ranks: продвиж* AND служб* /S
- карьера; карьерн*_лестниц*; карьеру; карьеры; номенклатур*

Teams
- Team 1: команда NOT NEAR сверху /S 5
- Team 2: командой NOT NEAR сверху /S 5
- Team 3: команду NOT NEAR сверху /S 5
- Team 4: команды NOT NEAR сверху /S 5
- клан*; прицеп*; свит*; скамейк*; цепоч*

Trust
- Trust within a team: довер* AND команд* /S
- Personalized trust: личн* AND довер* /S
- доверитель*; искрен*; Мюллер; не подв*; недовер*; но_проверяй; откровен*

Vocation
- Career in the state service: государствен* AND человек* /S; государствен* AND карьер* /S
- аппаратч*; государев*; государственник*; карьерны*; мисси*; призван*

Administrative reform
- Reforming the state service: реформ* AND аппарат* /S
- административ*_рефор*

Charisma
- Outstanding qualities: голов* AND выше /S
- Leadership: качеств* AND лидер* /S

- Personality: рол* AND личност* /S
- талантлив*; харизм*

Constellation of interests
- Power and business: бизнес* AND власт* /S
- Domination on the market: доминиров* AND рын* /S
- Partnership: партнерств* AND *государств* /S
- административн*_барьер*; административн*_рент*; Газпром*; крышева*; монополи*; олигарх*; преференц*

Elections
- *выборн*; выборы; избират*; парламентар*; политическ*_парти*

Ideology
- Liberalism: либерал* AND иде* /S; либерал* AND вер* /S
- идейн*; идеологическ*; коммунист*_иде*; либералы; ментальност*; мировоззрен*; национальн*_иде*; прав*_иде*; принципы; яблочник*

International
- Prices on the world market: миров* AND цен* /S
- External danger: угроз* AND внешн* /S; угроз* AND военн* /S
- америка*; европ*; запад*; НАТО; оранж*; штаты

Law
- Law 1: закон* AND уважен* /S; закон* AND выполнен* /S
- Law 2: закон* AND подчинен* /S; закон* AND требован* /S
- Law 3: закон* AND служб* /S
- Violation of the law: закон* AND нарушен* /S
- Judiciary system: судебн* AND власт* /S; судебн* AND систем* /S
- законодательств*; конститу*

Peer control
- Everyone knows: все AND *зна* /S
- Be like everyone else: не AND высов* /S
- Don't oppose yourself to the others: противопост* AND коллект* /S
- бел*_ворон*; выпа*_из; как_все

Popular protests
- Protests: обществ* AND акци* /S
- бунт*; Бутов*; забастовк*; монетизаци*; протест*; революц*; рельс*

Press
- аккредитац*; Ведомости; Коммерсант; массовой_информации; пресс*; сми

Private property
- Redistribution: собственн* AND *дел* /S; собственн* AND отбир* /S
- Privatization: приватиз* AND *спор* /S; приватиз* AND пересмот* /S
- рейдерст*; частн*_собственн*

Regulations
- Procedures of decision-making: технолог* AND решен* /S
- инструкци*; методик*; положен*_о; предписан*; процедур*; регламент*

Religion
- бог*; бож*; religи*

Resources
- Salary of the office holder: зарплат* AND *чиновн* /S
- баррел*; бонус*; газ*; нефт*; преми*

Rivals
- Former associates: зам* AND были /S; зам* AND бывш* /S
- Rivals: полит* AND конкурен* /S
- оппозиц*

Traditions
- Soviet heritage: советск* AND систем* /S
- *наслед*; инерц*; привыкл*; привычк*; ритуал*; стереотип*; традиц*

Vertical of power
- Compliance: исполн* AND дисципл* /S
- Mechanisms of control: контрол* AND орган* /S; контрол* AND отдел* /S
- вертик*_власт*; доминиров*; проверк*; проверяющ*

Why trust
- Involuntary trust 1: довер* AND *нуж* /S; довер* AND надо /S
- Involuntary trust 2: довер* AND обязан* /S; довер* AND долж* /S
- Start by trusting: довер* AND до_перв* /S

Relatives
- Trust in close relatives: родствен* AND довер* /S
- Mutual support: родствен* AND за_друг* /P
- Conflicts between close relatives: родствен* AND конфликт* /P
- Covering up: родствен* AND не_сда* /S
- Additional problems: родствен* AND неприятн* /S
- Close relative as a subordinate: родствен* AND подчинен* /S
- Problematic compliance: родствен* AND требов* /S

Information exchanges
- Feedback loops: обратн* AND связ* /S
- Public councils: обществ* AND совет /S & обществ* AND министерст* /S
- Petitions: пис* AND гражд* /S; пис* AND населен* /S
- Deliberate leaks: информац* AND дозиров* /S; информац* AND сли* /S
- State secrets: гос* AND тайн* /S
- Leaks: информац* AND *крыт* /S; информац* AND утечк* /S
- жалоб*; секретн*; статистик*

Us/Them
- Citizens and power holders: гражд* AND начальн* /S; гражд* AND обычн* /S
- Us and Them: мы OR нас & мы AND они /S
- Ordinary people: прост* AND челов* /S; прост* AND люд* /S
- Force majeure: правит* AND форс-мажор* /S
- Outsider: человек* AND со_сторон* /S; человек* AND с_улиц* /S
- каст*; Розенбаум*; Рублевк*

IV.2 Power

Information field entry control
- Seen on TV: телев* AND вид* /S; телев* AND картин* /S
- Newspapers: газет* AND пи* /S
- Vertical of information: информ* AND вертик* /S
- Information control: информац* AND контрол* /S
- Control of the press: пресс* AND контр* /S; пресс* AND подчинен* /S
- Control of the mass media: контр* AND сми* /S
- Negative information: журналист* AND негатив* /S
- Control of TV: контрол* AND тв /P; контрол* AND телев* /P
- What they show: телев* AND показ* /S; телев* AND говор* /S
- *цензур*; аккредит*; замалчив*; Пушков*

Legal field entry control
- Amnesty: амнист* AND капитал* /S; амнист* AND приватиза* /S
- Endorsement: получ* AND виз* /S; получ* AND подпис* /S

- Inclusion in a government program: включ* AND програм* /S; включ* AND конкур* /S
- Entry: вход* AND выход* /S
- Consultative council: совет* AND бизнес* /S
- Lobbying regulations: лоббир* AND закон* /S; лоббир* AND поправк* /S
- Tax administration: сво* AND налог* /P; сво* AND инспекц* /P
- Single window (streamlining the procedure of establishing a business): одн* AND окн* /S
- Legal field: правов* AND пол* /S
- Preparing laws: пров* AND закон* & пров* AND поправк* /S
- Registering business/political party: *регистр* AND фирм* /S; *регистр* AND парт* /S
- Protection of property: собств* AND сохран* /S; собствен* AND допуск* /S
- Bribing judges: суд* AND тыс* /S; суд* AND взят* /S
- Manipulating law: закон* AND понят* /S; закон* AND разобр* /S
- Legal language: язык* AND закон* /S; язык* AND документ* /S
- лицензи*; пропуск*; справк*; справочк*; удостоверен*

Market entry control
- Vertical integration: вертик* AND интегр* /S
- Entry ticket: вход* AND цен* /S; вход* AND билет* /S
- Gazprom: газпром* AND бизнес* /S; газпром* AND независ* /S
- State purchases: распред* AND заказ* /S
- Auction: аукц* AND *пуст* /S
- Market entry control: рын* AND доступ* /S; рын* AND контролир* /S
- State capture: захв* AND регулят* /S
- Information about an auction: информац* AND аукцион* /S; информац* AND конкурс* /S
- Monopoly: монопол* NOT NEAR естеств /P 3; монопол* NOT NEAR власт* /P 3
- Preferences: бизнес* AND субсид* & бизнес* AND преференц* /S
- Rent: рент* AND адм* /S; рент* AND созд* /S
- *закупк*; госзакуп*; картель*; полян*; слиян*; тендер*

Territory entry control
- City: город* AND бизнес* /S; город* AND предпр* /S
- Governor: губернат* AND рынок* /S
- Foreign investor: иностр* AND инвест* /S; иностр* AND прод* /S
- West: запад* AND полиц* /S; запад* AND посад* /S
- Region: област* AND бизнес* /S; област* AND предпр* /S
- Area: регион* AND работ* /S; регион* AND приход* /S
- Letting in: рынок* AND *пуск* /S

- Agreements between the administration and businesses: соглашен* AND социал* & соглашен* AND сотрудн* /S
- Customs: тамож* AND догов* /S
- Territory: территор* AND деятель* /S; территор* AND хозяин* /S
- Territory entry control: территор* AND работ* /S; территор* AND приход* /S
- протекц*; пятне; пятно; субаренд*; участке; участок

Asymmetrical
- Lack of responsibility: ответствен* AND не* /S; ответствен* AND без /S
- Highest level: уров* AND верхн* /S; уров* AND вы* /C
- Hierarchy: иерарх* NO NEAR цел* /P 4
- Initiative: иници* AND *верх* /S; иници* AND не_люб* /S
- Initiative 2: иници* AND исход* /S; иници* AND ид* /S
- Subordinate: испол* AND прост* /S; испол* AND предан* /S
- Concentration of power: концентр* AND власт* /S
- Monopoly of power: власт* AND моно* /S; власт* AND полнот* /S
- No rights: не* AND прав* /S; не* AND обязат* /S
- Work horse: рабоч* AND сил* /S; рабоч* AND лошад* /S
- Close control: спр* AND силь* /S; спр* AND больш* /S
- Top-down: сверху AND идет /S; сверху AND спуск* /S
- Narrow circle: узк* AND круг* /S
- Guided democracy: управл* AND демокр* /S
- Define the course of actions: *формир* AND курс* /S; *формир* AND интерес* /S
- авторитар*; беззащит*; ведомы*; всевласт*; доминир*; командов*; монарх*; на_колен*; перв*_лиц*; пирамид*; подлежащ*; рулит*; сверху_вниз; униж*; унитар*; цар*; централиз*

End in itself
- Power struggle: бор* AND за_власть /S
- Power-property: власт* AND собствен* /S
- Survival of the organization: струк* AND выжив* /S; струк* AND сохран* /S
- Office entrenchment: кресл* AND держ* /S; кресл* AND расста* /S
- Continuity of power: преем* AND власт*
- Self-reproduction: власт* AND сохранен* /S; власт* AND получен* /S
- End in itself: власт* AND цел* /S; власт* AND получен* /S
- Status: статус* AND повы* /S; статус* AND мотив* /S
- Power entrenchment: власт* AND *держ* /S; власт* AND остат* /S
- Power lust: хо* AND власт* /S

- властолюб*; временщ*; самосохранен*; самоутвежд*; самоценн*

No feed back
- To whom to send letters: не* NEAR *пис* /S 3; не* NEAR обратит* /S 3
- Opinion of ordinary people: мнени* AND гражд* /S; мнени* AND populationн* /S
- On the ground: мест* AND с* /S; мест* AND на /S
- No advice: совет* AND не /S
- No dialogue: нет AND диалог* /S; нет AND дискус* /S
- No contact: контакт* AND нет /S; контакт* AND теря* /S
- No control: контрол* AND не* /S
- Feedback loops: обратн* AND связ* /S
- No sense of reality: жизн* AND отрыв* /S; жизн* AND оторв* /S
- Alienation: отчужд* AND власт* /S
- Hour glass society: обществ* AND раскол* /S; обществ* AND разрыв* /S
- Self-sufficiency: самодост* AND чиновн* /S; самодост* AND аппарат* /S
- No bottom-up movement: снизу AND нет /S; снизу AND не /S
- без_оглядки; в_реальности; о_реальност*; референд*

Self-justifiable
- No limits: беспредел* NEAR власт* /D 10
- Willful decision: волев* AND реш* /S; волев* AND указан* /S
- Stupid orders: глупост* AND вышестоящ* /S
- Priests: жре* AND закон* /S
- Changes in the constitution: конституц* AND *мен* /S
- Violations of the law: закон* AND наруш* /S; закон* AND плев* /S
- No discussion: не AND обоснов* /S; не AND обсужд* /S
- Shut up: рассужд* AND не /S
- Discretion: произвол* AND власт* /S
- Boss is always right: начальн* AND дурак* /S
- Force majeure: форс* AND правит* /S
- под_раздач*; самодур*

Coercion
- Afraid 1: боит* NOT NEAR не /S 3
- Afraid 2: боят* NOT NEAR не /S 3
- To coerce: вынужд* AND бизн* /S; вынужд* AND предпр* /S
- To put pressure: давлен* AND *верх* /S; давлен* AND власт* /S
- To open a criminal case: дел* AND заве* /S; дел* AND возб* /S
- Threaten: другим AND неповадно /S
- To force: застав* AND работ* /S; застав* AND дел* /S
- Procuracy 1: *прокур* AND провер* /S; *прокур* AND выз* /S

- Procuracy 2: *прокур* AND отка* /S; *прокур* AND возб* /S
- Fear: страх NOT страхов* /S
- Fear of being fired: увольн* AND стра* /S; увольн* AND угр* /S
- Yukos case: дел* AND ЮКОС* /S; дел* AND Ходорк* /S
- вымогател*; запуг*; кнут*; компромат*; наез*; наеха*; напуг*; рэкет*; угро*; шантаж*

Force, physical violence
- Staff applying violence: насил* AND аппар* /S
- To twist arms: выкруч* AND рук* /S
- Screw-tightening: гай* AND закруч* /S; гай* AND завинч* /S
- To initiate an investigation: операт* AND мероприят* /S
- To apply force: сил* AND подчинен* /S; сил* AND использ* /S
- Solving a problem by applying force: сил* AND реш* /S
- *убив*; войн*; драк*; за_решет*; застрел*; колони*; кров*; нагиб*; погром*; посад*; пригиб*; принуд*; принужд*; расстрел*; репресс*; тюрьм*; убийств*; убил*; убит*; Чечн*

Legitimation
- Law: соответст* AND закон* /S; соответст* AND положен* /S
- Monarchy: традиц* AND монарх* /S
- Public support: *нар* AND поддерж* /S; *нар* AND люб* /S
- Justified solution: решен* AND опирает* /S
- Force of arguments: сил* AND аргумент* /S
- Traditions: традиц* AND власт* /S; традиц* AND президент* /S
- авторитет*; аргументир*; легитим*; обоснов*; от_бог*

Manipulation
- Leaking information: вбр* AND информ* /S
- Limiting information: информац* AND дозир* /S
- Paid article: заказ* AND стат* /S
- Paid publications: заказн* AND публик* /S; заказн* AND расслед* /S
- To whisper: добе* AND до /S
- Orchestrate protests: акц* AND организ* /S
- Political technologies: полит* AND технолог* /S
- Crafting information: информац* AND дозиров* /S; информац* AND сли* /S
- Hiding information: информ* AND сокрыт* /S; информ* AND утечк* /S
- PR*; имитац*; интриг*; манипул*; пиар*; подтасов*; политтехн*

Positive incentives
- Business-like motivation: бизнес* NEAR мотив* /P 3
- To give money: ден* AND предл* /S; ден* AND да* /S

- Salary: зарплат* AND повыс* /S; зарплат* AND увелич* /S
- Apartment: кварт* AND получ* /S
- Pay: подн* AND зарплат* /S; подн* AND оклад* /S
- Payment: оплат* AND труд* /S
- Pension: пенс* AND повыш* /S; пенс* AND госслужб* /S
- Increases in pensions: пенс* AND подн* /S; пенс* AND повыш* /S
- Increases in salaries: зарплат* AND подн* /S
- Bonuses: преми* NOT NEAR не* /D 3
- Social insurance benefits: социал* AND пакет* /S
- Stimulus: стимул* AND финанс* /S; стимул* AND денеж* /S
- бабл*; бонус*; вознагражд*; допл*; Жуковк*; занес*; занос*; поощр*; привелег*; пряник*; соцпакет

Structural bias
- Adaptation to the environment: адапт* AND сред* /S
- Bureaucratic laws: бюрократ* AND закон* /S; бюрократ* AND принцип* /S
- To keep oneself within limits: рамк* NEAR в /P 3
- Natural monopolies: монопол* AND естеств* /P; монопол* AND жкх* /P
- Consolidation: структ* AND консолидац* /S; структурир* AND выстр* /S
- Corporate solidarity: корпора* AND солид* /S; корпора* AND интер* /S
- Logics of the system: систем* AND взаимоотн* /P; систем* AND логик* /P
- On the rails: накат* AND рельс* /S
- Crude oil: нефт* AND распред* /S
- Returning services: услуг* AND ответ* /S; услуг* AND услуг* /S
- Adverse selection: отрицат* AND селекц* /S; отрицат* AND отбор* /S
- Outcomes of a particular policies: определ* AND политик* /S
- Rules of the game: правил* AND игр* /S; правил* AND поведен* /S
- Legal regulation: прав* AND регулир* /S
- Job description 1: регламент* AND адм* /S; регламент* AND долж* /S
- Job description 2: регламент* AND функц* /S; регламент* AND инструк* /S
- Lever: рычаг* AND влиян* /S
- System bias: систем* AND завис* /S; систем* AND специфик* /S
- Build a system: систем* AND *строит* /S; систем* AND специфик* /S
- Mining industries: сырьев* AND сект* /S; сырьев* AND отрас* /S
- Communal charges: тариф* AND телеф* /S; тариф* AND коммун* /S

- водоканал*; квот*; конъюнктур*; не_высов*; по_течен*; принор*; приспосаб*; стае; стая; электроэнерг*

Symbolic violence
- Impose a world-view: вдалб* AND идеи* /S; вдалб* AND голов* /S
- Military education: воен* AND образов* /S
- Symbol: знак* NOT знаком* /S
- National idea: национальн* AND иде* /S
- Create images: созда* AND представ* /S; созда* AND образ* /S
- Teach how to live: учи* AND жи* /S
- Learning: школ* AND про* /S
- большеви*; воспит*; государственни*; зомбир*; идеалистич*; идеолог*; коммунизм*; либерализм*; лозунг*; марксизм*; пропаганд*; фашизм*

IV.3 Crisis

Actions of power elite
- Fight of clans: борьб* AND клан* /S; борьб* AND групп* /S
- Actions of the government: действ*_правит* AND не* /S
- Avoiding responsibility: отвевств* AND не_хо* /S
- Conflict of interest: интерес* AND конфликт* /S; интерес* AND противореч* /S
- Corruption: коррупци* AND интер* /S
- Personal relationships 1: личн* AND отнош* /S; личн* AND контакт* /S
- Personal relationships 2: личн* AND предан* /S; личн* AND лоял* /S
- Personal connections: личн*_связ* NOT NEAR бизнес* /P 30
- Incompetence: *компетентн* AND мало /S; *компетентн* AND недостаточн* /S
- Lack of professionalism: непрофес* NOT журнал* /P
- New generation: покол* AND нов* /S; покол* AND мол* /S
- Conflicts between elites: раскол* AND элит* /S
- временщ*; коррупци*; кумов*; некомпетентн*; неподготовлены*; разворовыв*; слабовольн*

Administrative reform
- Changing the system: систем* AND слом* /S; систем* AND разруш* /S
- административн*_рефор*

Deficit of ideas
- Crisis of ideas: иде* AND криз* /S; иде* AND деф* /S

- No ideas: иде* NEAR не* /S 3; иде* AND отсутств* /S 3

Economy and infrastructure
- Lack of investments: инвестиц* AND мало /S; инвестиц* AND не* /S
- High inflation: *инфляц* AND *% /S
- Taxes: налог* AND систем* /S; налог* AND политик* /S
- Resource dependence: нефт* NOT #RESOURCES /S
- инфраструк*

Popular protests
- Riot: бунт NOT #ACTIONS OF POWER ELITE /S
- Strike: забаст* NOT NEAR итал* /P 15
- Protests: протес* AND ак* /S; протес* AND выст* /S
- Social explosion: взрыв* AND соц* /S
- Бутов*; на_улиц*; недовольст*

Succession
- The 2008 problem (presidential elections): 2008 AND год* & 2008 NOT NEAR *комит* /S 3
- New bosses: начал* AND нов* /S; начал* AND смен* /S
- Rotating power-holders: смен* AND руков* /S; смен* AND власт* /S
- преемник*

Vertical of power
- To depend on the superiors: завис* AND ли* /S; завис* AND рук* /S
- To depends on particular personalities: завяз* AND личн* /S
- Compliance: исполн* AND *% /S; исполн* AND проц* /P
- Problems with compliance: не_идеал* AND чиновн* /S
- Italian strike: забаст* AND итал* /S
- Concentration of power: *концентрац* AND власт* /S; концентрац* AND моно* /S
- Corruption at the top: коррупц* AND наверх* /S; коррупц* AND вы* /S
- No initiatives: инициат* AND не* /S; инициат* AND отсут* /S
- No leverage: рычагов NEAR нет /S 2
- Delegation of responsibility: ответствен* AND презид* /S; ответствен* AND Путин* /S
- Guidelines are not important: установк* AND неважн* /S
- наш*_урод*; обратн*_связ*; саботаж*

Risk
- High probability: вероятн* AND больш* /S; вероятн* AND весьма /S

- Probability: вероятн* AND макс* /S; вероятн* AND высок* /S
- Assessing chances: оцен* AND шанс* /S
- Predictability: предсказуем* NOT #UNCERTAINTY /S
- Forecasting: прогноз* NOT NEAR труд* & прогноз* NOT NEAR не* /S 5
- Calculating risks: риск* AND просчит* /P
- Forces at play: расклад* NEAR при /S 4
- Minimizing risks: риск* AND минимиз* /P; риск* AND просчит* /P
- Excessive risks: риск* AND чрезмерн* /S

Uncertainty
- No forecasts: не* AND *прогноз* /S; не* AND просчит* /S
- Capital flight: капитал* AND отток* /S; капитал* AND экспорт* /S
- Difficult to predict: прогноз* AND труд* /S
- в_любой_момент; неопределен*; непредсказуем*; случайност*; форс_мажор*; форс-мажор*

Enlightened bureaucrats
- Administrative reform: административн*_рефор* NOT #ADMINISTRATIVE REFORM /S
- Good intentions: намерен* AND благ* /S
- Kozak (the senior official responsible for drafting the program of administrative reform): Козак NOT # ACTIONS OF POWER ELITE & Козак NOT #UNCERTAINTY /S
- Young and active: молод* AND инициативн* /S; молод* AND кандид* /S
- Young talents: молод* AND толк* /S; молод* AND одарен* /S
- Renewing the government body: обновл* AND минист* /S
- Devotion: преданн* AND дел* /S; преданн* AND работ* /S
- Enlightened: просвещ* AND мон* /S; просвещ* AND нач* /S
- Mission: сво*_мисси* NOT NEAR бизнес* /P 5
- To be driven by ideas: человек* AND иде* /S
- гуманист*; молод*_талант*; подвижник*; романти*; служен*; эрудирован*

Manipulation
- Control of the press: контр* AND газет* /S
- Control of the mass media: сми AND под* /S; сми AND контр* /S
- Control of the TV: телев* AND вид* /S; телев* AND показ* /S
- *цензур*; аккредитац*; манипулир*; пропаганд*; фальсифи*

Popular support
- Trust in the president: довер* AND президент* /P; довер* AND Путин* /P

- Trust in the governor: губерн* AND довер* /S; губерн* AND люб* /S
- Trust in the local administration: довер* AND местн*_власт* /S
- Popularity of power holders: популярн* AND власт* /S; популярн* AND губернат* /S
- рейтинг*

Resources
- Crude oil: нефт* NOT NEAR комп* & нефт* NOT нефтяни* /C 30
- Stabilization fund: стаб* AND фонд* /S
- махорк*; стабфонд*

Legend: * refers to the "wild card" (any character or a combination of characters); /S—two words co-occur in the same sentence; /P—two words co-occur in the same paragraph; NOT NEAR—two terms should not co-occur within a sentence (/S); &—three words co-occur; NEAR—two terms should be separated by no more than N words.

References

Afanasiev, Mikhail. (2000). *Klientelizm and rossijskaia gosudarstvennost'* [Patron-Client relationships and Russian statehood] (2nd ed.). Moscow: MONF.
Ailon, Galit. (2006). What B Would Otherwise Do: A Critique of Conceptualizations of "Power" in Organizational Theory. *Organization*, 16 (6), 771-800.
Akhiezer, Aleksandr. (1997 [1991]). *Rossiia: kritika istoricheskogo opyta* (Tom 1: Ot proshlogo k budushchemu) [Russia: Criticism of its historical experience (Vol. 1: From the past to the future)] (2nd ed.). Novosibirsk: Sibirsky khronograf.
Aksenov, Vasily. (1993 [1991]). *Moskovskaia Saga* (Tom 2: Vojna i tjurma) [Generations of Winter (Vol. 1: War and prison)]. Moscow: Tekts.
Albats, Yevgenia. (2005). Rynok bjurokraticheskikh uslug [Market of bureaucratic services]. working paper *WP4/2005/01*. Moscow: the State University – the Higher School of Economics.
Albats, Yevgenia. (1994). *The State within a State: the KGB and Its Hold on Russia – Past, Present, and Future*. New York: Farrar, Straus and Giroux. Translated by Fitzpatrick, Catherine A.
Alchian, Armen A. & Demsetz, Harold. (1972). Production, Information Costs and Economic Organization. *The American Economic Review*, 62 (5), 777-795.
Analitichesky tsentr Yuriia Levady. (2007). *Obshchestvennoe mnenie – 2007: ezhegodnik* [Public opinion – 2007: Yearbook]. Moscow.
Andreff, Wladimir. (2003). *La mutation des économies postsocialistes: Une analyse économique alternative*. Paris: l'Harmattan.
Andreff, Wladimir. (1993). *La crise des économies socialistes: la rupture d'un système*. Grenoble: Presses Universitaires de Grenoble.
Andreff, Wladimir. (1992). Convergence or congruence between Eastern and Western economic systems. In Dallago, Bruno, Brezinski, Horst Dieter & Andreff, Wladimir (Eds.), *Convergence and System Change: The Convergence Hypothesis in the Light of Transition in Eastern Europe* (pp. 48-78). Aldershot: Dartmouth.
Aoki, Masahiko. (1991). *Economie japonaise: Information, motivations et marchandage*. Paris: Economica. Translated by Bernard, Henri.
Arendt, Hannah. (1969). *On violence*. New York: Harcourt, Brace & World.
Arlacchi, Pino. (1986). *Mafia et compagnies: L'éthique mafiosa et l'esprit du capitalisme*. Grenoble: Presses Universitaires de Grenoble. Translated by Del Forno, A.
Arnaud, André-Jean (Ed.). (1993). *Dictionnaire encyclopédique de théorie et de sociologie du droit* (2nd ed.). Paris: L.G.D.J.
Arthur, W. Brian. (1988). *Self-Reinforcing Mechanisms in Economics. In* Anderson, Philip W., Arrow, Kenneth J. & Pines, David (Eds.), *The economy as an evolving complex system* (pp. 9-31). Boulder, CO: *Westview Press.*
Aslanov, L. (2009). *Mentalitet i vlast': russkaia tsivilizatsiia* [Mentality and power: Russian civilization] (Vols. 1-3). Moscow: TEIS.

Avdasheva, Svetlana, Alimova, Tat'yana & Yusupova, Guyzel. (2005). Vozmozhnosti ispol'zovaniia statisticheskoi informatsii dlia identifikatsii gruppy lits. *Voprosy statistiki*, 5, 9-17.
Babbie, Earl & Benaquisto, Lucia. (2002). *Fundamentals of Social Research*. Scarborough, ON: Nelson.
Badie, Bertrand. (2000 [1992]). *The Imported State: The Westernization of the Political Order*. Stanford, CA: Stanford University Press, 2000. Translated by Royal, Claudia.
Bakhtin, Mikhail. (1979). *Problemy poetiki Dostoevskogo* [Problems of Dostoevsky's Poetics]. Moscow: Sovetskaia Rossiia.
Bandura, Albert. (1990). Mechanisms of moral disengagement. In Reich, Walter (Ed.), *Origins of Terrorism: Psychologies, Ideologies, Theologies, States of Mind* (pp. 161-191). Washington, D.C.: Woodrow Wilson International Center for Scholars and New York: Cambridge University Press.
Barrey, Sandrine. (2006). Formation et calcul des prix: le travail de tarification dans la grande distribution. *Sociologie de travail*, 48, 142-158.
Basilevsky, Alexander. (1994). *Statistical Factor Analysis and Related Methods*. New York: John Wiles & Sons.
Beck, Ulrich. (1992 [1986]). *Risk Society: Towards a New Modernity*. London: SAGE Publications. With an introduction of Lash, Scott and Wynne, Brian.
Becker, Gary S. (1993). Nobel Lecture: The Economic Way of Looking at Behavior. *The Journal of Political Economy*, 101 (3), 385-409.
Beetham, David. (1991). *The Legitimation of Power*. Atlantic Highlands, NJ: Humanities Press International.
Benton, W. C. & Maloni, Michael. (2005). The influence of power driven buyer/seller relationships on supply chain satisfaction. *Journal of Operations Management*, 23, 1-22.
Bibler, Vladimir. (1991). *Mikhail Mikhailovich Bakhtin, ili Poetika Kultury* [Mikhail Bakhtin, or Poetics of Culture]. Moscow: Progress.
Black, R. D. Collison. (2008). Utility. In Durlauf, Steven & Blume, Lawrence (Eds.), *The New Palgrave: Dictionary of Economics* (2nd ed.) (Vol. 8, pp. 577-581). New York: Palgrave Macmillan.
Blomley, Nickolas K. (1994). *Law, Space, and the Geographies of Power*. New York: The Guilford Press.
Boeri, Tito, Castanheira, Michael, Faini, Riccardo & Calasso, Vincenzo. (2006). *Structural Reforms without Prejudices*. Oxford: Oxford University Press.
Bogoiavlensky, Sergei. (2006 [1946]). *Moskovsky prikaznoi apparat and deloproizvodstvo XVI-XVII vekov* [Moscow administrative staff and clerical work in the XVI-XVII centuries]. Moscow: Yazyki slavianskoi kul'tury.
Bol'shakov, V. & Ermachkov, E. (1999). *Russkaia sobornost', obshchinnost' i derzhavnost': istoriko-sotsiologichesky analiz* [Russian communitarian traditions and attitudes toward the state]. Moscow: RITs ISPI.
Boltanski, Luc & Thévenot, Laurent. (2000). The reality of moral expectations: a sociology of situated judgment. *Philosophical Explorations*, 3 (3), 208-231.
Boltanski, Luc & Thévenot, Laurent. (1991), *De la justification: les économies de la grandeur*. Paris: Gallimard.
Bourdieu, Pierre. (2005 [2000]). *The Social Structures of the Economy*. Cambridge: Polity. Translated by Turner, Chris.
Bourdieu, Pierre. (1994). Rethinking the State: Genesis and Structure of the Bureaucratic Field. *Sociological Theory*, 12 (1), 1-18.
Bourdieu, Pierre. (1984). *Homo Academicus*. Paris: Editions de Minuit.
Bourdieu, Pierre. (1980). *Le sens pratique*. Paris: Editions de Minuit.

Bourdieu, Pierre. (1979 [1963]). *Algeria 1960*. Cambridge: Cambridge University Press and Paris: Editions de la MSH. Translated by Nice, R.
Bourdieu, Pierre & Passeron, Jean-Claude. (1970). *La reproduction: Eléments pour une théorie du système d'enseignement*. Paris: Editions de Minuit.
Bowles, Samuel & Gintis, Herbert. (2008). Power. In Durlauf, Steven & Blume, Lawrence (Eds.), *The New Palgrave: Dictionary of Economics* (2nd ed.) (Vol. 6, pp. 565-570). New York: Palgrave Macmillan.
Bowles, Samuel & Gintis, Herbert. (1993). A Political and Economic Case for the Democratic Enterprise. *Economics and Philosophy*, 9, 75-100.
Boycko, Maxim, Shleifer, Andrei, & Vishny, Robert. (1995). *Privatizing Russia*, Cambridge, MA and London: The MIT Press.
Boyer, Robert & Orléan, André. (1990). La convention salariale fordienne: Les obstacles d'une innovation locale dans la transformation du mode de régulation. *Couverture Orange No. 9029*. Paris: Centre d'études prospectives d'économie mathématique appliquées à la planification (CEPREMAP).
Brenner, Reuven. (1994). *Labyrinths of Prosperity: Economic Follies, Democratic Remedies*, Ann Arbor, MI: the University of Michigan Press.
British Petroleum. (2008) *Statistical Review of World Energy 2008: Workbook of historical data*. Retrieved from http://www.bp.com/liveassets/bp_internet/globalbp/globalbp_uk_english/reports_and_publications/statistical_energy_review_2008/STAGING/local_assets/downloads/spreadsheets/statistical_review_full_report_workbook_2008.xls.
Broman, Thomas. (1998). The Habermasian Public Sphere and "Science *in* the Enlightenment." *History of Science*, 36, 123-149.
Brym, Robert & Gimpelson, Vladimir. (2004). The Size, Composition, and Dynamics of the Russian State Bureaucracy in the 1990s. *Slavic Review*, 63 (1), 90-112.
Brym, Robert, Lie, John & Rytina, Steven. (2008). Networks, Groups, Bureaucracies, and Societies. In Brym, Robert (Ed.), *New Society* (5th edition) (online chapter). Toronto: Nelson. Retrieved from http://www.newsociety5e.nelson.com/student/pdf/Online%20Chapter%2021%20-%20Networks,%20Groups,%20Bureaucracies,%20and%20Societies.pdf.
Bryman, Alan. (2004 [2001]). *Social Research Methods* (2nd edition). Oxford and New York: Oxford University Press.
Buchanan, James M. (1980). Rent-Seeking and Profit Seeking. In Buchanan, James M., Tollison, Robert D. & Tullock, Gordon (Eds.), *Toward a Theory of the Rent-Seeking Society* (pp. 3-15). College Station, TX: Texas A & M University Press.
Byzov, Leonty. (2006). Bjurokratiia pri V. Putine – sub'ekt razvitiia ili ego tormoz? [Bureaucracy under V. Putin's rule: a force of development or stagnation?]. *SOCIS*, 3, 21-28.
Centre for Study of Globalization and Regionalization. (2004). Democratizing the Global Economy: The Role of Civil Society. *Research report*. Coventry: University of Warwick.
Chandler, Andrea. (2008). The Social Promise: Rights, Privileges, and Responsibilities in Russian Welfare State Reform Since Gorbachev. In Lahusen, Thomas & Solomon, Peter H. (Eds.), *What is Soviet Now? Identities, Legacies, Memories* (pp. 192-213). Berlin: LIT Verlag.
Chester, Lynne. (2010). Actually existing markets: The case of neoliberal Australia. *Society of Heterodox Economics Working Paper No. 2010-09*. Sydney: University of New South Wales.
Churkin, V. E. (2006). Gosudarstvenny organ kak juridicheskoe litso [Government body as a juristic person]. *Trudy Instituta Gosudarstva i Prava RAN*, 2, 89-99.

Coase, Ronald H. (1988 [1937]). The Nature of the Firm. In *The Firm, the Market and the Law* (pp. 33-55). Chicago, IL and London: the University of Chicago Press.
Cohen, Joshua. (1986). Structure, Choice, and Legitimacy: Locke's Theory of the State. *Philosophy and Public Affairs*, 15 (4), 301-324.
Colander, David C. (1984). Introduction. In: Colander, David C. (Ed.), *Neoclassical Political Economy: The Analysis of Rent-Seeking and DUP Activities* (pp. 1-13). Cambridge, MA: Ballinger.
Coleman, James S. (1990). *Foundations of Social Theory*. Cambridge and London: The Belknap Press of Harvard University Press.
Coleman, James S. (1974). *Power and the Structure of Society*. New York: W. W. Norton.
Collins, Randall. (1995). Prediction in Macrosociology: The Case of the Soviet Collapse. *American Journal of Sociology*, 100 (6), 1552-1593.
Colton, Timothy J. (2006). Introduction: Governance and Postcommunist Politics. In Colton, Timothy J. & Holmes, Stephen (Eds.), *The State after Communism: Governance in the New Russia* (pp. 1-20). Lanham, MA: Rowman & Littlefield.
Commons, John R. (1939). *Legal Foundations of Capitalism*. New York: Macmillan.
Commons, John R. (1931). Institutional Economics. *The American Economic Review*, 21 (4), 648-657.
Cook, Linda J. (2006). State Capacity and Pension Provision. In Colton, Timothy J. & Holmes, Stephen (Eds.), *The State after Communism: Governance in the New Russia* (pp. 121-154). Lanham, MA: Rowman & Littlefield.
Cooter, Robert D. (1987). Coase Theorem. In Eatwell, John, Milgate, Murray & Newman, Peter (Eds.), *The New Palgrave: A Dictionary of Economics* (Vol. 1, pp. 457-460). New York: Stockton Press.
Cornell, Stephen & Kalt, Joseph P. (1995). Where does Economic Development Really Come From? Constitutional Rule among the Contemporary Sioux and Apache. *Economic Inquiry*, 33, 402-426.
Corsten, Daniel & Kumar, Nirmalaya. (2005). Do Suppliers Benefit from Collaborative Relationships with Large Retailers? An Empirical Investigation of Efficient Consumer Response Adoption. *Journal of Marketing*, 69, 80-94.
Cox, Andrew. (2004a). The art of possible: relationship management in power regimes and supply chains. *Supply Chain Management: An International Journal*, 9 (5), 346-356.
Cox, Andrew. (2004b). Business relationship alignment: on the commensurability of value capture and mutuality in buyer and supplier exchange. *Supply Chain Management: An International Journal*, 9 (5), 410-420.
Cox, Andrew, Furlong, Paul & Page, Edward. (1985). *Power in Capitalist Societies: Theory, Explanation and Cases*. Brighton, Essex: Wheatsheaf Books.
Cox, Andrew, Watson, Glyn, Lonsdale, Chris & Sanderson, Joe. (2004). Managing appropriately in power regimes: relationship and performance management in 12 supply chain cases. *Supply Chain Management: An International Journal*, 9 (5), 357-371.
Crook, T. Russel & Combs, James G. (2007). Sources and consequences of bargaining power in supply chains. *Journal of Operations Management*, 25, 546-555.
Crozier, Michel. (1963). *Le phénomène bureaucratique*. Paris: Editions du Seuil.
Dahl, Robert. (1990 [1970]). *After the Revolution? Authority in a Good Society* (revisited edition). New Haven, CT and London: Yale University Press.
Dahl, Robert A. (1985). *A Preface to Economic Democracy*. Berkeley and Los Angeles, CA: University of California Press.
Dal', Vladimir (1955 [1880]). *Tolkovy slovar' zhivogo velokorusskogo iazyka* [Explanatory dictionary of Great Russian language]. Moscow: Gosudarstvennoe izdatel'stvo inostrannykh i natsional'nykh slovarei.

Dasgupta, Partha & Serageldin, Ismail (Eds.) (2000). *Social Capital: A Multifaceted Perspective*. Washington, D.C.: The World Bank.
Davis, Lance & North, Douglass C. (1970). Institutional Change and American Economic Growth: A First Step Towards a Theory of Institutional Innovation. *The Journal of Economic History*, 30 (1), 131-149.
Dementiev, Vyacheslav. (2006). Problema vlasti i ekonomichesky analiz [Problem of power and economic analysis]. In Nureev, Rustem (Ed.), *Postsovetsky institutsionalizm: vlast' i biznes* [Post-Soviet institutionalism: Power and Business] (pp. 77-98). Rostov-on-Don: Nauka-Press.
Dementiev, Vyacheslav. (2004). Vlast' i transformatsionnaia ekonomika [Power and the economy in transition]. *Ekonomichesky Vestnik Rostovskogo Gosudarstvennogo Universiteta*, 2 (4), 74-86.
Denzau, Arthur & North, Douglass C. (1994). Shared Mental Models: Ideologies and Institutions. *Kyklos*, 47 (1), 3-31.
Derrida, Jacques (1967). *De la grammatologie*. Paris: Editions de la Minuit.
Dexter, Lewis Anthony. (2006 [1970]). *Elite and specialized interviewing* (2nd ed.). Colchester: ECPR Press.
Djankov, Simeon, La Porta, Rafael, Lopez-de-Silanes, Florencio, & Shleifer, Andrei. (2002). The Regulation of Entry. *The Quarterly Journal of Economics*, 117 (1), 1-37.
Douglas, Mary. (1986). *How Institutions Think*. Syracuse, NY: Syracuse University Press.
Douglass, Dorothy W. (1972 [1953]). *Transitional Economic Systems: The Polish-Czech Example*. New York and London: Monthly Review Press.
Dowding, Keith M. (1996). *Power*. Minneapolis, MN: University of Minnesota Press.
Dowding, Keith M. (1991). *Rational Choice and Political Power*. Aldershot: Edward Elgar.
Duhamel, Luc (2004). The Rise of Moscow Trade Organizations during the 1980s and its Impact on the Russian Society. *Paper presented at the annual meeting of the American Political Science Association*. Chicago, IL.
Earle, Timothy. (1997). *How Chiefs Come to Power: the Political Economy in Prehistory*. Stanford, CA: Stanford University Press.
Eckstein, Harry. (1966). *Division and Cohesion in Democracy: A Study of Norway*. Princeton, NJ: Princeton University Press.
Eco, Umberto. (1990). Introduction. In: Lotman, Yuri. *Universe of the Mind: A Semiotic Theory of Culture* (pp. vii-xiii). Bloomington and Indianapolis, IN: Indiana University Press.
Economist, the. (2008). Send me a number (pp. 10-12). January 5.
Eggertsson, Thráinn. (1990). *Economic Behavior and Institutions*. Cambridge: Cambridge University Press.
Ekelund, Robert B. Jr. & Hébert, Robert F. (2007 [1997]). *A History of Economic Theory and Method* (5th edition). Long Grove, IL: Waveland Press.
Ekelund, Robert B., Jr. & Tollison, Robert D. (1984). A Rent-Seeking Theory of French Mercantilism. In Buchanan, James M. & Tollison, Robert D. (Eds.), *The Theory of Public Choice – II* (pp. 206-223). Ann Arbor, MI: The University of Michigan Press.
El-Qorchi, Mohammed. (2002). Hawala. *Finance & Development: A Quarterly Magazine of the IMF*, 39 (4). Retrieved from http://www.imf.org/external/pubs/ft/fandd/2002/12/elqorchi.htm.
Emerson, Richard M. (1976). Social Exchange Theory. *Annual Review of Sociology*, 2, 335-362.
Energy Charter. (2007). *Energy Charter Protocol on Transit*. Draft. Retrieved from http://www.encharter.org/fileadmin/user_upload/document/CC251.pdf.

Ermakov, S., Kim, I., Mikhailova, T, Osetrova, E. & Sukhovol'sky S. (2004). *Vlast' v russkoi iazykovoj i ethnicheskoi kartine mira* [Power according to Russian linguistic and ethnical worldview]. Moscow: Znak.
Etzioni, Amitai. (2003). Toward a New Socio-Economic Paradigm. *Socio-Economic Review*, 1, 105-134.
Etzioni, Amitai. (1988). *The Moral Dimension: Toward a New Economics*. New York and London: The Free Press.
Etzioni-Halevy, Eva. (1993). *The Elite Connection: Problems and Potential of Western Democracy*. Cambridge: Polity Press.
European Commission. (2008). An EU Security and Solidarity Action Plan. *Commission Staff Working Document SEC (2008) 2871.*
European Commission. (2007). EU Energy Policy Data. *Commission Staff Working Document SEC (2007) 12.*
Fadeev, Valeri. (2008). Infantilizm intellektualov [Infantilism of intellectuals]. *Vedomosti*, 104 (2126) from June 7, A4.
Farnsworth, Kevin & Holden, Chris. (2006). The Business-Social Policy Nexus: Corporate Power and Corporate Inputs into Social Policy. *Journal of Social Policy*, 35 (3), 473-494.
Federal State Statistics Service. (2008a). *Regiony Rossii – 2008 g.* [Regions of Russia – 2008], Moscow.
Federal State Statistics Service. (2008b). *Sostav rabotnikov, zameshchavshikh gosudarstvennye dolzhnosti i dolzhnosti gosudarstvennoi grazhdanskoi skuzhby* [Composition of staff occupying state positions and positions in the state service]. Retrieved from http://www.gks.ru/bgd/regl/b08_99/Main.htm.
Federal State Statistics Service. (2008c). *Rossiisky Statisticheski Ezhegodnik – 2008* [Russian Statistical Yearbook 2008]. Moscow.
Federal State Statistics Service. (2006a). *Promyshlennost' Rossii – 2005: statisticheskii sbornik* [Industry of Russia: statistical data]. Moscow.
Federal State Statistics Service. (2006b). *Rossiisky Statisticheskii Ezhegodnik – 2006* [Russian Statistical Yearbook – 2006]. Moscow.
Federal'naia i regional'naia elita Rossii: kto est' kto v politike i ekonomike [Federal and regional elites in Russia: who is who in politics and economy]. (2004). Moscow: Tsentr Politicheskoi Informatsii.
Fink, Matthew P. (2008). *The Rise of Mutual Funds: An Insider's View*. Oxford and New York: Oxford University Press.
Fisun, Oleksandr. (2003). Developing Democracy or Competitive Neopatrimonialism? The Political Regime of Ukraine in Comparative Perspective. *Paper presented at the workshop "Institution Building and Policy Making in Ukraine."* Toronto: Centre for Russian and East European Studies, University of Toronto. Retrieved from http://www.utoronto.ca/jacyk/files/Fisun-CREES-workshop.pdf.
Fligtsein, Neil. (1996). Markets as Politics: A Political-Cultural Approach to Market Institutions. *American Sociological Review*, 61, 656-67.
Fligstein, Neil & Dauter, Luke. (2007). The Sociology of Markets. *Annual Review of Sociology*, 33, 105-128.
Foucault, Michel. (1984a). *Histoire de la sexualité* (Volume 3: Le souci de soi). Paris: Gallimard.
Foucault, Michel. (1984b). *Histoire de la sexualité* (Volume 2: L'usage des plaisirs). Paris: Gallimard.
Foucault, Michel. (1976). *Histoire de la sexualité* (Volume 1: La volonté de savoir). Paris: Gallimard.
Foucault, Michel. (1975). *Surveiller et punir: Naissance de la prison*. Paris: Gallimard.

Frey, Bruno S. & Buhofer, Heinz (1986). A Market for Men, or: There is no such Thing as a Free Lunch. *Journal of Institutional and Theoretical Economics*, 142 (4), 739-744.
Friedman, James W. (1987). Bilateral monopoly. In Eatwell, John, Milgate, Murray & Newman, Peter (Eds.), *The New Palgrave: A Dictionary of Economics* (Vol. 1, pp. 242-243). New York: Stockton Press.
Frye, Timothy. (2004). Credible Commitment and Property Rights: Evidence from Russia. *American Political Science Review*, 98 (3), 453-466.
Fukuyama, Francis. (1996). *Trust: The Social Virtues and the Creation of Prosperity*. New York: The Free Press.
Gaddy, Clifford. (2004). Perspectives and Potential of Russian Oil. *Eurasian Geography and Economics*, 45 (5): 346-351.
Gaddy, Clifford & Ickes, Barry. (2005). Resource Rents and the Russian Economy. *Eurasian Geography and Economics*, 46 (8), 559-583.
Gaidar, Yegor. (2006). *Gibel' imperii: uroki dlia sovremennoi Rossii* [Collapse of an Empire: Lessons for Modern Russia]. Moscow: ROSSPEN.
Galbraith, John K. (1967). *The New Industrial State*. London: H. Hamilton.
Galitsky, Efim & Levin, Mark. (2007). Korruptsionnye vzaimootnosheniia biznesa i vlasti [Relationships between business and authorities based on corruption]. *Voprosy Ekonomiki*, 1, 19-32.
Gaman-Golutvina, Oxana. (2006 [1998]). *Politicheskie elity Rossii: Vekhi istoricheskoi evolutsii* [Power elites of Russia: milestones of their historical evolution] (2nd ed.). Moscow: ROSSPEN.
Gambetta, Diego. (1993). *The Sicilian Mafia: The Business of Private Protection*. Cambridge, MA: Harvard University Press.
Garfinkel, Harold. (1967). *Studies in Ethnomethodology*. Englewood Cliffs: Prentice-Hall.
Gazprom. (2007). *Godovoi Otchet 2007* [Annual Report 2007]. Moscow.
Geertz, Clifford. (1988). *Works and Lives: the Anthropologist as Author*. Stanford, CA: Stanford University Press.
Gernet, Mikhail. (1941). *Istoriia czarskoi tjurmy* [History of czarist prison] (Vol. 1). Moscow: Yuridicheskoe izdatel'stvo NKYu SSSR.
Gerschenkron, Alexander. (1992 [1952]). Economic Backwardness in Historical Perspective. In Granovetter, Mark & Swedberg, Richard (Eds.), *The sociology of Economic Life* (pp. 111-130). Boulder, CO: Westview Press.
Giddens, Anthony. (1984). *The Constitution of Society: Outline of the Theory of Structuration*. Cambridge: Polity Press.
Gimpelson, Vladimir & Magun, Vladimir. (2004). Na sluzhbe gosudarstva rossiiskogo: perspektivy i ogranicheniia kar'ery molodyh chinovnikov [Serving the Russian state: prospects and constraints of the career of young state servants]. Working paper *WP3/2004/07*. Moscow: the State University – the Highest School of Economics.
Gintis, Herbert. (2000). *Game Theory Evolving: A Problem-Centered Introduction to Modeling Interactions*. Princeton, NJ: Princeton University Press.
Golden, Marissa Martino. (2000). *What Motivates Bureaucrats? Politics and Administration During the Reagan Years*. New York: Columbia University Press.
Gosudarstvenny komitet Rossijskoj Federatsii po statistike. (2003). *Prestupnost' i pravoporiadok v Rossii* [Crime and order in Russia]. Moscow.
Gosudarstvenny komitet Rossijskoj Federatsii po statistike. (2002). *Sostav rabotnikov, zameshchavshikh gosudarstvennye i munitsipal'nye dolzhnosti po poly, vozrasty, stazhy raboty, urovnju obrazovaniia* [Composition of employees holding offices in the state and municipal service, by gender, age, work experience, level of education] (Vol. 1). Moscow.

Granovetter, Mark. (1985). Economic Action and Social Structure: The Problem of Embeddedness. *The American Journal of Sociology*, 91 (3), 481-510.
Gray, Judy & Densten, Iain. (1998). Integrating Quantitative and Qualitative Analysis Using Latent and Manifest Variables. *Quality & Quantity*, 32, 419-431.
Grazhdan, V. (Ed.). (2005). *Rossiiskaia grazhdanskaia sluzhba* [Russian state service]. Moscow: Yurkniga.
Gregory, Paul R. (1990). *Restructuring the Soviet economic bureaucracy*. Cambridge: Cambridge University Press.
Gribovsky, V. (1912). *Gosudarstvennoe ustroistvo i upravlenie Rossiiskoi imperii (iz lektsy po gosudarstvennomy i administrativnomu pravu)* [Constitution and management of the Russian empire (excerpt from a course on constitutional and administrative law)]. Odessa: Tekhnik.
Grosse, Robert. (1996). The bargaining relationship between foreign MNEs and host governments in Latin America. *The International Trade Journal*, 10 (4), 467-499.
Grossman, David & Frieder, Ophir. (2004). *Information Retrieval: Algorithms and Heuristics* (2nd ed.). Dordrecht: Springer.
Gudkov, Lev, Dubin, Boris & Levada, Yuri. (2007). *Problema elity v segodniashnei Rossii: razmyshleniia nad rezul'tatmi sotsiologicheskogo issledovaniia* [Problem of the elite in today's Russia: interpreting results of a sociological study]. Moscow: Fond Liberal'naia Missiia.
Guo, Yong & Hu, Angang. (2004). The administrative monopoly in China's economic transition. *Communist and Post-Communist Studies*, 37, 165-280.
Harsanyi, John C. (1977). *Rational Behavior and Bargaining Equilibrium in Games and Social Situations*. Cambridge: Cambridge University Press.
Hayek, Friedrich von. (1967). *Studies in Philosophy, Politics and Economics*. Chicago: the University of Chicago Press.
Hedlund, Stefan. (2005). *Russian Path Dependence*. London and New York: Routledge.
Hegy, Pierre. (1974). Words of Power: The Power of Words. *Theory and Society*, 1, 329-339.
Hellie, Richard. (2005). The Structure of Russian Imperial History. *History and Theory*, 44, 88-112.
Herbert, Steve. (1997). Territoriality and the Police. *Professional Geographer*, 49 (1), 86-94.
Herrera, Yoshiko M. (2006). The Transformation of the State Statistics. In Colton, Timothy J. & Holmes, Stephen (Eds.), *The State after Communism: Governance in the New Russia* (pp. 53-86). Lanham, MA: Rowman & Littlefield.
Heywood, Andrew. (2002). *Politics* (2nd ed.). New York: Palgrave.
Hodgson, Geoffrey M. (2006). What Are Institutions? *Journal of Economic Issues*, 40 (1), 1-25.
Hoffman, Elizabeth & Spitzer, Matthew L. (1982). The Coase Theorem: Some Experimental Results. *Journal of Law and Economics*, 23 (1), 73-98.
Hofstede, Geert. (1980). *Culture's Consequences: International Differences in Work-Related Values*. Beverly Hills, CA and London: SAGE Publications.
Hofstede, Geert & Hofstede, G. J. (2005). *Cultures and Organizations: Software of the Mind* (2nd ed.). New York: McGraw-Hill.
Hofstede, Geert & Bond, Michael H. (1984). Hosftede's culture dimensions: An independent validation using Rokeach's value survey. *Journal of cross-cultural psychology*, 15 (4), 417-433.
Hogenaraad, Robert, McKenzie, Dean & Péladeau, Normand. (2003). Force and Influence in Content Analysis: The Production of New Social Knowledge. *Quality & Quantity*, 37, 221-238.

Holmes, Larry. (1994), *Sotsial'naia istoriia Rossii: 1917-1941* [The Social History of Russia: 1917-1941]. Rostov-on-Don: Izdatel'stvo RGU.
Huntington, Samuel P. (1968). *Political Order in Changing Societies*. New Haven, CT: Yale University Press.
Ilyenkov, Evald. (1982 [1960]). *Dialectics of the Abstract and the Concrete in Marx's Capital*. Moscow: Progress. Translated by Kuzyakov, Sergei.
Ingerform, Claudio Sergio. (1996). Entre le mythe et la parole: l'action. Naissance de la conception politique du pouvoir en Russie. *Annales HSS*, July-August, 733-757.
Inglehart, Robert. (1997). *Modernization and Postmodernization: Cultural, Economic and Political Change in 43 Societies*. Princeton, NJ: Princeton University Press.
Inglehart, Robert. (1995). Modification des valeurs, développement économique et évolution politique. *Revue Internationale des Sciences Sociales*, 145: 433-460.
Institut Sotsiologii RAN. (2005). Bjurokratiia i vlast' v novoi Rossii: poziciia naseleniia i otsenki ekspertov [Bureaucracy and power in new Russia: the perception by the population and experts' evaluations]. *Final research report*. Moscow.
Ivanovsky, V. (1895). *Gosudarstvennoe pravo* [Constitutional law] (Vol. 1: Verkhovnaia vlast' i eia organy [Supreme power and its bodies]). Kazan': Tipo-litografia Imperatorskogo universiteta.
Jick, Todd D. (1979). Mixing Qualitative and Quantitative Methods: Triangulation in Action. *Administrative Science Quarterly*, 24 (4), 602-611.
Jonge, Jan de. (2005). Rational Choice Theory and Moral Action. *Socio-Economic Review*, 3, 117-132.
Kagel, John & Roth, Alvin (Eds.). (1995). *The Handbook of Experimental Economics*. Princeton, NJ: Princeton University Press.
Karamzin, Nikolai. (2003 [1815]). *Istoriia gosudarstva rossiiskogo* [History of the Russian state]. Moscow: OLMA Press.
Karamzin, Nikolai. (1991 [1811]). *Zapiska o drevnei i novoi Rossii v ee politicheskom i grazhdanskom otnosheniiakh* [Memoir on Ancient and Modern Russia]. Moscow: Nauka.
Kemerovostat. (2008). *Kemerovskaia oblats': istoriia v tsifrakh* [Region of Kemerovo: history in figures]. Kemerovo: Kemerovostat.
Keohane, Robert O. & Nye, Joseph S. (2001). *Power and Interdependence* (3rd ed.). New York: Longman.
Keynes, John M. (1936). *The General Theory of Employment, Interest and Money*. London: Macmillan.
Kharkhordin, Oleg. (2001). What is the State? The Russian concept of *Gosudarstvo* in the European context. *History and Theory*, 40, 206-240.
Khasis, Lev. (2006). Na rossijskom rynke postavshchiki dominirujut nad roznitsei [Suppliers dominate over retailers in the Russian market]. *Profil'*, 47 (508) from December 18. Retrieved from http://www.profile.ru/items/?item=21155.
Khlopin, Aleksandr. (1997). Stanovlenie grazhdanskogo obshchestva v Rossii: institutsional'naia perspektiva [Emergence of civil society in Russia: institutional approach], *Pro et Contra*, 2 (4), 60-76.
Khlopin, Aleksander. (1994). The Phenomenon of "Double-Thinking": Specific Features of the Role Behavior. *Social Sciences* (Quarterly Review), 25 (4), 68-83.
Kirdina, Svetlana. (2001 [2000]). *Institutsional'nye matritsy i razvitie Rossii* [Institutional matrixes and the development of Russia] (2nd ed.). Novosibirsk: IEiOPP SO RAN.
Kleiner, Georgi. (2001). Osobennosti formirovaniia i evoljutsii sotsial'no-ekonomicheskih institutov v Rossii [Particularities of the emergence and evolution of economic institutions in Russia]. Working paper *WP/2001/126*. Moscow: TsEMI.

Klyuchevsky, Vasily. (1958 [1905]). Kurs russkoi istorii [Course on Russian history]. In *Sochineniia* [Collected works] (Vol. 4). Moscow: Izdatel'stvo social'no-ekonomicheskoi literatury.
Klyuchevsky, Vasily. (1957 [1904]). Kurs russkoi istorii [Course on Russian history]. In *Sochineniia* [Collected works] (Vol. 2). Moscow: Izdatel'stvo social'no-ekonomicheskoi literatury.
Klyuchevsky, Vasily. (1956 [1903]). Kurs russkoi istorii [Course on Russian history]. In *Sochineniia* [Collected works] (Vol. 1). Moscow: Izdatel'stvo social'no-ekonomicheskoi literatury.
Konovalov, Aleksandr. (2006). *Partijnaia nomenklatura Sibiri v sisteme regional'noi vlasti (1945-1991)* [The party's nomenklatura in Siberia and its place in the system of regional governance (1945-1991)]. Kemerovo: Kuzbassvuzizdat.
Konovalov, Aleksandr. (2004). *Istoriia Kemerovskoi oblasti v biographiiakh partijnykh rukovoditelei* [History of the region of Kemerovo through the lens of biographies of the party's leaders], Kemerovo: Kuzbassvuzizdat.
Kordonsky, Simon. (2006 [2000]). *Rynki vlasti: administrativnye rynki SSSR i Rossii* [Markets for Power: administrative markets in the USSR and Russia] (2nd ed.). Moscow: OGI.
Kornai, János (1980) *Economics of Shortage* (Vols. 1-2). Amsterdam: North Holland.
Kostomarov, Nikolai. (2008 [1863]). *Russkaia respublika: severnorusskie narodopravstva vo vremena udel'no-vechevogo uklada* [Russian Republic: North-Russian states governed by the people at the time of appanage]. Moscow: Firma STD.
Kostomarov, Nikolai. (2007 [1872]). *Russkaia istoriia v zhizneopisaniiakh ee vazhneishikh deiatelei* [Russian history through life stories of its key actors] (Vol. 1). St. Petersburg: Lenizdat, Leningrad.
Kreps, David. (1990a). Corporate Culture and Economic Theory. In Alt, James & Shepsle, Kenneth (Eds.), *Perspectives on Positive Political Economy* (pp. 90-143). Cambridge: Cambridge University Press.
Kreps, David. (1990b). *Game Theory and Economic Modeling*. Oxford: Clarendon Press of Oxford University Press.
Krivosheev, Yuri. (2008). *Russkaia srednevekovaia gosudarstvennost'* [Russian statehood in the Middle Ages]. St. Petersburg: Izdatel'stvo Sankt-Peterburgskogo Universiteta.
Krugman, Paul. (2009). *The Return of Depression Economics and the Crisis of 2008*. New York and London: W. W. Norton.
Kryshtanovskaya, Olga. (2005 [2004]). *Anatomiia rossiiskoi elity* [Anatomy of the Russian elite]. Moscow: Zakharov.
Kuhn, Thomas S. (1972 [1963]). Scientific Paradigms. In Barnes, Barry (Ed.), *Sociology of Science: Selected Readings* (pp. 80-104). Harmondsworth: Penguin Books.
Kurbatova, Margarita & Aparina, Natalia. (2008). Sotsial'ny kapital predprinimatelia: formy ego proiavleniia i osobennosti v sovremennoi rossiiskoi ekonomike [Social capital of the entrepreneur: its forms and manifestations in today's Russian economy]. *Ekonomichesky Vestnik Rostovskogo Gosudarstvennogo Universiteta*, 6 (4), 45-61.
Lamont, Michèle & Molnár, Virág. (2002). The study of boundaries in the social sciences. *Annual Review of Sociology*, 28, 167-95.
Langlois, Richard. (1986). Rationality, Institutions and Explanation. In Langlois, Richard (Ed.), *Economics as a Process: Essays in the New Institutional Economics* (pp. 225-255). Cambridge: Cambridge University Press.
Lawson, Tony. (1997). *Economics and Reality*. London and New York: Routledge.
Ledeneva, Alena V. (2006). *How Russia Really Works*. Ithaca, NY: Cornell University Press.

Ledeneva, Alena V. (1998). *Russia's Economy of Favours: Blat, Networking and Informal Exchange*. Cambridge: Cambridge University Press.
Ledyaev, Valeri G. (2009). Domination, Power and Authority in Russia: Basic Characteristics and Forms. In Oleinik, Anton (Ed.), *Reforming the State without Changing the Model of Power* (pp. 18-37). London and New York: Routledge.
Ledyaev, Valeri G. (1997). *Power: A Conceptual Analysis*. Commack, NY: Nova Science Publishers.
Levada, Youri. (1993). *Entre passé et l'avenir: L'homme soviétique ordinaire. Enquête*. Paris: Presses de la Fondation Nationale des Sciences Politiques. Translated from Russian by Tordjman, J. and Berelowitch, A.
Lincoln, W. Bruce. (1990). *The Great Reforms: Autocracy, Bureaucracy and the Politics of Change in Imperial Russia*. DeKalb, IL: Northern Illinois University Press.
Lindenberg, Siegwart. (1990). A New Push in the Theory of Organization: A Commentary on O. E. Williamson's "Comparison of Alternative Approaches to Economic Organization." *Journal of Institutional and Theoretical Economics*, 146 (1), 76-84.
Livet, Pierre & Thévenot, Laurent. (1994). Les catégories de l'action collective. In Orléan, André (Ed.), *Analyse économique des conventions* (pp. 139-167). Paris: Presses Universitaires de France.
Livshin, Aleksandr & Orlov, Igor. (2002). *Vlast' i obshchestvo: dialog v pis'makh* [Power and society: dialogue through letters]. Moscow: ROSSPEN.
Lotman, Yuri. (1990). *Universe of the Mind: A Semiotic Theory of Culture*. Bloomington and Indianapolis, IN: Indiana University Press. Translated by Shukman, Ann. With an Introduction by Eco, Umberto.
Lubarsky G. (2005). Chinovniki i gossluzhashchie [Office holders and state servants]. Retrieved from http://bd.fom.ru/report/map/gur050407.
Luhmann, Niklas. (1990 [1982]). *Amour comme passion: De la codification de l'intimité*. Paris: Aubier. Translated from the German by Lionnet, A.-M.
Luhmann, Niklas. (1979 [1973-1975]). *Trust and Power*. New York: John Wily & Sons. With an Introduction by Poggi, Gianfranco.
Lukes, Steven. (2005 [1974]). *Power: A Radical View* (2nd ed.). Houndmills, Hampshire and New York: Palgrave Macmillan.
Lukes, Steven. (2002). Power and Agency. *British Journal of Sociology*, 53 (3), 491-496.
Macaulay, Stewart. (1963). Non-Contractual Relations in Business: A Preliminary Study. *American Sociological Review*, 28 (1), 55-67.
Machiavelli, Niccolò. (1940 [1513]). *The Prince and the Discourses*. New York: Random House.
Makarenko, Viktor P. (1998). *Russkaia vlast': teoretiko-sotsiologicheskie problemy* [Russian power: theoretical and sociological aspects]. Rostov-on-Don: Izdatel'stvo Severo-Kavkazskogo Nauchnogo Tsentra Vyshej Shkoly.
Malia, Martin. (1999). *Russia under Western Eyes: From the Bronze Horseman to the Lenin Mausoleum*. Cambridge, MA and London: The Belknap Press of Harvard University Press.
Malinin, Yu. (1995). "Korolevskaia troitsa" vo Frantsii IV-XV vekov ["Royal Trinity" in France of the IV-XV centuries]. In *Odissei: chelovek v istorii* [Odyssey: human being and history] (pp. 20-36). Moscow: Nauka.
Mann, Michael. (1993). *The sources of social power* (Vol. 2: The Rise of Classes and Nation States, 1760-1914). Cambridge: Cambridge University Press.
Mann, Michael. (1986). *The sources of social power* (Vol. 1: A history of power from the beginning to A.D. 1760). Cambridge: Cambridge University Press.
Manning, Nick. (2003). *International Public Administration Reform: Implications for the Russian Federation*. Washington, DC: World Bank Publications.

Marshall, Alfred. (1920 [1890]). *Principles of Economics* (8th ed.). London: Macmillan.
Marx, Karl. (1998 [1894]). Capital (Vol. 3). In Marx Karl & Engels Frederic. *Collected Works* (Vol. 37). New York: International Publishers.
Marx, Karl. (1936 [1867]). *Capital: A critique of political economy* (Vol. 1). New York: Modern Library. Translated from the third German edition by Moore, Samuel and Aveling, Edward.
Ménard, Claude. (2005a). Transaction Cost Economics: From the Coase Theorem to Empirical Studies. In Oleinik, Anton (Ed.), *The Institutional Economics of Russia's Transformation* (pp. 45-64). Aldershot, Hampshire and Burlington, VT: Ashgate.
Ménard, Claude. (2005b). Theory of Organizations: The Diversity of Arrangements in a Developed Market Economy. In Oleinik, Anton (Ed.), *The Institutional Economics of Russia's Transformation* (pp. 88-111). Aldershot, Hampshire and Burlington, VT: Ashgate.
Ménard, Claude. (1993 [1990]). *L'économie des organisations* (New ed.). Paris: La Découverte.
Merton, Robert K. (1995). The Thomas Theorem and the Matthew Effect. *Social Forces*, 74 (2), 379-424.
Merton, Robert K. (1938). Social Structure and Anomie. *American Sociological Review*, 3 (5), 672-682.
Meyer-Sahling, Jan-Hinrik. (2006). The Institutionalization of Political Discretion in Post-Communist Civil Service Systems: The Case of Hungary. *Public Administration*, 84 (3), 693-716.
Meyer-Sahling, Jan-Hinrik (2004). Civil Service Reform in Post-Communist Europe: The Bumpy Road to Depolitization. *West European Politics*, 27 (1), 71-103.
Mills, Wright Charles. (1957). *The Power Elite*. New York: Oxford University Press.
Mitchell, Timothy. (1990). Everyday metaphors of power. *Theory and Society*, 19 (5), 545-577.
Mitrokhin, Nikolai. (2000). Russkaia pravoslavnaia tserkov' kak sub'ekt ekonomicheskoi deiatel'nosti' [Russian Orthodox Church as an economic subject]. *Voprosy Ekonomiki*, 8, 54-70.
Morozov, Yuri. (1991). *Puti Rossii: Modernizatsiia neevropeiskikh kul'tur* [Trajectories of Russia: On modernization of non-European cultures] (Issues 1-4). Moscow.
Morriss, Peter. (2009). Power and Liberalism. In Clegg, Stewart R. & Haugaard, Mark (Eds.), *The SAGE Handbook of Power* (pp. 54-69). Los Angeles, CA: SAGE.
Morriss, Peter. (1987). *Power: a Philosophical Analysis*. New York: St. Martin's Press.
Munro, J. E. (1987). Principal and Agent. In Eatwell John, Milgate Murray & Newman Peter (Eds.), *The New Palgrave: A Dictionary of Economics* (p. 966). New York: Stockton Press.
Muratbekova-Touron, Maral. (2002). Working in Kazakhstan and Russia: Perception of French Managers. *International Journal of Human Resource Management*, 13 (2), 213-231.
Nelson, Richard R. & Winter, Sidney G. (1982). *An Evolutionary Theory of Economic Change*. Cambridge, MA: The Belknap Press of Harvard University Press.
Neuendorf, Kimberly A. (2002). *The Content Analysis Guidebook*. Thousand Oaks, CA, London and New Delhi: SAGE Publications.
Newman, W. Lawrence. (2006). *Social Research Methods: Qualitative and Quantitative Approaches* (6th ed.). Boston, MA: Allyn and Bacon.
Ngo, Tak-Wing. (2008). Rent-seeking and economic governance in the structural nexus of corruption in China. *Crime, Law and Social Change*, 49, 27-44.
North, Douglass C. (1990). *Institutions, Institutional Change and Economic Performance*. Cambridge and New York: Cambridge University Press.

North, Douglass C. (1981). *Structure and Change in Economic History*. New York: W. W. Norton.
Nyam-Osor, Namsrain. (2003). *Mongol'skoe gosudarstvo i gosudarstvennost' v XIII-XIV vv* [Mongol state and statehood in the XIII-XIV centuries]. Ulan-Ude: Izdatel'stvo Buriatskogo nauchnogo tsentra SO RAN.
Obshchestvennoe mnenie – 2008: ezhegodnik (2008) [2008 Yearbook of public opinion]. Moscow: Levada-Tsentr.
Obshchestvo "Memorial." (1998). *Sistema ispravitel'no-trudovykh lagerei v SSSR: 1923-1960* [System of penitentiary camps in the Soviet Union: 1923-1960]. Moscow.
Oleinik, Anton. (2010). Uses and Abuses of Sexuality in Social Interactions: Empirical Evidence from Russia. *Europe-Asia Studies*, 62 (5), 749-778.
Oleinik, Anton (Ed.). (2009a). *Reforming the State without Changing the Model of Power? On Administrative Reform in Post-Socialist Countries*. London and New York: Routledge.
Oleinik, Anton. (2009b). Introduction: Putting Administrative Reform in a Broader Context of Power. In Oleinik, Anton (Ed.), *Reforming the State Without Changing the Model of Power? On Administrative Reform in Post-Socialist Countries* (pp. 1-17). London and New York: Routledge.
Oleinik, Anton. (2009c). Inquiring into communication in science: alternative approaches. *Science in Context*, 22 (4), 613-646.
Oleinik, Anton. (2009d). Gazovy konflikt: torg neumesten [Conflict around gas supplies: bargaining is not appropriate]. *Vedomosti*, 2 (2272) from January 12, A4.
Oleinik, Anton. (2008a). On Negative Convergence: The Metaphor of Vodka-Cola Reconsidered. *Telos*, 145, 31-46.
Oleinik, Anton. (2008b). Lessons of Russian in Afghanistan. *Society* (Social science and modern society), 45 (3), 288-293.
Oleinik, Anton. (2008c). Zapiski puteshestvennika po Regionu.SU [Travel Notes from Region.SU]. *EKO – Ekonomika i Organizatsiia*, 2, 3-22.
Oleinik, Anton. (2008d). Deux modèles de pouvoir: une étude empirique dans le milieu carcéral russe. *Revue d'études comparatives Est-ouest*, 39 (4), 185-212.
Oleinik, Anton. (2008e). Teoremy Kouza: institutsional'nye predposylki [The Coase theorems: institutional assumptions]. *Ekonomicheskaia nauka sovremennoi Rossii*, 2 (38), 21-39.
Oleinik, Anton. (2008f). Torgovlia kak dvigatel' vlasti [Retail trade as a weapon in hands of power holders]. *Nezavisimaia Gazeta* from November 28, 7.
Oleinik, Anton. (2008g). Face-kontrol dlia investora [Face-control for the investor]. *Vedomosti*, 97 (2119) from May 29, A4.
Oleinik, Anton. (2008h). Skromnoe obaianie etatizma [Discreet charm of etatism]. *Vedomosti*, 107 (2129) from June 11, A4.
Oleinik, Anton. (2007a). Minimizing Missed Opportunities: A New Model of Choice? *Journal of Economic Issues*, 41 (2), 547-556.
Oleinik, Anton. (2007b). Le système pénitentiaire Russe. In Céré, Jean-Paul & Japiassú, Carlos Eduardo A. (Eds.), *Les systèmes pénitentiaires dans le monde* (pp. 295-320). Paris: Dalloz.
Oleinik, Anton. (2006a). A Plurality of Total Institutions: Towards a Comparative Penology. *Crime, Law and Social Change*, 46, 161-180.
Oleinik, Anton. (2006b). The More Things Change, the More They Stay the Same: Institutional Transfers seen through the Lens of Reforms in Russia. *Journal of Economic Issues*, 40 (4), 919-940.
Oleinik, Anton. (2005a). "Small society" and networks: on the meaning lost in semiotic translation. *Journal of Economic Issues*, 39 (3), 813-818.

Oleinik, Anton. (2005b). A Distrustful Economy: An Inquiry into Foundations of the Russian Market. *Journal of Economic Issues*, 39 (1), 53-74.

Oleinik, Anton (Ed.). (2005c). *The Institutional Economics of Russia's Transformation*. Aldershot, Hampshire and Burlington, VT: Ashgate.

Oleinik, Anton. (2005d). Institutional Traps in the Post-Privatization Development of the Russian Economy. In Oleinik, Anton (Ed.), *The Institutional Economics of Russia's Transformation* (pp. xiii-xxviii). Aldershot, Hampshire and Burlington, VT: Ashgate.

Oleinik, Anton. (2004a). A Model of Network Capitalism: Basic Ideas and Post-Soviet Evidence. *Journal of Economic Issues*, 38 (1), 85-111.

Oleinik, Anton. (2004b). On Universal versus Specific Categories of Network Capitalism: A Reply to V. Barnett's Note. *Journal of Economic Issues*, 38 (4), 1040-1046.

Oleinik, Anton. (2003). *Organized Crime, Prison and Post-Soviet Societies*. Aldershot: Ashgate. Translated by Curtis, Sheryl. With a Foreword by Touraine, Alain.

Oleinik, Anton. (2002a). The Costs and Prospects of Reforms in Russia: An Institutional Approach. *Teme*, 26 (4), 491-517.

Oleinik, Anton. (2002b). "Business According to Understandings": An Institutional Model of Russian Capitalism. *Problems of Economic Transition*, 44 (11), 3-35.

Oleinik, Anton, Aparina, Natalia, Clément, Karine, Gvozdeva, Eugenia, Kashturov, Aleksandr, & Minin, Mikhail. (2005). *L'analyse socio-économique du blanchiment: L'example des capitaux illicites Russes en France et d'autres pays occidentaux*. Saint-Denis-La-Plaine: Institut National des Etudes de Sécurité.

OPEC (Organization of the Petroleum Exporting Countries). (2009). *Monthly Oil Market Report: September 2009*. Retrieved from http://www.opec.org/home/Monthly%20Oil%20Market%20Reports/2009/pdf/MR092009.pdf.

Orléan, André. (1994). Vers un modèle général de la coordination économique par les conventions. In Orléan, André (Ed.), *Analyse économique des conventions* (pp. 9-40). Paris: Presses Universitaires de France.

Orléan, André. (1988). L'autoréférence dans la théorie keynésienne de la spéculation. *Cahiers d'Economie Politique*, 14-15, 229-242.

Ostrom, Elinor. (1998). A Behavioral Approach to the Rational Choice Theory of Collective Action. *American Political Science Review*, 92 (1), 1-22.

Ostrom, Elinor. (1990). *Governing the Commons: The Evaluation of Institutions for Collective Action*. New York: Cambridge University Press.

Ovchinnikova, Julia. (2006). Strategii vystraivaniia konkurentnyh otnoshenii na rynke roznichnoi torgovli v sovremennoi Rossii [Strategies for building competitive relationships in the Russian retail trade]. *Undergraduate research paper*. Moscow: the Higher School of Economics.

Padovani, Marcelle. (1987). *Les dernières années de la Mafia*. Paris: Gallimard.

Peach, Jim & Dugger, William. (2006). An Intellectual History of Abundance. *Journal of Economic Issues*, 40 (3), 693-706.

Peristeras, Vassilios & Tsekos, Theodore. (2004). e-Governance as a Public Policy Framework. *NISPAcee Occasional Papers in Public Administration and Public Policy*, 5 (2), 4-10.

Petukhov, Vladimir. (2006). Bjurokratiia i vlast' [Bureaucracy and power]. *SOCIS*, 3, 9-15.

Pipes, Richard. (2005 [1959]). *Karamzin's Memoir on Ancient and Modern Russia: A Translation and Analysis* (New ed.). Ann Arbor, MI: The University of Michigan Press.

Pipes, Richard. (2000 [1999]). *Property and freedom*. New York: Vintage Books.

Pipes, Richard. (1974). *Russia under the Old Regime*. London: Weidenfeld and Nicolson.

Pivovarov, Yuri S. (2006a). *Russkaia politicheskaia traditsiia i sovremennost'* [Russian political tradition and current situation]. Moscow: INION RAN.
Pivovarov, Yuri S. (2006b). *Russkaia politika v ee istoricheskom i kul'turnom otnosheniiakh* [Historical and cultural aspects of Russian politics]. Moscow: ROSSPEN.
Pivovarov, Yuri S. (2004). *Polnaia gibel' vseriez* [Talking seriously about prospects of Russia's downfall]. Moscow: ROSSPEN.
Pivovarov, Yuri S. & Fursov, Andrei. (1998). Pravopreemstvo i russkaia vlast' [Succession of power and Russian power]. *Politiia – Vestnik fonda ROPTs*, 1, 68-80.
Pobedonostsev, Konstantin P. (1965 [1869]). *Reflections of a Russian Statesman*. Ann Arbor, MI: Ann Arbor Paperbacks of the University of Michigan Press. With a new foreword by Polner, Murray.
Polanyi, Karl. (1957 [1944]). *The Great Transformation: The Political and Economic Origins of Our Time*, Boston, MA: Beacon Press.
Poliakov, Leonid. (2007). Suverennaia demokratiia: politicheskii fakt kak teoreticheskaia predmetnost' [Sovereign democracy: theorizing a political fact]. *Obshchestvennye nauki i sovremennost'*, 2, 59-68.
Polterovich, Viktor. (2001). Transplantatsiia ekonomicheskih institutov [Transfers of economic institutions]. *Ekonomicheskaia nauka sovremennoi Rossii*, 3, 24-50.
Posner, Richard. (1977). *Economic Analysis of Law* (2nd ed.). Boston, MA: Little & Brown.
Presnyakov, Aleksandr. (1998 [1918]). *Obrazovanie Velikorusskogo gosudarstva* [Formation of the state of Great Russia]. Moscow: Bogorodsky pechatnik.
Publichny disput 19.3.1860 o nachale Rusi mezhdu gg. Pogodinym i Kostomarovym (1860) [Public dispute about the origin of Russia between Mr. Pogodin and Mr. Kostomarov]. *Sovremennik*, 80 (3), 257-292.
Putterman, Louis. (1988). The Firm as Association versus the Firm as Commodity: Efficiency, Rights and Ownership. *Economics and Philosophy*, 4 (2), 244-267.
Radaev, Vadim. (2007). *Zakhvat rossiiskih territorii: novaia konkurentnaia situtsiia v roznichnoi torgovle* [Annexation of Russian territories: a new competitive situation in retail trade] (2nd ed.). Moscow: Izdatel'skii dom GU-VShE.
Radaev, Vadim. (2005). Dinamika delovyh strategii rossiiskikh roznichnykh kompanii pod vozdeistviem global'nykh torgovykh setei [Changes in strategies of Russian retailers under influence of global retailers]. *Rossiisky zhurnal menegmenta*, 3 (3), 3-26.
Raeff, Marc. (1984 [1982]). *Understanding Imperial Russia: State and Society in the Old Regime*. New York: Columbia University Press.
Raeff, Marc. (1983). *The well-ordered police state: social and institutional change through law in the Germanies and Russia: 1600-1800*. New Haven, CT: Yale University Press.
Redmond, P. W. D. & Shears, Peter. (1993 [1964]). *General Principles of English Law* (7th ed.). London: Pitman Publishing, the M & E Handbook Series.
Remington, Thomas. (2006). Democratization, Separation of Powers, and State Capacity. In Colton, Timothy J. & Holmes, Stephen (Ed.), *The State after Communism: Governance in the New Russia* (pp. 261-297). Lanham, MA: Rowman & Littlefield.
Reporters Without Borders. (2004). *Internet Under Surveillance*. Retrieved from http://www.rsf.org/rubrique.php3?id_rubrique=433.
Richardson, Amanda. (2003). Corridors of Power: A Case Study in Access Analysis from Medieval England. *Antiquity*, 77 (296), 373-384.
Robbins, Paul. (2000). The Rotten Institution: Corruption in Natural Resource Management. *Political Geography*, 19, 423-443.
Roberts, Carl W. (2000). A Conceptual Framework for Quantitative Text Analysis. *Quality and Quantity*, 34, 259-274.

Rodriguez, Peter, Siegel, Donald S., Hillman, Amy & Eden, Lorraine. (2006). Three Lenses on the Multinational Enterprise: Politics, Corruption and Corporate Social Responsibility. *Journal of International Business Studies*, 37, 733-746.
Rose, Richard. (1995). La liberté, valeur fondamentale. *Revue Internationale des Sciences Sociales*, 145, 519-536.
Rose, Richard & Mishler, William. (1995). What Are the Alternatives to Democracy in Post-Communist Societies? *Studies in Public Policy*, 248.
Rose, Richard, Mishler, William & Haerpfer, Christian. (1997). Getting Real: Social Capital in Post-Communist Societies. *Studies in Public Policy*, 278.
Rose, Richard, Mishler, William & Munro, Neil. (2006). *Russia Transformed: Developing Popular Support for a New Regime*. Cambridge: Cambridge University Press.
Rose, Richard, Mishler, William & Munro, Neil. (2004). Resigned Acceptance of an Incomplete Democracy: Russia's Political Equilibrium. *Post-Soviet Affairs*, 20 (3), 195-218.
Roshé, Sébastian. (1993). *Le sentiment d'insécurité*. Paris: Presses Universitaires de France.
Rossiia: Khronika osnovnikh sobytii. IX-XX veka [Russia: Milestones. IX-XX centuries] (2002), Moscow: ROSSPEN.
Rusakov, N. P. (1969). *Iz istorii sitsiliiskoi mafii* [Essays on the History of the Sicilian Mafia]. Moscow: Nauka.
Ryavec, Karl W. (2003). *Russian Bureaucracy: Power and Pathology*. Lanham, ML: Rowman & Littlefield.
Sack, Robert D. (1986). *Human Territoriality: Its Theory and History*. Cambridge: Cambridge University Press.
Salton, Gerard & McGill, Michael. (1983). *Introduction to Modern Information Retrieval*. New York: McGraw-Hill.
Samuelson, Paul & Scott, Anthony. (1966). *Economics: An Introductory Analysis*. Toronto: McGraw-Hill.
Samye vliiatel'nye ljudi Rossii – 2003 [Most influential people in Russia in 2003] (2004). Moscow: Institut situatsionnogo analiza i tekhnologii.
Sandler, Todd. (1992). *Collective Action: Theory and Applications*. Ann Arbor, MI: The University of Michigan Press.
Sapir, Jacques. (1990). *L'économie mobilisée*. Paris: Editions La Découverte.
Sappington, David E. (1991). Incentives in Principal-Agent Relationships. *Journal of Economic Perspectives*, 5 (2), 45-66.
Sassen, Saskia. (2000). Territory and Territoriality in the Global Economy. *International Sociology*, 15 (2), 372-393.
Saussier, Stéphane. (2005). Theory of Optimal Contract: Contractual Relationships. In Oleinik, Anton (Ed.), *The Institutional Economics of Russia's Transformation* (pp. 65-87). Aldershot, Hampshire and Burlington, VT: Ashgate.
Schelling, Thomas S. (1960). *The Strategy of Conflict*. Cambridge, MA: Harvard University Press.
Schotter, Andrew. (1981). *The Economic Theory of Social Institutions*. Cambridge: Cambridge University Press.
Schutz, Alfred. (1987 [1954]). Formation du concept et de la théorie dans les sciences sociales. In *Le chercheur et le quotidien: Phénoménologie des sciences sociales* (pp. 65-88). Paris: Méridiens Klincksieck. Translated by Noschis-Gilliéron, Anne.
Schuetz, Alfred. (1953). Common Sense and Scientific Interpretation of Human Action. *Philosophy and Phenomenological Research*, 14 (1), 1-38.
Scott, John. (2001). *Power*. Cambridge: Polity Press.
Sedova, Natalia. (2006). Effektivnost' bjurokratii v otsenkah rossiian [Effectiveness of the bureaucracy in evaluations of Russians]. *SOCIS*, 3, 15-20.

Serrano, Roberto. (2008). Bargaining. In Durlauf, Steven & Blume, Lawrence (Eds.), *The New Palgrave: Dictionary of Economics* (2nd ed.) (Vol. 1, pp. 370-380). New York: Palgrave Macmillan.
Shachtman, Max. (1962). *The bureaucratic revolution: the rise of the Stalinist state*. New York: The Donald Press.
Shervani, Tasadduq A., Frazier, Gary & Challagalla, Goutam. (2007). The Moderating Influence of Firm Market Power on the Transaction Cost Economics Model: An Empirical Test in a Forward Channel Integration Context. *Strategic Management Journal*, 28, 635-652.
Shkaratan, Ovsey et al. (2009). *Sotsial'no-ekonomicheskoe neravenstvo i ego vosproizvodstvo v sovremennoi Rossii* [Social-economic inequality and its reproduction in today's Russia]. Moscow: OLMA Media grupp.
Shlapentokh, Vladimir. (1995). Russian Patience: A Reasonable Behavior and a Social Strategy. *Archives européennes de sociologie*, 36 (2), 247-280.
Shlapentokh, Vladimir. (1989). *Public and Private Life of the Soviet People: Changing Values in Post-Stalin Russia*. New York and Oxford: Oxford University Press.
Sieca-Kozlowski, Elisabeth & Daucé, Françoise (Eds.). (2006). *Dedovshchina in the Post-Soviet Military: Hazing of Russian Army Conscripts in a Comparative Perspective*. Stuttgart: Ibidem-Verlag. With a foreword by Herspring, Dale.
Simon, Herbert A. (1978). Rationality as Process and as product of Thought. *The American Economic Review*, 68 (2), 1-16.
Simon, Herbert A. (1953). Notes on the Observation and Measurement of Political Power. *The Journal of Politics*, 15 (4), 500-516.
Simon, Herbert A. (1951). A Formal Theory of the Employment Relationship. *Econometrica*, 19 (3), 293-305.
Skinner, Quentin. (2002a). *Visions of Politics* (Vol. 1: Regarding Method). Cambridge: Cambridge University Press.
Skinner, Quentin. (2002b), *Visions of Politics* (Vol. 2: Renaissance Virtues). Cambridge: Cambridge University Press.
Smith, Adam. (1818 [1776]). *An Inquiry into the Nature and Causes of the Wealth of Nations* (11th ed.). Hartford: Cooke & Hale.
Smith, John Maynard. (1982). *Evolution and the Theory of Games*. Cambridge: Cambridge University Press.
Sokolov, A. (2005). Prinuzhdenie k trudu v sovetskoi ekonomike: 1930-ye – seredina 1950-h [Forced labor in the Soviet economy: the 1930s – the mid-1950s]. In Borodkin, L., Gregory P. & Khlevniuk, O. (Eds.), *Gulag: ekonomika prinuditel'nogo truda* [Gulag: the economics of forced labor] (pp. 17-66). Moscow: ROSSPEN.
Solomon, Peter H. (2004). Socialist Bureaucracy and the Law-Based State. *Paper presented at the conference "Real Socialism and the Second World" (April 30 – May 1)*. Toronto: University of Toronto.
Solomon, Peter H. (1996). *Soviet Criminal Justice under Stalin*. Cambridge: Cambridge University Press.
Solzhenitsyn, Aleksandr. (1973). *Arkhipelag Gulag* [The Gulag Archipelago] (Vols. 1-2). Paris: Ymca-Press.
Soto, Hernando de (2005 [1989]). *The Other Path: The Economic Answer to Terrorism*. New York: Basic Books.
Soto, Hernando de (2000). *The Mystery of Capital: Why Capitalism Triumphs in the West and Fails Everywhere Else*. London: Bantam Press.
Statistics Canada. (2008). *Report on the demographic situation in Canada, 2005 and 2006*. Retrieved from http://www.statcan.gc.ca/pub/91-209-x/91-209-x2004000-eng.pdf.

Stewart, Agnus. (2001). *Theories of Power and Domination: The Politics of Empowerment in Late Modernity*. London: SAGE Publications.
Stiglitz, Joseph E. (1994). *Whither Socialism?* Cambridge, MA: The MIT Press.
Stiglitz, Joseph E. (1987). Principal and Agent. In Eatwell John, Milgate Murray & Newman Peter (Eds.), *The New Palgrave: A Dictionary of Economics* (pp. 966-971). New York: Stockton Press.
Strange, Susan. (1996). *The Retreat of the State: The Diffusion of Power in the World Economy*. Cambridge: Cambridge University Press.
Sugden, Robert. (1989). Spontaneous Order. *Journal of Economic Perspectives*, 3 (4), 85-97.
Summa ideologii: mirovozzrenie i ideologiia sovremennoi rossiiskoi elity [Sum of ideologies: the worldview and ideology of the contemporary Russian elite] (2008). Moscow: Institut obshchestvennogo proektirovaniia.
Surkov, Vladislav. (2006). Natsionalizatsiia budushchego: paragrafy pro suverennuju demokratiju [Nationalizing the future: theses on sovereign democracy]. *Ekspert*, 43.
Swanson, Jacinda. (2007). Rower and Resistance: Perpetuating and Challenging Capitalist Exploitation. *Contemporary Political Theory*, 6 (1), 4-23.
Swedberg, Richard. (2003). *Principles of Economic Sociology*. Princeton, NJ: Princeton University Press.
Sykes, Gresham. (1958). *The society of captives: A Study of a Maximum Security Prison*. Princeton, NJ: Princeton University Press.
Taylor, Scott & Spicer, André. (2007). Time for Space: A Narrative Review of Research on Organizational Spaces. *International Journal of Management Reviews*, 9 (4), 325-346.
Thévenot, Laurent. (2007). The plurality of cognitive formats and engagements: moving between the familiar and the public. *European Journal of Social Theory*, 10 (3), 409-423.
Thévenot, Laurent. (2000). L'action comme engagement. In Barbier, Jean-Marie (Ed.), *L'analyse de la singularité de l'action* (pp. 213-238). Paris: Presses Universitaires de France.
Thévenot, Laurent, Eymard-Duvernay, François, Favereau, Olivier, Orléan, André & Salais, Robert. (2005). Values, Coordination and Rationality: The Economy of Conventions. In Oleinik, Anton (Ed.), *The Institutional Economics of Russia's Transformation* (pp. 21-44). Aldershot, Hampshire and Burlington, VT: Ashgate.
Thoumi, Francisco E. (1995). *Political Economy and Illegal Drugs in Columbia*. Boulder, CO and London: Lynne Rienner Publishers.
Tikhomirov, Lev. (2006 [1905]). *Monarkhicheskaia gosudarstvennost'* [Monarchical statehood], Moscow: Iris-Press.
Tikhonova, Natalia. (2006). Bjurokratia: chast' obshchestva ili ego kontragent? [Bureaucracy: a part of the society or a separate group?]. *SOCIS*, 3, 4-8.
Tilly, Charles. (2004). Terror, Terrorists, Terrorism. *Sociological Theory*, 22 (1), 5-13.
Tilly, Charles. (1995). Contentious Repertoires in Great Britain, 1758-1834. In Traugott, Mark (Ed.), *Repertoires and Cycles of Collective Action* (pp. 15-42). Durham, NC and London: Duke University Press.
Tilly, Charles. (1985). War Making and State Making as Organized Crime. In Evans, Peter B., Rueschemeyer, Dietrich & Skopol, Theda (Eds.), *Bringing the State Back In* (pp. 169-191). Cambridge: Cambridge University Press.
Timofeev, Lev. (1993). *Cherny rynok kak politicheskaia sistema* [Black market as a political system]. Vilnius and Moscow: VIMO.
Tirole, Jean. (2007). *The Theory of Industrial Organization* (16th ed.). Cambridge, MA: MIT Press.

Tishkov, Valery. (2004). *Chechnya: Life in a War-Torn Society*. Berkley, CA: University of California Press.
Touraine, Alain. (1999). *Comment sortir du libéralisme*. Paris: Fayard.
Touraine, Alain. (1995 [1992]). *Critique of Modernity*. Oxford: Blackwell. Translated by Macey, David.
Touraine, Alain. (1988). *La parole et le sang: Politique et société en Amérique Latine*. Paris: Editions Odile Jacob.
Traugott, Mark. (1995). Recurrent Patterns of Collective Action. In Traugott, Mark (Ed.), *Repertoires and Cycles of Collective Action* (pp. 1-14). Durham, NC and London: Duke University Press.
Trepavlov, Vadim. (1993). *Gosudarstvenny stroi mongol'skoi imperii XIII v.* [Mongolian statehood in the XIII century]. Moscow: Nauka.
Tronev, Konstantin. (1972). K voprosy ob abstraktnom i konkretnom v politicheskoi ekonomii [On the Abstract and the Concrete in Political Economy]. *Vestnik MGU. Seriia 'Ekonomika,'* 4.
Trotsky, Lev. (1972 [1937]). *The Revolution Betrayed: What is the Soviet Union and Where is it Going?* New York: Pathfinder Press.
Tsentral'noe Statisticheskoe Upravlenie SSSR. (1978). *Narodnoe khoziaistvo SSSR v 1977 g.* [National economy of the Soviet Union in 1977]. Moscow: Statistika.
Tullock, Gordon. (1984). The Backward Society: Static Inefficiency, Rent Seeking, and the Rule of Law. In Buchanan, James M. & Tollison, Robert D. (Ed.), *The Theory of Public Choice – II* (pp. 224-237). Ann Arbor, MI: The University of Michigan Press.
Tullock, Gordon. (2005). *Public Goods, Redistribution and Rent Seeking*. Cheltenham, UK: Edward Elgar.
Turk, Austin T. (1976). Law as a Weapon in Social Conflict. *Social Problems*, 23 (3), 276-291.
Turner, Jonathan H. (2000). The formation of social capital. In Dasgupta, Partha & Serageldin, Ismail (Eds.), *Social Capital: A Multifaceted Perspective* (pp. 94-146). Washington, D.C.: The World Bank.
Ulfelder, Jay. (2007). Natural-Resource Wealth and the Survival of Autocracy. *Comparative Political Studies*, 40 (8), 995-1018.
Uporov, Ivan. (2004). *Penitentsiarnaia politika v Rossii v XVIII-XX vv.* [Penitentiary policy in Russia in the XVIII-XX centuries]. St. Petersburg: Yuridichesky tsentr Press.
Uri, Ra'anan & Lukes, Igor (Eds.). (1990). *Inside the Apparat: Perspectives on the Soviet Union from Former Functionaries*. Lexington, MA: Lexington Books.
US Energy Information Administration. (2009). *International Petroleum (Oil) Reserves and Resources*. Retrieved from http://www.eia.doe.gov/emeu/international/reserves.xls.
US Energy Information Administration. (2005). *Major Non-OPEC Countries' Oil Revenues*. Retrieved from http://www.eia.doe.gov/emeu/cabs/opecnon.html.
Uznadze, Dmitrii. (1966 [1961]). *The psychology of set*. New York: Consultants Bureau. Translated from Russian by Haigh, Basil.
Vasiliev, Vladimir. (2003). *Neirolingvisticheskoe programmirovanie v uchebno-vospitatel'nom protsesse i sotsial'nom obshchenii* [Neuro-linguistic programming in education and social communications]. Moscow: Gruppa 62.
Veblen, Thorstein. (1939 [1915]). *Imperial Germany and Industrial Revolution*. New York: The Viking Press. With an introduction by Dorfman, Joseph.
Veblen, Thorstein. (1934 [1899]). *The Theory of the Leisure Class: An Economic Study of Institutions*. New York: The Modern Library.
Vlast' i vlastnye otnosheniia v sovremennom mire: materialy IX nauchno-prakticheskoi konferentsii [Power and power relationships in contemporary world: proceedings

of the IXth academic conference] (Vols. 1-2). (2006). Yekaterinburg: Gumanitarny universitet.

Vogt, Paul W. (2007). *Quantitative Research Methods for Professionals*. Boston, MA: Allyn and Bacon, Pearson.

Volkov, Vadim. (2002). *Violent Entrepreneurs: The Use of Force in the Making of Russian Capitalism*. Ithaca, NY: Cornell University Press.

Voslensky, Michael. (1984 [1980]). *Nomenklatura: The Soviet Ruling Class*. Garden City, NY: Doubleday. Translated by Mosbacher, Eric.

Wacquant, Loïc. (2001). Deadly symbiosis: When ghetto and prison meet and mesh. *Punishment and Society: The International Journal of Penology*, 3(1), 95-133.

Walzer, Michael. (1983). *Spheres of Justice: A Defense of Pluralism and Equality*. New York: Basic Books.

Warner, Rebecca M. (2008). *Applied Statistics: From Bivariate Through Multivariate Techniques*. Thousand Oaks, CA: SAGE Publications.

Wartenberg, Thomas E. (1990). *The Forms of Power: From Domination to Transformation*. Philadelphia, PH: Temple University Press.

Weber, Max. (1968 [1922]). *Economy and Society: An Outline of Interpretative Sociology*. New York: Bedminster Press. Edited by Roth, Guenther and Wittich, Claus.

Weber, Max. (1949 [1904]). "Objectivity" in social science and social policy. In: *The Methodology of the Social Sciences* (pp. 49-112). Glencoe, IL: The Free Press. Translated and edited by Shils, Edward and Finch, Henry.

Weber, Max. (1946 [1915]). The Social Psychology of the World Religions. In Gerth, Hans & Mills, C. Wright (Eds.), *From Max Weber* (pp. 267-301). New York: Oxford University Press.

Weil, Philippe. (1989). Increasing Returns and Animal Spirits. *The American Economic Review*, 79 (4), 889-894.

Weinthal, Erika & Luong, Pauline Jones. (2006). The Paradox of Energy Sector Reform. In Colton, Timothy J. & Holmes, Stephen (Eds.), *The State after Communism: Governance in the New Russia* (pp. 225-260). Lanham, MA: Rowman & Littlefield.

Welch, Catherine & Wilkinson, Ian. (2005). Network perspectives on interfirm conflict: reassessing a critical case in international business. *Journal of Business Research*, 58, 205-213.

White, Marilyn D. and Marsh Emily E. (2006). Content analysis: a flexible methodology. *Library trends*, 1 (55), 22-45.

Williamson, Oliver E. (1991). Comparative Economic Organization: The Analysis of Discrete Structural Alternatives. *Administrative Science Quarterly*, 36 (2), 269-296.

Williamson, Oliver E. (1985). *The Economic Institutions of Capitalism: Firms, Markets, Relational Contracting*. London and New York: Macmillan and the Free Press.

Williamson, Oliver E. (1975). *Markets and Hierarchies, Analysis and Antitrust implications: A Study in the Economics of Internal Organization*. New York: The Free Press.

Wilson, Andrew. (2005). *Virtual Politics: Faking Democracy in the Post-Soviet World*. New Haven, CT and London: Yale University Press.

Wolf, Charles Jr. (1988). *Markets or Governments: Choosing between Imperfect Alternatives*. London and Cambridge, MA: The MIT Press.

World Bank, the. (2007). *World Development Indicators 2007 CD-ROM*. Washington, DC: the World Bank.

World Values Survey Association, the. (2009). *The World Value Survey: 1999-2004 wave*. Retrieved from http://www.worldvaluessurvey.org/.

Wrong, Dennis H. (1980). *Power: Its Forms, Bases and Uses*. New York: Harper Colophon Books.

References

Yakovlev, Aleksandr. (1988). *Sotsiologiia ekonomicheskoi prestupnosti* [Sociology of economic crime]. Moscow: Nauka.

Yaney, George L. (1973). *The Systematization of Russian Government: Social Evolution in the Domestic Administration of Imperial Russia, 1711-1905*. Urbana, IL: University of Illinois Press.

Yaney, George L. (1966). Bureaucracy and Freedom: N. M. Korkunov's Theory of the State. *The American Historical Review*, 71 (2), 468-486.

Yefimov, Vladimir. (2003). *Economie institutionnelle des transformations agraires en Russie*. Paris: l'Harmattan.

Zhang, Li. (2001). *Strangers in the City: Reconfigurations of Space, Power, and Social Networks Within China's Floating Population*. Palo Alto, CA: Stanford University Press.

Zinoviev, Alexandr. (1994 [1981]). *Kommunizm kak real'nost'* [The Radiant Future]. Moscow: Tsentrpoligraf.

Zweynert, Joachim. (2009). The role of the State in catch-up modernization: The post-1789 reforms in the Germanies and the Russian 'Great reforms' in comparative perspective. In Oleinik, Anton (Ed.), *Reforming the State without changing the model of power? On administrative reform in post-socialist countries* (pp. 215-235). London and New York: Routledge.

Index

Ableness 34, **149**, **152-154**, 156, 162, 168-169, 171-173, 216
Access control (see also Entry control) 136, 155, 197, 204, 212, 217, 219, 222, 229-230, 235, 291
Action
    justifiable 23, 44, **52-53**, 55, 57, 67, 69, 72, 285
    familiar 34, 44, **52**, 54-57, 59, 67-69, 71, 84, 285
    normal 34, 44, **52**, 54-57, 63, 67-68, 72, 84, 285
    social **1-5**, 24, 34, 37, 44, 52-53, 65, 102, 110, 114, 145, 155, 174, 179, 284, 287-288, 301
Administrative barrier **187**, 204, 222, 333
Administrative reform 243-244, 259, 271-272, **278-282**, 332, 336, 340, 343, 352, 354
Afghanistan 248, 264, 298
Agency **10-14**, 46, 59, 68, 72, 143, 148-150, 152, 158, 230
Alexander I 79, 129
Alexander II 129-130
Analytical philosophy 13, 36, 143, 175, 296
Authority **53**, 55, 58, 66, 69, **72**, 75, 78, 83, 130, 152, 251, 286, 289, 339
    conjoint **52**
    disjoint **52**, 57, 61
    traditional 55, 57, 79, 81, 83, 99, 129, 263
    rational-legal 51, 55, 57, 69-71, 104, 121
    charismatic 55, 57

Bargaining power **186**, 155
"Bench" **31**, 331, 336
Berlusconi, Silvio 249, 289
Bogoljubsky, Andrei 119-120

Boundary (of the field) 36, 156-157, 163-164, 173, 201, 291, 338
    institutional 36, 158, 161, 163-164, 169, 171, 202, 216, 220-221, 223, 233, 235
    spatial 36, 158-159, 161, 164, 221
    financial 36, 158-159, 161, 164, 221
    symbolical 158, 161, 164
Brinkmanship 243, **249**
Byzantium 78, 119, 139
Bureaucracy 17, 57, 61, **80**, 85, 131, 214, 237-238, 252, **265**, 335

"Capture" theory 37, 206, **297**, 347
Catherine II 128-130, 135
Chechnya 250, 298
China 160, 207, 229, 233-234, 291
Communist party 16, 33, 111, 131, 135, 139
Compulsory cooperation **3**, 62
Content analysis 23, 37, 86, 90, 137-138, 189, 197, 201, 211, 218, 223, 226, 240, 242-244, 265, 293, **301-325**
Coordination device **3-4**, 7, 11, 24, 31, 34, 43-44, 46-47, 49, 102, 114, 118, 130, 187, 287
Corruption 88, 136, 159, 169, 191, 193, **206-207**, 227, 232, 253, 261, 266, 279, 333, 339-340, 352-353
Credible threat 2, 60, 134, 185, 194, 259
Crisis (started in October 2008) 6, 36, 39, 175, 195, 197, 230, 275, **290-295**
Critical case **3-4**, 7, 211
Critical situation **238**, 314, 335, 337
Critical sociology 13, 56, 89, 138, 144-145, **149-150**, 152, 157, 172
Czar, tsar 16, 33, 79, 95, 98-99, 111, **123-124**, 126-127, 129-130, 263, 282

Deficit, also shortage (as a resource of power) 114-115, 120, **135-136**, 165, 340

Despotism (see also Tyranny) 57, **62**, 66, 68-69, 77-79, 106, 108-109, 120, 123, 125-128

Discourse 16, 26-27, 35, 71, 90, 97, **102-104**, 106-110, 113-119, 123, 126-128, 133, 136-139, 141, 149, 162, 191, 200, 202, 240, 252, 267, 298

Division of powers, as opposed to Hierarchy of powers 50, 105, 157, **244-245**

Domination **52-54**, 73, 143-144, 146-159, 161-163, 167, 169, 172-175, 177-178, 188-190, 195, 202-204, 206-207, 219-220, 226-227, 229, 232-233, 246-247, 257, 266, 282-283, 344

Domination by virtue of a constellation of interests 34-37, 43, 55, 57-58, 69, 90-91, 93-95, 119-120, 127, 135-137, **145-153**, 157-159, 161-162, 166, 171-173, 175, 177-178, 181-196, 201-202, 206-207, 211-212, 218, 223, 225-233, 242-244, 253, 256-257, 266, 274-275, 283, 291-292, 315, 336, 338

Edinaia Rossiia (political party) 192, 213, 254, 262

Elective affinity 37, 83, 94, 127, 160, 165, 175, 195, 202, 234, 306, 324

Elite **14-20**, 37, 40, 81, 86, 98, 128, 182, 230, 235, 248-250, 252, 267, 269, 273-275, 283, 285, 288-290, 297, 313, 332, 336, 352-354

sub-elite 17, 19-21, 23, 24-34, 128, 275

Eltsin, Boris 8, 33, 141, 164, 250, 264, 267

Emic **76-77**, 79, 83, 97

Empowerment **71**, 73

Entry control (see also Access control) 7-8, 39, **154-158**, 161-162, 173, 190, 222, 231, 338, 346-348

Entry ticket 94, 156, 170, 176, 189, 191, 201, 293, 347

Etic **76-77**, 79, 83, 97

European Court of Human Rights 262, 275

European Union 9, 230, 298

Exit control 160, 162

Field (of transactions) **154-155**, 158, 166-172, 212
    territorial **203-204**, 213, 217, 220, 224-226, 233, 238
    information **202**, 213, 217, 219, 224-226, 233, 238

    legal **202-203**, 213, 217, 221, 224-226, 233, 238
    market **204-208**, 213, 217, 221, 224-226, 233, 238

Force (as a technique for imposing will) 5, 26, 35, 50, 53, **57-58**, 62, 69, 73, 78, 83, 90-91, **92-93**, 116, 121, 123, 126-127, 133-134, 137, 154, 159-161, 181, 224-226, 241-243, 247, 249-250, 338, 350

Ford, Henry 61, 160

Freedom 3, 10-11, 45-46, 48, 51, 57, 69, 75, 87, 98, 115, 133, 124, 134, 143, 146, 148, 151, 159, **174-175**, 185, 195, 239, 241, 243, 250-251, 253, 255, 257-258, 270, 275, 285, 289, 333, 338

FSB (also KGB) 26, 134-135, 249, 263, 336

Game
    zero-sum **65**, 72, 149, 195
    non-zero-sum **65**, 184

Gate-keeper 6-7, 155-157, 159, 165-167, 169-170, 173, 175, 189, 205-206, 221-222, 239, 291-292

Gazprom 252-254, 290, 298, 347

Globalization 145, 163

Gorbachev, Mikhail 8, 33, 264, 267

Justification 35, 51-53, 56-57, 63, 66, 69, 79-81, 83-85, 87-88, 93, 99, 103, 106, 110, 115, 124, 130, 181-182, 186-187, 193-195, 237-238, 256, 301, 337

Head (bureau, department) 19, 21, 25, 29, 211, 260, 272, 274, 292, 327-330, 332, 335

Hybrid, also Hybrid form 57, **61**, 148, 197, 317, 325

Ivan III 121-124, 139
Ivan IV 8, 107, 124-125

Keynes, John 293-295
KGB (see FSB)
Kievan Rus', Kievan State 111, 118

Levada-Center 17, 22-23, 210
Liberals **26-28**, 41, 275
Luck **13-14**, 39, 59, 153

Manipulation 53-54, **57-58**, 69, 90-91, 93, 129-130, 133, 135, 137, 154, 181,

Index

224-227, 241, 250-252, 267-270, 339-340, 350, 354
Market power **146-148**, 196, 206, 253, 274, 290
Marx, Karl 4-5, 10, 46, 63, 175, 293-295
Marxism 6, 12, 46, 49, 98, 132-133, 269, 294
Mass-media 58, 93, 113, 202, 214, 219, 252, 293-294, 337-338, 340, 346, 354
Medvedev, Dmitry 33, 40, 42, 298
Monarchy **78-79**, 104, **106-110**, 140, 350
Mongol yoke **120-121**
Monopoly 5-7, 14, 55, 57-58, 61, 87, 133, 146-147, 160-161, 163, 178, 181, 190, 196, **204-207**, 229, 253-255, 278, 290, 347-348
Moscow, Grand Duchy of 103, 111, 122-123, 139

Neoclassical economics 4, 10-12, 26, 36, 39, 47, 71, **144-151**, 172-173, 175, **177-178**, 182, 184, 186, 196, 199, 204-207, 232, 293-294, 296-297, 338
New Institutional Economics 13, 38, 157, 164, 197
Novgorod 99, 120, 123, 141
Not letting in 146, 156, **159-162**, 171, 175 176, 200 201, 204, 347
Not letting out **159-160**, 338

Obshchina 131, 141
Oil and natural gas industries 8-9, 39, 114, 135, 163, 188-189, 192, 197, 200, 229, 234, **253-258**, 272, 274, 289-290, 298, 336, 340, 351, 355
Oligopoly 8, 135, 173, 204, 253, 290
OPEC (Organization of Petroleum Exporting Countries) 8, 39
Opportunism 18, 57, **61**, 67, 107, 185-186, **238-247**, 254-255, 259, 263, 265, 268, 271, 289, 295, 336-337

Path-dependence 104, **110-120**, 124-125, 128, 130, 133, 140-141, 150, 278, 282-287, 298
Patrimonialism 35, 55, 77, **79-83**, 88, 98, 108-109, 122, 140, 155, 157
Peter I 8, 125-128, 264
Presidential Executive Office 16, 19-20, 25, 98, 111, **244-245**, 248, 254, 259, 327-329, 336, 343

Principal 61, 66, 143, 175, 177-178, **180-188**, 192-196, 238-239, 273, 339
Prison vii, 60, 89, 93, 113, 116-117, 124, 127, 129, 134, 149, 166, 175, 338
Police 160, 252-253, 336
Police state 106, 139, 175
Power
    definition 2-4, **43-48**, 72, 11, 13-14, 18, 50-52, 56-59, 66-67, 75, 78, 83, 102-104, 143, 149-150, **177-179**, 186, 241, 273, 296
    as a means to achieve other ends 4, 11, 13, 34, 44, **64-67**, 72, 83, 85, 88, 107, 280, 293, 338
    as an end-it-itself 11, 34-35, 44, **64-67**, 72, 83, **85**, 89, **91**, 95-96, 224-226, 280, 289, 293, 338, 348
    dyad 45, 75, **155-156**, 171-172, 175
    power-centered society **3-4**, 10-12, 14-15, 17-18, 20, 24, 78, 101-102, 288, 297
    power over 2, 5, 10, 54, 59, **64-65**, 71, 80, 143, **149-151**, 170, 174, 339
    power-property **80-81**, 83, 86, 88-89, 257, 337, 348
    power to **64-65**, 114, **149**, 151, 174, 222, 250
    Russian **34-37**, 43, 69, 75-89, 91-92, 97-99, 102-104, 107, 240, 280-283, 286, 288-290
    Supreme **16-21**, 24, 33, 40, **104-105**, 106-116, 118-141, **244-245**, 272, 274, 283, 285-286
    triad 36, 45, **155-157**, 175, 283, 291-292, 297
Property rights **54**, 62, **72**, 81, **86**, 109, 122, 126, 128, 141, 155, 157, 167, **175**, 199, 203-204, 206, **256-258**
Putin, Vladimir 8, 28, 33-34, 40, 42, 93, 95, 244, 298-299

Realistic democracy 55, 269
Rent **187**, 199
    administrative 36, **199-201**, 204, 207-208, 221-223, **226-229**, 232, 253, 272
    protection 140, **187**
    resource 36, 163, **199-200**, 204, 208, 213, 215, 229, 232, 234, 340
Rent-seeking 200, 205-206, 232
Repertoire of

techniques for imposing will 35-36, 43, 104, **113-114**, 118, 124, 127-130, 133-137, 226, 257, 263, 338-339
coordination devices 3
Retail trade 7, 136, **166-171**, 176, 212-213, 215, 217, 219-220, 222, 235
Revolution
    October 1917 46, 99, 111, 130-131, 175, 263-264, 282-283
    Orange 94
    of Supreme power 113, 122, 125
Rosneft 254, 258
RuNet **26**, 252

Samoderzhavie 35, **78-80**, 83-84, 98, 104, **108-109**, 113, 119-120, 123, 125-126, 131, 137, 263
Samovlastie **78-79**, 83-84, 104, **108**, 113, 119-121, 123, 125-127, 137
Satisficing 182-184
Schröeder, Gerhard 249, 289, 298
Service
    state 12, 17-21, 23, 25, 27-31, 40-41, 85, 91-92, 112, 191, 231, 240-243, 246-247, 259-260, 263, 265-266, 268, 271, 274, 278-279, 282, 296, 313, 331-337, 341, 343
    public 17, 256, 296
Shleifer, Andrei 298
Small society 34, 277
Sovereignty 78, 98, **104-105**, 109, 120, 123, 151, 163
Stalin, Joseph 66, 130-131, 133-134, 140, 264

Structural bias (also Bias of the system) 7, 13-14, 27, **57-61**, 63, 90, 135-137, 152-153, 167, 172-175, 181, 189, 219, 224-226, 230, 240, 242-243, 255-256, 290-291, 293, 295, 299, 339, 351
Structure (versus Agency) 10-14, 152, 162, 239
Symbolic violence 35, **76**, **86**, 89-92, 94, 138, 161, 224-226, 339, 352

Team **28-29**, 31-34, 37, 41, 62, 242, 246, 272, 331, 333, 336, 342-343
Triangulation 37, 242, **303-306**, 310-311, 313, 318, 324
    within-methods 201, 211, 303-304, 310, 316, 322
    between-methods 201, 211, 240, 304, 311, 316, 322
Television (TV) 219, 244, 252, 337-338, 346, 354
Tyranny (see also Despotism) 78-79, 108, 120, 123

Ukraine 41, 94, 196, 290
United States 40, 49, 160, 248, 287-289, 292, 298

Vocation (also *Beruf*) 27, 41, 265, 331, 336, 343, 271

Weber, Max 3-6, 35-36, 44, 47, 49, 51, 55, 61, 77, 80-81, 83, 98, 144-146, 152, 155, 265, 301

Yukos 81, 94, 248, 254, **258**, 350

NN
49
.P6
O44
2011